Routledge Revivals

South Wales Miners: Glowyr de Cymru

First published in 1975, *South Wales Miners* starts with the War of Empires, when nearly 50,000 Welsh miners, almost one-fifth of the total manpower of their coalfield, responded to the call and voluntarily enlisted in the British armed forces. The author uncovers how the coalowners in the meantime took advantage of the war emergency to deny the remaining miners a fair recompense for their toil and of the bitter strife that followed. The book tells the story of what led up to the General Strike and here the author uses hitherto hidden sources of information. The picture is revealed of what was a virtual conspiracy between the Baldwin-Churchill Government and the mineowners, not only to cut wages and lengthen hours, but to cripple British trade unionism. When the miners held out through a seven-month lockout the efforts of these highly placed conspirators recoiled on their own heads and on the whole economy of British Empire. This book will be of interest to students of history, labour studies, economics and political science.

South Wales Miners: Glowyr de Cymru

A History of the South Wales Miners' Federation (1914-1926)

R. Page Arnot

First published in 1975
By Cymric Federation Press

This edition first published in 2023 by Routledge
4 Park Square, Milton Park, Abingdon, Oxon, OX14 4RN
and by Routledge
605 Third Avenue, New York, NY 10017

Routledge is an imprint of the Taylor & Francis Group, an informa business

Publisher's Note
The publisher has gone to great lengths to ensure the quality of this reprint but points out that some imperfections in the original copies may be apparent.

Disclaimer
The publisher has made every effort to trace copyright holders and welcomes correspondence from those they have been unable to contact.

A Library of Congress record exists under ISBN: 0950457701

ISBN: 978-1-032-53917-1 (hbk)
ISBN: 978-1-003-42920-3 (ebk)
ISBN: 978-1-032-55142-5 (pbk)

Book DOI 10.4324/9781003429203

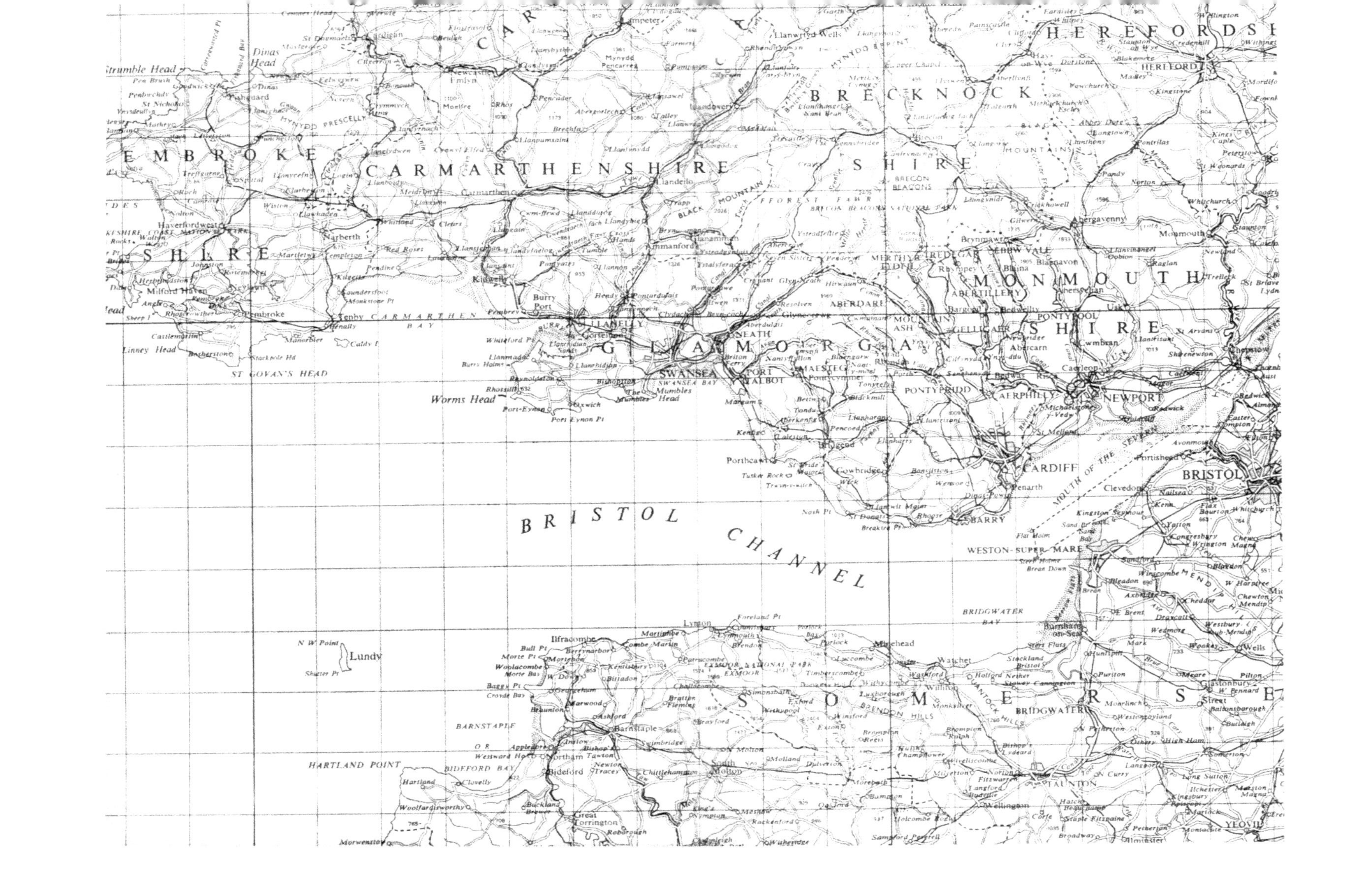

HEREFORDSHIRE
BRECKNOCKSHIRE
CARMARTHENSHIRE
PEMBROKESHIRE
GLAMORGAN
MONMOUTHSHIRE
SOMERSET
BRISTOL CHANNEL
CARMARTHEN BAY
SWANSEA BAY
BRIDGWATER BAY
BARNSTAPLE OR BIDEFORD BAY
MOUTH OF THE SEVERN
BLACK MOUNTAIN
BLACK MOUNTAINS
BRECON BEACONS
FFOREST FAWR
MYNYDD PRESCELLY
EXMOOR NATIONAL PARK
BRENDON HILLS
QUANTOCK HILLS
MENDIP HILLS
Strumble Head
Dinas Head
Fishguard
Haverfordwest
Milford Haven
Pembroke
Tenby
Narberth
Whitland
Cardigan
Newcastle Emlyn
Lampeter
Llandovery
Llandeilo
Carmarthen
Llanelly
Burry Port
Kidwelly
Ammanford
SWANSEA
NEATH
PORT TALBOT
ABERDARE
MERTHYR TYDFIL
PONTYPRIDD
CAERPHILLY
CARDIFF
Penarth
BARRY
Bridgend
Cowbridge
Porthcawl
Maesteg
EBBW VALE
ABERTILLERY
PONTYPOOL
NEWPORT
Abergavenny
Monmouth
Chepstow
Brecon
Hay-on-Wye
HEREFORD
BRISTOL
Clevedon
Portishead
Avonmouth
WESTON-SUPER-MARE
Burnham-on-Sea
BRIDGWATER
TAUNTON
Wells
Glastonbury
Street
YEOVIL
Minehead
Watchet
Lynton
Ilfracombe
Barnstaple
Bideford
Great Torrington
South Molton
Lundy
Worms Head
The Mumbles
HARTLAND POINT
ST GOVAN'S HEAD
Linney Head

1 A. J. COOK SPEAKING AT A MEETING IN TRAFALGAR SQUARE

SOUTH WALES MINERS

GLOWYR DE CYMRU

A History of the
South Wales Miners' Federation
(1914-1926)

BY

R. PAGE ARNOT

FIRST PUBLISHED IN 1975

PRINTED IN WALES
in 10 on 11 point Times type
BY THE CYMRIC FEDERATION PRESS
CARDIFF

FOREWORD

Once more we are proud and honoured to present the history of the South Wales Miners' Federation. Glowyr de Cymru in this second volume covers the years of ordeal from 1914 to 1926: throughout the War of Empires (1914-18) and its revolutionary aftermath, throughout the slump of 1921 and the first seven years between the wars.

The story is told of how our forebears struggled to safeguard their living standards against ruthless exploitation by the coalowners, of how Welsh and British coalowners, now an extinct species, happily forgotten by the younger generation, received full backing from a Government of political fossils who imagined that coal could not be won or wound to the surface without the existence of the coalowning parasites. It tells how successive British Prime Ministers—Lloyd George and Baldwin personally intervened against the miners to save the coalowners.

It tells how our forebears strove to win back a militant policy, and how one of our Agents, Arthur James Cook, triumphantly carried that policy into effect throughout the British coalfield.

In this volume Robin Page Arnot puts events into the framework of the development of capitalism, internationally, with that same accuracy and skill as in the presentation of his other writings which have made the past come to life.

In addition, his long personal acquaintance with so many families in the coalfields and especially with those who came to the fore in the ten years of ordeal, enables him to give a sympathetic portrayal of the never ending class struggle of the mineworkers.

GLYN WILLIAMS, President.

EMLYN WILLIAMS, Vice-President.

DAVID FRANCIS, General Secretary

Pontypridd,
October, 1973

PREFACE

Many years ago, equipped with a letter from Beatrice Webb, I visited trade union and Co-operative offices mainly in order to gather records for the Labour Research Department. On more than one occasion I was told that, if only they had known earlier that their old records would have been of use to Mrs. Webb they would certainly have been kept for her. But offering them to some middle class library (public or private) was outside their reckoning: and, indeed, there was reluctance to make disclosures to any outsider. The smaller the organisation, the more tenaciously they were inclined to withhold from any inspection that might turn out to be hostile. There was a dread of inspection from above of which they had had enough in their private lives. This suspicion was repaid in some institutions with contempt for proletarian records, some of which might turn out to be little better than seditious libels.

What with one thing or another there has resulted a continuous erosion of sources, so that the last hundred years, with spread of literacy, profusion of periodicals and deluge of printed pages, may turn out to have been also a prodigal and squandering century in this respect.

With the beginning of this century there set in an accelerated process of destruction of working-class records, nowhere seen more clearly than in the coalfields where, as I have recorded, it is impossible to write a full and true history of the Amalgamated Association of Miners from 1869-1875 until all its half-yearly reports, printed in thousands of copies, have been recovered. Then, following on the savage zealots of 1939-45, there was extensive pillage by unscrupulous collectors. Happily, this process has undergone a check, partly through the help given since 1965 by the Social Science Research Council. In South Wales, the work undertaken by a number of graduates under the guidance of two professors of the University College of Swanea has already yielded results. In particular Hywel Francis, as reported in *The Times*, has taken action which has stopped the process of dispersal and/or destruction of miners' institute libraries, with the setting up of the South Wales Miners' Library at Swanea under the auspices of the National Union of Mineworkers (South Wales Area) and the College of Swansea.

If this counter-process of rescue develops elsewhere a prospect would open for researchers, annalists, chroniclers and historians to make up the back-log of what should have been done before the War of Empires of 1914-18, in the period when records of the working-class were treated in libraries and universities with neglect and contempt. Thus, there is now possible the compilation of effective records, beginning, where possible, with the annals of trade unionism from 1666 onwards.

These things said, I must now deal with the short-comings of this volume. The space of a dozen years envisaged was a miscalculation, given the nature of the new events and new conditions in the country and the coalfields, especially during the War of Empires. It proved all too little. In the first six years, and again in the three last years, when the outstanding name is that of Arthur James Cook of the Rhondda, I have had to compress, excise and, in the final chapter, to leave out all but the bare essentials of the story.

That tenth chapter also suffered from the three-day week imposed by Mr. Heath against whose damages to industry there seems no remedy in English law or indeed in the Constitution—unless by resort to impeachment.

For instance, the reader will not find one of the most important activities, that of the Union in connection with the Labour College and the whole development of what was called "independent working-class education". Secondly, the Union's care for health and rehabilitation reached a high-point in the setting up in 1923 of Tal-y-garn, where the work by its staff has been the admiration of miners' leaders from other countries. Thirdly, the work done by the South Wales Miners' Federation in the fight against the incidence and effect of pneumoconiosis in conjunction with hospitals, such as Llandough outside Cardiff, has been of the highest importance. Fourthly, the consistent fight for the prevention of accidents, as well as to diminish other occupational diseases. All these I have had to leave for others to write: and I am happy to say that David Smith and Hywel Francis, both at the University College of Swansea, have undertaken to continue the work of writing the history of the union.

A comprehensive bibliography of the South Wales Miners' Federation, thanks to librarians and archivists, is now more possible than was the case a dozen years ago: and its inclusion in "a later volume" (to which I postponed bibliographical details in 1966) will now have to be undertaken by succeeding chroniclers.

Throughout my task I have had the utmost courtesy and help from the members and officials of the National Union of Mineworkers. I have also to thank the many friends in Swansea and other universities who gave me help in so many ways—so many as to make this really a co-operative effort. I found I could get considerable help from those in the National Coal Board—in strong contrast to the behaviour of the Trustees of the Monmouthshire and South Wales Coal Owners' Association who, in the early sixties, sought to impede my research into their past records.

I must, however, single out Idris Cox, Maurice Dobb, George Jerrom, Owen Parsons, Andrew Rothstein, Maelgwyn Byrdon Thomas (commonly called Mel), Angela Tuckett and Beulah Walker who came to my aid by reading the proofs most thoroughly: and, finally, my wife, who continued her critical help throughout.

R. PAGE ARNOT.

46 Byne Road,
London, S.E.26.
25th April, 1974.

CONTENTS

ACKNOWLEDGMENTS

To the trustees and staff of the British Museum for their courtesy and help in the matter of books and periodical press.

To the staff of the Public Records Office.

To Mrs. Nan Green for her skill and care in compiling the Index.

To Edgar Evans for the generous loan of the minute book of "The Bedlinog Council of Action".

To Hywel Francis and his friends for choosing and captioning of the Illustrations.

To the Press and Publicity Department of the Trades Union Congress for the photograph of A. J. Cook in the frontispiece.

ACKNOWLEDGMENTS FOR ILLUSTRATIONS, ETC.

To the Social Sciences Research Council Coalfield History Project and Mr. Roger Davies, L.R.P.S., (for technical assistance)—all of the University College, Swansea.

To Mr. C. Batstone (Ystrad, Rhondda).

To Miss M. Hughes (Cardiff) who was in turn secretary to A. J. Cook, W. H. Mainwaring, James Griffiths, A. L. Horner, Alf Davies and Will Paynter.

To Mr. W. Rees (Cwmtwrch).

To Mr. J. M. Phillips (Ammanford).

To Mr. S. Watts (Glyn-Neath).

To Mrs. S. O. Davies (Merthyr Tydfil).

To Mrs. Vol Tofts (London).

To Mrs. Phyllis Bell (London).

To the National Coal Board.

LIST OF ILLUSTRATIONS

CHAPTER ONE

THE OUTBREAK OF WAR

1 FUEL FOR THE NAVY REFUSED

One week before Britain declared war on Germany a significant notice was issued in Whitehall from the Board of Admiralty, whose First Lord was Winston S. Churchill. The public were told that the Grand Fleet, assembled at Portsmouth since mid-July, 1914, for the naval review by King George V, was not being demobilized, but was proceeding to its war base. Jubilantly Churchill recorded it: "The King's ships were at sea."

Thereafter all went forward smoothly to Armageddon—as laid down beforehand in the War Book. In advance of "The Warning Telegram," premonitory messages went out to ships in all the seven seas. Each had his part assigned in the war preparations: and all went merry as a marriage bell—but for one technical hitch. The coal miners of South Wales, on whom the Royal Navy depended for its fuel, refused to play the part assigned them by the Lords of the Admiralty.

The roots of this unexpected obstacle lay on the one hand in the preceding decade of intense war preparation in the rivalry between the Triple Alliance headed by Imperial Germany and the Triple Entente of Russia, the French Republic and the British Empire—to which last Japan was attached: and on the other hand in the historic standpoint in opposition to war of the whole Socialist International, part and parcel of which was the Labour Party with its many scores of affiliated trade unions. But only one of these trade unions, the South Wales Miners' Federation, was in a position of peculiar responsibility for supply of the needed fuel.

Naval rivalry had been a main determinant for Britain in the arms race that led up to the war: and it was the effectiveness of the naval arm which was to be a decisive factor in bringing about the defeat of Prussia and her partners.

For over half a century the navies of the world had been driven by engines whose motive force was steam, generated from boilers above furnaces stoked with coal. Although oil was soon to take the place of coal as a fuel for raising steam and, through internal combustion engines, to take the place of steam as a motive force, its day was not yet come. Coal, still supreme, was made available from a multitude of coaling-stations and depots throughout the seven seas. In the South Wales coalfield, producing no less than one-fifth of the island's total output, was to be found the coal the Navy wanted. The combustible minerals grouped under the common name of coal fell readily into three classes in South Wales, namely, steam coal, bituminous coal, anthracite. Of these, anthracite coal, as shown by a typical analysis, would be nine-tenths of it fixed carbon, less than one-twentieth of it volatile matter, and finally small amounts of sulphur, water and ash. A bituminous coal on the other hand might be seven-tenths fixed carbon over two-tenths volatile matter and finally a considerable amount of sulphur, water or ash. Between these extremes lay the steam coals which in their thirty-odd different kinds (half of them from the Rhondda valleys) exactly suited naval requirements. Typically, a steam coal would be made up of eight-tenths fixed carbon, but with twice as much volatile matter as anthracite and very much less sulphur, water or ash. It was by far the best for its purpose : and its price was correspondingly high. Advertisements of colliery companies proclaimed their product to be "Welsh Smokeless Steam Coal" as used by the great oceanic steamship lines or "as supplied to the French, German and Italian Navies."

Of this first class coal there had already been considerable consumption that summer as warships of all kinds came together for the great naval review at Portsmouth which began on Saturday, 18th July, 1914. Ten days later, as the Apostolic Emperor of Austria-Hungary, Franz Josef, declared war on Serbia,[1] the order was made public that the British Fleet was proceeding to its war base. Other measures, as planned, were taken : and within three more days the Executive Council of the South Wales Miners' Federation meeting in Cardiff on Saturday, 1st August, 1914, learned of a request from the Board of Admiralty that "the miners employed at collieries supplying Admiralty contracts should work on Tuesday and Wednesday next, two of the three days arranged as holidays by the Conciliation Board."

What answer were they to give ? After a long discussion the following resolution was unanimously adopted :

"That this Council having, at a special meeting called for the purpose, very carefully considered the present international conditions and the suggestion of the Board of Admiralty that the miners employed

[1] *Cardinal Dates in* 1914.

June 28 : Assassination of Archduke Franz Ferdinand, heir to the throne.
July 23 : Austria-Hungary sends ultimatum to Serbia.
July 28 : Austria-Hungary declares war on Serbia.
July 30 : Tzar of Russia orders general mobilization.
August 1 : German Kaiser declares war on Russia.
August 2 : General mobilization in process in France.
August 3 : Germany declares war on France.
August 4 : Great Britain declares war on Germany.

In the remainder of August, Austria-Hungary declared war on Russia on the 5th, France on Austria-Hungary on the 10th, Britain on Austria-Hungary on the 11th : while Japan declared war on Germany on the 23rd.

Three months later Great Britain and France declared war on Turkey (the Ottoman Empire) on the 5th November and on the same day Great Britain annexed Cyprus. On the 23rd November the Sultan of Turkey, as Caliph of all the Muslim believers, declared a Holy War (*Jehad*) on the Entente Powers. On the 17th December, Egypt was declared a "Protectorate" and the Sultan's sovereignty over it came to an end.

at the collieries supplying Admiralty contracts should work on Tuesday and Wednesday next, two of the three days arranged as holidays by the Conciliation Board.

"We do not consider it necessary for defensive purposes to ask the miners to work on these two days, and we decline to encourage or in any way countenance the policy of active intervention by this country in the present European conflict, and we are also strongly of the opinion that there is no necessity for Great Britain in any degree to become involved in the war between Austria and Serbia, and we call upon the Government to continue its position of neutrality and to use all its power in the attempt to limit the area of the present conflict and to bring it to a speedy termination" (1 viii 1914).

Finally, they considered that it was now the moment for "the miners of Europe" to endeavour "to enforce their views upon the governments implicated" and told their secretary what he had to do.[1]

It was further resolved : "That a copy of the resolution be sent to the Prime Minister, the First Lord of the Admiralty, and Sir Edward Grey" (1 viii 1914).

On the day this resolution was passed, Great Britain's participation in the war did not seem to be a foregone conclusion. A couple of days earlier the two-score Labour Members in the House of Commons had unanimously called "upon all labour organisations in the country to watch events vigilantly so as to oppose, if need be, in the most effective way any action which may involve us in war" (30 vii 1914).

In Cardiff the Executive Council, with their President and Secretary (William Brace, M.P., and Tom Richards, M.P.) closely in touch with Westminster, certainly hoped that the terms of their own resolution were a clear response to the call "to watch events vigilantly" so as to oppose "in the most effective way"—just as they hoped would also be done by working-class organisations in other countries of Europe.

2 THE HISTORIC STANDPOINT

The refusal of the miners' leaders in South Wales to accede to the request from the Board of Admiralty had its origin not in a sudden petulance but in an established conviction and a political outlook. This standpoint had grown greater over a decade ever since George Plekhanov of Russia and Sen Katayama of Japan had clasped their

[1] "Further, that as the Miners' International Congress has, at its meetings, adopted a resolution condemnatory of war between the nations represented, we think the present moment opportune for the miners of Europe to make an endeavour to enforce their views upon the governments implicated in the conflict and the pending complications, and to this end the General Secretary shall at once get into communication with the President and Secretary of the International Miners' Organisation, requesting that an international conference of miners shall immediately be convened to consider the attitude to be adopted by the affiliated miners in the present crises."

hands together at the Sixth (Amsterdam) International Socialist Congress in 1904 at the height of the Russo-Japanese War.

That same year saw the signing of the Entente Cordiale between Britain and France, which settled disputes about their colonial empires. Four months later the question of "Peace or War" came up at the Sixteenth Miners' International Congress, held at Liège in Belgium, where they unanimously resolved that "all international questions be settled by arbitration: and also expresses its warmest sympathy to the Russian workmen in their struggles for industrial freedom, and wishes them every success" (7 viii 1905).

The signing in August, 1907, of an Anglo-Russian Convention (usually referred to as "the partition of Persia") brought the Triple Entente into existence; and with it an increased danger of war. The Seventh International Socialist Congress meeting from 18th to 24th August, 1907, in Stuttgart proclaimed "that the struggle against militarism cannot be separated from the socialist class struggle in general"; and dealing with "the efforts of the working class against war," drew lessons from the past, stating that "since the International Congress at Brussels,[1] the proletariat has employed the most diverse forms of action with increasing emphasis and success in its indefatigable struggles against militarism by refusing the means for naval and military armaments, and by its efforts to democratise the military organisation—all for the purpose of preventing the outbreak of wars or of putting a stop to them, as well as for utilising the convulsions of society caused by war for the emancipation of the working class."

Four weeks later a dozen representatives of the South Wales Miners' Federation attended the Eighteenth Miners' International Congress. It was held at Salzburg, the gateway to the huge Austro-Hungarian Empire, which with twice the acreage of the United Kingdom was soon to annex a Balkan province that was more than twice the size of Wales. There the French miners had tabled a resolution, that the International Miners should define their attitude "in case of a war breaking out" (20 ix 1907). William Brace, M.P., then argued that the Congress should then and there instruct the committee that "in the case of a threatened war, they should meet" and if need be "convene an international congress of miners."

When their twenty-second international congress was held in the last week of July, 1911, it was the summer of "the Agadir crisis" between Germany and France, and a week after the Chancellor of the Exchequer, in a speech on 21st July at the Mansion House, had used words indicating that the whole weight of Britain's power would be thrown upon the scales. The German Foreign Office was so angered by this that Sir Edward Grey in the last week of that July warned the Admiralty against the possibility of a surprise attack upon the British

[1] 16th to 23rd August, 1891.

fleet. The Agadir crisis, bringing Britain to the brink of war, lasted on through the autumn of 1911 till the end of September, in which month bridges and tunnels on the main railway lines in Kent were guarded by troops.

Then came the Italo-Turkish war, followed immediately by the first Balkan War in mid-October, 1912. The International Socialist Bureau took emergency steps and hastily convened an anti-war congress of the Socialist International, held at Basle in Switzerland on 24th and 25th November, 1912. Its manifesto recalled that at its congresses at Stuttgart and Copenhagen the International had formulated for the working class of all countries "these guiding principles for the struggle against war"; and then stated that "the Congress views as the greatest danger to the peace of Europe the artificially cultivated hostility between Great Britain and the German Empire," and pin-pointed the arms race in "naval armaments."

The Basle Manifesto ended with a stirring appeal for action by the workers to prevent "the annihilation of the flower of all peoples" and for this purpose to "use every means that the organisation and the strength of the proletariat place at your disposal." The leaders of the parties (including the Labour Party) who subscribed to this manifesto had hopes and fears for the future: but they could not foresee that the opening of the cataclysm to bring about "annihilation of the flower of all peoples" on land and sea lay just twenty months ahead.

3 NEARING THE BRINK

On the same day, 1st August, 1914, that the SWMF categorically refused the request of the Admiralty, Sir Edward Grey was speaking to the French Ambassador and horrifying him with the information that France must not count upon receiving from Britain "assistance which we were not now in a position to promise." Peace or war for Britain seemed to be still trembling in the balance. But when the refusal from Cardiff was told to the First Lord of the Admiralty in London there was no equivocation in his telegram to T. Richards:

"The situation is very grave. We have done our best to ward off this immeasurable catastrophe. We have no selfish interests to pursue, no territory to acquire, no quarrels to avenge, but we must be prepared to meet the dangers that are so near, with courage and with comradeship, and to do our duty. South Wales will help us. We are all in this together."

Winston Churchill was never one to take no for an answer: and the terms of his message were so urgent that it split up the previous unanimity. There was protracted discussion on Monday, 3rd August, in the Executive Council. The first proposition was to stand pat on their previous decision. An amendment repeated the main tenor of their Saturday resolution but also accepted Churchill's statement. Thus it reiterated the protest against active intervention in the war, again uttered the need for the calling of an international miners' congress to bring the war to an end; but relying on the "assurance that it is not the intention of the Government to participate in the war either for the acquisition of territory, quarrels to avenge or any other selfish interest", it then set forth "our duty in the interests of the nation to secure a sufficient supply of coal to enable ample protection to be given to our food supplies and the protection of our shores" ; and asked the miners at a dozen named colliery companies, "and any other requested to do so, to return to work tomorrow." This amendment received six votes only. Twelve voted for the proposition "that we reaffirm the resolution passed on Saturday last." The majority were not prepared to give up holidays for a purpose which they disapproved, indeed viewed with abhorrence.

That same day in Parliament (Monday, 3rd August) Sir Edward Grey was to make his statement, the outcome of which was anxiously awaited in the Foreign Office. There was, as it turned out, no need for their apprehensions. The Members of Parliament, except for a small number, accepted the Foreign Secretary's explanation and cheered him approvingly. The British ultimatum to Germany followed. The ultimatum expired on Tuesday, 4th August, at 11 p.m. : and from that hour a state of war existed between the two countries.

All sections of the British labour movement had striven to prevent this happening. They had been united in their desire and their efforts, in thus carrying out the first of the "guiding principles" enjoined upon the working class of all countries in the struggle against war. Now all their efforts had failed. Six great nations were now locked in combat, before long to be joined by others. The British declaration of war had at once altered the situation and brought into prominence in Britain the second of the "guiding principles." What was to be done ?

On the day after the declaration of war there began a special meeting of the Executive Committee of the Labour Party to consider the European crisis. The miners' unions received the resolutions. These resolutions, which ended with the advice to concentrate on relief and other measures "to mitigate the destitution which will inevitably overtake our working people while the state of war lasts", clearly showed that the Labour Party Executive had receded quite a way from its earlier pronouncements as part of the British Section of the International.

Amongst the miners' leaders there was a rapid shift of opinion. At a third specially summoned meeting, on Thursday, 6th August, 1914, the Executive Council learned that the Admiralty had intimated their desire "in order to get immediate additional supplies of the best Welsh coal for the Navy," either for suspension of the Eight Hours Act, or for advantage to be taken of the "Sixty Hours Clause" to work an additional hour per day. In that Act, passed six years earlier, the fourth section ran as follows :

"His Majesty may, in the event of war or of imminent national danger or great emergency, or in the event of any grave economic disturbance due to the demand for coal exceeding the supply available at the time, by Order in Council suspend the operation of this Act to such extent and for such period as may be named in the Order, either as respects all coal mines or any class of coal mines."

The outbreak of war, written into the Act as a contingency, had now come upon them as an actuality. What was to be done? To suspend the Act might throw them back for a generation. Neither in South Wales nor in any other coalfield was there any wavering on this issue, which was to be brought forward more than once in the course of the 1914/18 war and from time to time urged very strongly. The alternative under Section 3 of the Act of an extra hour "on not more than sixty days in any calendar year" was preferable, if they were to grant the request. Grant it they did: and by 18 votes to one the Council recommended the miners "to work an additional hour per day" at whatever colliery they were requested to do so, "for the time the present emergency lasts." A reasoned amendment, that "this Council respectfully submit that the purposes of the Admiralty will be amply served, if necessary, by putting additional Steam Coal Collieries on the Admiralty list" received the solitary vote of Noah Ablett.

There was still some concern at Naval headquarters about coal supply, as appears from the entry in the SWMF Executive Council Minutes for Thursday, 13th August, 1914.[1] On this occasion "Mr. Jenkins, representative of the Admiralty" attended the Council, and gave "a lengthy explanation" of the Admiralty requirements of coal. The request was agreed to without argument pro or con.[2]

[1] *Collieries working Sunday.* This was a Special Meeting called to consider the following letter:

Admiralty,
11th August, 1914.

"Sir,

I am commanded by My Lords Commissioners of the Admiralty to acquaint you that it would be a very great convenience in regard to the prompt dispatch of the supplies of coal for His Majesty's Navy if, by mutual arrangement between the owners of the collieries concerned and the South Wales Miners' Federation, the pits could be worked on Sunday next. It may not be necessary to work them on the following Sunday.

"My Lords will be glad to learn that you are able to meet their wishes in this matter.

"Copies of this letter are being sent to the Home Office and to W. G. Dalziel, Esq., the Secretary of the Monmouthshire and South Wales Coal Owners' Association.

I am, Sir, Your Obedient Servant,
(Signed) W. Graham Greene."

Resolved:

"That we agree to the request and advise the workmen to work on Sunday next."

[2] "The war fever had now got well into the minds of the South Wales leaders, and at that time it appears that they were prepared to sacrifice all their hard-won conditions in order that little Belgium might be saved from the rapacious Hun. In one week all their old working-class ideas had been swamped" —so wrote the Rt. Hon. Ness Edwards, M.P., when a miners' agent, in 1938.

Thereafter, too, the Admiralty had other matters than coal to cause them concern : for in the first three months of the naval war six of their major vessels were sunk, four by German submarines in home waters and two by Admiral Von Spee at the battle off Coronel in the Pacific, without as yet any corresponding effective retaliation upon the vessels of the Kaiser's High Sea Fleet.

4 COLLAPSE OF THE SOCIALIST INTERNATIONAL

The horror and repugnance with which the miners' leaders in South Wales regarded the imminent deadly breach of civilization in Europe and their efforts to make those feelings effective in the only way open to them and to maintain the historic attitude and outlook of the labour movement lasted for a few days. Then came stunned bewilderment as all preconceptions and established standpoints were first dwarfed by the magnitude of the catastrophe and then for the most part swept into a limbo of oblivion. The event affected all the inhabitants of Europe, all the households of the United Kingdom, all forms of activity both below and above ground. Amid the confusion and disorder of departing peace and the novel activities of war the miners' leaders turned to those matters of the people's livelihood in which they had full understanding and could immediately play a useful part. Consequently, the Executive Council found the effect of the cataclysm presenting itself as a series of problems of industrial dislocation, sudden unemployment, higher prices and consequent widespread distress.[1] So on Thursday, 6th August, they resolved :

"That this Council desires to enter its most emphatic protest against the action of tradesmen in taking advantage of the Declaration of War by raising the price of goods in stock, notwithstanding the cost price of such goods to them has remained the same."

In order to discourage hoarding the Council urged tradesmen "to refuse to supply customers except in the usual quantities" (6 viii 1914). Three weeks later the Council convened a special conference to consider what kind of help could be given to "people thrown out of work or in any other way adversely affected by the war." Meeting in Cory Hall, Cardiff, on Tuesday, 1st September, the special conference (of

[1] Industrial dislocation had been an immediate effect. On August 5th, 1914, the day after the Declaration of War between Great Britain and Germany, the Customs Authorities received orders to prohibit the export from the United Kingdom ports of large steam coal and manufactured fuel to all foreign ports in Europe and on the Mediterranean and the Black Sea with the exception of France, Russia (except for Baltic Ports), Spain and Portugal. The exception was afterwards extended to Italy. Exporters had to give a bond before moving for any friendly or neutral country with securities for three times the value of the cargo. Immediate consequence was widespread unemployment at the pits. Representations were made to the Government by exporters, to withdraw the prohibition and bond, and on August 20th, 1914, the prohibitions and bond were removed.

201 accredited delegates representing 143,508 members) was addressed by the President upon the decisions of the Council respecting the working of the extra hour and the proposal to raise funds by levies for the support of the workmen thrown out of employment. William Brace explained the extra hour, and also the attempt made to get an international conference of miners' representatives.

The delegates had to consider whether to deal with their own local difficulties, or join in the national effort for dealing generally with the distress in the country. It was proposed, seconded and carried unanimously that the conference endorse the whole of the decisions of the Council for dealing with matters arising out of the war.[1] No further special conference was held that year or indeed during the first six months of the war.

Nationally the effect of the widespread distress had been countered by the setting-up on 5th August, on the initiative of the Labour Party, of an all-embracing "War Emergency: Workers' National Committee." This committee embraced organisations covering every sphere of labour activity, among the bodies represented on its executive committee being the Trades Union Congress, the Co-operative Congress, the Labour Party, Co-operative Wholesale Society, Co-operative Union, General Federation of Trade Unions, Women's Co-operative Guild, Women's Trade Union League, the National Union of Teachers, various large trade unions and socialist societies, the Scottish Trades Union Congress, and the London Trades Council. From amongst the three representatives from the Miners' Federation of Great Britain (more than from any other union) President Robert Smillie was elected Chairman. The other two were Vice-President Herbert Smith and the President of the South Wales Miners' Federation, William Brace, M.P.

This body, for the first year or two of the war, played no small part in concentrating the attention of the trade union and other working-class bodies on social and industrial issues arising from the war. Problems arising in Wales that were suitable for national handling were dealt with readily and effectively in this new national body. It was

[1] Details were in seven resolutions, viz:—

"That we contribute a levy for meeting the distress caused by unemployment."

"That the amount be 6d. per man and 3d. per boy per week."

"That the levy be raised through the colliery offices and that it be paid into the Prince of Wales Fund through the local committees."

"The deduction to be made in all collieries working more than 3 days per week."

"That the employers be asked that any contribution they make to the Prince of Wales Fund should be paid through the local committees."

"That we send to the President of the Local Government Board requesting that South Wales and Monmouthshire be considered one unit in the calculation of the amounts received by the Prince of Wales Fund."

"That this Conference are of the opinion that all men called to service in the army or navy should be given a much higher rate of pay to ensure that their wives and children should not be impoverished and caused unnecessary suffering, believing that the financial resources of the Government and the leisured classes are such that no difficulty would be experienced by so doing."

the most all-embracing body that had existed hitherto in the labour movement: and its setting up on 5th August turned out to be the last unanimous decision of the Labour Party chiefs.

Thereafter the cleavage of opinion widened. Within the British Section of the International, made up of the Labour Party and the three Socialist organisations (Fabian Society, British Socialist Party and Independent Labour Party) a gulf had opened. By 12th August the Independent Labour Party set out their separate standpoint in an anti-war manifesto, whose brave words, "Out of the darkness and the depth we hail our working-class comrades of every land", were echoed to some extent in the Welsh valleys. But the majority in the South Wales Miners' Federation, as in nearly every other union, might ruefully ponder the derisive editorial of "The Times" (if they read it at all) on that second week of August: "The class war of Socialism and the international peace movement associated with it have evaporated into words and are in process of collapsing altogether." The words of socialism in their mouths had turned to dust. That autumn, dealing in the *Sotsial-Demokrat* with official representatives of European Socialism who had "succumbed to bourgeois nationalism, to chauvinism," Lenin added his mordant comment that "with good reason the bourgeois press of all countries writes of them, now with derision, now with condescending praise."

Within the anti-war minority there were some around the Welsh mines who adhered to the standpoint put forward by James Connolly in mid-August, 1914: "If these men must die, would it not be better to die in their own country fighting for freedom for their class, and for the abolition of war, rather than go forth to strange countries and be slaughtering and slaughtered by their brothers that tyrants and profiteers may live." A similar, if less explicit standpoint was contained in a slim pamphlet entitled "War and the Welsh Miner" published in Tonypandy under the name of W. F. Hay, part-author of "The Miners' Next Step" (1912), the product of the Unofficial Reform Committee."[1]

[1] This stated:

"We know that the only defence of the British capitalist against the clutching hands of his fellow pirates across the channel is the British Navy. The effectiveness of this depends upon a continuous and ample supply of Welsh steam coal. This can only be produced with the consent of the Welsh collier." Then addressing "My Lords and Gentlemen, the capitalist class," the pamphlet continued in a somewhat rhetorical vein: "Yours is indeed a satirical fate. The Welsh collier, defeated in many a bitter conflict to obtain human conditions, cheated in his work by unscrupulous managers, speeded up by an iniquitous system of piecework, under price lists instituted by a process of unvarnished swindling, victimised and hounded from pillar to post, thrown on the road and blacklisted for demanding simple justice, robbed by the decisions of so-called 'impartial' chairmen, murdered by the hundred and thousand through the neglect of elementary precautions, cheated by judge-made law from the scanty 'compensation' for the 'accidents' which greed of profit made inevitable, the victim of a thousand extortions and villainies, this grimy slave of the lamp can hold the British Empire to ransom. Such as he is you have made him. In your heartless pursuit of a profit, you cared not if he became a veritable Caliban. You degraded him to the level of the first pony, and now expect him to immolate himself on the altar of your menaced Mammon God."

5 ARMY RECRUITING AND ENLISTMENT

In the last week of August, 1914, there came hard and heavy tidings to Britain of military disaster, of German armies surging through Belgium and across France, of the British Expeditionary Force pushing forward to meet the enemy on 23rd August near Mons whence with heavy losses the British Army was soon in rapid retreat. Following on this news came a series of decisions, a transformation of outlook, all taken within a very different atmosphere from that of the first week of August: of these the most significant was the Labour Party's resolution on recruiting for the army:

"That, in view of the serious situation created by the European War, the Executive Committee of the Labour Party agrees with the policy of the Parliamentary Party, in joining the campaign to strengthen the British Army, and agrees to place the Central Office organisation at the disposal of the campaign, and further recommends the affiliated bodies to give all possible local support" (29 viii 1914).

Not only did the South Wales Miners' Federation fall in with the rest of the trade unions in carrying out the policy for recruiting as put forward by the Labour Party and then by the Parliamentary Committee of the Trades Union Congress, but leading officials took an active and ardent part in "the campaign to strengthen the British Army." William Brace's oratorical powers were now at the service of the recruiting authorities: and he was ably seconded by Tom Richards, M.P., and most of the agents.

This autumn campaign raised problems of soldiers' pay and separation allowances, compensations, etc., etc., and the magnitude of these problems arose from the size of the response to the slogan "KITCHENER WANTS YOU!" Out of the whole of Wales, there were proportionately more enlisted than in England or Scotland. Of the total number of working miners in the South Wales coalfield in July, 1914, there was drained away nearly a fifth within less than nine months. Manpower was seriously depleted. But this "nearly a fifth" was withdrawn from mining personnel between the ages of 18 and 40, and in the first place from those just entered upon their manhood years. Of these it was well over a half who rushed to enlist in the armed forces.[1]

[1] "Our own industry has probably contributed the largest number, proportionately to our members, to any trade or industry in the country. Special efforts, I think at recruiting have gone on in the mining districts, and from the point of view of the heads of the Army there is some reason, a reason well known to many of us that they believe in securing the miner, they have already secured a man whose muscles are as hard as wood with hard work; a man who does not require an extraordinary amount of training to make him fit for the privations of a campaign; a man generally speaking whose whole life from early boyhood has brought him face to face with dangers almost as great as the battlefield. This being so, it is recognised that the miners make splendid soldiers, that the miners have proved they are not behind others in their patriotism and in their desire to do their share." (From Smillie's presidential address at Nottingham, 5th October, 1915).

Such was the power of the appeal to patriotic feeling, such the torrential force that swept these many into uniform. It applied to the people as a whole who, in the words of Robert Smillie's address to the MFGB Annual Conference "have answered the call and have gone forth to defend their country and their country's flag." None of his hearers at that moment wanted to remember what had been a fundamental tenet of socialism that "the working men have no country."

6 STRUCTURE OF THE SOUTH WALES MINERS' FEDERATION

The onset of war after its initial dislocation of markets could change the lives of those engaged in coal mining, deplete the manpower, slacken the old tensions between master and man, and for many months put a truce to industrial strife. But the form and functioning of the South Wales Miners' Federation remained as it had been since its formation fifteen years earlier—and was to be for another score of years. With an unusually high degree of autonomy in districts and lodges the union remained ineluctably federal in its functioning as well as in its structures.[1] Any one could be nominated when an agency fell vacant: but once selected the miners' agent was in a permanency. "Every agent is a Czar in his own district more or less," confessed Tom Richards some three years before the war began, "and no one else dares to interfere with him." The members of the Unofficial Reform Committee such as Noah Ablett, checkweigher in Mardy from 1909-1918, might make headway with some of their proposals (e.g., in the effort to absorb the coalfield craft organisations) : but not in their successive schemes for centralised reorganisation. The autonomy, natural in an industry with many hundreds of pits separately sunk and owned at a time when communications were poor and the use of the electric telephone was a novelty, was not so well suited to a developed coalfield dominated by one of the most formidable employers' combinations in Europe, the Monmouthshire and South Wales Coal Owners' Association. Hence the mordant utterance of Noah Ablett feeling the frustrations of a quarter of a century : "We have got the tribal system in operation, with all the little chieftains. We do not desire to continue institutions that are ossified and fossilised. We don't want the little tribes. We want one Union" (12 vii 1932).

LOCAL AUTONOMY VERSUS CENTRALISATION

The aim of the miners' Unofficial Reform Committee, born from the

[1]"The rules dealing with the election of officers and of the Executive Council with their several duties, made it clear that a federal constitution was the aim and that the source of effective power remained very largely in the districts. These twenty districts in the main corresponded to the valleys that were such a distinctive feature of the Welsh coalfield, each separated from its neighbour by a mountain and each with its own traffic in coal through a railway running up to the valley head. In each district the miners' agent held the key position". (*South Wales Miners, Glowyr De Cymru*, by R. Page Arnot. Vol. I, p 74).

1910-11 strike struggle in the Rhondda, was to make the South Wales Miners' Federation into a militant form of organisation. After the ballot votes of autumn 1911 had inflicted a signal defeat on their President (Rt. Hon. William Abraham, M.P.) and on his fellow office-bearers (Brace, Richards and Onions), Lib-Lab miners' agents for over a quarter of a century, a campaign was launched to alter the constitution. By September, 1912 (as told in a previous volume) the campaign had resulted in a decision by ballot vote for "Abolition of Districts and Centralisation of Funds and Administration"—only to have the consequent Reorganisation Scheme reversed by another ballot in the spring of 1913. Three months later Noah Ablett put the case in a paper contributed to a Barrow House conference in July, 1913, on "The Control of Industry" presided over by Beatrice Webb, who was then making preparations for the public launching of the Fabian Research Department that autumn. In two succinct paragraphs Ablett sought to clarify the "ORIGIN AND MEANING OF THE TWO IDEAS" viz:

AUTONOMY. In the first place we may bluntly put it down to the ambition of petty or local leaders who, being unable to be kings, adhere jealously to a dukedom with the fullest possible privileges. They exploit the parochial spirit. On the other hand this parochial spirit arises from a much nobler source. There is the horror of bureaucracy and uniformity commingled with the desire to govern as much as possible the conditions under which one has to live, or to put it after the manner of Ibsen—to find oneself by expressing one's individuality in as many ways as possible. This is at first view more easily capable of accomplishment in a small restricted area where the conditions and customs are the same, and where the individuals concerned are known to each other, than a larger area with a remote central government.

CENTRALISATION. Firstly, the idea is to obtain power to be a huge massive force. From the head officials' standpoint such increment added to the general body augments their importance and gives the greater social prestige. No doubt it also increases the efficiency and wage-earning capacity of the organisation, so that progress and great leadership seem to be in harmony. On the other hand, however, it will be found that the most advanced, militant and anti-leadership section in the S.W.M.F. are enthusiastic advocates of centralisation. Their motives, as will appear later, are: to kill parochialism, to increase the power of democracy by extending its sphere of influence, to kill leadership by destroying petty leaders, and to replace the functions of the great leaders into that of mere servants by transferring their power into the organisation and thus to find oneself in a still larger sense by synthesising the differences between autonomy and centralisation.

There was no prescriptive right of "the little chieftains" to sit upon the Executive Council: but each of them was nearly always a first choice from his district and from "his own members." Each district numbering 3,000 was entitled to one representative on the Executive Council and an additional representative for every 6,000 additional members. By the beginning of 1914 there were some thirty-two members of the Executive Council of whom nearly two dozen were miners' agents and the remainder mostly checkweighers.

South Wales with its great diversity of coals produced one fifth of British output, a proportion fully maintained in war-time.[1] Within the coalfield there was great diversity in the twenty districts of the South Wales Miners' Federation from tiny Saundersfoot at the eastern tip of Pembrokeshire, so small (333 miners) that John Williams, M.P., could take it on as well as his agency for the Western miners centred in Swansea, to the hundredfold more numerous Rhondda Valleys. A dozen districts ranged from two thousand to some six thousand and half as many more could count nearly a myriad miners each.

The numbers fluctuated from year to year. The total before the war was given as 154,000 members in the South Wales Miners' Federation. This, together with the 11,000 in other unions, made a total of 165,000 organised workers in an industry where the total employed counted 226,000. The fluctuation of membership was countered from time to time either by "showcard" days which induced the laggards to pay up and the lapsed members to repent. This ebb and flow of membership was particularly to be seen in the Rhondda, where it was affected by unemployment or by long duration of strikes or lockouts which left little money in the household. Fluctuation, indeed, seemed more constant than membership until the events of the war filled the pits and an agreement with the employers ended non-unionism.

In 1920 the total organised in Rhondda No. 1 district reached 40,000 with thirty-two lodges, some of them, as shown in the table given below, being larger than the lesser-sized S.W.M.F. districts:

Name of Lodge	Membership	Name of Lodge	Membership
Bodringallt	475	Ferndale	2,730
Maindy	855	Llwynypia	2,752
Cilely	700	Albion	1,631
Maerdy	2,020	Ynysfeio	1,108
Fernhill	1,127	Standard	1,143
Naval	2,264	Blaenclydach	385
Tylorstown	3,140	Cymmer	1,700
Coed Ely	1,322	Lewis Merthyr	1,753
Caerlan	63	Cambrian	3,806
Gelli Steam	105	Tydraw	735
Parc and Dare	2,124	Lady Lewis	1,039
Gelli House	336	Hendrewen	281
National	1,150	Bute Merthyr	722
Tynybedw	602	Nantdyrus	135
Eastern	698	Tylcha Fach	313
Penrhiwceiber	1,069		
Abergorky	1,800		40,083

[1] See Appendix IV to this chapter.

In the history of the South Wales Miners' Federation the foremost part at the beginning was played by the men from Monmouthshire—William Brace, Tom Richards, and very many others who became agents outside Monmouthshire, including Vernon Hartshorn and Frank Hodges. After the first decade, however, strong trade union activity in Glamorgan followed upon the growing tendency to monopoly as exemplified by the increasing power of D. A. Thomas, M.P., in the mid-Rhondda. With the growth of these "chain-pits" there came another feature not allowed for in the building up of the unions. This was the creation of "combine committees" which covered all collieries under a single ownership. Of these the most remarkable up to the war had been the famous Cambrian Combine whose committee conducted the struggle at Tonypandy and in the whole of mid-Rhondda.[1] Other combines presently were to be set up and their embryonic growth became visible during this war of 1914-18.

This, then, was the shape in war-time of the South Wales coalfield and of its chief trade union. In that trade union the miners reposed nearly all their hopes, and though five years earlier they had entered the Labour Party it was not to supply a long-felt need. This they had already met themselves by four members whom they had in Parliament from early on in the century and who formed part of a miners' group separate from the Labour Party. It was not until 1910 that they fought a general election as part of the Labour Party. Similarly, while in the second decade of the 20th century they operated through the Labour Party there was scarcely any of the candidates for the local government who were not from the minefields. A special example, again the Rhondda No. 1 District, lists in the 1918 annual report its representation upon public bodies.

This covered the eleven areas namely: the Trades Councils of Treherbert, Treorchy, Pentre, Mid-Rhondda, Tonyrefail, Porth, No. 9 Ward, Ferndale, Maerdy, Penrhiwceiber and Cilfynydd. These returned eleven members of the Board of Guardians; thirteen members of the County Council and no less than twenty in the District Council.

But it is impossible even by those examples to convey the extent to which this union differed from unions in industries that were less concentrated such as printing, building, engineering, scattered through every part of Britain. The life of the Welsh people in the valleys, largely channelled through "the Federation" was often of a different quality and a greater intensity than elsewhere. This, at any rate before 1914, was true also of the chapel. Few families there were in the valleys, at any rate of believers, that had not attended one or other of the dissenting chapels, Methodists, Baptists, Wesleyans or Independents.

Lastly, in those mining valleys, there was strong national feeling which for a time Lloyd George and others had sought to canalise

[1] See *South Wales Miners: Glowyr De Cymru* by R. Page Arnot.

into a "home rule" party. But when, in 1905, Lloyd George, the Welsh attorney was chosen rather than D. A. Thomas the coalowner by Campbell-Bannerman to be in the Liberal Cabinet, Lloyd George endeavoured to persuade his fellow countrymen that national aspirations were being partly satisfied in the promotion of his own person. Thus, to some extent, both chapel and union tended to carry a class outlook and a national feeling which had not yet found expression in other ways. But the main vehicle of a common national feeling was in the clear accents of those whose fathers had learned English and whose ancestry had spoken Welsh, the ancient language of the Roman province that was Britannia. Their vowels, diphthongs and consonants make a common bond, whether in the Celtic original or carried over into an English utterance that in most European ears is more sweetly sounding than the many pronunciations of Southern England.

APPENDIX I

THE SOCIALIST PRESS, 1914-18

With the almost complete collapse of socialism and of the associated international peace movement when the majority leaders of the European parties (with the exception of those in Hungary, Russia and Serbia) had gone back on their pledged word, there was in each country and in each working class body a minority. But those who steadfastly adhered to the Basel Manifesto were few : and their forces were feeble. Attempted public meetings were soon rendered very difficult by "jingo mobs" : and soon, apart from private meetings of branches or other units, most could find effective expression only in the written word. Apart from daily and weekly newspapers (even before 1914 beginning to be called "the capitalist press") the journals readily available to members of the South Wales Miners' Federation were few and meagre in comparison with continental countries.

From spring, 1912, the *Daily Herald*, edited latterly by G. Lansbury, sustained by H. D. Harben, and widely publicised by the cartoons of Will Dyson, was a stimulant to all kinds of socialist, syndicalist, anti-imperialist and feminist propaganda : but by September, 1914, it folded up into a weekly. The *Daily Citizen*, officially blessed by the Labour Party and by the Independent Labour Party and heavily supported from trade union funds (including from the Miners' Federation), ran from autumn, 1912, till early summer of 1915 when it ceased publication. Socialist penny weeklies with a national scope were *Justice*, founded in 1884 (with the help of Edward Carpenter and William Morris) as the paper of the Social-Democratic Federation : and the *Clarion*, founded in 1891 by Robert Blatchford. The *New Age*, a threepenny weekly of Fabian socialist dissenters, had from the spring of 1912 carried on the propaganda of Guild Socialism. In April, 1913, the sixpenny *New Statesman*, representing the majority Fabian standpoint, had been launched by Beatrice Webb. After August, 1914, both of the dailies and all of the above national socialist weeklies could be classed as pro-war socialist periodicals. Only one tenth of the adherents of the *Daily Citizen* manifested opposition to the war, and a little over four tenths in the case of the *Daily Herald*.

The *Labour Leader*, founded by Keir Hardie and representing from 1893 the standpoint of the Independent Labour Party, had at the outset of the war (with Fenner Brockway as editor) adhered to the Basel Congress (1912) standpoint. The same was true of the *Merthyr Pioneer* published from Keir Hardie's constituency of Merthyr Tydfil. The Scottish *Forward*, less overt, sought to maintain circulation, under the editorship of Tom Johnston, by appearing in part as an "open forum."

There were also irregular anti-war periodicals of seceders from the Socialist International parties amongst them those in which James Connolly was writing such as *The Socialist*, edited by George Harvey of Tyneside for the small Socialist Labour Party. These were joined by the *Women's Dreadnought* (afterwards the *Workers' Dreadnought*) edited by Sylvia Pankhurst: and in February, 1916, by *The Call*, the organ three months later of the British Socialist Party, when that body had rejected its pro-war leadership: and finally by *The Tribunal*, organ of the No-Conscription Fellowship edited alternately by Lydia Smith and Joan Beauchamp.

The monthly *Plebs*, organ of "independent working-class education" was widely read in the Federation, which had in the summer of 1914 become responsible together with the National Union of Railwaymen for the maintenance of the Central Labour College in London, at 13 Penywern Road, near Hammersmith.

There were other fugitive publications, both in English and Welsh, mostly so short-lived that their very names can scarcely be remembered while it will require most diligent search to find surviving copies. Anti-war pamphlets and leaflets too there were, both of established parties and also of short-lived *ad hoc* bodies such as the "British Stop-the-War Committee" which was promoted by C. H. Norman, a frequent contributor to the pre-war socialist press.

APPENDIX II

NAVIES AND COAL PRODUCTION OF BELLIGERENT POWERS

Country	FLEETS at January 1914		OUTPUT OF COAL
	Battle-ships	All ships	for year 1913 (in million tons)
United Kingdom	58	580	287
South Wales	–	–	57
France	21	339	39
Russia	8	152	30
Germany	35	328	188
Austria-Hungary	14	115	17
Japan	17	152	21
Italy[1]	9	177	Belgium 22

[1] The place of Italy which had scarcely any coal output is taken by Belgium (also one of the belligerents) which had very little in the way of a navy.

A

APPENDIX III

OFFICERS AND EXECUTIVE COMMITTEE OF THE SOUTH WALES MINERS' FEDERATION, 1915

Acting President: J. Winstone, J.P. [1]
Secretary: Ald. Thomas Richards, M.P.
General Treasurer: Alfred Onions, J.P., C.C., Tredegar.

Anthracite	J. D. Morgan, M.P., Ystradgynlais.
	John James, Cwmgorse.
Aberdare	C. B. Stanton.
Afan Valley	Wm. Jenkins, C.C., J.P., Cymmer, Pt. Talbot.
Blaina	James Manning, J.P.
Dowlais	J. Davies.
Eastern Valleys	W. L. Cook, The Old Oak, Blaenavon.
East Glamorgan	Hubert Jenkins, J.P., Abertridwr.
Ebbw Vale	Wm. Vyce.
Garw	Frank Hodges, Bridgend.
Maesteg	Vernon Hartshorn, J.P.
Merthyr	J. Williams, 8 Fairview Terrace, Merthyr.
Monmouthshire, Western	George Barker, Alexandra Road, Abertillery.
Valleys	Chas. Edwards, J.P., Wattsville, Cross Keys.
	G. Daggar, 25 High St., Six Bells, Abertillery.
Ogmore and Gilfach	Thos. Lucas, J.P., 3 "Nythfa," Ogmore Vale.
Pontypridd and Rhondda	Ben Davies, J.P.
	Rt. Hon. W. Abraham, M.P.
Rhondda No. 1	D. Watts Morgan, J.P., Porth.
	William John, Tonypandy.
	Noah Rees, 60 Thomas Street, Tonypandy.
	Noah Ablett, Glanville St., Mardy, Rhondda.
	Tom Smith, 248 Cemetery Road, Trealaw.
Rhymney Valley	Walter Lewis, J.P., Bargoed.
	Albert Thomas, Bargoed.
Taff and Cynon	E. Morrell, J.P., Troedyrhiw.
Tredegar Valley	Oliver Harris, Rhiw Syr, Dwia, Blackwood.
Western (& Saundersfoot)	John Williams, M.P., Sketty, Swansea.

[1] William Brace, M.P., did not function as President while in the Coalition Governments from 30th May, 1915, to 18th December, 1918.

APPENDIX IV

COAL OUTPUT, BY COUNTIES (in million tons).
(figures as given in South Wales Coal Annual, 1924)

County	1915	1916	1917	1918	1919	1920	1921	1922
Glamorgan ...	33.1	34.1	32.1	30.8	31.05	30.2	19.7	32.8
Monmouth ...	14.2	14.8	13.6	13.1	13.5	13.1	8.5	14.3
Carmarthen ...	2.4	2.4	2.2	2.2	2.3	2.3	1.7	2.5
Brecon ...	.655	.580	.384	.414	.481	.501	.429	.562
Pembroke ...	.056	.057	.046	.046	.063	.053	.038	.052
S. Wales and Mon. ...	50.4	52.080	48.50	46.7	47.5	46.2	30.5	50.3
All Other Counties ...	202.7	204.2	199.9	181.03	182.2	183.2	132.6	199.2
United Kingdom ...	253.2	256.3	248.4	227.7	229.7	229.5	163.2	249.6

It will be seen that Glamorgan produced roughly two-thirds of the total output and Monmouth rather more than a quarter. Carmarthen never reached more than a twentieth and together with Brecon made up about a seventeenth of the coalfield. Pembroke was never more than the very small amount here extracted from the eastern tip of the contorted anthracite seams.

CHAPTER TWO

TROUBLES ON THE HOME FRONT

1 A COAL SHORTAGE?

In the first week of the new year 1915 it was possible for Robert Smillie, who was also chairman of the all-embracing War Emergency: Workers' National Committee, to greet a special conference of his national Federation of 945,000 organised mineworkers with the sincere hope of so early an end to the war that "this year will rid us of the terrible struggle at present going on on the Continent of Europe" (7 i 1915). By the close of February, when the war had already lasted seven months, any such illusion had disappeared. The facile hopes of early victory had gone. The Allies' superiority in sea power and manpower had come up against the German superiority in fire power and in military organisation. On "the home front" in that first quarter of 1915 the infirmities in the economy of each Power began to be realised—in the United Kingdom as shortages of fuel, of food, of arms and all the munitions of war.

Meanwhile, the South Wales Miners' Federation, like all other unions, had to fit in to the strange and novel conditions of a major war. The miners' agents and lodge officials could only do what came to hand in the way of helping their members in case of hardship; but their essential trade union function, to maintain and improve the standard of life, had no longer behind it the sanctions of industrial conflict. These had been freely given up in August, 1914, when the industrial truce was spontaneously declared at a special national conference: "That an immediate effort be made to terminate all existing trade disputes, whether strikes or lock-outs, and whenever new points of difficulty arise during the war period a serious attempt should be made by all concerned to reach an amicable settlement before resorting to a strike or lock-out" (24 viii 1914).[1] The declaration was from one side

[1] How effective this industrial truce was may be seen from the following table of disputes before and after the declaration of war in 1914:

	Number of new disputes	Number involved in thousands
January ...	54 ...	30.6
February ...	67 ...	16
March ...	105 ...	17.6
April ...	99 ...	25.2
May ...	140 ...	34.5
June ...	118 ...	33.6
July ...	99 ...	45.7
August ...	15 ...	1.9
September ...	23 ...	2.9
October ...	27 ...	5
November ...	25 ...	4.6
December ...	17 ...	1.2

only of industry but the majority of the South Wales agents felt themselves bound by it. Moreover, several of them of military age volunteered for the Army, notably D. W. Morgan[1] the Rhondda agent.

Those against the war were in a minority that had seemed more and more negligible as the weeks passed by. Indeed, after six months of the war the question of the rights or wrongs of British participation in it disappeared underground : and only the Christmas, 1914, fraternisation of the "Tommies" with the "Fritzes" in the trenches served to show, like the shapes of a dissolving dream, that it had once been held that the workers of each country had no quarrel with one another.

Scarcely had the new year 1915 begun when "new points of difficulty" to jeopardise the industrial truce arose as the coalowners began to press for a suspension of the Eight Hours Act. Thereupon the Executive Committee of the Miners' Federation of Great Britain (on which sat four members from South Wales) "emphatically protested against the movement at present being engineered by the mine-owners, manufacturers, Chambers of Commerce, Gas Committees and other interested parties to bring about the suspension of the Eight Hours Act" (2 ii 1915).

Pressure followed by counter-pressure upon a government department had the usual outcome, namely, an inquiry into the facts and potentialities to be held by a departmental committee with equal representation upon it of owners and miners. Suddenly on Wednesday, 24th February, this was publicly announced as a committee "for enlistment from the mines." Immediately, the fat was in the fire. The miners' executive committee, in their wrath, questioned Hartshorn from South Wales, Smillie from Scotland and Walsh from Lancashire : and on the morrow, at an MFGB special conference, delegates also asked questions. Smillie explained in detail how he had been approached by the Chief Inspector of Mines about the committee. "I asked him if there was any connection with the proposal to suspend the Eight Hours Act. He said 'No'." Then, "to our astonishment an official report appeared in all the newspapers yesterday pointing out that the real object of this committee was to inquire whether or not it was possible to have such a combination of action between miners and mine-owners so as to arrange matters in order to set at liberty for enlistment further men from the mines of this country" (22 ii 1915). Smillie ended by

[1] David Watts Morgan had previously been criticised for his recruiting activities by Tydraw Lodge which, however, was defeated at the Rhondda District meeting by 21 votes to 11 : and a little later, on 26th October, 1914, he was congratulated on his commission by 23 votes to 4. It was agreed in mid-February, 1915, that Watts Morgan's pay in his absence on service be made up by the Rhondda District : and he continued to pop up at meetings during 1915 and first half of 1916 when he is referred to as Captain. On 7th May, 1917, he is congratulated on becoming Major, just before he goes on active service to France. On 1st January, 1918, the District Meeting congratulated him on his Distinguished Service Order won "for bravery on the Field of Battle." In the Rhondda Reports after the 1914-18 war their chief agent appears as Colonel D. Watts Morgan, D.S.O., M.P.

saying that, either by the fault of the Home Secretary or the Government or of the Chief Inspector of Mines, "We have been hopelessly and shamefully misled."

Meanwhile, at the Home Office, the terms of reference had been hastily amended : and that same evening the MFGB executive committee resolved that "in view of the amended terms of reference [1] we advise our three members to serve on the committee" : but they added a caution that "in the event of circumstances proving to them that the committee is to be used in the interests of recruiting, or for any purpose which they consider to be inimical to the interests of the Federation, our members shall resign their positions on the committee" (25 ii 1915).

The facts found by the inquiry about enlistment and output are significant. The number of workers in the coal mines before the war was 1,116,648. Up to the end of February, 1915, 191,170 had enlisted. This was a total of 17.1%. By the end of April it was estimated that the number of miners with the colours was over 220,000. The estimate was that the decrease in coal production for the whole year 1915 would be fully 36 million tons. But such a loss of output did not mean a shortage to the like extent: for fully 18 million tons, normally exported to Germany, Austria-Hungary, Turkey, Russia and Belgium would be liberated by the closing of those markets.

In the course of the inquiry the following means were suggested as calculated to counteract the effect of shortage: suspension of the Eight Hours Act: introduction of labour from outside (by which Robert Smillie suspected was meant Chinese coolie labour) : employment of women to perform the lighter work on the surface of the mines: reduction of the age limit for boys to work underground or on the surface.

The conclusions of the committee's first report[2] did not fall in with any of these four suggestions: and, actually, a power of veto on the vexed question of hours of labour was suggested for the workmen, viz:

"With reference to the Eight Hours Act, we suggest that the owners and workmen should confer together and determine to what extent, if

[1] "To inquire into the conditions prevailing in the coal mining industry with a view to promoting such organisation of work and such co-operation between employers and workmen as, having regard to the large number of miners who are enlisting for naval and military service, will secure the necessary production of coal during the war."

[2] Cd. 7939 of May, 1914. Seven months later, in the Second General Report, paragraph 13 ran: "**The Eight Hours Act.** At a conference between the representatives of the coalowners of Great Britain and the Miners' Federation of Great Britain on matters arising out of our First Report, held at the Home Office on the 2nd September last, at which our Chairman presided, the question of the suspension of the Eight Hours Act during the period of the war was discussed. The workmen's representatives were of the opinion that the question of suspension should not be considered until it was seen how far the joint efforts of owners and workmen to increase output which were to be made had been successful, and the coalowners' representatives recognised that suspension could not be usefully employed until the time had arrived when co-operation between the parties on the question was possible" (10 xii 1915).

at all, the Act should be suspended in individual districts, i.e., to what class of labour the suspension should apply, and the amount in point of time the suspension should cover" (7 v 1915).

The Miners' Federation of Great Britain, it was also suggested, should alone deal with curtailment of holidays and "stop-days" as well as with absenteeism; while the owners were urged "in the highest interests of the nation" to co-operate with the representatives of the workmen on such questions as "non-unionism, or other questions likely to lead to any friction or stoppage during the present unprecedented circumstances." This last recommendation was later to have its effect in South Wales where disputes over non-unionism had been particularly prevalent for over a decade. In 1906 disputes through refusal to work with non-union men were "the highest on record." Out of 50,750 workers affected the Government report (Cd. 3711 of 1907) states that "no less than 45,995 were coal miners in South Wales and Monmouthshire, where a determined effort was made by members of the South Wales Miners' Federation to compel all non-unionists to join the Federation." By the spring of 1915 the reluctance of the South Wales owners to co-operate with the unions on non-unionism brought about local disputes. Out of 30 disputes in the six months after February, 1915, no less than ten were in the coal mining industry and of these some half-a-dozen were in South Wales, mostly over non-unionism.[1] The industrial truce was wearing thin.

2 A NEW WAGE AGREEMENT?

At this time the need for discussion with the coalowners about the revision and renewal of wage agreements, which were due to expire in the spring of 1915, was taken up in South Wales. These agreements were the main content of the conciliation boards by which for a dozen or more years a measure of peace if not of industrial harmony had been maintained in the British coalfield. The South Wales Executive Council looked forward to a friendly discussion between the two sides of the industry, whose representatives had been brought into closer relations by the impact of the war crisis. But the owners in South Wales turned out to have quite a different viewpoint about the revision of the

[1] **Labour Disputes (March to August, 1915)**

Month		Duration in Days
March	2,136 miners, Merthyr Tydfil (against employment of non-unionists)	2
April	850 miners, Pontardawe (against employment of non-unionists)	7
June	1,084 miners, near Pontypridd (refusal to work with non-unionists)	3
June	1,538 miners, Rhondda Valley (refusal to work with non-unionists)	2
August	1,500 miners, etc., Pontypridd (refusal to work with non-unionists)	1

conciliation board: and from this there was to develop a serious situation in the summer of 1915.

Back in October, 1913, at the Scarborough conference of the Miners' Federation of Great Britain, important decisions on this matter had been taken, arising from their experience of the 1912 national strike. One was to make the national Federation much stronger and tighter by assimilating its numerous conciliation boards one to another so that they would be able to move to the long desired goal of one single conciliation board, one single national negotiating unit. The actual resolutions of Scarborough were to the following effect: (1) That all new agreements entered into by the conciliation boards must terminate at one and the same time, subject to three months notice : (2) That a new standard of wages be created in place of the present obsolete standards 1877, 1879 and 1888 by merging into the new standards all bonuses and percentages not less than the existing minimum percentages recognised by the present boards: (3) That a minimum wage of not less than 5/- per day for all adult surface workers be asked for: (4) That notice be given to terminate all existing agreements regulated by conciliation boards on 1st April, 1915.

Ten months thereafter, the war made its impact upon Britain, dislocating the programmes of the trade unions. Much of the energies of the mining unions was channelled into other activities, such as raising funds in relief of Belgian miners. In these harassing circumstances the Scarborough resolutions appeared for a time to have dropped out of memory. They had not been forgotten, however, in the Welsh Valleys. At the last council meeting in Cardiff of the year 1914 a letter was read from the Garw District on the termination of the conciliation board agreement, whereupon it was resolved "that the matter of the possibility of terminating the general wage agreement in the Federation areas next year be raised by our representatives on the MFGB committee with a view to a uniform procedure being adopted in all districts" (23 xii 1914). In London, this request was remitted from 7th January to a special discussion one month later when the initiative taken by South Wales resulted in the following resolution :

"That for the guidance of districts in the negotiation of new wages agreements the executive committee recommends that no such agreement be finally settled until it has been submitted to the executive committee for confirmation in order to ascertain whether or not the principles laid down by the Federation of Great Britain are embodied in the terms of the agreement" (4 ii 1915).

It looked as though in spite of war difficulties the Scarborough resolutions on new agreements were now to be tackled in earnest. So the very next day, on Friday, 5th February, the executive council at Cardiff drafted proposals for a programme to be put on the morrow to the coalfield conference in Cory Hall, Cardiff, the first of 1915. There the following three resolutions were put to the 274 delegates:

"1. That notices be given on April 1st to terminate the Conciliation Board Agreement.

"2. That the council be authorised to open negotiations with a view to a new agreement.

"3. That the proposals of the council be accepted as the terms for negotiations, viz. (a) All surface workmen be paid a minimum rate of wages of not less than 5/- per day. (b) That workmen employed on the afternoon and night shifts be paid at the rate of a turn and a fifth for each shift worked. (c) That 50 per cent be merged in the present standard rate to form a new standard. (d) That 10 per cent above new standards be the minimum rate of wages. (e) That a uniform rate of wages be paid all hauliers whether employed by day or night" (6 ii 1915).

The resolutions were carried unanimously : and on 13th February, 1915, six council members together with the officials were appointed to prepare draft proposals for submission to the owners. A fortnight later the draft of the proposals "for a revision of the Conciliation Board Agreement" was adopted and sent to the employers with a request for "a joint meeting for its consideration" (1 iii 1915).

The letter the coalowners sent in reply, dated the 9th March, 1915, was as follows:

"Dear Sir, The owners' representatives on the conciliation board have considered your letter to me of the 3rd instant, intimating the intention of the workmen employed at the collieries embraced in the Conciliation Board Agreement to give three months notice on the 1st April next to terminate the agreement, and putting forward the schedule of the workmen's proposals for a revision of the agreement.

"In reply to your letter I am instructed to say that confidently appealing to the same spirit of loyalty as was displayed by the workmen and their representatives in the early stages of the war the owners most seriously urge the desirability of continuing the existing agreement for the duration of the war so as to maintain the output and avoid disputes and possible cessation of work at the collieries.

"If the workmen's representatives agree to this proposal the owners recognising that there has been some increase in the cost of living (although not so great to miners as to other classes of labour in the country because of the old established custom of the men receiving cheap coal at prices which under the agreement cannot be altered) are prepared to offer to the men a war bonus of 10 per cent on the existing standard rates until peace is declared, such bonus to apply as from the 1st April next.

"In making this concession the owners wish to point out some of the difficulties which they have to contend with. The bulk of the output of South Wales coal was contracted for at prices very much lower than prices now ruling in the open market. A reduction of from 15 to 20 per cent has taken place in the output of the collieries, owing to large numbers of colliery workmen having joined the colours involving a corresponding increase in the cost of working. A very large increase has occurred in the cost of materials necessary for the working of the collieries."

The letter, addressed to "Thomas Richards, Esq., Secretary to the Workmen's Representatives on the Board of Conciliation for the Coal Trade of Monmouthshire and South Wales" was signed, as usual, by W. Gascoyne Dalziel, secretary of The Monmouthshire and South Wales Coal Owners' Association.

This employers' association, originating half a century earlier "to resist unjustifiable demands on the part of the colliers"[1], set up "a sliding scale" for wages from the year 1875 when it had caused the dissolution of the Amalgamated Association of Miners. Some four years after the formation in 1898 of the South Wales Miners' Federation a Conciliation Board was reluctantly conceded by the owners, who made the workmen pay heavily for it in the terms of the first wages agreement (31st March, 1903, to 31st December, 1905). The second Conciliation Board ran for four years from 1st January, 1906 to 31st December, 1909.

Under a Wages Agreement, dated 8th April, 1910, a third Board of Conciliation was "established to determine the general rate of wages to be paid to the workmen, and to deal with disputes at the various collieries of the owners." It was set forth in Clause 26 that "this Agreement shall continue in force" from the 1st April, 1910, until the 31st March, 1915, and thenceforth "until either party gives to the other three calendar months notice terminating the same." Upon the termination of agreement, it was stated "all contracts of service" between the owners respectively and their workmen "shall cease," when, presumably, unless there were negotiated in the meantime another agreement, there would be a resumption, not of the sliding scale, but of the earlier condition of unregulated industrial conflicts.

To most of the SWMF Executive Council, when the epistle from Gascoyne Dalziel was read to them, it seems never to have occurred that there would be a possibility of the owners refusing to negotiate. Tough bargaining they had expected, but refusal to negotiate seemed to be a reversion to the period of the Boer War and the late nineties when Sir William Lewis, afterwards Baron Merthyr of Senghenydd, had declined to have a Conciliation Board at all, and indeed would not recognise the trade unions.

Welsh miners' leaders were therefore astounded at this apparent reversion to an earlier standpoint : and this in wartime when trade unions had been prepared to give up so much and had proclaimed an industrial truce. They regarded the attitude of the employers as a breach of that truce, a break with the normal procedures of industrial relations and an attempt on the pretext of the war to shuffle out of solemn engagements. Their feeling on this was all the keener as they knew that the

[1] See *South Wales Miners, Glowyr De Cymru*, by R. Page Arnot, Chapter I.

employers were "doing well out of the war" as shown by the rising prices on the coal market. The offer of 10 per cent seemed to them merely a device by the employers to forestall the inevitable concession of a war bonus then being agitated for on a national scale.

In the biblical language to which so many of them were accustomed, the miners were being asked to barter away their birthright for a mess of pottage in the shape of a war bonus which they were going to have in any case. It was therefore with restrained indignation that the council briefly took its decision. The owners, holding out the bait of the 10 per cent bonus, had refused to negotiate. They in turn refused the bait and stuck to their previous engagements. Their decision was "that the council cannot consider any offer of an advance in wages which is made conditionally upon a postponement of the revision of the Conciliation Board Agreement" (12 iii 1915). On the 1st April, three months notice was given by the workmen's side of the South Wales Board of Conciliation.

From mid-March onwards when, if not earlier, negotiations should have been taking place, there was no response from the owners. Throughout the next three months the owners maintained their refusal to negotiate, while the Government, afterwards to play a prominent part in the dispute, seems to have taken no heed of the situation that was developing in South Wales.

Ten weeks after the owners had been notified by the special conference of 5th February of the terms desired by the miners for the new Conciliation Board, and three weeks after formal notice had been given on 1st April, there was still no shift shown in their attitude. It was an attitude peculiar to the Monmouthshire and South Wales Coal Owners' Association. The whole matter was reported to a South Wales special conference. It was felt that their only possible recourse was to put the situation to the Miners' Federation of Great Britain which had already indicated how and in what way the 1913 decisions of Scarborough were to be put into effect. So a unanimous decision was taken by 292 delegates, representing 142,993 members. "In face of the South Wales coalowners refusing to meet for negotiating an agreement, that we oppose the signing of an agreement for any period by any district in the Federation, until the whole of the district agreements have been negotiated" (19 iv 1915).

The speeches in the discussion showed that the valleys were seething with rage, valleys, so many of whose families had made what was then termed "the supreme sacrifice." This mood amongst the colliers was presently to be reflected in the conference of 22nd April in London when each district was called upon to report what degree of success they had had in carrying out the Scarborough resolutions each with their own Conciliation Board. All other districts had had negotiations with the employers, and in each they could report, at any rate, some accommodation reached with the other side of the Conciliation Board.

William Brace began by telling that in a meeting with the coalowners over "the ordinary troubles of the coalfield" the Conciliation Board met on 17th April. He had, at the request of his colleagues, asked the employers to give a date when they might meet to discuss the making of an amended Conciliation Board Agreement. Brace then had to undergo the humiliation of revealing with what scant courtesy the owners had behaved. He said:

"I regret to have to report that the coalowners' chairman was instructed to tell us that under no consideration would the coalowners give us a date to discuss the making of an amended wages agreement to take the place of the agreement that is now terminating.

"I need hardly say what was pointed out when they adopted that extraordinary attitude, that attitude must mean disaster unless something was done to change that phase of things. They said they were quite aware of the seriousness of their reply but a stoppage of work was not going to terrify them at all into doing what they do not want to do, that they had made up their minds during the war period this agreement must stand and nothing I could say or my colleagues, or anyone else presumably, would change their view."

Fred L. Davis, the chairman on the owners' side of the Conciliation Board, had said:

"If you put it to me, you are technically within your right in asking for a meeting. I am not going to refuse to meet but I should only tell you then what I am telling you now, that we will not discuss the making of an agreement following the one now terminating."

To this the President of the South Wales miners had returned a placable answer, as he did not want "to create further embarrassment to an embarrassing position." He said: "We put it quite courteously, and quite respectfully, but without avail."

William Brace concluded:

"We are at the maximum, and unless something is done to remove the maximum and amend the agreement, no matter how the selling prices advance, we cannot advance.

"You need not be very much surprised that the Welsh coalfield is seething with agitation.

"I make this report, we are part and parcel of this organisation. We have given notice upon the instructions of the national organisation, and on our part, we say we have endeavoured to find ways and means for a peaceful solution. But that is the position of the owners.

"It is now out of our hands and in the hands of the national organisation" (22 iv 1915).

As it turned out, the national organisation was not ready at that stage to take it over from the district: and eleven weeks later, when they were ready to do so, it was entirely out of their hands.

3 HIGH PRICES FOR FOOD AND FUEL

War brought a speeding-up of the inflation that had begun nearly twenty years earlier—so much so that the pound sterling, worth 20 shillings in 1896, was worth only 14/7d by 1914. From August, 1914, this kind of inflation was accelerated. After six months of food prices soaring upward at an increasing rate—due partly to war profiteering by shipowners—the matter came up at the MFGB executive committee. A resolution, drafted by Hartshorn, Straker and Walsh, and unanimously adopted, urged the Government (which so far had refused to move) "to take immediate steps" so as to "prevent the community being exploited" (2 ii 1915). The resolution was sent both to the Prime Minister and to the "War Emergency Committee," which had already been carrying on a vigorous campaign.[1] This forced, on 9th February, 1915, a Food Prices Debate in the House of Commons, which made it clear that the Government was not ready to respond. Prime Minister Asquith would not give the immediate help that was needed : and, in his speech, somewhat callously advised that the workers should "wait till June." Thereupon it was realised that the workers must prepare to help themselves.

The South Wales contingent—over a quarter of the delegates, 38 out of 138—who attended the national miners' conference on 25th February, 1915, joined in the unanimous decision that the MFGB executive committee should consider "the serious increase in the cost of living." When, some three weeks later, they were summoned once more to the Westminster Palace Hotel they were again part of the unanimous decision that the Miners' Federation of Great Britain "make a demand as a national organisation for an advance in wages in consequence of the increased cost of living" (17 iii 1915). The demand made was for an immediate increase of 20 per cent "on present earnings." This was to be obtained through an "immediate national joint meeting of the representatives of the owners and workmen." To this proposal, however persuasively it was put to them and however cogently argued by the MFGB secretary, in the second half of March, the coalowners in the Mining Association of Great Britain would not agree. Their refusal to come to the proposed national meeting appears to have put a considerable strain on the patience of the miners' leaders.

Another two weeks passed by and the miners were no nearer to securing the national joint meeting with the coalowners. Meantime the tension in the coalfields was mounting higher and higher. Already food prices stood well above the high February level which had led the miners to table their "modest proposal" for 20 per cent.

In mid-April in Cardiff at a fully attended executive council meeting the main business was this demand, on which a number of letters had been received from districts and lodges. After a report had been given

[1] For this campaign in South Wales see Appendix I.

by the members of the MFGB committee upon the attempts made to secure a national conference, there was keen discussion and a whole range of proposals as is shown by the following excerpt from the minutes:

"*Proposed*: That conference on Monday be recommended to instruct the delegates to the national conference on Wednesday to move that in face of the coalowners' refusal to co-operate for a national joint meeting, that each conciliation board be authorised to meet the respective coalowners to arrange an advance upon the 20 per cent resolution of the national conference. 6 votes.

"*Amendment*: That we reaffirm our demand for a national joint conference of owners and workmen, to get this matter settled. 18 votes. This was carried.

"*Further proposed*: That failing a national conference, the Government be asked to intervene at once with a view to getting a settlement. 12 votes.

"*Amendment*: That failing a national conference, we tender 14 days notice to terminate contracts. 13 votes. This was carried".

Within three days the feelings of dissatisfaction had grown greater in the valleys: and reached a climax of tension, on Monday, 19th April, 1915, when 292 delegates (representing 142,993 members) of the South Wales Miners' Federation gathered for the union's annual conference in Cory Hall, Cardiff. The first item on the agenda was the demand for "war bonus": whereupon six proposals were made amid the tumult of debate: (1) "That we tender 14 days notice to terminate contracts": (2) "That failing a satisfactory answer to our claim by the 21st or 22nd of this month, that we down tools at once": (3) "That the Government be asked to demand the books of the coalowners, that we may secure what is due on the selling price since the commencement of the war, or that 14 days notice be given": (4) "That any advance secured be retrospective to the 1st of April, and made subject to three months notice": (5) "Unless the bonus is paid before 1st May and made retrospective, notices be given on the 1st May": (6) "That the Government be asked to call a joint conference at once to deal with our application." At length, after a whole morning of debate, the following resolution was carried:

"That the South Wales delegation to the National Conference be instructed to move a resolution to tender 14 days notice to terminate contracts to enforce our claim for a war bonus of 20 per cent."

Clearly, the industrial truce which was to last for the whole period of the war was now nearing its term in South Wales. Seven months and more had passed and already some new development was quickening in the womb of time.

As the third week of April drew near there began to be some perturbation in Whitehall. By Tuesday, 20th April, as the miners' leaders assembled in Westminster in preparation for their special conference there were emissaries from the Board of Trade and particularly from its Labour Department (soon to become the nucleus of the Ministry of Labour) seeking to find out exactly what was the standpoint of the miners and what policy they were likely to pursue : but they got very little change out of Smillie or Ashton. So the chief permanent official of the Board of Trade wrote that night a letter which was personally brought round by Isaac Mitchell, the one-time boilermakers' secretary, who was almost the first of trade union leaders to have been given "a post in the Board of Trade." The letter ran as follows :

Sir, 20th April, 1915.

I am directed by the Board of Trade to advert to your letter addressed to the Chancellor of the Exchequer during the recent Treasury conferences with trade union representatives, and to the offer on the part of your executive contained therein to hold themselves at the disposal of representatives of the Government if at any time they should desire to confer with them. With reference thereto, I am to say that Mr. Runciman will be very glad if representatives of your executive could make it convenient to meet him tomorrow, Wednesday, afternoon at 5.30 o'clock, at the Board of Trade.

I am, Sir,

Your obedient servant,

H. Llewellyn Smith.

Thos. Ashton, Esq.,
General Secretary,
Miners' Federation of Great Britain.

4 THEY CONFER WITH WALTER RUNCIMAN

On the afternoon of Wednesday, 21st April, 1915, the members of the MFGB executive entered No. 7 Whitehall Gardens and met for the first time the new President of the Board of Trade, Walter Runciman junior, eldest son of the millionaire shipowner Sir Walter Runciman. From the time he left Cambridge, Walter Runciman had been dedicated to a life of "public service." So at the age of 28 he contested the double-barrelled constituency of Oldham where his opponents were the cotton-spinner James Mawdsley, who stood as a Tory trade unionist and a young aristocrat who stood as the Tory candidate, W. S. Churchill. The son of the capitalist Runciman defeated both of them. As a sufficiently gifted and enormously wealthy young Liberal he was given, in mid-December, 1905, the post of Parliamentary Secretary to the Local Government Board. By 1908 Runciman was taken into the Cabinet as President of the Board of Education, kept there as President of the Board of Agriculture and Fisheries, and then on the outbreak of war, as President of the Board of Trade. Thereafter he was seldom out of office in the later Coalition Governments until 1937 when he went to the House of Lords.[1]

At the outset of the meeting Runciman had the hardihood to make the suggestion that the attitude of the miners as expressed in resolutions could easily be a comfort if not an aid to the enemies of Britain, citing an instance from one coalfield as having been "circulated throughout the country by the German wireless messages." Then he stressed the anxieties of the Government who were "anxious that nothing should be published or in any way made public by way of resolutions or otherwise which would cause apprehensions in France, and possibly in other countries that may be associated with us,[2] and simultaneously rejoicing in Berlin" : and finally asked the miners to explain, as "I do not know exactly what is the attitude of the Miners' Federation, and what their feelings are at the present moment : to put it in a vulgar form what are they out for ?"

Robert Smillie explained the situation and the attitude of the Miners' Federation. He recounted also what steps they had taken in their quest for a 20 per cent bonus to meet a rise in the cost of living—which that month had gone up to 26 per cent above the already high level of July, 1914. But before he ended he made the following retort to the "offensive insinuation" voiced by Walter Runciman about the effect abroad of trade union resolutions :

"I wonder whether or not any reports get into the foreign newspapers to the effect that the mine-owners of this country, who have raised the price of coal on current prices by from 2/-d. to 10/-d. per ton, have refused at the same time to meet the miners who are wishing to meet them to discuss the wages question with them.

"A report of that kind, that the mine-owner has refused to meet us nationally even to discuss the wages question, surely would have the effect which you mention here, both on this nation's enemies abroad and also upon the tens of thousands and hundreds of thousands of miners who have gone abroad, and who may read reports of this kind.

"I only say that to remind you that if there is any blame or any danger arising from reports it should not be confined to the workmen's side of the thing" (21 iv 1915).

Early next day at the executive committee bitter words were spoken about the behaviour of Runciman : but to the conference, Smillie said he would not embitter the debate; and therefore merely remarked :

"Mr. Runciman did not seem to meet us as an outside intelligent Government official who was going to try to have a national settlement, but rather struck us, struck the whole of the executive, as being a

[1] In his biography in *Who's Who* he proudly listed his "Munich" activity in 1938 as being that of "Head of Mission to Czechoslovakia 1938." It was on his return that he was made Lord President of the Council on the last day of October, 1938. On the outbreak of war a year later Viscount Runciman of Doxford retired. (See *The Munich Conspiracy* by Andrew Rothstein, 1958.)

[2] Runciman was referring to Italy which four weeks later adhered to the Entente and declared war on Austria-Hungary.

capitalistic partisan, who felt it his first duty to put the employers' position rather than have very much sympathy with us" (22 iv 1915).

5 "UP TO THE PRESENT TIME WE HAVE FAILED"

The morning of 21st April, 1915, in somewhat cramped quarters (the lesser conference room of the Westminster Palace Hotel) had begun almost the largest and perhaps the longest of all the special conferences held in the twenty-five years of the Miners' Federation of Great Britain. Out of 162 delegates 41 came from the South Wales coalfield, amongst them ten Justices of the Peace and four Members of Parliament.

President Smillie, opening the conference, told how so far they had been unable to get the desired meeting with the owners. "Mr. Ashton," he said "has used all his persuasive powers and has also used the personal friendship that exists between himself and Sir Thomas Ratcliffe Ellis in addition: that, in itself, would have been sufficient to have secured such a conference had it been at all possible, but Mr. Ashton has failed."

Smillie then told how the miners had incurred much odium and widespread abuse, saying: "Personally I have received a considerable number of letters; some of them signed. Most of them were full of abuse, full of blame of the miners' side of the movement, and especially their leaders. Most of the letters were written by perfectly earnest people who did not know the full facts of the case; but I have had no letter from any source in which any blame at all was attached to the mine owners of this country; all the blame was to be attached to the miners, they were charged with want of patriotism and everything of that kind . . . . I do not think public opinion of that kind ought in any way to interfere with us doing what we believe to be our duty to our people" (21 iv 1915).

Smillie then asked for discussion, whereupon three main standpoints were put forward. The first (moved by Yorkshire) was to abandon hope of national action, and for each district to do the best they could according to their power. Before this could be fully discussed, the chairman ruled that a vote for or against rescission of the previous conference's resolution must be taken first. This resulted in 50 delegates for rescission and 85 against. The second (moved by Northumberland) was to ask the Government to convene a national conference between owners and miners. Third came the "fourteen days notice" motion from South Wales which had so agitated the officials of the Board of Trade. It had been carried by a single vote after a long discussion in the executive council in Cardiff: but then had been adopted in the SWMF annual conference by a very large majority. William Brace, M.P., was compelled to move a resolution to which he had, in council and conference, put up the strongest opposition. Frank

Hodges, however, supported the South Wales resolution [1] in his most eloquent manner. He attacked the Liberal Government, and particularly Runciman, for its partiality towards capitalist interests, and said:

"Who will be the people responsible for the result of notices being given? Can it be the miners, can it be us, can it be laid at the door of South Wales district of this Federation if it is carried into effect? Gentlemen, the onus of responsibility will fall on the capitalists in the first instance, and the Government in the second instance, for not having the courage to remove the capitalists' objection."

Replying for Northumberland, William Straker said:

"Let me say that I wept bitter tears when I knew that war was declared, and now if we, the miners of England, Scotland and Wales, were to decide to stop coal supplies, and thereby stopping munitions of war being sent out to the poor fellows in the trenches who are laying down their lives for us, I would weep tears of blood . . . Will not the capitalistic coalowners be responsible? Granted that the capitalistic owners are what we say they are, absolutely unpatriotic, and that they are not doing their share as patriots, does that justify us in following their example?"

Noah Ablett, answering Straker with his usual speed of utterance and brevity, reiterated the standpoint of the majority both on the Executive Council and in the SWMF annual conference on the issue of the war bonus.

"I may say that the most extreme man in South Wales does not contemplate a strike. Why? Because they know that the Government is in charge of this country at the present time, and they know full well they would do all they possibly could to prevent that.

"One of the delegates has given expression about 'my brother who is in the trenches' at present. I have more regard to the mother with three or four children here who is weak and defenceless. I want to ask you why should we be more patriotic than the coalowners?"

Then, looking around at the scores of delegates from the English coalfields where sat several former Lib-Lab Members of Parliament, and not without a glance at the older members of his own delegation, Noah Ablett voiced his suspicions:

"Then again with regard to the Government, I may be deemed offensive in saying—I feel strongly on this matter—I will say, assuming that a Tory Government had been in power, would the same regard have been paid to the Government as is exercised today had there been no Liberal Government in power?

"I think we ought to look at this question from our point of view, and use the power of this organisation as much as we possibly can to

[1] "That in face of the persistent refusal of the coalowners to meet in national conference to negotiate and settle the workmen's claim for a 20 per cent advance in wages to cover the increase in the cost of living, this conference of the Miners' Federation of Great Britain advise its members to tender fourteen days notice to terminate contracts failing the conceding of the 20 per cent advance upon existing wages by the employers" (22 iv 1915).

get our demands for our men, because experience has shown us that the authorities will not move unless you tell them in a definite manner what is going to happen if they do not. The most diplomatic course to take is to convince the Government of the country that we mean business."

Smillie from the chair criticised Ablett's argument, his own standpoint being that "if we are forced on strike because we cannot get a joint meeting to negotiate our claim for a 20 per cent advance, the strike will be for our claim for 20 per cent increase and not Government interference or anything else . . . . I have thought from beginning to end we should have to have a strike to secure it."

He was himself criticised by Steve Walsh, M.P. of Lancashire, who said :

"I think everybody will agree that at the very beginning very little consideration was given to the point as to whether a 20 per cent war bonus was justified or not. The President brought the matter forward without the slightest consultation with any of his colleagues on the executive. He approached the matter at the time by saying he hoped Mr. Ashton would not rule him out of order. He let him go on and there was not a single objector."

The South Wales resolution was then put to the vote and was completely defeated, every other district voting against. There was now left the resolution from Northumberland which commanded the general assent of the delegates. It ran as follows :

"That, as the coalowners have refused to agree to our request for a national conference in order to discuss with them our demand for a 20 per cent special advance on present wages, we instruct the executive committee to ask the Government to convene a national conference between the representatives of the coalowners and the representatives of the miners for this purpose and that this conference stand adjourned for one day to wait the Government's reply" (22 iv 1915).

The Northumberland resolution was transmitted that same Thursday evening to the Prime Minister. On Friday, 23rd April, there came a reply; and it was arranged for the executive committee to meet the Prime Minister immediately.

Late that afternoon Smillie reported back to the conference and told the substance of the discussion with the Prime Minister who, he said, "seemed to receive us in a very kindly spirit, and tried to make us at home. We put our position before him, and we gave additional reasons why there should be a joint conference between the mine-owners and ourselves. He seemed to be possessed of the opinion that we ought to endeavour to settle locally. We pointed out to him, however, that if this was settled it would have to be settled on national lines." Smillie then told how after they had made out the strongest case they could the Prime Minister asked them to retire and that when he had come back he said to the miners that obviously he could not peremptorily call a meeting without consultation with the owners; but he would get in touch with them.

So the delegates adjourned until Monday, 26th April. In the meantime preparations were made for the discussion with the coalowners and with the Government. The conference which Prime Minister Asquith had promised to call was held at the Home Office in Whitehall between "representative coalowners of Great Britain" and the MFGB representatives, with Asquith presiding and Runciman present on Thursday, 29th April. It resulted in deadlock: and on Saturday, 1st May, the miners' conference by 438 votes to 279 resolved "to refer this question to the Prime Minister for settlement."

In his letter to the Prime Minister that afternoon, Thomas Ashton stated: "It was decided to accept your suggestion made at the joint meeting of owners' and workmen's representatives, held at the Home Office on April 29th, over which you presided, and to remit to you the miners' claim for a 20 per cent advance in wages to meet the increased cost of living. The conference expresses an earnest hope that the settlement of this national question be retained in your own hands."

Four days later the Prime Minister telegraphed his decision that he was "for an immediate advance of wages to coal miners," but that "owing to the great variety of local conditions it is not possible for me to fix an amount which shall apply uniformly to all the coalfields."

So the Prime Minister's award referred the matter for settlement to the conciliation boards in each coalfield. It had turned out in the end even as Smillie had feared.

On 7th May the MFGB committee resolved: "The Prime Minister having decided that the special advance in wages owing to the increased cost of living shall be determined by the existing conciliation boards and sliding scale committees, we recommend that each district shall at once put forward the claim recommended by conference, namely, 20 per cent on current earnings."

The result of the local negotiations, as might have been expected, was that some districts were fairly satisfied while others did very badly. Northumberland and Durham, for example, only got 15 per cent on the standard which was less than half of what had been demanded by the claim for 20 per cent on earnings. The federated districts, which included Lancashire and Cheshire, Yorkshire, Midlands and North Wales, gained 15½ per cent on earnings. On their standard of 1888 the Scottish miners received 18¾ per cent. In South Wales the miners received 17½ per cent on their basic standard. Nowhere, however, was there conceded the full 20 per cent on earnings.

It was on the 11th May that the Conciliation Board for the South Wales Coal Trade met for the first time since August 1914 to fix the amount of the war bonus for the coalfield. The independent chairman Viscount St. Aldwyn reserved his decision but two days later fixed it as 17½ per cent on standard rates. When the board met on 17th May it was to receive from Viscount St. Aldwyn his wish to resign. This did not suit either side : and so the joint secretaries were instructed to write him to reconsider his decision. Before the board could meet again at the end of May, there were great changes in Westminster.

6 COLLAPSE OF THE LIBERAL GOVERNMENT

In its tenth year the Liberal Government that began on December 5th, 1905, came to a sudden and inglorious end. H. H. Asquith, who had given his award on the miners' war bonus demand on 5th May, found himself three weeks later no longer the head of a Liberal Cabinet : but Prime Minister in a Coalition Government made up mainly from the Tory and Liberal "front benches" in the House of Commons. The Labour Party, numbering 40 out of the total House of Commons of 670 members, now was given the offer of three posts : Arthur Henderson, leader of the Labour Party, to be President of the Board of Education, G. H. Roberts to be a Junior Whip, and William Brace, President of the South Wales Miners' Federation, to be Under-Secretary to the Home Office. All three accepted. Out of a total administration of some 75 Government members three posts were held by the Labour Party, now to be a junior partner in Government from 25th May onwards.

In the new administration there was to be a new Ministry to deal with the supply of munitions, and the Minister of Munitions was to be Lloyd George who immediately began to push forward his plans for the organisation of industry and of labour. The Defence of the Realm Acts (DORA) gave power to commandeer any private works and to order the worker, so long as he remained in employment, to work exactly as directed. They gave no power, however, to prevent the worker leaving his job either individually or in concert with others. DORA gave no power either to constrain the individual worker (by industrial conscription) or to prohibit strikes. To achieve the latter end and if possible the former was now Lloyd George's aim, in his new Munitions of War Act, which became law on 2nd July, 1915.

Part One of this Act was designed to deal with strikes by compulsory arbitration with the stipulation that a refusal to accept an arbitration award or the participation in a strike would be an offence. It was this which particularly concerned the miners of Britain. Section 14(1)(c), for example, said that any person guilty of an offence under the Act "shall, if the offence is a contravention of the provisions of this Act with respect to the prohibition of strikes, be liable to a fine not exceeding £5 for each day or part of a day during which the contravention continues." Efforts were made throughout June by the Miners' Federation of Great Britain's executive committee and officials to make sure that the mining industry was exempt from these new offences to be created by the proposed new law.

On the last day of May, 1915, William Brace, taken the previous day into the new Coalition Government, presided at the executive council in Cardiff where his colleagues made it their first business to pass a resolution "that we tender to Mr. Brace our hearty congratulations upon his appointment as Under-Secretary to the Home Office." A week later when a letter from him was read asking to be "released from his position as President until after the war," the request was granted and regret expressed at not having his services during the "negotiations for a new Conciliation Board Agreement." Meantime Vice-President James Winstone took over the duties both in South Wales and on the MFGB executive committee.

7 "REFUSAL OF THE OWNERS TO NEGOTIATE"

The conciliation board had run into difficulties as soon as they had met on 31st May when Fred L. Davis, spokesman for the owners, had raised so many questions that the discussion was postponed for ten days. Then on 9th June negotiations for a new wage rate agreement had been broken off : the owners at the conciliation board that day had declined "to negotiate during the war." The miners were back at square one. The next day (the third successive day of council meetings) there was anxious discussion, at the end of which it was resolved to call a special conference "to consider the situation created by the failure of the negotiations for a new Conciliation Board Agreement," and

"That a report be presented that we see no reason for any modification in our proposals, and that the conference be asked to authorise the council to conduct any further negotiations necessary" (10 vi 1915).

When the 268 delegates in Cory Hall on Tuesday, 15th June, had fully discussed the deadlock that had arisen, the following resolution was passed on the claim (set out on page 24) :

"That having heard the report from our representatives upon the negotiations for a new wage agreement, the conference expresses its astonishment and dissatisfaction at the refusal of the coalowners to negotiate during the period of the war for a new agreement, and refuses to accept the responsibility for any stoppage which will take place as the result of this attitude on the part of the coalowners.

"Further, it reaffirms its previously expressed conviction that the amendments put forth by the workmen for a new agreement are eminently reasonable, and such as can be conceded by the coalowners apart from the inflated coal prices caused by their taking advantage of circumstances created by the war.

"Further, we authorise our representatives to hold themselves ready to continue negotiations on the said proposals for a just and satisfactory settlement and that the delegates hold themselves ready to be called together in conference for consultative purposes" (15 vi 1915).

The South Wales Miners' Federation had reaffirmed their original claim for the new wage agreement. A further meeting of the conciliation board was held on Monday, 21st June. But it was fruitless. The employers were aware of what was being planned in Whitehall to prevent stoppages : and indeed Leonard Llewellyn, general manager of Cambrian Collieries and a prominent member of their conciliation board, had earlier that month been appointed Director of Matériel in the Ministry of Munitions. No settlement was arrived at : and the same day, when the executive council had been given a report by their MFGB committee members on the suggested Bill for dealing with "labour disputes", they resolved "that we confirm our opposition to any system of compulsory arbitration and other compulsory measures intended by the Government Bill." With this the course seemed set for a headlong collision not only with the mineowners in Wales but with the Coalition Government.

Could anything be done in London to avert this ? From Tuesday, 22nd June, onwards till the end of the month, the trio of South Wales leaders on the miners' national committee were meeting their colleagues in Westminster day after day or traversing the corridors of Whitehall seeking to reach some settlement through the Board of Trade. The full seriousness of the situation was apparently not realised in Government circles until within a few days of the expiry of the three months notice and not even then.

8 NEGOTIATIONS OR COMPULSION

At the MFGB executive committee Robert Smillie on 23rd June read aloud two letters received by Thomas Ashton. The first was from Sir John Simon, the new Home Secretary. A fortnight earlier Smillie had told the executive committee that "Mr. Brace, M.P., had been sent by Sir John Simon, the Home Secretary, to see the officials of the Federation" and to propose, in view of the national need for coal, that there be held in London a national joint meeting of coalowners and mineworkers ("the Government would furnish each delegate with a railway pass to and from his home to London"). The miners were very much in favour of such a meeting, provided no question of compulsion was brought in. There had been talks between the Home Secretary on the one hand and Hartshorn, Walsh and himself on the other, and they now had a letter from Sir John Simon of 15th June in which it was made clear that all would be "on the basis of voluntary goodwill and harmonious co-operation between employers and workmen." The three members had "told Sir John that while they were willing to do everything to increase the supply of coal they must have some guarantee that there was no intention to apply compulsion. He then agreed to give such a pledge in his letter."

The second letter was from Arthur Henderson who, although occupying the post of President of the Board of Education, was busying himself with questions of munitions. Headed "Ministry of Munitions of War, 6 Whitehall Gardens, S.W." and dated 17th June, 1915, the letter stated that "The Minister of Munitions, Mr. Lloyd George, is exceedingly anxious to have an interview with the executive committee of your Federation and has requested me to extend to you in his name an invitation to meet him on Thursday, the 24th of June, at 11.30 a.m. at 6 Whitehall Gardens."

Smillie went on to tell how William Brace had been with them at the close of the interview with the Home Secretary and had said that on the same day a meeting had been held at which "compulsory arbitration had been talked about." "It seems," went on Smillie, "that a representative body of trade union leaders had met Lloyd George with Brace and Henderson present. Not only had they pledged themselves to compulsory arbitration but they had also insisted that the miners should be included." He went to the House of Commons to pick up Steve Walsh, M.P. The two of them had then met John Hill of the boilermakers and William Mosses of the patternmakers (chairman and secretary of what was now called the Labour Advisory Committee) who had "indulged in some plain speaking." These men complained that the miners ought to and should be included : that if the miners did not agree to attend the meetings to which they had been invited they would have to put up with it. "We then met Arthur Henderson and we told him we were not going to be included in the Bill." Henderson said he did not see how they could be out of it. Henderson had then asked if Lloyd George could come and see the miners' committee. "We told him that he might take it that that would be of no use, for the miners will not go into the Bill." They then parted with Mr. Henderson who asked them to go and see Lloyd George : but they had told him they could not.

However, on the following day Smillie decided to ask for "an interview with Mr. Lloyd George" and there he asked : "What have the miners done that you want to put them in your Bill ?" Thereupon Lloyd George denied that he had done it, and said that it was their own fellow trade unionists who had done it.[1] Lloyd George promised he would not put them in.

After this information the chairman then read to the committee certain clauses in the Bill in regard to penalties and imprisonment and penalties for striking or inciting to strike. There was discussion. Finally it was decided to write direct to Lloyd George but to make it clear that their fellow trade unionists, even if now Ministers of the Crown, Arthur Henderson and William Brace, were to be ruled out from these talks. The wording of their letter to Lloyd George dated 23rd June made this abundantly clear :

"I am instructed to say that our committee gladly accept your kind invitation and will attend at 6 Whitehall Gardens at 11.30 tomorrow, Thursday morning, to meet you.

[1] Smillie informed his committee that he had had a note of the meeting between the trade union leaders and Lloyd George and knew the names of those who had proposed even stronger measures than were contained in the Munitions of War Bill as drafted.

"We have no desire to meet any other Minister or officials outside your own department.

"I am, sir, your obedient servant, Thomas Ashton, Secretary."

The committee took a decision in advance of the meeting "that our attitude be one of uncompromising opposition to the inclusion of the miners in the Bill," and that further consideration of the proposed national meeting (to be arranged by the Home Office) should be left over in the meanwhile. On the next day they met Lloyd George but were not able to get very far with him that morning. In the early afternoon they were asked by their Welsh colleagues (part of the delegation of the executive council of the South Wales Miners' Federation then meeting Walter Runciman at the Board of Trade) to postpone the discussion until later. When the MFGB executive committee got to their evening discussion they found that the South Wales situation (of which Thomas Ashton had been informed a fortnight earlier) was not only grave in itself but also a serious complication in the negotiations they were carrying on with Lloyd George. James Winstone reported "a courteous interview with Walter Runciman" who was "very anxious to bring about a settlement" with the South Wales employers. A meeting had been arranged for Saturday, 26th June. Runciman had undertaken that the employers would be there while he himself would take the chair "to act as mediator but with no power to settle." Having heard this the national committee discussed their interview with Lloyd George and finally passed the following resolution :

"That this executive committee meet Mr. Lloyd George in the morning at eleven o'clock and the President be instructed to inform him that while every consideration had been given to the suggestion that if the Federation were left out of the Bill they would do everything possible to assist him in maintaining peace during the war, and while there was a general feeling that the existing machinery might be used to that end, we cannot at the moment come to any definite decision on the matter owing to the situation at present existing in South Wales" (24 vi 1915).

What happened the next day when Smillie informed the Minister of Munitions of this hold-up caused by the blockage next door (in the Board of Trade offices at No. 7 Whitehall Gardens) is recorded with laconic brevity, and duly signed "Thos, Ashton, secretary, 1461 Ashton Old Road, Manchester," in the MFGB committee minute of Friday, 25th June, as follows :

"The committee met again after the interview with Mr. Lloyd George and, after some discussion, it was resolved : 'that this committee stand adjourned until six o'clock tomorrow (Saturday) evening'."

Throughout that Saturday, 26th June, the South Wales representatives were engaged at the Board of Trade till long after 6 o'clock. Late that evening at the Westminster Palace Hotel, James Winstone reported on their "very hard day" at the joint meeting. The workmen's representatives had put the case : then the owners had put their case, and in so doing took very good care to rebut so far as they could the case put by the workmen's representatives. Negotiations were carried on backwards and forwards until the afternoon. The owners were then asked to retire into a room by themselves, while the workmen's representatives remained in the room in which they had been all the time. Eventually the employers had declined to come back into the room where the joint meeting had been held unless the workmen's representatives were prepared to drop what was for all a vital issue, namely, the merging of the percentages into a new standard. Walter Runciman, still there as "mediator", had come in with that proposal from the owners. To overcome the difficulty caused by the owners' refusal to come into the room the South Wales executive council appointed four or five as a sub-committee to meet the employers. When they did get to the owners they found the same attitude was maintained.

Winstone went on to state how Runciman had told the owners "pretty bluntly" that he thought they should make much more serious efforts to bring about a settlement. The final result was that "Mr. Runciman, who was a very busy man," had undertaken to allow them "to get some more information" to be put before him on Monday morning. Runciman would try and reach a decision thereafter and let them have it by Tuesday morning (29th June).

It was late at night. Eventually the Miners' Federation of Great Britain leaders adjourned till the next day. It was unusual for them to meet on a Sunday. But meet they did : and there was a lengthy discussion of all phases of the matter. It was a perplexing and critical state of affairs. Eventually their decision was to meet Lloyd George "in the morning at eleven o'clock" when the President was charged to inform him that "Mr. Runciman has reached a stage in the negotiations in regard to South Wales which might be gravely prejudiced by any definite pronouncement on our part, and we cannot therefore give him anything definite." Lloyd George was to be asked "to postpone any statement on the miners' position in the House of Commons until it is known what is going to take place in South Wales." If, however, a settlement were reached a guarantee against any wartime strikes by miners would be given him.

Meantime, they took the precaution, on that Sunday, 27th June, to send "telegrams at once" to their half-dozen most influential Members of Parliament asking them "to be in their places at the House of Commons on Monday, and during the whole time that the Munitions Bill is before the House" (27 vi 1915). They were taking no chances with Lloyd George.

When on the next day the MFGB leaders met Lloyd George, he jumped at the notion of "a guarantee" and immediately made the suggestion that he "might be permitted" to put the suggested guarantee as a clause into the Bill. They retired. They took the decision that "we cannot see our way to put the guarantee into the Bill but we give Mr. Lloyd George the resolution moved by Mr. Straker as a guarantee on behalf of the Federation." With slight reformulation from the previous day the resolution ran as follows:

"That, in order to prevent all miners' strikes during the period of the war, we are prepared to enter into an arrangement with the colliery owners in every district by which all disputes can be settled by the representatives of the owners and of the workmen and, in case of the two sides failing to settle any dispute, an independent chairman to be called in with full power to settle" (28 vi 1915).

They felt they had gone to the limit, and having done this they went back to their hotel and thence to their homes, knowing that the discussion on South Wales was now in the forefront and that everything depended on its outcome.

APPENDIX I

The circular given below was issued under the joint signatures of Arthur Henderson and J. S. Middleton (on behalf of the War Emergency: Workers' National Committee) and of Thomas Richards, General Secretary, South Wales Miners' Federation, and J. E. Edmunds, Secretary, Cardiff Trades Council:

HIGH PRICES FOR FOOD AND FUEL

February 2nd, 1915.

Dear Sir or Madam,

Under the auspices of the above organisations, a Conference of Representatives of Trade Union Branches, Socialist Societies, Co-operative and Industrial Women's Organisations will be held in the Congregational Church, Windsor Place, Cardiff, on Saturday, February 13th, 1915, at 2.30 p.m., for the purpose of discussing the following proposals for the Reduction of Food and Fuel Prices, recommended by the Workers' National Committee:

(1) "That the most effective action that the Government can now take to reduce wheat prices is to intervene to remedy the deficiency in carrying-ships; and that the Government should at once take steps to obtain the control of more ships and itself bring the wheat from Argentina and Canada at the bare cost of transport."

(2) "That maximum prices for coal should be fixed by the Government."

(3) "That railway trucks, belonging both to the separate railway companies and to private traders, should be pooled and run to their fullest economic use."

(4) "That in fixing shipping freights for vessels under their control, the Government should have regard to normal rates rather than to the excessive rates inflicted by private shipowners."

(5) "That the Government commandeer coal supplies and distribute to household consumers through municipal or co-operative agencies."

CHAPTER THREE

A CLIMACTERIC YEAR

1 THE LAST TRIUMPH OF THE LIBERALS

In summer 1915 came the first climacteric of the European war. It was marked by the fall of the Liberal Cabinet occasioned by shortages and shortcomings, both at home and on the foreign field, and by industrial troubles notably in the coal mining industry of South Wales. The issue of the war either in victory or defeat for the Allied Powers was seen to depend not so much on the strategy of admirals and generals with their fleets and armies, as on the men and women at home who could furnish supplies of all that was most essential. Henceforth it was a question, both in quantity and quality, of manpower and munitions. It was a question of relations in industry or, put more broadly, of relations between economic classes.

The outbreak of war had witnessed the supreme triumph of the Liberal Party. Liberal Ministers putting forward tentatively their plea that only the violation of Belgium's neutrality had brought them reluctantly into the war (to which they had been committed for nearly ten years—and by such detailed commitments as Sir Edward Grey dared not divulge to his cabinet colleagues) suddenly found themselves acclaimed at the head of a united nation and their policy almost universally accepted.

Differences between classes, differences within classes—all seemed forgotten. At Westminster in that autumn of 1914 the Liberal Party whips, already counting on the four score votes of the Irish Nationalist Party and the three dozen votes of the Labour Party to maintain them in office, could now count on 272 Tories, with votes exactly equal to their own in 1910, to back their foreign policy in that crucial first month. A truce to "party warfare" was announced while all elections were to go uncontested. In the House of Commons the number of avowed socialists either in the Labour Party or the Liberal Party amounted to little more than one per cent of the whole assembly : and these socialists were not unanimous on carrying out the Basle Resolution of the Socialist International. Since the few critical questionings in Parliament went mostly unreported in the patriotic press, the Liberal politicians found themselves carried up by the hot wind of popular esteem, as in a thermal current, on to a very pinnacle of admiration. There was as it were a transfiguration on the mount. All of them became great statesmen and war leaders within the space of a few editions of the evening newspapers. To criticise them was a form of blasphemy.

It was 100 years since the last great war, well on towards a thousand since destructive hordes had invaded England, a country for two centuries without a standing army, a population unused to arms, innocent of warfare, whose manhood had never been conscripted. While Ministers of the Crown were seeking for precedents, and their acolytes were finding them, for the wording of the Defence of the Realm Act the verdict of the nation was given not to any instructed realisation of the causes or the magnitude of the event but to the case as put before them by the forensic skill of Asquith : they were a jury that had been conditioned by anti-German propaganda for nearly a generation. The support of the Liberal Party's war aims and war policies was interpreted and popularised in various slogans. The response to these was undiscriminating and well-nigh universal. The general literacy, the daily newspaper and the electric telegraph had wrought this marvel and were the proximate causes of what appeared to outsiders as a stampede.

With only a small number of dissentients (but including the main membership of the ILP and others staunch in adherence to the Basle Resolution) an overwhelming majority in every class declared their enthusiastic support: they expressed themselves immediately and even dramatically in favour of the Liberal Party's policy. They voted with their feet in its favour : in swelling numbers everywhere they walked into hastily arranged recruiting offices and marched out as volunteer soldiers. The call from Field Marshal Earl Kitchener of Khartoum—installed as Secretary of State for War through the clamour of the Press—the call for a hundred thousand volunteers went out on August 7th, 1914. By Christmas ten times that number had voluntarily enlisted. In no other country in Europe had there been such extensive political freedom as then existed in the United Kingdom, and in no other country was such an enlistment possible or even conceivable.

The Liberal ministers responsible for the hidden commitments to France sought from the first to present their case for declaring war *(casus belli)* as an affair of honour (Sir Edward Grey) and as a vindication of international law (H. H. Asquith). But soon it was presented as a moral issue. All the Dominions and Dependancies, Colonies and Protectorates of the vast British Empire had been thrown into the war and were called upon to defend British interests in the name of truth, honour and justice. The British nation outraged by the breach of the 1839 treaty for Belgian neutrality, itself "a scrap of paper" that was soon to be treated as Holy Writ, was asked to be at once jury, judge and executioner. By such means as these and as the result of an electioneering virtuosity that had grown up for over a century, politicians of all parties induced in their hearers a stolid belief in the justice of their cause and were able to rouse an unselfregarding enthusiasm for righteous vengeance against law-breakers—who were to be designated as the Huns. Not only the ten thousand journalists and writers but also the clergy of all the main churches gave full backing to the statesmen.

The enemy was not only in the wrong but wicked and sinful: and the righteous vengeance of heaven was also invoked. By the last week of November, 1914, when the Sultan of Turkey as Caliph of Islam proclaimed a *Jehad* against the infidel Powers of the Triple Entente, the British slogans and sermons had already generated the cult of an Holy War against the Huns—and also against the Turks.[1]

Thus, even before that November ended with the punitive legislation of the Defence of the Realm Act, giving an extraordinary extension of the power of the State, there had already been manifested a hundred days of willing surrender of personal, party and class interests to State authority. It seemed like the fabled condition of the ancient Roman Republic

Then none was for a party
Then all were for the State.

It was not only the supreme triumph of the Liberal Party. Within that ruling party it was the triumph of their right wing, of the Liberal Imperialists. It was Asquith, Grey and Haldane who, as a Liberal Imperialist group formed in the late 'nineties, had supported the Conservative Government's war in South Africa (the Boer War of 1899 to 1902) against their own leader Campbell-Bannerman and their colleagues in the Commons. It was they who, despite the efforts of Prime Minister Campbell-Bannerman in December, 1905, to break up their cabal, now held key posts in the Cabinet—in the Treasury, the Foreign Office and as Secretary of State for War—and so were able to ensure that continuity in foreign policy so much desired by the Tories and at the court of King Edward VII. When this policy had ripened to the establishment of the Triple Entente in August, 1907 (the point at which the Socialist International Congress at Stuttgart gave a signal of alarm) the Liberal Imperialists ruled the roost; and by summer 1911 had secured the support of the "left-wing" Lloyd George. The Liberal Imperialists had every reason to congratulate themselves on their triumph especially when, at the critical moment in August, 1914, they found only two members of the Cabinet, John Burns and Viscount Morley, had resigned the seals of office. They had pulled it off. They had inflicted defeat on the neutralist, pacific and anti-imperialist standpoint within their own party by winning the overwhelming majority to the belief that that standpoint had been wrong and that the Liberal Imperialists had been in the right. They had won over also, without difficulty but at the price of postponement of the Home Rule Act, the Conservative Party whose foreign policy of preparation for war they had so assiduously carried out. The Irish Nationalists and the Labour Party showed themselves similarly convinced that the Liberal Imperialists were the rightful leaders of a party which included many radicals

[1]God heard the embattled nations sing and shout
"Gott strafe England!" and "God save the King"
God this, God that and God the other thing.
"Good God," said God,
"I've got my work cut out." (J. C. Squire).

and Lib-Labs, non-conformist preachers and temperance reformers, defenders of small nationalities and of civil liberties, upholders of the "English radical tradition."

The Liberal Imperialists felt confident about the Empire, and first about the white Dominions of Australia, Canada, Newfoundland, New Zealand and South Africa as so many extensions overseas of Britain itself : and with the exception of the rising of the Boer General De Wet in South Africa their expectations were fulfilled : nor was there at that time a movement from Quebec within Canada. The great dependancies of India and Egypt were another matter. Would the leaders of Indian opinion and the potentates of that great dependency respond ? In Hindustan the disaffection of some Muslims, after the Caliph of Islam had proclaimed a *Jehad* against the infidel British and French, as well as the attempts at insurrection of the Ghadr party of revolutionary Sikhs, were regarded as of little moment (and in any case went almost entirely unreported in the British Press); while the Nizam of Hyderabad, the greatest Moslem Monarch outside Turkey, publicly proclaimed his support of the Entente powers and headed the list of the Princes who gave lavish promises of support and aid. The Rajahs and the Maharajahs rallied to the support of the British Raj. They stood staunchly in support of the Kaisar-i-Hind, their King-Emperor George against Kaiser Wilhelm of the German Reich.

In Egypt however the Khedive Abbas Hilmi whose wavering had inclined him to support his suzerain lord the Sultan of the Ottoman Empire had to be deposed and a new monarch had to be installed by the British, Husein Kamel. Thus, the British Empire (comprising a quarter of mankind) "on which the sun never sets" had accepted the Liberal Imperialist policy and was arrayed in arms in all the continents : and when, on September 7th, 1914, the House of Commons and the House of Lords heard the telegram from the Viceroy of India announcing the lavish support from the Princes and parties of the Indian sub-continent there was the utmost gratification and content. The triumph of the Liberals reached a new height.

On the other hand this same highly developed political freedom, greater than in any other big power in the Old World, which compelled the rulers to resort to every instrument and agency of propaganda to win over most of the working class and the common people to a crusade of self-sacrificial enthusiasm, made it possible for oppositional shades of ruling class opinion to find easy expression, at any rate in the opening years of that war. Apart from the clear-cut standpoint of John McLean in Scotland and James Connolly in Ireland, neither of which were made widely known, it was indeed from within circles of the Liberal Party that opposition first appeared effectively in public print. From amongst some of the Whig families there were dissentient aristocrats who set up immediately the Union of Democratic Control with a critical standpoint on Liberal policy. E. D. Morel, a Liberal candidate and a first-rate propagandist against imperialism, was chosen to be its secretary. This action brought upon these pioneers of the Union of Democratic Control (which soon included Ramsay Macdonald and a couple of other socialist M.P.s) the fury of the millionaire Press, for their exposures of the pretensions of the Liberal Government, and their criticism of beloved and trusted Liberal statesmen who were now speaking with the tongues not of men but of archangels.[1] The UDC standpoint found expression not only in their own publications but also in the organ of the Independent Labour Party, the *Labour Leader*, in which E. D. Morel, until his imprisonment by the Government on a trumped-up charge, was able to pen a weekly article exposing Liberal diplomacy and the part played by the armament rings.

The enthusiasm which had conceived of the war as a short summary punishment for wrongdoers that would last until Christmas when Winston Churchill would be riding down the Unter den Linden—this and all the other absurdities were undampened by Kitchener's chilling announcement that the war would last four years. The euphoria was proof against such blows of reality as the British retreat from Mons and the disasters to the British fleet: the allies were invincible, and the proof was to hand, in the fantastic widespread and widely credited rumour that myriads of Russian soldiers ("with snow on their boots") had been landing in the north of Scotland and passing by train south to reinforce the Western front in Flanders.

This acceptance of the leadership of the Liberal Party and the ending or apparent ending of all class differences, was the Liberal heaven which the party had striven for on its formation sixty years earlier and was now to be briefly achieved in the year 1914.

2 THE TRUCE WEARS THIN

The mood that prevailed in autumn 1914 could not last; the willing sacrifice of all lesser interests upon the altar of a supreme need, of an unexampled national emergency, could not be sustained—unless buttressed to meet changing circumstances. The atmosphere of unbounded trust in the country's rulers, with all the accompanying fantasies, began to be dispersed after six months of war. By February, 1915, thick-coming troubles caused economic and industrial and military problems: and with these the country's rulers proved unable to cope.

[1] For a short time an even more intense attack was directed against Bernard Shaw, as the outstanding socialist (and indeed founding father of socialism in the 'eighties) who would not sing in the chorus of adulation of the Liberal Ministers. In his "Commonsense about the War", a supplement to *The New Statesman*, he had torn away the romantic illusions that were being cherished or created: and again in his "Last Spring of the Old Lion" (12 xii 1914) had arraigned the ruling class, with a scorn that could not be mitigated by his final verdict supporting the war effort—given, as he himself had once said of John Stuart Mill, against the evidence.

Nowhere was this more obvious than in the supply industries where the hollow nature of "the industrial truce" declaration of 24th August, 1914, was soon to become apparent. The effect of it had been real enough in that autumn of 1914, so that Ministers of the Crown could be happy over an unexpected situation[1] which they had done nothing to bring about, when they found the stress and storm of pending industrial disputes had subsided, leaving them tranquil at Christmas, halcyon days "while birds of calm sit brooding on the charmed wave."

But it had not been a real "truce" in any normal sense of the word. A truce has to be negotiated. It is an agreement reached after negotiation between two opposing sides. But this had not been the product of such meetings. The conference of 24th August, representing the Parliamentary Committee of the Trades Union Congress, the Management Committee of the General Federation of Trade Unions, and the Executive Committee of the Labour Party had been specially called for the purpose of making two requests to the Government: (1) to prevent unemployment by forbidding overtime, (2) to provide relief for the victims of inevitable unemployment. There were no employers present nor government representatives. The "industrial truce" was a unilateral declaration, one-sided, unconditional: and the employers could, in the Scottish phrase, make either a kirk or a mill of it: or they could take no notice of it whatever.

In the sequel the employers, or at any rate many of them, interpreted the declaration not only for what it was—namely an aspiration for harmony and unity in industry against the foreign foe—but also as a declaration that the trade unions would now retire from the field and leave it to the employers to operate in industry as they chose without hindrance. Subsequent proceedings suggest that a number of employers thought that these trade union and labour leaders had recognised that in time of war the laws and rules and stipulations of trade unionism should be silent: that trade unionism was something which could only be allowed to function in times of peace and must be suspended in times of national emergency—as many other customs, laws and stipulations were suspended and indeed had in empowering Acts of Parliament provisions for their suspension in war time. The Government, too, even the members of it who had in any way been brought into contact with trade union leaders, seemed not to have perceived that a truce expressed as a cessation of industrial hostilities on one side only was not likely to be either binding or lasting. This may be ascribed partly to sheer ignorance of the conditions of life of the majority of the population and of the various institutional means to safeguard that standard of life, but also because in so far as they were not utterly aloof from the working class they shared the infatuation of the employers with the progress and profits of the industrial firms.

[1] "The autumn of 1914, which had seemed likely to be a period of great industrial unrest, was, in fact, a period of almost unbroken tranquillity."—G. D. H. Cole, *Labour in War Time.*

2 POTATO CLEANING FATIGUE FOR ENLISTED TONYPANDY MINERS IN 1914

3 LLOYD GEORGE, FLANKED BY HENDERSON AND RICHARDS. AT CONFERENCE OF SWMF (21 v 1915)

Actually as was shown in the discussions of the War Emergency: Workers' National Committee there was considerable ground for discontent amongst the workers. Many employers, mostly in the smaller trades and in commerce, took advantage of the situation to reduce salaries and staff: and the government contractors, or many of them, were soon notorious in their unfair treatment of employees.

In the main industries, however, the employers were glad of the aspiration uttered on August 24th. It enabled them to maintain the *status quo*, to go on as they had been doing, paying the same wages as before, at a moment when circumstances urgently required a raising of wages. Moreover particularly in the most important fields of industry there was such a boom as yielded an unexpectedly large increase in profits so that the position of the employers was improving while the workers were steadily becoming worse off during that autumn and early winter of 1914-15. The comment within the labour movement critical of the leaders came a little later, after the first shock of the stampede into acceptance of the Liberal Government's war policy had receded, and also came from some who had been part of the stampede. Their criticism was that any industrial truce should have been granted from the workers side only on condition that the standard of living would be maintained either by reducing prices or by raising wages to keep pace with the rise in prices: also that in all the new situations the trade unions would be consulted by the government and taken into its confidence in problems arising from the war. Furthermore, they might well (given increased strength of trade unionism notably in the five years preceding the war) have asked that that strength should be recognised by prior consultation and by a modification of unfettered capitalist control of the economy. Only the British Socialist Party on the parallel question of entering into an inter-party recruiting campaign wished to insist on the workers' demands being put from the inter-party platforms as well as the ordinary capitalist standpoint.

Later the comment grew more and more sharp and it was felt that in their declaration the ageing leaders of trade unionism had represented the feeble "friendly society" type of trade unionism in which they themselves had grown up in the 'eighties and 'nineties, twenty and thirty years earlier and had not measured up as they should have done to the new situation that had matured from 1910 to 1914. They had not negotiated: they had abdicated from their responsibility.

In all these circumstances it was not surprising that the stresses and strains to break up industrial harmony should have appeared first in this matter of the industrial truce.

We have seen in the previous chapter how the coal owners took the war-time opportunity to mount an offensive against the Eight Hours Act which they had always regarded as a blot on the Statute Book and used arguments for substitute labour in the pits which the miners saw as a retrogression to the worst years of the 19th century. In other cases demands or attitudes which employers considered both reasonable and seasonable were seen by workers as an unwarranted incursion on their cherished rights as well as a gross infraction of the industrial truce which they wrongly believed to be binding on the employers. It was in February, 1915, that the breaking-point was reached. It came on the Clyde, the world-famous centre of engineering and shipbuilding, to which in that winter the words of Shakespeare's *Hamlet* might well apply :

> "Why such impress of shipwrights, whose sore task
> Does not divide the Sunday from the week,
> What might be toward that this sweaty haste
> Doth make the night joint-labourer with the day ?"

Within a week a strike of engineering and shipbuilding workers broke out on the Clyde, where the employers were held to have repeatedly and persistently dishonoured the industrial truce. In June, 1914, the Amalgamated Society of Engineers (Glasgow District) had decided to ask for an increase of twopence on their standard rate of 8½d. per hour as from January, 1915, when the three year agreement, which had kept their wages fixed amid rising prices, would terminate. The behaviour of the employers, followed by their offer of one farthing per hour, together with the readiness of the union's Executive Committee in an access of "patriotism" to accept an improved but still quite insufficient agreement on three farthings (rather than be accused of any infringement upon the industrial truce) brought about a strike. Shop after shop came out on 16th February, 1915, and the strike lasted for two weeks, while a Central Withdrawal of Labour Control Committee, made up largely of shop stewards, kept the men of all the different unions together until direct intervention by the Government brought about an arbitrated settlement of one penny per hour as a "war bonus". A penny advance was "not sufficient even to bring the Clyde standard rate up to the level obtaining in other parts of Britain, let alone to meet the rise in the cost of living prior to the war, while it did nothing whatever to make up for the increase in the cost of living due to the war" *(Labour Year Book,* 1916*)*.

This Clyde strike was a portent. It had a profound effect throughout the Labour movement, not least amongst the mineworkers of South Wales. In the conditions on the Clyde they saw a certain similarity to their own situation : and in the unexampled abuse hurled upon strikers they recognised not the patriotic intentions of the scribes and the speakers but a manifestation of class antagonism and class prejudice with which they had been all too familiar in the recent past. Two months later, after the experience of similar dilatory tactics by their own employers, the miners in South Wales decided at their annual conference to press for a national coal strike.

In the same month as the first big break in the industrial truce, the final breakdown of the Socialist International was made manifest by fragmented sectional meetings. Socialist leaders from Belgium, Britain, France and Russia held a meeting in London at which the representative of the Russian Social-Democratic Labour Party (Maxim Litvinov) attended to reprobate the sectional gathering[1] as itself a breach of international socialism and to present the declaration on the war of his Central Committee, based on Lenin's draft.[2] Litvinov was present under the name of Maximovitch; while I. M. Maisky, on behalf of the Organising Committee, attended to express (though in less forthright terms) the Menshevik disagreement with the "Allied Socialist" parties on their overall attitude towards the war.

Throughout January, 1915, there was still something surviving of the halcyon days of December and the euphoria of the Liberal triumph : but February proved to be the month of new beginnings, and of the ending of the old songs of Liberalism. It began with food prices showing a 23 per cent increase from the level of July, 1914—a rise of nearly a quarter in six months. It was on February 4th that the government at last appointed a Committee on Production in Engineering and Shipbuilding Establishments "to inquire and report forthwith, after consultation with the representatives of employers and workmen, as to the best steps to be taken to ensure that the productive power of the employees in engineering and shipbuilding establishments working for Government purposes shall be made fully available so as to meet the needs of the nation in the present emergency."

Four days later, the War Office publicly indicated that all was not well but that it knew the remedy : in a debate in the House of Commons the Rt. Hon. Harold J. Tennant, Parliamentary Under-Secretary to Lord Kitchener and brother-in-law of the Prime Minister, asked the Labour Party members if they would kindly secure the relaxation of trade union rules. To the expostulations of Labour members, who knew that his speech was blatantly an employers' utterance and as such would be resented throughout the world of labour, H. J. Tennant did not even deign to reply. It was the turning point.[3]

The abyss opened, the rainbow bridge thrown to the Liberal Valhalla began to crumble away and across the gulf there stood in rock-like confrontation employer and employee, trade unionist and industrialist, proletarian and capitalist. Not that H. J. Tennant himself was a capitalist, any more than his brother-in-law the Prime Minister or his sister Margot or any other of the brotherhoods and cousinhoods that for years had made up so much of the two Front Benches in Parliament. They were barristers, publicists, ex-officers and country gentlemen, all

[1] The author witnessed for a short time this meeting on February 14th, 1915, in Central Hall, Westminster (headquarters of the Methodist Church).

[2] "*The War and Russian Social-Democracy*" in Lenin Collected Works Vol. 21.

[3] G. D. H. Cole wrote that summer : "Only a few weeks before, the Government had been overflowing with compliments to the workers : now there was a sudden change of face. Mr. Tennant's speech was the beginning of a series of attacks on Trade Unionism."

with a way of life which placed them aloof (apart from ownership of stocks and shares) from the grime and clangour of extractive or manufacturing industry. Many were peers of the realm or younger sons of the aristocracy : for although a half century had elapsed since Palmerston's cabinet of Dukes and Earls, alloyed only by two commoners, Gladstone and Sir James Graham, there were long memories in the ruling circles and the great Whig families still had a stake in each administration.[1] But whatever the origin of this aloofness from the life and institutions of the majority of their fellow countrymen, Ministers of the Crown at this crucial stage tended to adopt the presuppositions, presumptions and prejudices of the industrial magnates.[2] They jettisoned bit by bit whatever remained of the traditional *laissez-faire* attitude of Liberalism and drove towards compulsion as the solution for their difficulties.

In utter contrast to his Liberal colleagues was "the little Welsh attorney", hymned as "the people's own Lloyd George." As President of the Board of Trade from 1905 to 1908 he had plunged into problems of industrial relations : and later in the launching of his "made-in-Germany" schemes for social insurance had dealt with friendly societies and trade unions. In February, 1915, he observed "while the whole Press is describing the war as an unbroken success, the facts are precisely the contrary."[3] Lloyd George, supple as an eel (and as slippery)

[1] The Liberal administration which was constructed in December, 1905, was scornfully hailed as "Lady Aberdeen's Cabinet" by disgruntled Tory opponents.

[2] Thus the Engineering Employers' Federation on 17th December, 1914, had approached the trade unions in order to overcome the shortage of skilled labour (largely caused by lack of foresight on the part of the employers and the government) and had made proposals for scrapping most trade union rights and regulations as to skilled and unskilled, demarcation of work, introduction of female labour, limitation of overtime, employment of non-union labour. The guarantees they offered for resumption of the old conditions at the end of the war were found insufficient. So the unions put forward counter proposals which would have gone a good way to easing the shortage "without encroaching upon the hard-won trade rights of the operative engineer."

The employers, making light of these proposals, replied with a rather nasty epistle in which they much regretted that the unions (namely the Amalgamated Society of Engineers and four other skilled unions) "appear to regard the strict adherence to their rules, regulations and restrictions as of greater importance than the supply to the nation of its requirements in this crisis" and added in an arrogant (and untruthful) paragraph : "The employers further desire to place on record their disappointment that their proposals to assist the country should have met with no response."

The union officials replied placably, repudiating the suggestion that they were unpatriotic and offering to meet the employers again. The employers answered that provided only that the unions would first concede all demands, they were willing to resume the conference. Despite this stipulation a further conference was held on January 13th, 1915, but reached no agreement. The employers' final word was "the proposals and suggestions of the unions" (practically all of which had afterwards to be adopted by the government) "did not in any way afford the remedy required." Three weeks later, and after the employers had communicated their attitude to their anxious customers in the War Office, Tennant made his February 8th speech, with no mention in it of guarantees nor of even the possibility of any *quid pro quo* in the form of limitation of profits.

[3] *Politicians and the War* 1914-1916 by Lord Beaverbrook.

knowing that his Liberal colleagues were as hide-bound as the War Office, was driving for a solution to the manifold problems, either through a final effort for continued harmony in industry or through some drastic measure of compulsion. As Chancellor of the Exchequer he summoned the Treasury Conference of 17th March in which he besought the trade union representatives to give up their hard-won rights, to accept a measure of compulsion in industry in return for a special tax on the excess profits of the employers. As we have seen the MFGB Executive Committee indignantly refused to consider their members being brought under compulsion and abruptly withdrew their representatives. But when other trade union leaders yielded to the pressure the Treasury Conference decisions were sealed and signed. A few weeks later the sequel was seen in the setting up of the Ministry of Munitions in a new Coalition Government which would be able to ensure compulsion alike in industry and in military service. It was not so much the run of failures abroad or the duplicity of admirals and generals as the menacing background of the Treasury Conference that brought down the Liberal Cabinet and led to the events that constituted the first climacteric of the 1914-18 war and indeed of the British Empire.

With this necessary explanation we resume the narrative of the earlier chapters.

3 DEADLOCK AND FRUSTRATION

In midsummer of 1915, at the Board of Trade offices, the attendance of the two dozen or more members of the SWMF Executive Council had begun on Tuesday, 22nd June, and went on for day after day. Employers' representatives were there also : but it could hardly be said that the two sides at any point got together for such a mutual interchange as would lead to a new agreement. From day to day also the officials of the Board of Trade were in attendance but neither they nor their President were effective in bringing matters to an issue. The daily conferences had little apparent result. Various solutions were proposed, but none that could be accepted by the Executive Council. No matter how much pressure was put on them (and some of them had already shown themselves to be highly malleable) they knew that no decision of theirs would be operative in the coalfield or have democratic assent until it had been ratified by a conference of delegates from the lodges. But the men they were meeting in Whitehall were aloof from this conception of trade union procedure or of response to democratic pressure. For the Welshmen it was a week of frustration.

Some clue to their quandary may be found in a voluminous record (printed for use inside the Ministry of Munitions) where an account of the South Wales troubles serves to explain also something of the standpoint with which the old administrative class of the Civil Service approached problems of this kind. A section, significantly headed "The Control of Labour 1915-1916", deals with the miners' national demand for a war bonus of 20 per cent on earnings (wrongly quoted as 25 per cent) and then adds, as though it were consequential, the following paragraph :

"The Welsh miners. however, continued to press for their original proposals for a new agreement. Their object was partly to simplify the old system, which was exceedingly complicated, but principally to take advantage of their strong position in order to secure a high minimum after the war when they feared a depression, and to claim at once an advance in wages should the price of coal rise still higher in the course of the war."

Clearly, these highly-placed government officials had not grasped how important a new agreement was for the miners nor had they a realisation of how much the old agreement in all its implications was hated[1] throughout the coalfield. Their phrases could be read as suggesting that the miners were greedy ("to take advantage of their strong position") and simply wanted more money immediately as well as some security for the future by a rise in the minimum wage. The official account proceeds :

"The owners refused to accede to these demands, and a stoppage throughout the coalfield seemed inevitable on 30th June, unless the government could avert it. For, although the owners had intimated their willingness to refer the whole matter to the Committee on Production, the men's representatives declined to have it settled by arbitration."

There was no parallel attempt to penetrate into the motivation of the employers' refusal to negotiate, or to set it down that "the object" of the coalowners was "to take advantage of their strong position" due to the war emergency in order to hold on to an obsolete agreement which, for just twenty-three months, had clamped wages down to the maximum of 60 per cent over 1879 level while prices (and profits also) had been rising rapidly. Their next sentence is so worded as to impute some degree of censure on the miners for declining arbitration of an outside body when their own Board of Conciliation provided for arbitration by the Independent Chairman whenever mutual agreement had not been reached; and that the owners (whose refusal to allow the conciliation machinery to function was the cause of the crisis) had been reasonable men, "willing" to refer the matter to an outside Committee, set up primarily for purposes other than the powers of arbitration which they had assumed. Moreover, the MFGB standpoint had always rejected compulsory arbitration as had been made

[1]Vernon Hartshorn, who took an active part in these "frustrations" wrote : "When the last agreement was entered into, in 1910, it was literally forced down the throats of the men by the coal owners' threat of a lockout. It was accepted by the men under bitter protest. It has been probably the most unpopular agreement ever entered into in the South Wales coalfield. Throughout the five years that it ran, the men longed for the day when its shackles would be thrown off" (23 vii 1915).

emphatically clear to Ministers both in mid-March and throughout the discussions in June. Not only therefore did each sentence seem to be loaded against the miners but the whole thinking of the higher civil service seems to have been "slanted" in favour of the owners.

From these tell-tale phrases of the official record it can easily be imagined in what atmosphere the President of the Board of Trade and his officials on Saturday 26th June held their meetings with both the parties.[1]

After an exhaustive discussion it was obvious that no settlement could be reached. It was only four days to the expiry of the notices on 30th June. It was only three days to the special conference summoned for 29th June in Cardiff when, if no alternative was available, the delegates were bound to sanction a stoppage to ensure that the "law and order" of a Wages Agreement was restored in the coalfield under a new Board of Conciliation. At last, in order to escape a deadlock, the men's representatives consented to have the difference reported on by the Chief Industrial Commissioner, and undertook, if his report was acceptable to them, to recommend its acceptance by the miners' delegates.

Accordingly on 27th June Sir George Askwith[2] was asked to inquire "into the whole circumstances of the miners' demand" and to report to the Government not later than the morning of 29th June "with a recommendation as to what the settlement should be."

Sir George, fully instructed as to his duties, had behind him the experience of the Clyde strike of February 1915 and later problems of the munitions industries that were discussed and summed up in another portion of the Ministry of Munitions record under the heading "The Failure of the Treasury Agreement", as follows:

"Nor must it be forgotten that, while profits and prices were left free to rise, the burden of sacrifice was thrown wholly on the workman, who knew that the fruits of that sacrifice, to a large extent, were reaped by private capitalists, and that nothing but an undertaking of doubtful value stood between the temporary surrender of cherished rights and a permanent deterioration of his standard of living."

In his report Sir George laid down two principles, which in his opinion should govern the consideration of the whole subject: "(1) that during the present grave national emergency no section of the

[1]Ten years later, also amid the tension that precedes industrial strife, it was written by a secretary to the Cabinet "It is impossible not to feel the contrast between the reception which Ministers give to a body of owners and a body of miners. Ministers are at ease at once with the former, they are friends jointly exploring a situation . . . . whether it were better to precipitate a strike or the unemployment which would result from continuing the present terms. The majority clearly wanted a strike." (*Whitehall Diary* 1925-1930 by Thomas Jones).

[2]G. R. Askwith (1861-1942); Marlborough and Oxford (Brasenose); barrister 1886; K.C. 1908; Chief Industrial Commissioner 1911-1919; created Baron in 1919; President Middle Classes Union 1921-29; President of a dozen other organisations, including Institute of Arbitrators 1933-41; Vice-President Federation of British Industry.

community should take advantage of the needs of the nation to make a profit beyond what is normal in times of peace; (2) that if there is a movement of profits, due to war conditions, such movement cannot equitably take place without a movement of wages, and if the selling price of coal should rise so that coal owners make additional realised profits, the miners should get a share of such profits."

The increases in the selling price of the more expensive classes of coal were not disclosed. When Tom Richards in the House of Commons asked the First Lord of the Admiralty "if he will state the increase in the price of coal supplied by the South Wales collieries for Admiralty purposes for the month of May as compared with the price paid in July 1914" (16 vi 1915) the answer given was a refusal on the ground that the prices paid under contracts "are treated as confidential." A day later Sir A. B. Markham, M.P., himself a prominent owner of collieries in Derbyshire, asked the President of the Board of Trade whether he was aware that the price of Welsh coal "is 35s. per ton as against 17s. to 18s. during last year," and small Welsh coal "22s. per ton as against 5s. to 8s.", to which Walter Runciman replied that he was aware that the price of Welsh coal[1] had risen considerably; but he was not prepared as yet to undertake regulation of prices—a matter on which he had to change his tune before the summer was out.

In accordance with the principles he had laid down Sir George Askwith recommended a settlement as follows : removal of the maximum limit to wage claims; the Board of Conciliation to settle wage claims or as an alternative "some persons or tribunal" to be made available with "power to take into account all relevant circumstances"; no new Wage Agreement, the claim for which "is in my opinion impracticable"; no lowering of existing rate of wages until a new minimum be agreed upon.

According to the official account, when Sir George Askwith's report was submitted to the men's representatives on 29th June, the date promised by Runciman, "they at once intimated that nothing could prevent a stoppage throughout the coalfield if the report was made public. Its publication was therefore postponed."

[1]Actually the selling price for coal (Coalowners' Auditors' Report Average Price F.O.B.) had reached 15/11½d. by 31st March 1913 and wages two months later were raised to the maximum of 60 per cent. During the next year the price rose to 16/- and by the spring of 1914, for the first time since the Conciliation Board came into existence, the price per ton reached just over 17/-. On 31st December 1914 it was nearly 17/11½d. By 31st March 1915 it had jumped up to 19/2½d. Thereafter, the prices rose still higher in certain classes of coal. For example, of the steam coal prices (large coal F.O.B. Cardiff) "bests" with a 1914 pre-war average of just under 20/- rose by the first half of March 1915 to 30/- a ton. Similarly, the quality called "best seconds" with an average of 18/10d. for the year 1914 rose, by the second half of March to 34/6d. and by the first half of April 1915 to 36/6d.—at which date practically the whole of those classes of coal were taken by the British Admiralty so that there were no market quotations thereafter. There was a still steeper rise in the cheaper classes of coal which considerably more than doubled in the first six months of 1915.

With the hasty suppression of the Askwith report, Runciman and the parties were now "back to square one"—with this difference that the embattled delegates from the lodges were meeting that same morning at Cardiff in their Special Conference. What was to be done? Was the Board of Admiralty to be told that, only seven weeks after the sinking of the transatlantic liner *Lusitania* by a German submarine, the British navy could no longer be assured a full supply of its essential fuel? Was the President of the Board of Trade to tell his Cabinet colleague of the Home Office that he had failed to avert the impending stoppage? Yet he had done his best according to his lights. Like Aladdin in the *Thousand-and-One-Nights* he had summoned to his aid the Slave of the Lamp, the powerful genie who could settle all disputes; and Sir George Askwith had proved powerless, had only made matters worse. It seemed an impasse.

The next day the Under-Secretary, Home Office (William Brace) stated that from enquiries he had made of two of the miners' principal leaders, he was confident that if certain concessions were made the strike could be averted. These concessions in effect were: (1) the establishment of a new standard 50 per cent above that of 1879, subject to the proviso that the alteration of the standard should not in itself effect an immediate change in wages; (2) the abolition of the maximum and minimum provided for in the 1910 Agreement; (3) the levelling up of the rates for surfacemen, night-men and hauliers.

Now the junior minister at the Home Office (which for a century had always more to do with the coal mining industry than the Board of Trade) had produced a plan. Would it be accepted? Runciman swallowed it, but with rather an ill grace; he stipulated that these "concessions" were his last word. The miners must take it or leave it; and the same would apply to the owners. On that last day of June the question remained: would the miners accept?

4 RUNCIMAN'S "TERMS OF SETTLEMENT"

All through the spring and summer, and indeed for over six months since December, 1914, the democratic processes of the trade union had been carried on, deliberately and carefully and in accordance with the terms of the 1910-1915 Wages Agreement that governed the industry. But ever since the special conference early in February there had been frequent signs of real unrest and perturbation in the coalfield. The attitude of the owners as we have seen was that a solemn binding agreement could be swept aside by a unilateral decision on their part, on the ground of the national emergency created by a European war. Procrastination by the owners and dilatoriness by the government had brought a mood of bitter resentment already voiced in the April wrangles over the war bonus when the SWMF Annual Conference could contemplate a national coal strike; and keenly expressed at the Special

Conference of mid-June by "astonishment and dissatisfaction at refusal of the coal owners to negotiate" in a resolution which threw the responsibility for "any stoppage which will take place" back upon their employers. Now a still further stage of exasperation was reached in the blank refusal of the owners to meet in the same room even when brought together in the same building by the tardy intervention of the Board of Trade.

When at length the Special Conference had met in Cardiff on Tuesday morning, 29th June, it was only to learn that their Executive Council in London was "unable to attend before the afternoon": and when the delegates, back at 3 o'clock, had heard a telegram from their General Secretary Richards regretting "meeting President Board of Trade prevented us leaving in time to attend conference today" they could do nothing but adjourn. Next day their Vice-President Winstone, after apologising for all the inconvenience caused to the delegates, had given a report of the proceedings in London from Tuesday the 22nd right up to the previous day: and so explained why the conference had had to be postponed. But when he had asked for a further postponement "consequent upon the Council not having received Mr. Runciman's reply to their proposals", the delegates realised that so far their officers and councillors had come back empty handed. Hearing, however, of "intimation received" that a "Deputation had left London by special train with his reply," they duly resolved "that the Conference stand adjourned."

The mystery of "a Deputation" was solved that same afternoon, when the "special train" from Paddington disgorged the three new Labour ministers (Arthur Henderson, G. H. Roberts and William Brace) upon Cardiff Central platform. They were accompanied by Isaac Mitchell who "had been sent by Mr. Runciman, M.P." to convey his proposed Terms of Settlement to the Executive Council. It might have seemed at first as though they had been taken into His Britannic Majesty's Government a month earlier and kept there as three hostages for the good behaviour of the Labour movement. Actually, though it is true Arthur Henderson had aroused some ill-feeling through his readiness at the Treasury Conference of 17th March to barter away the hard-won rights of the trade unions, nevertheless the three trade unionists were much more likely to get on good terms with the colliers than the "capitalistic partisan" who presided at the Board of Trade. The following were Runciman's terms for the revision of the Conciliation Board agreement:

"South Wales Coal Mines.

Terms of Settlement made by the Government on the 1st July, 1915.

1st—The rates of surfacemen which are below 3/4 per day to be advanced to 3/4 per day.

2nd—Nightmen to receive six turns for five.

3rd—Hauliers employed in afternoon and night shifts to be paid the same rate of wages as those employed on the day shift.

4th—A new standard of 50 per cent on the 1879 standard to be established. Any standards in operation other than the 1879 standard to be correspondingly adjusted. (It is not intended that the alteration of the standard shall in itself effect an immediate change in wages.)

5th—The maximum and minimum provided for in the 1910 agreement not to be operative.

6th—Any question of interpretation of these terms to be submitted in writing."

The Executive Council members saw at a glance through Runciman's sheet of notepaper, brought to them under this heavy escort, that the six points on it were utterly insufficient. But they listened to the three Labour ministers : and then made this recommendation :

"That this Council recommend the conference to treat the general propositions of the Government as forming the basis for negotiations for a settlement, and that work be continued under a day-to-day contract until the completed agreement has been submitted to and ratified by a further conference; such agreement to be submitted to the further conference on or before the 14th July, 1915" (30 vi 1915).

The Executive Council had been unanimous: but the Special Conference was not. Reassembled that evening, delegates accepted the recommendation by 123 votes to 112. The narrowness of this majority at the conference might have been a warning signal to the Board of Trade and other ministries that time was running out. It was now half-way through 1915.

5 AN ULTIMATUM FROM THE COALFIELD

The first twelve days of July, 1915, seemed to be passing in relative calm after storm; with a new government of coalition, constructed amid the screams of the *Daily Mail* that "Lord Kitchener has starved the army of high explosive shell", with the new Ministry of Munitions and the new Munitions of War Act, with a Liquor Control Board set up to handle Lloyd George's April scare about "the lure of drink."[1] It was calm enough for the leaders of the Miners' Federation of Great Britain to return to their districts, having given their guarantee—not endorsed by South Wales—against strike action in the hope of being thereby exempt from the procedures and penalties of the Munitions Act.

[1] King George was deeply affected and on 6th April, 1915, had commanded that no wine, spirits or beer should be consumed in any of his houses, setting an example which proved mandatory for Ministers of the Crown—at any rate till later that year when medical advice could be taken and, in at least one case (a former Lord Chancellor, "the keeper of the King's conscience") abstinence from customary vintages was pronounced detrimental to bodily health.

Compulsion in industry had been achieved : and preparations for military compulsion (the National Registration Act of mid-July) were going ahead. The columns of the newspapers were mainly devoted to war news, such as the setback on the Eastern Front balanced by the first battles of the new Italian ally, while the heavy reinforcement in Gallipoli of the Turkish troops (at whose hands the soldiers of the British Empire were to suffer defeat) was offset by the capitulation on 9th July of German South West Africa to General Botha.

Suddenly, on the evening of Monday, 12th July, the newspaper offices learned that an ultimatum had been delivered to the Government and the coal owners by the sovereign body of the South Wales Miners' Federation. Earlier that evening the delegate conference at Cardiff had given notice of a coalfield strike unless the interminable bickering and shuffling of the last twenty weeks were brought to an issue within three days. The delegates had overruled the recommendations of their own Executive Council.

During the first week of July the Executive Council of the South Wales Miners' Federation pressed Walter Runciman for such an interpretation of these terms as might make them more palatable even considered merely as a basis for negotiations. Meantime from their side the owners were putting forward demands of an opposite nature.

It was not until Friday, 9th July, three days before the assembling of the delegate conference called for Monday, 12th July, that Walter Runciman gave his interpretations on the points that had been raised. These interpretations were eight in number and in the opinion of the Executive Council they were extremely unfavourable to the miners. Runciman, for example, on the question of the rates of surfacemen made a restriction to apply it only to "able-bodied workmen." Secondly, Runciman made it clear that men on afternoon and night shifts should be paid at the rate of six turns for five and not, as had been demanded, at the rate of one turn and a fifth for each turn worked. Thirdly, the rates paid to underground daywagemen were left to the consideration of the Conciliation Board instead of being raised to a uniform 5/- minimum. Fourthly, the question as to what workmen were covered by the terms of the 1st July was left to the decision of the independent chairman of the Conciliation Board. The miners' demand that the agreement should apply to those workers who were or might become members of the South Wales Miners' Federation (so that non-unionists and members of "sectional" societies would not be able to benefit) was a fifth point for interpretation. On this Runciman shelved a decision. The reply was that "As this may affect other trade unions, it requires more investigation and inquiry into local circumstances than Mr. Runciman can at present undertake." Runciman's failure to grapple with this point was, perhaps, more fruitful of dissension than anything else.

Finally, the note that ran through Runciman's interpretations was that of reference to the independent chairman of the Conciliation Board.

This did not satisfy the miners who wanted an immediate decision and who knew that a question shelved was frequently a question lost.

The Executive Council now realised that it would be well nigh impossible to prevent a stoppage of the coalfield immediately the nature of the Runciman interpretations was made public. In effect the Government had given a decision which practically invited a strike. Nevertheless, the Executive Council decided by 15 to 11 to put forward a recommendation of a kind that might secure a further continuance of work. The resolution ran :

"That the Council cannot advise the workmen to agree to Clause D of the interpretations of the Board of Trade, as it might involve the possibility of the perpetuation of the old standard rates as the basis of the new standard, and are still in doubt as to the precise meaning to be attached to several of the interpretations which have been given; but are willing to meet the Owners at a further meeting to be presided over by the President of the Board of Trade, with a view to endeavouring to arrive at an agreement satisfactory to the Workmen, and that pending this meeting taking place and a decision being arrived at, recommends the Workmen to continue work on the understanding that any Terms which are come to shall relate back to the 1st day of July, 1915; it being further distinctly understood that before any Agreement is entered into, that the same shall be submitted to and be ratified by the Workmen." (10 vii 1915).

By this time, however, the patience of the miners was exhausted. For five years they had been bound down by an agreement in many ways unfavourable to their interests. Notice had run for three months after its termination without the owners being willing of their own accord to enter the negotiations for the new agreement. Finally, for fourteen days they had extended the period of working. Despite this extended notice they were as far off a decision as ever. Indeed, the interpretations by Runciman of his own document had only strengthened the opposition to that document itself. Thus the conference delegates resolved to wait no longer but at once to bring matters to a head. The Executive Council recommendation was rejected by 1,894 votes to 1,037, a majority which was equivalent to nearly 43,000 out of the 156,000 workmen, there represented by 303 delegates. The Special Conference of the South Wales Miners' Federation had rejected the terms of settlement put forward by the Government and passed the following resolution : "That we do not accept anything less than our original proposals, and that we stop the collieries on Thursday next until these terms are conceded." There were three days before the wheels would cease to turn in the South Wales coalfield.

6 THE PRESS BARRAGE BEGINS

The miners' ultimatum of 12th July 1915 was "headline news" the next day throughout the British Empire : and for the whole of the next week it was given "full coverage" by the newspaper Press. What this meant in practice may be conveyed by a comparison with an earlier great war (of Britain and her allies against the French Revolution) when a few petty sheets of newsprint circulated slowly throughout the towns and the shires—so that, outside the areas affected, some might know of the Luddites only from Byron's speech on their behalf in the House of Lords. A hundred years later the newspaper Press coursed throughout the United Kingdom in a single day with a circulation transformed from hundreds or thousands into millions and tens of millions, with its owners turned into limited liability companies headed by millionaires; while upon the utterances of its journalists there had been bestowed something of the authority that for ten successive generations had been accorded to the printed columns of the "King James' Bible", so that while it would be an overstatement to say that by 1900 the British public was largely governed by the newspaper Press, nevertheless its readers were daily persuaded to be governed nationally and locally by the Queen-in-Council and the Queen-in-Parliament by the two-party system of Liberal and Conservative (Whig and Tory "writ large")—and persuaded to form their opinions along lines provided not only by the weighty editorials but by the selection of news that seemed to its producers to be "fit to print."

By 1915 there were still newspapers that straddled "the dark backward and abysm of time" between the 18th and the 20th centuries : and they were as ready to denounce the German Emperor Wilhelm as they had been to fulminate against Napoleon Bonaparte. Amongst these the *Morning Post*, born in 1772 and still going strong throughout the 1914-18 war, was foremost in response to the threatened strike.

The editorial, headed "Of our own household", began :

"The Germans are no doubt rejoicing over the situation in South Wales. Probably they have had some hand in bringing it about, for there is good ground for the belief that agents of the enemy are busy everywhere stirring up labour troubles . . . . There are German agitators and German money at work, and the Government, which for some mysterious reason is still protecting the enemy in our midst, is much to blame" (13 viii 1915).

But the enemy was not the only "instigator of industrial strife." On the contrary, said the *Morning Post* :

"For years South Wales has been a hotbed of class hatred, radicalism, syndicalism and socialism. The miners of South Wales have gone from one crisis to another. They have talked violence and done violence; they have cost themselves, the industry and the country many millions by their bitter disputes."

These miners, stated the editorial, could not say that they are ill-paid; for, on the contrary, "they make high wages and live well." But, starved of good counsel, "they have been as sheep without a shepherd;" for "their politicians" have poured out to them the "raw and fiery liquors of envy, uncharitableness and class hatred."

After this somewhat envious and almost uncharitable allusion to the Liberals and Lib-Labs who had held mining constituencies in Wales (and indeed of all but three of the Welsh parliamentary seats) the *Morning Post* went back to three years earlier, when "we ventured to predict" that the Minimum Wage Act of 1912 "would bring not peace but a sword"; and continued confusedly with a farrago that proved nothing beyond the writer's unawareness of the facts of the dispute. But the *Morning Post* did more than exclaim in horror at the strike ultimatum or provide what it believed to be an analysis of the situation. It proposed, if persuasion failed, immediate stern, swift measures against the miners, the union funds to be "sequestrated", a food blockade (such as was actually then being operated against the German enemy) of the Welsh valleys; the whole coalfield to be put under martial law.[1]

"A strike, like an army, needs supplies; if the funds are sequestrated and the shops closed the strike cannot proceed. If need be, the whole of the mining district will have to be placed under military law and administered as a military area. The Government have the necessary powers, and the country, which has willingly surrendered all powers to the Coalition, will expect the Coalition to do its duty" (13 vii 1915).

A day later *The Times* began its editorial significantly headed "The Test of Government" with the words:

"The South Wales miners have brought the labour crisis to a head and forced the Government to take action . . . . It had to come, and the Government must go through with it. No experienced observer who knows the facts can have expected the present labour difficulties to pass away without some shock which will convince the men concerned that the situation is serious and the Government in earnest" (14 vii 1915).

The editorial then harked back to the opposition speech of Philip Snowden, M.P. (on the second reading of the Munitions of War Bill on Monday, 28th June) who had stated: "Socialism, of which I have been an advocate for a great many years, is a system of industrial and social organisation. I believe that I am the only one among the Members of the Labour Party in this House who has been an advocate of compulsory State arbitration. I have always regarded that as being the logical outcome of the Socialist principles which I have professed. I have never said that with State compulsory arbitration you should destroy all trade union rights. I do not believe in strikes: I think that strikes are unthinkable at a time like this."

The Times commented:

"The other day, while Mr. Snowden was pronouncing strikes 'unthinkable' in the House of Commons, Mr. Hartshorn, who knows something about it, said that the Welsh miners were going to strike, no matter what the Government did, unless all their demands were conceded.

[1]Further details of how this compulsion was to be applied (by ordering that each single collier was accompanied underground by two soldiers with fixed bayonets presumably) the *Morning Post* left to the imagination of its reader.

He has been proved to be right . . . . So now the clash has come, and the Munitions Act will be put to the test."

A brief resumé of the events was followed by reflections on the perils of democracy in the trade union movement:

"The President of the Board of Trade has been negotiating with the executive of the miners' union, and what the delegates rejected on Monday was the proposal to continue negotiations on the lines laid down by him—a proposal endorsed by their own executive. The delegates declared by a large majority their intention of waiting no longer for any negotiations and of stopping work on Thursday. And they did this in the teeth of the Munitions Act, which they knew might be applied.

"This is clearly an open challenge, not to the Government only, but to all government."

Then after stating that "the action of the South Wales miners" showed that no guarantee given by parliamentary representatives "or heads of the union is worth anything" and they could not guarantee the behaviour of their members "over whom they exercise no control", it went on:

"They exercise none because they have abandoned it, and because they depend for their own offices on the favour of the men. This is democracy. It is being tested by the war as it never has been before. And, so as far as trade unionism is concerned, it has failed. Hence the necessity for the Munitions Act."

Finally, the old "Thunderer" reckoned that there might be "further trouble on a larger scale" and concluded:

"The one thing certain is that, if there is to be trouble, it must be resolutely met. The question is no longer one of wages but of governing the country. Any notion that concessions would put the matter right may be dismissed. They would only be the signal for further demands by the Welsh miners and for similar demands by all the others. That is clear from the case of the Scottish miners, who have just received an advance under a conciliation board award and have immediately proceeded to formulate fresh demands."

7 THE KING "PROCLAIMS" THE COALFIELD

The news of an ultimatum, of an imminent stoppage in time of war of the most important coalfield may have come to the news agencies of Fleet Street and to the Members of Parliament as a thunderclap, sudden and unexpected. It was not so in Whitehall where the measures to be taken if a strike were threatened had already been concerted between the Board of Trade and the Ministry of Munitions. But their answer appeared as something equally sudden and drastic, namely, to "proclaim" the whole South Wales coalfield under the new Munitions of War Act, which had become law on 2nd July. By this it became a criminal offence for anyone in the coalmining industry of South Wales

4 FUNERAL DEMONSTRATION BY MINERS OF PARK AND DARE

5 PENYRENGLYN SOUP KITCHEN, 1921 LOCKOUT

to take part "in a strike or lockout" : and compulsory arbitration under "the Board of Trade" was put into force. This was conveyed on the morning of Tuesday 13th July to Tom Richards, M.P., in a telegram from the Minister of Munitions as follows :

"In view of the seriousness of the situation created by the apprehended coal strike in South Wales, His Majesty the King approves the issue of a Proclamation under Section 3 of the Munitions of War Act, 1915, declaring that the existence or continuance of the difference which has arisen in the South Wales coal mining industry is prejudicial to the manufacture, transport, and supply of munitions of war, and applying Part 1 of the Act to that difference. The effect of this Proclamation, which is issued today, is to make it an offence punishable under the Act to take part in a strike or lock-out unless the dispute has been reported to the Board of Trade, and the Board have not within 21 days of such report referred it for settlement in accordance with the Act" (13 vii 1915).

A Royal Proclamation was a formal announcement made under the Great Seal, of some matter which the King-in-Council desired to make known to his subjects, e.g., the declaration of war, the dissolution (or the summoning) of Parliament, the statement of neutrality; or it might be, as it was in this case, the bringing into operation of the provisions of some statute the enforcement of which the legislature (the King-in-Parliament) had left to the discretion of the King-in-Council. The style in which a proclamation was printed, usually in large type on big sheets of not less than 26 × 36 inches, with its unvarying two-line heading

"BY THE KING
A PROCLAMATION"

had been calculated in past times to impress the beholder with the awful authority of His Britannic Majesty, acting "by and with the advice of Our Privy Council." It was printed for wide distribution, to be stuck up on every parish notice board.

The wording of the proclamation, after a recital in full of Section 3 of the Munitions of War Act, 1915, refers first to "a difference" about terms of "a proposed agreement" between the Monmouthshire and South Wales Coal Owners' Association and the South Wales Miners' Federation, and "Whereas the Minister of Munitions is not satisfied" that it could be settled without a stoppage prejudicial to supply of Munitions of War : "Now Therefore," it concludes, "We, by and with the advice of Our Privy Council are pleased to proclaim direct and ordain" that Part One of the Act "shall apply."[1]

Just after three of the clock that same Tuesday in the House of Commons, in reply to a "private notice" question (usually a question which a Minister has arranged should be asked) Walter Runciman said that a "serious situation" had been created when the Cardiff conference of delegates "rejected the terms of settlement" and that the Government "have decided to apply by Proclamation the provisions of

[1]Full text in Appendix to this Chapter.

Part 1 of the Munitions of War Act, 1915". Thereupon Edgar Jones, senior Member for Merthyr Tydfil, put supplementary questions: and, according to the report in *The Times*, asked: "Will the Right Hon. Gentleman have copies of the Proclamation affixed at every coal pit tomorrow?" To this Runciman replied: "Certainly."

It was clear that the Government's decision had the assent of the House of Commons; nor was there any dissent in the House of Lords. The newspaper Press, in these opening years of the century, often hailed as "the Fourth Estate," having been given full information at the same time as the statement was made in Parliament, was equally satisfied. On the next day the headlines ran: "Government dealing in right way with the coal strike threat"; "No strike by Royal Proclamation"; "Powers of Munitions Act to be enforced against Welsh miners—£5 a day penalty" (*Daily Express*). "Miners must not strike"; "Royal Proclamation"; "South Wales Under New Act"; "£5 a day penalty for strikes"; and also "Effect in South Wales—Miners glad at State Action" (*Daily Mail*). "Swift action in the Coal Crisis—Munitions Act applied"; "Strike Forbidden by Proclamation"; "Leaders appeal to South Wales men to go on working" (*Daily Telegraph*). "Government to be congratulated for having placed South Wales miners under Munitions Act" (*Evening News*). "Miners Strike Forbidden"; "Commendable promptitude applying Munitions Act" (*The Standard*). "Government orders miners to remain at work" (*The Daily News and Leader*).

At the same time it was generally put about that the Government, completely taken by surprise, had nevertheless reacted with "commendable promptitude". But, as we have seen, the action had been premeditated. There was a sequence of events that was not published in the streets.

Under the powerful urging of the three Labour Ministers on 30th June the SWMF Executive Council had recommended the adjourned conference "to treat the general propositions of the Government as forming the basis for negotiations for a settlement" and for work to be continued "under a day-to-day contract" in the expectation of speedy completion of the agreement. The Executive Council in drafting this recommendation felt that they had met the situation in such a manner as to avoid a strike: and so they had—but by a narrow majority—and, added the official Ministry account, "after an acrimonious discussion."

The matter was very differently viewed in Whitehall, where on the same day the President of the Board of Trade had met the coalowners and told them of the terms: and the owners, says the official history, "though very reluctant to accept the terms, ultimately bowed to the express wish of the President." The President then received the reply of the South Wales miners and took it in a very different way from that which the Executive Council had hoped would be the result. In the official history the position as seen from the Board of Trade is described as follows:

"The Miners' Executive then proceeded to demand further concessions in the form of interpretations of the Government's terms, and intimated that unless they were made the men would cease work." But Mr. Runciman would not yield. He therefore wrote (M.W.20552) on 7th July to Mr. Lloyd George asking whether he was prepared to deal with the crisis which might arise.

" 'I am still in touch with the parties', he said, 'and the men are unlikely to take any drastic action prior to receiving from me the interpretations of the proposals I made to both sides on 30th June. As, however, the interpretations the men want are really in the nature of a demand for further concessions, and as I have already gone very far in compelling the owners to accept conditions which are very distasteful to them, and as my proposals on 30th June were definitely made for acceptance or rejection without alteration, I feel it extremely difficult to reopen the matter.' "

"Mr. Lloyd George replied (M.W.20552) the next day that he should not hesitate, if unfortunately the necessity should arise, to advise the issue of a Proclamation bringing the difference within the scope of Part 1 of the Munitions of War Act."

8 DISCUSSIONS IN THE MINING CAMP

The decision by the Cardiff conference on Monday, 12th July, to set a time limit to these protracted negotiations with the Board of Trade had caused perturbation throughout the island, and particularly in the Westminster Palace Hotel. There the MFGB Executive Committee was meeting for the first time since Monday, 28th June, when to avoid compulsion they had offered Lloyd George their guarantee against miners' strikes: but the resolution containing this guarantee had not been accepted by the South Wales representatives. Lloyd George had then conceded that he would not apply the Act if he saw no need to do so: and with this nugatory concession the miners' leaders had perforce to be satisfied. But now a fortnight later there seemed little they could do but anxiously ponder the situation and send a wire summoning their Welsh colleagues to be with them on the morrow.

Tuesday, 13th July, was a day of discussion. One after another the three agents from Wales explained the matter to their fifteen colleagues on the national committee. Vernon Hartshorn told how the Runciman terms had arrived on 30th June. From these terms "certain vital matters" had been omitted: nor did the Executive Council understand what was entailed in some of the proposals. Was the "six shifts for five for night men" to apply to every shift? Had their figures (which were to be the basis for the 50 per cent) been accepted? As the Wages Agreement was due to expire that evening after 5½ years, the Executive Council had "advised the men to go on working on day-to-day contracts until further interviews with Mr. Runciman": and by a very narrow majority the conference had accepted that recommendation.

Then Hartshorn told of the further negotiations with Runciman until "they had got his interpretation of his own proposals" which proved to be unacceptable; of the division in the Executive Council "as to whether or not the men should continue working" (10 vii 1915); and of the previous day's decision not to accept the Executive Council's recommendations. He said:

"They passed a resolution that Wednesday night shift (14th July) should be the last shift to be worked until agreement has been reached, Wednesday being the last day according to the decision of the conference on 30th June, on which they would work on day-to-day contracts. On Thursday morning, the whole coalfield will be idle" (13 vii 1915).

Hartshorn went on to point out some things "the men would not accept"—matters which had been discussed "for five or six hours" before the conference delegates rejected what was put before them. Nor would they go on working from day to day but decided "to insist on their original terms being put forward as the basis of fresh negotiations."

George Barker in his manner drew a somewhat lurid picture of "the last time we saw the face of the owners . . . . in Mr. Runciman's room at the Board of Trade." It was after negotiations had been broken off and when half a dozen of the Executive Council met the owners. He recalled the utterances of F. L. Davis, their spokesman: before discussion of any terms the men must withdraw the demand for a minimum rate of wages, or for the fixing of an equivalent selling price, or for the three year period suggested for the duration of the agreement: moreover the claim for a new standard should be withdrawn.

When Runciman then acted as intermediary, they had found that, with a single exception "every one of the demands made by the owners had been granted."

Barker considered it a singular feature that although Runciman had drawn up a series of paragraphs supposed to be terms of settlement "he refuses to interpret those terms." While his proposal to refer them to somebody else to interpret "was the subject of much mirth and ridicule at our conference yesterday." They found that except for two points, "the whole of the South Wales miners are placed absolutely in the hands of the arbitrators." Then George Barker gave details of what had been discussed by the 303 delegates at the Cory Hall. He said:

"By 94,700 to 51,850 it was decided at the conference not to accept either the recommendation of the Executive or the terms. A great amount of indignation has been caused in the coalfield by statements that the delegates did not represent the men. That suspicion is very ill founded. Delegates are appointed and paid by their own lodges to attend the conference, and came with mandates from their lodges. The proposal for a ballot vote was defeated by an overwhelming majority: but if it had been carried it would certainly have meant a stoppage while the ballot was being taken as the delegates had already decided not to go on working from day to day."

He ended by saying that after three months spent in urging the owners to negotiate, and after fourteen days in day-to-day contracts "the patience of the men was exhausted" as there was no finality at all.

"Their secretary had been authorised to send the resolution to Mr. Runciman, with an expression of opinion that they were still prepared to negotiate upon the terms of settlement. At present the terms, meagre as they were, were so vague and indefinite that no one knows what their meaning really is! If Mr. Runciman desired to settle he had forty-eight hours in which to do it.

"To grant the whole of their terms would only cost the owners 4.43d. per ton."

Vice-President James Winstone, a newcomer compared with his two senior colleagues, elected to the national committee in 1911, said he did not think he had anything to add, except to express his regret at the unfortunate position. He did not know that anybody was more to blame than the coalowners and Mr. Runciman had simply fooled them. They had heard the decision of the Welsh men, and he could not depart from it.

Replying to a question by the chairman, Winstone said that the Executive Council of the South Wales Miners' Federation had decided by resolution that the matter was not to come before the Miners' Federation of Great Britain.

"George Barker said there were three essential demands: (1) No compulsory arbitration; (2) A minimum of 10 per cent on the new basis; (3) A satisfactory equivalent selling price, and further the duration of the agreement must be satisfactory.

"The matter was discussed at great length. Several resolutions were before the meeting suggesting that the men should continue at work, and that the Miners' Federation of Great Britain be allowed to assist the South Wales representatives in their negotiations.

"George Barker said whatever resolution this committee may carry the South Wales Federation will not allow this Federation to interfere".

Ultimately, the following resolution was passed and sent immediately by telegram to Tom Richards:

"That we express our deep regret that a settlement has not been secured in the South Wales coalfield. We believe that the South Wales coal masters are mainly responsible for the deadlock. In view, however, of the serious national crisis existing at the present time caused by the war, we appeal for the South Wales miners to go on working from day to day until a satisfactory settlement is arrived at. Ashton." (13 vii 1915).

Next day in Cardiff the full thirty of the Executive Council (except their president) met to deal with an unprecedented situation. The SWMF councillors had been called together to consider the telegrams of Tuesday, one from Lloyd George and one from Thomas Ashton. They discussed the whole situation created by the 48-hour ultimatum of the conference, the subsequent Royal Proclamation and the resolution passed by the Miners' Federation of Great Britain Executive Committee. It was an anxious session, which began at half past ten in the morning and adjourned for an hour before an afternoon session at 2 p.m. W. P. Nicholas, solicitor, was called in to explain the legal position of the workmen under the Proclamation. George Barker gave his report of what took place the previous day in the Westminster Palace Hotel where the first item on the agenda had been "the South Wales Dispute" and "part of the committee thought they ought to have this matter in their hands." Smillie had referred to the pledge given to Lloyd George but had admitted that South Wales had refused to be bound by that pledge : "South Wales was not in the pledge."

The difference of opinion was now extreme, from some of the older agents (making up five-sixths of the council) and from founding fathers, such as Ben Davies of Pontypridd (whose declamation that "the whole world" was against the Welsh miners "except in Germany, Austria and Turkey" was to be widely reported in the newspapers) or former firebrands like Stanton of Aberdare to the younger lodge secretaries and checkweighers, such as Noah Rees and Noah Ablett, keen socialists whose training had been at Ruskin College and at the Central Labour College.

Finally, a resolution for an immediate summons to a special conference was moved and carried by 13 votes to 10 :

"That we call a conference tomorrow to consider the whole situation, and that we try and get into communication with the Government" (14 vii 1915).

What recommendation, if any, should go from the council on the morrow ? A further proposal, which received 19 votes to 4 for an amendment ("That we make no recommendation other than the workmen shall stick to their proposals") ran as follows :

"That if the Government is prepared to meet this Council to consider the Workmen's Proposals, we agree to recommend the Workmen to resume work until this is done" (14 vii 1915).

It was well on in the afternoon of Wednesday, 14th July, before the Executive Council reached the end of its deliberations. But Tom Richards immediately sent off a telegram to the Rt. Hon. W. Runciman at the House of Commons in the hope of a speedy reply by telegraph or telephone.

"Workmen's Executive Council desire to know if you are prepared to meet them again to consider the Workmen's Proposals. The Council are prepared, if this is done, to recommend the Workmen to resume work on Friday, and continue working while a further attempt to arrive at a satisfactory settlement is being made. Council awaiting reply. Richards, General Secretary, Cardiff."

Some time elapsed, however, before there came an O.H.M.S. telegram signed by "Private Secretary, Board of Trade."

"In reply to your Telegram, President of Board of Trade is prepared to meet representatives of Workmen to promote a settlement of the difference in the South Wales Coal Trade. His Majesty's Government confidently expect that your Executive will use their influence to prevent a breach of the Munitions of War Act by men ceasing work tomorrow. Private Secretary, Board of Trade."

It was too late, and all Tom Richards could do was to tell Runciman that the private secretary's response had been ineffective. The telegram ran as follows:

"Very much regret. I am afraid your Telegram received too late to prevent stoppage tomorrow, but hope Conference will be able to secure resumption of work tomorrow night and Friday. Richards, Miners' Secretary" (15 vii 1915).

Before these hopes of resumption of work could be tested, the three hundred and more elected delegates had been "briefed" for the conference by their experience at the pit.

On that Wednesday, 14th July, 1915, the colliers in seven hundred mines, as they went toward their task in underground workings, farther down into the bowels of the earth than in any English coalfield,[1] saw posted up, staring them in the face at the pit gates, the Royal Proclamation: and they learned that they were now to be under compulsion—"GOD SAVE THE KING."

Each of them would be liable if they disobeyed the proclamation to a fine of £5 per day (over twice their weekly wage). It is stated by men up in years that as boys and young fellows they were incensed to a degree by this spectacle at their place of work. They were not, as some chronicled, unimpressed. They were furious and in their fury more and more began to think that those in the valleys who said that the Government and the State was an executive organ of the capitalist class had the truth of it. There was, according to these recollections, an access of class hatred against their rulers as well as their exploiters engendered by that Royal Proclamation posted on the pits.

9 THE IDES OF JULY

On Thursday the 15th, on the Ides of July "in the Sixth Year of Our Reign", there was a solitude in the collieries of South Wales: the great wheels were stopped: no coal was being won underground, no tonnage of fuel for the navy was rising from the depths: the strike of two hundred thousand mineworkers had begun. Later in the day it

[1]Seven years later they were found to be on average 275 fathom deep—or over twice the average depth of pits in Durham or Northumberland.

Employed underground (and never to see the light of day) were 17,000 horses whose plight could draw tears from royal personages: and normally fifteen times as many colliers, below and on the surface. But in 1915 statistics tell that there were 203,000 Welsh miners: a diminution caused by the withdrawal of 50,000 who had voluntarily entered the armed forces.

was a very full conference that met in the Cory Hall (321 delegates). The General Secretary read the messages sent to Runciman the previous day, and his reply. Then he called the attention of the delegates to "the prints of Telegrams" from the Ministry of Munitions and from Thomas Ashton. After it had been proposed and seconded "That the recommendation of the council be accepted" namely "to resume work" pending consideration of the "Workmen's Proposals", the debate began. There was very fierce interchange of opinion. Older leaders, aghast at the action of their members, and also aware of how hard it is to end a strike on the same day as it began, were nearly beside themselves with rage and frustration. Stanton of Aberdare gave free rein to his powers of invective—and was howled down for his pains. Despite the opening decision of the conference "that the Press be not admitted", what purported to be Stanton's utterance somehow found its way into the *Daily Express* where it was hailed as "a patriotic speech."

When the vote was taken the recommendation of the council was decisively rejected as follows:

For recommendation of council	113
Against recommendation of council	180
Majority against ...	67

Ness Edwards, afterwards to be a Minister of the Crown, pictured the situation after the Royal Proclamation:

"The mining villages were plastered with these Proclamations, evidently with the intention of frightening the Welsh miners into accepting the agreement. At the same time the MFGB sent a frantic message to the SWMF begging them to order the men to continue working. But these tactics had the opposite effect to that intended. Some of the leaders rose to meet the new situation with commendable courage, and asserted that an essential condition of remaining at work was that the Munitions Act be lifted off the mining industry, and the men followed this by striking on July 15th.

"The Press continued its mad shrieking against the miners; the politicians breathed fires of vengeance—yet the men remained calm and determined."

The recommendation of the Executive Council was "subject to the most bitter criticism and was rejected by the Conference" writes Ness Edwards, whose narrative continues thus:

"The Chairman, James Winstone, then raised the point of whether the Executive should go to London to continue the negotiations. The delegate who had moved the rejection of 'the Runciman rubbish' rose and delivered a homily to the Executive. 'No,' he said, 'you have been to London too often, that city of the Philistines, until you have become as bad as them.' Winstone then interjected 'Have a care, young man, for if this resolution is passed, it means that the Government has to bow the knee, and they do not bow the knee to such as you.' The delegate continued, 'You will put the resolution, Mr. Chairman, as moved from the body of this conference. We have stated our demands, and if the Government wants to negotiate, let them come to us here in South Wales. If I had my way, there would be no negotiations until their proclamation was repealed.' These sentiments were accepted by the conference, and it was understood that no deputation should go to London, but that the negotiations would have to take place in Cardiff.

"The strike proceeded with abundant enthusiasm, despite the rumours that abounded of Government prosecutions, and the suggestions of the Press that the miners should be called up and forced to work as soldiers at the point of the bayonet." *(History of the South Wales Miners' Federation.)*

10 EFFUSIONS OF PRINTERS' INK

Though the forebodings in some newspapers that the Royal Proclamation might not have the magical effect at first anticipated had been borne out in the event, nevertheless they printed every kind of condemnation of the lodge delegates who would not harken to their most experienced leaders. The treatment in half-a-dozen representative national newspapers varied little but in some a measure of responsibility is shifted on to supposed mischief-makers from Germany.

The Times also joined in the hunt for German agencies, but in a subordinate section in the editorial where they sought to find the origin of the strike and were "not inclined to judge the miners harshly":

> "They are evidently the cat's-paws of a small number of agitators. The hand of the men who have kept the South Wales coalfield—once the most peaceful in the Kingdom—seething for the last four years is plainly visible now.
>
> "They are clever fellows, and in the present case, by avoiding a genuine expression of opinion through the ballot, they have deliberately manoeuvred the men into a false position. That they have been backed, however unconsciously, by German agents is practically certain. Germans of high position have, in fact, boasted of it and predicted the strike."

Earlier the editorial had said "Strikes which endanger the safety of the realm cannot be tolerated" and then came the following passage:

> "The miners have defied and nullified it and are at this moment endangering the safety of the realm. It is no longer, therefore, a question of rights and wrongs in the dispute.
>
> "The very failure to recognise the change effected by the Munitions Act in the relations of employers and employed makes it imperative that the Government should not allow the error to persist. It must be removed by an unequivocal vindication of the Act. Otherwise the error will be justified and become general, the Act will be a dead letter, and the Government will have ceased to govern at the first challenge to their authority.
>
> "The announcement yesterday that a Munitions Court has

been set up for South Wales indicates that the Government regard the crisis in this light and are prepared to enforce the Act. There is nothing vindictive in doing so, and the Court is sure to take a 'first offence' view of test cases brought before it. Perhaps some method of amicably arranging penalties may be devised in the circumstances, but in any case the Act must be upheld."

The Standard, some twenty years earlier the favourite medium of Prime Minister Lord Salisbury, had fallen on evil days ever since it published its fatuous review of the Webbs' *History of Trade Unionism* in which it suggested their industriousness might have been devoted to some subject of more enduring interest such as the life of earthworms. Heedless of the worms already waiting for it, *The Standard* on the 16th July printed one of its last minatory utterances:

GERMANY'S ALLIES IN WALES

"Nearly all the pits in the South Wales coalfield were idle yesterday. The Munitions Act, under which the district has been proclaimed, declares that if men will not work they must be forced. Yet 200,000 Welsh miners declined to go down the pits yesterday . . . . the miners, by refusing work which is absolutely essential to the safety of the Navy and the nation, are playing Germany's game a good deal more effectively than if they were able to enlist *en masse* on the enemy's side. Welsh coal is the first necessity of a fleet in being."

After expressing the hope that the Government would "have nothing to do with the usual farce of conciliation", *The Manchester Guardian* stoutly affirmed that the strike, "a form of rebellion," must be suppressed; and that something far more drastic than a fine of £5 a day was needed to stop it:

"The enemy must be met literally by all the resources at the disposal of the State . . . . attach all the trade union funds and prohibit strike pay. Food supplies could be held up, and the whole area treated as if it were an enemy's country. The men affected might be placed, by special enactment, in the position of soldiers, and placed under military discipline. Finally, to deal with any open violence or defiance of law, the use of the military on a scale unexampled in ordinary times would be approved by the conscience of the community.

"No sensible person will talk lightly of shooting down strikers and dragooning a whole population."

The Daily Express, soon to come under the undisputed control of Max Aitken (later Lord Beaverbrook) devoted many column inches and a variety of views and themes to the events in South Wales. It began its editorial headed "A word to the South Wales Strikers" in persuasive style:

"Your most trusted leaders, men like Vernon Hartshorn,

C. B. Stanton, and James Winstone tell you that the national position is too grave for them to support you in your strike. The majority of your executive advise an immediate return to work. The executive of the Miners' Federation of Great Britain appealed to you to remain at work. And yet some 200,000 of you are on strike, and the Navy, on which the safety of our country depends, is threatened with a shortage of coal.

"They were afraid to let you express your opinion in a secret ballot, and have forced you to strike whether you agree or not."

The editorial was followed by verses entitled "The Kaiser's Black Guards" of which the final stanza ran:

"They've captured England's coal supplies,
The life-blood of her Fleet;
They'll stop her factories and works:
their triumph is complete.
They're better friends to me than my own
Guards could ever prove,
For all my vast battalions could not make
so fine a move.
As their occupation makes them black,
I'll show them my regards
By giving them the title of 'The Kaiser's
Own Black Guards'."

They handled the matter in a variety of ways. On Saturday, 17th July, the headline in very black ink and large letters ran as follows:

"£5,000 Reward is offered by the Daily Express for information leading to the Arrest and Conviction of any person responsible for instigating the Coal Strike, either through German or any other Enemy Alien Agency.

Address all communications in confidence to

The Editor,
The Daily Express,
8 Shoe Lane, E.C.4.

Envelope to be marked in left hand corner 'Coal Strike, Private'."

This headline was to be repeated and the theme of German agency was developed until within another three days the coalfield was "permeated by Germans" with speakers, pamphlets and papers for the miners and payments out of £60,000 (The *Financial News* said that this £60,000 "had been disbursed in gold coins").

But the column headed "German Agents and Money: influences that led to the strike" began with the words: "indications accumulate that German agents and German money have played a part in fomenting the strike."

Then it went on to say:

"Other influences, scarcely less harmful than those of

Germany, have also been at work. There are the baneful campaign of the Union of Democratic Control, which is allowed to proceed unchecked, the efforts of the Independent Labour Party, and the speeches and writings of many so-called pacifists, not least among whom has been Mr. Keir Hardie, the Member for Merthyr Tydfil.

"The notion of striking when the country's existence is at stake is by no means new to Welsh miners. It has been instilled into their minds for years by Mr. Keir Hardie that such a time is the most fitting and proper of all for a strike. Here are two typical statements by him :

> 'The moment war came within the range of possibility a conference of the workers of the two nations would be called to say that the moment war was declared they would cease work.' (At Birmingham, 18th October, 1910).
>
> 'An international conference would be held, and the workers of the world would pledge their faith to each other that they would stop finding soldiers or producing war material till the war came to an end.' (At Leicester, 31st January, 1911)."

On the same day, in the same column, a long list of horrific quotations was sharked up from the many speeches and writings of the Member for Merthyr Tydfil :

> "How Mr. Keir Hardie has sown the seed which has produced the strike may also be seen from the following utterances :
>
> 'We must not allow our children to be taught the hellish doctrine of shooting their brothers.' (October, 1906).
>
> 'Next to the Boys' Brigade, the most dangerous influence at work is Baden-Powell's Scouts.' (January, 1909).
>
> 'We belong to a party that is international.' (August 3, 1914).
>
> 'They had been led into the belief that the German naval and military preparations were designed for the subjection of Great Britain. Such was not the case.' (August 27th, 1914).
>
> "Such quotations might be multiplied a hundredfold. Mr. Keir Hardie's insults to our allies—despite the fact that his party is 'international'—are notorious. Is it any wonder that men fed on such poison should lack a sense of patriotism?"

In the next column a report written from Cardiff "on Friday night" ran as follows :

> "Most members of their executive council are in favour of peace, and the minority is composed of only four Syndicalist leaders.
>
> FOUL ADVICE
>
> "Mr. Keir Hardie's Syndicalist paper, the *Merthyr Pioneer* is adding fuel to the fire by urging the men to accept nothing less than their full demands. Another serious fact which I

learned today in the Rhondda Valley and Taff Vale districts is that the Union of Democratic Control is at work in all parts of the coalfield, and that Mr. 'Morel' has gained many disciples."

The *Daily News and Leader*, then one of a group of Liberal papers, often dubbed "the cocoa press" because of part ownership by Quaker families who manufactured chocolate, began with an eloquent address "to the men of South Wales":

TO THE MEN OF SOUTH WALES

"The decision of the South Wales Miners' executive last night to defy the Government and continue the strike will create a feeling of profound indignation throughout the country. It is a blow struck for the Kaiser against the nation of which these men are members."

After a reference to the miners' terms ("unconditional surrender by the State") in pursuit of which policy "they are prepared to stab the nation of which they are a part in the back, while it is fighting for its very existence against the greatest Power that has ever threatened its life," the newspaper adduced some "startling facts" viz:

"The very districts that have turned on the country in this moment of danger are the districts which have led the way in recruiting for the Army. There is no class in the land which has produced a larger proportion of soldiers during the last ten months than the miners of South Wales. They responded to the call so splendidly that their enthusiasm had to be checked lest the production of the mines should be gravely interfered with.

"Let us take another fact. This question of a strike has never been submitted to the men.

"The lodges have fallen into the hands of men with Syndicalist dreams, even if they have not more sinister motives, and with the votes of the members, thousands of whom are away serving their country, they are striking a blow against the life of the country in the hour of its gravest peril.

"The nation appeals from these men to the miners themselves."

The *Daily Mail*, created in 1896 by Alfred Harmsworth (Lord Northcliffe), who was feared and hated by Liberal journalists and politicians as the evil genius of Fleet Street—particularly after he had acquired by devious arts the control of *The Times*—did not differ from the other national papers in its condemnation of the South Wales miners as "unpatriotic" and "misled" in mid-July. But by Saturday, 17th July, the *Daily Mail* was seeking to find a way out of the impasse. This it did by broadening its target of attack to include the coalowners and the Government. In an editorial headed "The Shame of the Coal Strike—How to end it" it was said that the men "feel coalowners are making vast profits out of the war" and that the miners believe the owners to have been using the war "to deprive them of their liberty of negotiating";

while the coalowners were "discredited because they have not done their job properly." The Government too was "discredited" because it had failed to lead and govern—"has permitted poisonous literature to be scattered in South Wales in the shape of furious anti-war propaganda."

The *Morning Post*, which on Friday 16th still demanded the use of force "to compel them to work" and held that the miners were not "in the least affected by what is called patriotism," on the next day abruptly changed its editorial tune, declaring "We cannot believe that the Welsh miners as a body are traitors. They have recruited well."

But two days later a message purporting to come from its Swiss correspondent in Berne ran:

"THE ENEMY'S JUBILATION

> There is utmost rejoicing in Germany and Austria. If miners could see comments in enemy Press they would hide their heads in shame and lynch agitators who for doubtful motives have brought about such a situation."

It is clear that the abusive language of the newspapers day after day in that month of July—until the futility of Tuesday's Royal Proclamation had brought sobering thoughts by the Saturday morning issues—had an enormous effect, both upon what is called "public opinion" and on the men in the valleys.

In his comment on the Clyde strike of that year where "the men had a very real and serious grievance" G. D. H. Cole noted that "while the Government was congenially engaged in terrorising the Amalgamated Society of Engineers executive, the capitalist Press of both parties was no less congenially engaged in flinging mud" and that "journals vied with one another in applying such epithets as 'traitors.' The comments of the newspapers . . . . have taught the workers much about the real attitude of the governing class to Labour."

The South Wales miners had been alerted in their attitude by the happening of the Clyde strike, and were now being taught this same lesson.

A similar conclusion was reached in the comment that year of the authoritative *Labour Year Book* 1916 which in its account of coal mining in 1915 stated:

> "Meanwhile the strike had taken the chief place in public interest. Public opinion, being uninformed of the facts of the preceding delay, procrastination and deadlock was against the strikers: and, so far as public opinion is representative, it was still against them for many a long month afterwards. For this the daily newspapers were almost entirely responsible. The capitalist daily newspapers vied with one another in vilifying the miners of South Wales."

Perhaps the most penetrating comment on all the effusions up to 16th July was given in a relative newcomer to Fleet Street, the weekly

New Statesman, founded two years earlier by Beatrice Webb and at this stage receiving a frequent contribution from Sidney Webb as well as letters from Bernard Shaw. Its comment ran as follows :

> "There is probably nothing that does more to exasperate the rank-and-file Trade Unionist, and make him inclined to show the power of the one effective weapon he possesses than the knowledge that, whatever may be the merits of a dispute, the public (at the bidding of his employers and the newspaper proprietors) will assume that he is utterly in the wrong. In the South Wales coal dispute practically the only comment which has found public expression has taken the form of more or less violent and indiscriminate abuse of the men. They have been told daily that they are grasping, unreasonable and unpatriotic.
>
> "But what is the use of telling them that they are unreasonable, when the critic palpably neither knows nor cares anything about the actual merits of the dispute ? If, as *The Times* declares, the actual point at issue is 'absurdly small', why is it that the employers and the Government have thought it worth while to precipitate stoppage over it at so critical a moment ?
>
> "And what is the use of calling them grasping, when Mr. Runciman has just had to introduce a Bill to prevent mine owners asking prices more than from 25 per cent to 75 per cent in advance of those current last year ? As to being unpatriotic, in view of the fact that a great many of those who are thus accused are actually having to be prevented by the Government from enlisting in the Army, it is only natural that the charge falls somewhat flat" (17 vii 1915).

11 A WEEKEND OF TENSION

On Friday, 16th July, the day after the decisive rejection of their "resume work" recommendation, the SWMF Executive Council found themselves in a bit of a quandary. But they finally decided to act upon the decision of the special conference of Monday 12th, namely, that the President of the Board of Trade be informed that the Executive "hold themselves in readiness to negotiate upon the original proposals." So Runciman was told that "they would place themselves at the service of the Government in an effort to settle the strike". Runciman saw a deputation of coalowners earlier in the day. The owners, who had put their trust in Runciman, afterwards conferred at the Whitehall rooms and discussed his statements. When the miners' interview with Runciman at the Board of Trade offices in London began it was already 5.30 in the afternoon. It lasted for three hours; but no statements were issued, jointly or severally, that evening. The Press Association however circulated the newspapers as follows :

"It is understood that the miners' representatives intimated that they must ask that the original demands of the men should be conceded, and that in addition the Royal Proclamation bringing South Wales miners under the Munitions Act should be withdrawn.

"This suggestion did not bring about an approach towards a settlement. It was, therefore, put forward that Mr. Runciman might agree to allow the workmen to return to work on the condition that the original terms were granted meantime, and that the executive would discuss their incorporation in a new agreement, not necessarily to include the whole of the original proposals.

"Mr. Runciman declined these suggestions. He reminded the delegates that he had already put before them the best terms that the Government could see their way to concede. It was impossible for them to go further, and if they persisted in their attitude it was inevitable that a very serious situation must arise.

"The executive, rather than lead Mr. Runciman to think that a settlement was possible under the circumstances, decided to adjourn."

Prime Minister Asquith while taking no direct part in the interview remained at No. 10 Downing Street so as to be readily available if required. Little came of the encounter, but the Executive Council met again on the Saturday morning, 17th July, at the Westminster Palace Hotel, in the expectation of seeing Runciman once more in the afternoon.

It now seemed the deadlock was worse than before. This was the situation over a tense week-end : and on the Sunday night in Printing House Square it was decided "it is time to speak plainly." So *The Times* editorial on the morning of July 19th, after the Runciman week-end conversations had "come to nothing", stated that "neither the miners nor the Board of Trade nor the public appear to grasp the essential facts" because they still behaved "as if this were an ordinary strike," to be settled in the ordinary way by "negotiation and discussion of terms". But there could be no such discussion, ran the editorial, "until the men are back at work".

Welsh miners themselves could understand that it was "impossible" for the Government to yield to "an illegal strike". Nor could any Government "go on its hands and knees to men engaged in an illegal conspiracy" and retain any spark of authority.

The Times felt that the solution was a Government statement "which will be heard and read throughout the length and breadth of the land", to be made as soon as possible, "with all the weight demanded by the crisis" to the effect that strikes were "a form of treason to which there can be no concessions". The result would be that the strike, as in 1912, would break down "of its own weight". These were the guiding lines laid down by the paper of Lord Northcliffe which had just entered upon its fifth quarter century of editorialising.

Meantime, however, before this advice pressed upon them could have its full effect, another factor had entered into the situation. A stoppage of work on a large scale and a deadlock in negotiation is the opportunity for busybodies. All kinds of unofficial intermediaries get to work, sometimes privately stimulated by one side or another and sometimes out of sheer overflowing goodness of heart and unfailing propensity to meddle in matters outside their own affairs. Such an intermediary existed in the person of Clement Edwards, Liberal Member of Parliament for Glamorgan East, who had gone to see Runciman and as a result was able on the morning of Monday, 19th July, to present to Tom Richards a confidential memorandum.[1]

It was during the sitting of the Executive Council, who had met to consider further the situation after their talks with Runciman on the evening of Friday 16th, that Clement Edwards told his fellow parliamentarian Tom Richards that "he had seen Mr. Runciman" and had been informed by him that "if the Workmen returned to work" the basis along the following lines "for arriving at a settlement" could be agreed to. The older members of the Council had some experience of relations with East Glamorgan's M.P.

So the General Secretary was instructed by the Council to communicate with Runciman by telephone to ascertain whether Clement Edwards was correctly conveying the views of the President of the Board of Trade. In a conversation over the telephone Runciman replied

[1]Allen Clement Edwards (1869-1938), from 1910 one of three M.P.s of this name who, together with four called Jones, three called Williams and three called Davies made up a sizeable fraction of the thirty representatives of Welsh boroughs and counties. He was born in Radnorshire, called to the Bar, Middle Temple, in 1899, and at the end of his 16 years in Parliament became chairman of the "breakaway" National Democratic Party 1918-1920. He had played a prominent part at the 1914 inquiry into the Senghenydd disaster of October 1913.

"CONFIDENTIAL MEMORANDUM OF 19th JULY 1915.

Following upon my conversation with Mr. Richards, as a result of my inquiries Saturday and yesterday, I have reason to believe that if the men's representatives ask for a settlement on the following terms, they can obtain it:

1. Men to resume work at once.
2. All outstanding points between the men's full demands and the existing award of Mr. Runciman to be adjudicated by a new tribunal.
3. A firm undertaking given by the Federation that the award of such new tribunal to be abided by; but
4. Immediately the following terms to be conceded pending the decision of the tribunal:
   (1) Surfacemen—men's demands in full.
   (2) Nightmen—Mr. Runciman's proposals.
   (3) Hauliers—men's demands in full.
   (4) New standards of 1915. When the 5 per cent and 10 per cent advance respecting above standard, those amounts are to be merged in whatever increase in wage the men are entitled to in consequence of the increased selling price of coal.
   (5) Classes to be included in agreement—Enginemen's and Stokers' Union to be consulted.
   (6) Underground daywagemen. Application of St. Aldwyn's award to be adjudicated by the tribunal, otherwise the new standard of 50 per cent on 3/4 to be conceded.

(Signed) Clement Edwards."

that "speaking roughly" the terms "set forth by Mr. Edwards could form a basis of agreement", but that he could not discuss the terms over the telephone. Would he, however, again see the Executive Council asked Richards for that purpose of discussion? Runciman readily agreed. He "asked that as time was important he would see the Council tonight". Thereupon it was immediately resolved "That the Council proceed to London by the 3.5 train." Before the departure of the train the following telegram was received:

"Mr. Runciman wishes me to inform you that no useful purpose would be served by further interview between himself and representatives of South Wales miners, so long as representatives remain bound by resolution passed by conference of delegates on 12th July. A necessary preliminary to further interview must be that your Executive should be released from this resolution.

Private Secretary, Board of Trade."

It seemed that after the inviting tone of Runciman in his midday telephone talk with Richards, there had been second thoughts in the Board of Trade: and these had resulted in the counter-ultimatum of the private secretary's telegram, that no talks could take place so long as the democratic rules of the union (by which the delegate conference was the sovereign body) were strictly upheld. The Executive Council let the 15.05 train steam out of Cardiff Station. They did not go to London. They met again at the offices at 3.15 p.m. to consider the telegram received. What did it mean? They already felt from the atmosphere of their weekend discussions, confirmed by the tone of the morning's newspapers, that there would be no effective talks unless the men were back in the mines producing coal: and this had been the first stipulation in the "confidential memorandum" subscribed by A. C. Edwards, M.P.

But this new stipulation was like a counter-ultimatum. Had the President of the Board of Trade been influenced by the coalowners? The new refusal by Runciman to have a discussion until the Council had denounced the 12th July decision of their delegate conference might seem like a complete reversion to the attitude of leading coalowners seventeen years earlier, when Sir William Lewis had refused to meet the founders of the union so long as they considered themselves bound by delegate conference decisions.

During the sitting there was an interruption, indicating there had been further surprising developments in Whitehall. A telephonic communication was received that Messrs. Lloyd George, W. Runciman and A. Henderson were leaving London by the 6.10 train and desired to see the Executive Council." On hearing this they resolved—

"That the Council meet at the Park Hotel at 8.30 this evening" (19 vii 1915).

Later that evening at the Park Hotel the three Cabinet Ministers, together with Sir Llewellyn Smith, Sir Harry Verney and Mr. I. Mitchell (the "top brass" of the Board of Trade) attended the meeting, representing the Government: and, says the Council minute "they submitted proposals of the Government for the settlement of the present dispute." But, "after several hours musings" the meeting was adjourned to the morrow.

12 MAHOMET GOES TO THE MOUNTAIN

It had really happened. The old saying was that "if the mountain will not come to Mahomet, Mahomet will go to the mountain". In this case it was to a Welsh mountain, the *mynydd* with its seams of coal, that had the drawing power of the lodestone. The procedural stipulations of a Runciman and the stiffness of his staff which would have prolonged the stoppage to the extent of bringing about an early catastrophe were all swept aside. The legal penalties brandished by the Minister of Munitions, in the first flush of his industrial autocracy, were to be dropped like a hot brick. The constituted authority of the President of the Board of Trade could not be overridden, but in effect by the composition of the Government group it was overwhelmed.

In the Edwardian splendours of the Park Hotel, Cardiff, the Executive Council sat all day on Tuesday, 20th July, with "the Government deputation" as the three Cabinet Ministers and the high ranking civil servants were quaintly termed in the minutes. Eventually agreement was reached on Terms for a Settlement: and the adoption of that agreement by the Executive Council was unanimous. It might well have been, for the agreement (the achievement of which was considered at the time to be very largely due to Arthur Henderson) conceded those points on which the miners had laid most stress: and it promised that His Majesty's Government would see to it that the decisions were accepted by the coalowners. The opening words were:

"On receiving an assurance that the South Wales Miners' Federation accept a settlement on the following lines of the present dispute on behalf of those whom they represent, and that the men will immediately return to work on those terms, H.M. Government will undertake to secure the acceptance of these terms by the employers' representatives" (20 vii 1915).

The subsequent clauses (which are set out in full in the Appendix to this chapter) consisted of the "Runciman Terms" with a series of explanations and modifications—which pretty well modified several of the interpretations into complete nullity. For example, interpretations (d) (e) (g) were entirely deleted and new clauses substituted, while in the remaining five interpretations (a) (b) (c) (f) and (h) a significant change was made in each by omitting or altering the words of sentences found objectionable by the miners. There was to be no victimisation of anyone "for the part taken by him in the present dispute", while every effort was to be made to increase the output of coal "to meet the national needs during the present emergency".

The Terms of Settlement, thus provisionally agreed, had to be submitted to the special conference: and the final decision of the Executive Council in the Park Hotel began:

"The Council having considered the Terms of Settlement by His Majesty's Government, unanimously resolved to recommend the conference to accept such terms as a settlement of the matters in dispute.

Next morning, Wednesday, 21st July, 341 delegates gathered at the Cory Hall in Cardiff to hear their General Secretary, Tom Richards, explain the document that had emerged from the travail of Monday evening and of Tuesday. After additional explanations from the chairman, James Winstone, it was "decided by a large majority" that the Terms of Settlement be accepted. Thereafter the delegates sat back to absorb the unique experience of hearing three Cabinet Ministers addressing their conference in succession, which then concluded with a unanimous vote of thanks to Messrs. David Lloyd George, Arthur Henderson and Walter Runciman.

The miners were back at work on a new 1915 wage standard in accordance with the terms of the Scarborough resolutions of 1913: and their elected delegates, who had stood out against the arguments of the owners and of Liberal and Labour Members alike, and in the end of their own Executive Council majority, and who had withstood the threats of the Cabinet and a Royal Proclamation, could now afford to be generous in their applause of the Ministers of the Crown. Their demands had been conceded.

That same afternoon in the House of Commons the Prime Minister said: "I have received a telegram sent at a quarter to two this afternoon from Cardiff, and signed by the Minister of Munitions and the President of the Board of Trade, in these terms:

"Miners' Conference have decided to recommend their men to return to work forthwith, and urge their men to make up for lost time. The solution of the deadlock was rendered possible on the lines of agreement rather than of coercion by the public-spirited action of the coal owners, who placed themselves unreservedly in the Government's hands, for the purpose of securing a peaceful and reasonable settlement immediately."[1]

[1]The *New Statesman* scornfully commented that the "public spirit" of these gentlemen "would have been more valuable to the country if they had displayed it any time during the past three months by granting their employees terms similar to those which were long since agreed upon between owners and miners throughout the whole of the English coalfields.

"Also they might possibly have displayed it in connection with the price of coal by coming to an agreement with Mr. Runciman instead of having to be compelled by legislation to limit the excessive tribute they are levying upon the nation.

"But perhaps Mr. Asquith was moved to generosity by the consideration that his verbal tribute was the only consolation they were to get for their defeat" (24 vii 1915).

The coalowners themselves made no great to-do about the matter but nursed their grievances, if they still felt they had any, in seclusion and in comparative silence.

The Civil servants who had been so closely concerned were of a silent habit by nature of their office : but, at a later day (in the chapter already quoted from the *History of the Ministry of Munitions*) they had a last sour comment :

"In effect the miners obtained nearly everything they had demanded, and it was mutually agreed between the parties that no one should be penalised for the part he had taken in the dispute. The strike demonstrated the impotence of legal provisions for compulsory arbitration where a large body of obstinate men were determined to cease work rather than surrender their claims."

The daily newspapers lapsed into a comparative silence by the end of the week, treating these past events as "least said soonest mended," while continuing, most of them, to urge compulsion at home and abroad.

So by Saturday the 24th July the last word fell to the weekly papers. In an article headed "The Miners' Victory" the *New Statesman* which considered "they did wrong to strike in war-time" before every other expedient had been tried and had failed, nevertheless held that all the others, especially the Government, were "far more to blame". The best justification for the conduct of the miners was to be found firstly in the fact that "the Government might have settled the dispute, on terms which they now admit to be just, a fortnight ago" and secondly "in the columns of the anti-Trade Union Press", wherein "for the thousandth time" it was shown that "a strike is the sole means by which workmen can even get a hearing." On the deeper meaning of the struggle the *New Statesman* had this to say :

"The governing class and its spokesmen habitually allow their prejudices to override their common sense in matters of this kind. They would like to see the working classes disciplined and 'compelled' by means of martial law, and they allow the wish to be father to the belief that such methods are practicable. They thought that the Welsh miners could be bullied into surrender mainly because they wished to think so, but also because, being unable to imagine the possibility of the men being in the right, they overlooked the moral strength which comes from the possession of a just cause.

"What is less excusable is their failure to realise that if the miner could be browbeaten so easily he would not be the patriot and the splendid fighter he admittedly is.

"We most sincerely hope that we have now heard the last of this talk of compulsion in the industrial sphere."

In the *Cotton Factory Times* (1885 to 1937) the editorial supports the "very justifiable strike", whereby the miners "have defeated" what Smillie had described as "the Workers' Slavery Act" and stated :

"Nothing will prevent this unscrupulous exploitation of the country's dire needs by wealthy coalowners and middlemen except full State control of the production and distribution of coal. Instead of reviling we ought to compliment the colliers for making a stand against the monstrous extortion which is going on, and admire their modesty in merely asking for an advance of 4½d. a ton on their labour for getting coal " (23 vii 1915).

Justice which blamed Runciman's inability "to rise above the level of the mere business bureaucrat", or to see that "the needs of the nation stood before the profits of the coalowners", linked the matter mainly with the rise in prices:

"On Tuesday, Mr. Runciman introduced the Price of Coal (Limitation) Bill to the House of Commons . . . .

"If this Bill had been introduced a fortnight ago, there would have been little fear of a miners' strike in South Wales" (15 vii 1915).

The Clarion, with a similar attitude, chose as its exponent Vernon Hartshorn, whose proposals had been turned down by the Conference delegates.

Forward in its "Socialist War Points" of 24th July dealt with "the revolt against capitalism in Wales and the outrageous insolence of the Shareholders' Press", paid tribute to "the brave colliers who faced bluff, brag, abuse and slander in a week of trial" and slated Runciman, ending with the demand "Will the government take over the mines?" But their regular writer on the main editorial page in a general condemnation of coalmasters, Cabinet and colliers "in the order named" linked this "ugly incident" (where "the men were wrong" in rejecting their leaders' advice) with the question of socialist support or opposition to the war. Citing a June utterance from Emile Vandervelde, Chairman of the International Socialist Bureau (and Belgian Minister of State) who "deeply honoured Karl Liebknecht" (as well as Rosa Luxemburg and Clara Zetkin in Germany) but not "Bernstein, Kautsky or Haase" in their peace overtures, it went on to quote him as follows:

"Of the hard trials I have known since the German armies devastated and ruined my country, none has been more painful than to find here in England a certain number of my best comrades offering us only half-hearted support, seeking excuses for the crime of which we have been the victims, organising in favour of peace at any price, a propaganda which benefits only our aggressor . . . . In reality the extreme pacifism acclaimed by a minority, a small minority of the English proletariat, is not Socialism but Christianism" (24 vii 1915).

Writing from a pacifist standpoint ("I hate this war as I hate all wars") George Lansbury in *The Herald* concentrated his fierce invective on "the great armament trusts, the shipping rings, the coal and food monopolies, all of which are using the present crisis in order to fleece and rob the nation" and demanded ("Gaol the Coal Owners") that the Government "put the coal owners under lock and key until the end of the war" (17 vii 1915).

The *Labour Leader* with by far the largest circulation of the socialist weeklies[1] was edited by Fenner Brockway who had been drawing the attention of all the Socialists of Europe by printing E. D. Morel's exposures of British diplomacy. Its newly-appointed trade union correspondent in the last week of July welcomed the strike and its outcome, arraigned the Coalowners, "the Press Gang" and the Government whose quandary was described with relish.[2]

Jack Cade's conclusion was that the miners "have not been fighting for their own hand", but that "they were carrying on a double fight":

"They strove for their own demands and against compulsory arbitration. In this they were fighting for every Trade Union in the country" (27 vii 1915).

And what of the German spies and instigators? When on 21st July the Prime Minister read his reassuring telegram to the House of Commons, Hugh Edwards, Liberal Member for mid-Glamorgan (where in 1910 he had won electoral victory over Vernon Hartshorn) asked in great indignation "whether, in view of the fact that over 50,000 South Wales miners have joined the Colours since the outbreak of war, he, as the head of the Government, will associate himself with the protest against the base and malicious insinuation which has been made that this strike was in any way instigated by German influence?" To which the Prime Minister replied: "As far as I know, there is no foundation whatever for that." This did not satisfy Sir John Rees who earlier in the same Parliament had shown marked hostility to Keir Hardie. He asked the "President of the Board of Trade whether any evidence exists to the effect that German agency and German money have promoted, instigated, aided or abetted the strike in South Wales?" Mr. Runciman replied: "I know of no such evidence"[3] (26 vii 1915).

[1] Recollected by Lord Brockway in April 1970 as having been 80,000 weekly.

[2] "Having then put forward their farcical Coal Prices Bill, and having issued their terrible proclamation about the South Wales coalfield, the Government stood still and declared:

Who dares this pair of boots displace
Must meet Bombastes face to face.

The miners were not terrified: they went on in their own way even though that meant displacing the Governmental boots. They calmly met Bombastes face to face: and Bombastes has given way."

[3] Research on a considerable scale in the enemy papers of Germany and Austria (Turkey and Bulgaria were not researched) in that month of July 1915 failed to discover anything like the evidence of gleeful comment in the enemy Press which several of the British newspapers alleged to have existed. But in a sober review of "a year's war" the *Neue Freie Presse*, at the beginning of August, wrote: "The British Government has had to capitulate to 200,000 miners and already today sees itself confronted with the necessity of adopting compulsory service. What a confession of weakness! England began the war to destroy German militarism, and now sees herself constrained to turn to that . . . " and went on to use E. D. Morel's articles in *Labour Leader*.

APPENDIX I

SIR GEORGE ASKWITH'S DRAFT FOR SETTLEMENT
(29th June 1915)

"(1) If, and so soon as, prices rise so that the conditions on which Lord St. Aldwyn's award raising wages 17½ per cent was based, are materially altered, any claim made for an alteration of wages should be considered and discussed notwithstanding any previously existing maximum.

"(2) In the event of such claim not being settled by agreement, the claim should be adjusted either in accordance with the existing machinery, or, if it be preferred, by some person or tribunal agreed upon, who should have power to take into account all relevant circumstances (e.g., the question of increased cost of production and the state of trade, as well as prices and profits).

"(3) The claim that a new wage agreement should now be settled on normal peace lines, with an attempt to dismiss from the mind the conditions of war, is in my opinion impracticable. Certain essential features of such an agreement would be inoperative during the war, and the possible conditions after the war, to which it is thought the new wage agreement should apply, may be quite as abnormal as the present conditions. I suggest, therefore, that the conditions both during and for some time following the war are likely to be so different from ordinary peace conditions, to which it is admitted the wage agreement is intended to apply, that any such agreement would be in practice valueless.

"(4) In order that the position of the miners in respect to a new minimum may not be prejudiced by the deferment of the consideration of a new agreement, I am of the opinion that before any proposal for a reduction of wages below the present rate of 77½ per cent above standard is entertained, the question of what shall be the new minimum should be decided, by agreement or by some person or tribunal agreed upon."

APPENDIX II

RUNCIMAN INTERPRETATIONS
as submitted to Special Conference in Cory Hall, Cardiff,
on Monday, 12th July, 1915

SOUTH WALES COAL MINES
TERMS OF SETTLEMENT MADE BY THE GOVERNMENT ON THE 1st JULY, 1915

1st—The rates of surfacemen which are below 3/4 per day to be advanced to 3/4 per day.

2nd—Nightmen to receive six turns for five.

3rd—Hauliers employed in afternoon and night shifts to be paid the same rate of wages as those employed on the day shift.

4th—A New Standard of 50 per cent on the 1879 Standard to be established. Any Standards in operations other than the 1879 Standard to be correspondingly adjusted. (It is not intended that the alteration of the Standard shall in itself effect an immediate change in wages.)

5th—The Maximum and Minimum provided for in the 1910 Agreement not to be operative.

6th—Any question of interpretation of these terms to be submitted in writing.

Within ten days Runciman had sent down the following:

INTERPRETATIONS

The Owners' and Men's Representatives request interpretations on certain points respecting the meaning to be attached to some of the Clauses contained in the Terms of Settlement. The following are Mr. Runciman's answers on the points raised:

A. The Rates of Surfacemen which are below 3/4 per day to be advanced to 3/4 per day.

This means that at collieries where, prior to the 1st July, 1915, the Standard Rates of Surfacemen were below 3/4 per day on the 1879 Standard, they shall as from that date be advanced to a New Standard Rate of 5/- per day; and that at Collieries on Standards other than the 1879 Standard, where the rates were below 3/4 per day, they shall be raised to a New Standard Rate of 5/- per day.

This to apply to able-bodied workmen as understood at the various collieries.

B. Nightmen to receive Six Turns for Five.

This applies to men on Afternoon and Night Shifts. When a turn is lost in any working week and the loss is not due to the absence of the workman or to the inability of the workman himself to proceed with the work, he shall be paid at a proportionate rate for the turns worked by him in that week.

At collieries where the conditions of payment of Nightmen have been more favourable than those set out above, these conditions shall continue.

C. A New Standard of 50 per cent on the 1879 Standard to be established. Any Standard in operation other than the 1879 Standard to be correspondingly adjusted. (It is not intended that the alteration of the Standard shall in itself effect an immediate change in wages.)

It has been submitted to Mr. Runciman by the Men's Representatives that 50 per cent on the 1879 Standard equals 36 per cent on the 1877 Standard; whereas the Owners' Representatives place it at 35 per cent on the 1877 Standard. The terms of July 1st are definite, inasmuch as they state that "A New Standard of 50 per cent on the 1879 Standard is to be established. (Any Standard in operation other than the 1879 Standard is to be correspondingly adjusted.)"

In the event of any difference arising on this point or with regard to any other Standards which require adjustment, the chairman appointed under Clause (f) of this Memorandum shall decide the matter.

All equivalents mentioned in the late Agreement of Selling Prices opposite percentages are cancelled. In considering future alterations of wages, the independent chairman may consider what is a fair equivalent price for the New Standard in the circumstances then prevailing.

D. The question of the application of the New Standard to Underground Daywagemen who are under certain circumstances on rates below 3/4 has been raised, and inasmuch as the terms of 1st July state "It is not intended that the alteration of the Standard shall in itself effect an immediate change in wages," it will be for the consideration of the parties when they meet to decide as to how far it is feasible in harmony with this principle to adopt 3/4 plus 50 per cent as the uniform Standard in all cases. Failing decision, it shall be settled by the chairman appointed under Clause (f) of this Memorandum.

The question of the avoidance of fractional calculations is agreed to be a matter of minor importance, and may well be left to be settled in a similar manner, but it is intended that no workman shall be put in a less favourable position by any change made.

E. Workmen covered by the Terms of 1st July.

As the question of the inclusion of classes of workmen not covered by previous Agreements between the parties has been raised, and as this may affect other Trade Unions, it requires more investigation and inquiry into local circumstances than Mr. Runciman is able at present to undertake. In these circumstances the question should be discussed at the joint meeting, and, if necessary, settled by the chairman appointed under Clause (f) of this Memorandum.

F. Renewal of Agreement.

It has been pointed out to Mr. Runciman that the incorporation of the New Terms in the ordinary machinery under which the parties conduct their affairs will necessitate an Agreement. For this purpose Mr. Runciman considers that a joint meeting of the Owners' and Men's Representatives should be held forthwith, and as matters affecting these terms may arise, he purposes appointing a chairman to preside over the meeting, and to settle, after consultation with the Board of Trade, any questions upon which the parties fail to come to an agreement.

G. Duration of Agreement.

Mr. Runciman has given full consideration to this matter, which involves considerable difficulties at the present time, when it is impossible to forecast the conditions likely to prevail after the war is over. He has come to the conclusion that the question should be left to the Board of Trade to decide, on application from either party, what date is to be regarded for the purposes of the Agreement, as the date of the termination of war conditions, and also to settle what length of notice after that date should be given before the Agreement expires.

H. Further Questions of Interpretation.

Any further question of interpretation of these terms upon which the parties fail to agree shall be referred to the chairman appointed under Clause (f) of this Memorandum, who shall give a decision upon them after consultation with the Board of Trade.

APPENDIX III

"BY THE KING
A PROCLAMATION
UNDER THE MUNITIONS OF WAR ACT 1915.
GEORGE R.I.

WHEREAS in Section 3 of the Munitions of War Act, 1915, it is enacted :

'The differences to which this Part of this Act applies are differences as to rates of wages, hours of work, or otherwise as to terms or conditions of or affecting employment on the manufacture or repair of arms, ammunition, ships, vehicles, aircraft, or any other articles required for use in war, or of the metals, machines, or tools required for that manufacture or repair (in this Act referred to as munitions work); and also any differences as to rates of wages, hours of work, or otherwise as to terms or conditions of or affecting employment on any other work of any description, if this Part of this Act is applied to such a difference by His Majesty by Proclamation on the ground that in the opinion of His Majesty the existence or continuance of the difference is directly or indirectly prejudicial to the manufacture, transport, or supply of Munitions of War.

'This Part of this Act may be so applied to such a difference at any time, whether a lock-out or strike is in existence in connexion with the difference to which it is applied or not :

'Provided that if in the case of any industry the Minister of Munitions is satisfied that effective means exist to secure the settlement without stoppage of any difference arising on work other than on munitions work, no Proclamation shall be made under this Section with respect to any such difference.'

AND WHEREAS a difference within the meaning of this Section exists between employers and persons employed in the Coal Mining Industry of South Wales as to the rates of wages, hours of work or otherwise as to the terms or conditions of or affecting employment in connexion with the terms of a proposed agreement between the Monmouthshire and South Wales Coal Owners' Association and the South Wales Miners' Federation, for the settlement of differences of the nature aforesaid :

AND WHEREAS the Minister of Munitions is not satisfied that effective means exist to secure the settlement of the said difference without stoppage, being a difference arising on work other than munitions work :

AND WHEREAS in Our opinion the existence or continuance of the said difference is directly and indirectly prejudicial to the manufacture, transport, and supply of Munitions of War :

NOW, THEREFORE, We, by and with the advice of Our Privy Council, are pleased to proclaim, direct and ordain, that Part I of the Munitions of War Act, 1915, shall apply to the said difference.

Given at Our Court of **Buckingham Palace**, this thirteenth day of July, in the year of our Lord one thousand nine hundred and fifteen, and in the Sixth year of Our Reign.
GOD SAVE THE KING" (14 vii 1915).

APPENDIX IV

"RUNCIMAN TERMS"

as modified by Lloyd George and the "Government Deputation" on Tuesday, 20th July, 1915

On receiving an assurance that the South Wales Miners' Federation accept a settlement on the following lines of the present dispute on behalf of those whom they represent, and that the men will immediately return to work on those terms, H.M. Government will undertake to secure the acceptance of these terms by the employers' representatives.

(1) The terms of settlement made by the Government on the 1st July and the interpretation appended thereto (herein termed the "Runciman Terms") shall be adopted subject to the following explanations and modifications.

(2) The "Interpretations" shall be modified to the following extent:

A. The sentence referring to "able-bodied workmen" shall be omitted.

B. An accident in connection with a workman's employment shall be not a bar to his benefit by the bonus turn.

C. The new standard plus 10 per cent shall operate as a minimum. The last sentence of C shall read as follows:

"None of the equivalents mentioned in the late agreement of selling prices opposite percentages are to be inserted in the new agreement, but nothing shall prevent the independent chairman in determining future alterations of wages from considering what is a fair equivalent price for the new minimum."

The question of the avoidance of fractional calculations is agreed to be a matter of minor importance, and may well be left to be settled in a similar manner, but it is intended that no workman shall be put in a less favourable position by any change made.

D. This Clause shall be deleted. Standard rates for underground daywagemen which at present are less than 3/4 per day, shall be advanced to 3/4 per day plus 50 per cent.

The new standard rates for other underground daywagemen shall be either their existing rates or the rates applicable to them under the Minimum Wage Act, whichever are the higher, plus 50 per cent. Provided that where such last-mentioned new standard rates are determined by reference to a rate fixed under the Minimum Wage Act, they shall be subject to the rates applicable to such rates, pending the decision of an arbitrator appointed by the Board of Trade on the question what special rates, if any, shall apply in cases in which these rules are not observed.

E. This paragraph shall be deleted and replaced by the following:

"The Agreement shall apply to all workmen now employed or who might hereafter be employed at the collieries of the owners, and who may be members of the South Wales Miners' Federation."

F. All the words after "arise" shall be omitted, and the following words substituted :

"Any such matter upon which the parties fail to come to an agreement shall be referred to the President of the Board of Trade, whose decision shall be final."

G. This paragraph shall be deleted, and replaced by the following :

"This agreement shall continue in force until the expiration of six months after the termination of the war and thereafter until the lapse of three months, after notice has been given by one of the parties to terminate it."

H. The words from "Chairman" to the end of the clause shall be omitted, and the words "President of the Board of Trade, whose decision shall be final" substituted.

(3) The question of the rate for the Anthracite Collieries, as compared with those for other collieries, shall be the subject of inquiry.

(4) The whole of these Terms, including A of the Interpretations, shall operate as from the date of the resumption of work.

CHAPTER FOUR

THE AFTERMATH IN 1915 : WAR'S ALARMS IN 1916

1 CONTROVERSY

With the Prime Minister's announcement and benediction to the coal owners on 21st July, the general disposition of the chief parties to the dispute and of the newspapers was to treat the matter as finally settled. It was agreed to let bygones be bygones: and, as we have seen, "Least said soonest mended" was the motto of Fleet Street. But to obliterate it proved impossible : nor did any participant find himself saying

"So next day when the accustomed train
of things grew round my sense again"

that it had all subsided into oblivion. A fundamental antagonism had been laid bare: and Ness Edwards, one of the participants, concluded in his brief history that "the tone laid down in Hay's pamphlet was quietly permeating the rank and file of the organisation". That pamphlet, *War and the Welsh Miner*, had been circulating since August 1914.

A week after the settlement, in a parliamentary debate on Compulsory Military Service, there were many echoes : "What happened last week" was cited by J. H. Thomas, M.P., against the "sinister efforts of the conscriptionists" (28 vii 1915). Philip Morrell spoke also of the South Wales miners, saying "they will not listen to any idea of compulsion now . . . . " Llewellyn Williams, elected in mid-March for the Carmarthen District, referring to the strike in South Wales as "evidence of a spirit of victory" was interrupted by Joynson Hicks shouting "treachery" but went on to say that "last week compulsion in South Wales" had been tried and had failed.

Bitter arguments within the SWMF Executive Council were later transferred to the columns of newspapers. Vernon Hartshorn, J.P., regarded as their ablest member ("On union matters nobody could sustain an argument against old Tom Richards—except Hartshorn," was a fellow-member's recollection) had plunged into the *South Wales Daily News* with an article criticising the strike and the perils it had invoked for the Federation :

"Last week-end the very existence of the Federation as a Trade Union organisation hung in the balance . . . . on the very brink of the precipice . . . . in extreme peril, alone and absolutely unprotected . . . . abandoned by the whole of the Labour movement of the country, both industrial and political. The occasion was a unique opportunity for a bold stroke by bloodthirsty reaction . . . . the savage and crude old method of a 'whiff of grape shot' . . . . we were saved from that disaster not by any strength of our own, but by the wisdom, generosity and restraint of the Coalition Government" (24 vii 1915).

This brought a sharp rejoinder over the week-end in a letter from George Barker, his colleague on the board of the MFGB; and the controversy then continued with others, one of whom taunted Hartshorn about his frequent "paid articles". George Barker, hoary-headed zealot, had served seven years in the Buffs before getting the Zulu War Medal of 1879 after Isandhlwana. He was always most militant, a thorn in the flesh to his fellow agents and for this reason classed (quite wrongly) amongst "these wild young Syndicalists". In his letter Barker asked :

"Is it conceivable that any Government would be so stupid and monstrously wicked as to pour 'grape shot' on free men who were asking for a paltry 4½d. per ton from their greedy employers, who had raised the average price of large coal 6/1 per ton and small coal 5/1, and all this in the midst of a war which is taxing the united forces of the whole Empire? The idea is too foolish to merit the slightest consideration" (26 vii 1915).

Barker met the "wisdom, generosity and restraint of the Government" in Hartshorn's article with the gibe that "Here you have the vocabulary of the *adulator in excelsis*" and put the familiar rhetorical question : "Was there ever more confusion of thought and jumble of contradictions and inconsistencies in a single article than we have in this masterpiece of Hartshorn's?" Barker repudiated the argument that it was a "tactical slip" when the men "refused to continue working on day-to-day contracts." For 14 days they had tried that out and "the only fruit it produced was the proclamation under the Munitions Act. If they had gone to work under that Act they would have degraded themselves from free workers to slave labourers." Barker's conclusion that Hartshorn, by advising the men to continue working, "became the pet and idol of the enemies of the workmen and was quoted against them in most of the capitalist newspapers" ended with some old fashioned phrases :

"Now, forsooth, he is extolling and at the same time condemning the Government, and declares that by their blundering wisdom they saved the Federation from a peril that only existed in his own imagination. It is a strange world, my masters.—I am, &c., George Barker, Abertillery, Mon., July 24th, 1915."

Following upon this heated controversy came a soberly-worded article in *Justice* contributed by Executive Councillor Noah Rees, Secretary of the Cambrian Lodge, the greatest in the Rhondda District. Noah, at the end of a succinct explanation "of the peculiar methods by which the labour of the South Wales miners is exploited", made his own position clear on three points :

(i) on the issue of democracy : "in no other trade union is the opinion of the rank and file so fully felt and so quickly exercised and registered in any agitation"; (ii) on alienation of miners' leaders, "especially the brand that are citizens first and trade unionists some way after"; (iii) on nationalisation of the coal mining industry : "I am not personally prepared to say that the mines should be nationalised, and I very much doubt that the majority of the miners would favour nationalisation. I have yet to be convinced that the State would be a much more considerate employer than our present exploiters."

This last was in accord with the standpoint of other leading members of the Miners' Unofficial Reform Committee, expressed as early as winter of 1912-1913.

2 ANOTHER RUNCIMAN AWARD

While a joint sub-committee of coal-masters and colliers was working out the clauses of the new agreement (to be "in force from the 15th July, 1915 until the expiration of six months after the termination of the war") tempers flared up again in the coalfield—and also in Whitehall. Amongst a number of disputed points referred to the President of the Board of Trade was the question whether the agreement on the bonus turn (six turns paid for five worked) covered enginemen, pumpsmen, stokers, etc. In his award of 21st August, Runciman excluded these classes of workers from the benefit of the bonus turn. This appeared to the Executive Council, and certainly to the groups of men affected, to be a decision flatly against the terms of the award given by the three Ministers who came to Cardiff a month earlier : and so the following resolution was unanimously passed :

"That this Council accept the award with the exception of Clause (M) referring to the exclusion of the enginemen, pumpsmen, mechanical staff, stokers and banksmen, from the six turns for five payment, and that we inform the owners and the Government that we consider that Clause (M) is a withdrawal of the terms relating to this matter explicitly awarded by the representatives of the Government on July 20th, as set forth in Clauses (B) and (E) of the Government decisions of that date."

It was clear to them that a new crisis might easily develop when Runciman's latest award became known. So they called a conference for the last day of August and resolved (24 viii 1915) that a deputation of their leading members should "lay the foregoing resolution" before the three Ministers. If some colliers suspected Runciman to be the "capitalistic partisan" (Smillie's labelling) or believed him to be acting on the advice of the coal owners, it was a suspicion for which there could be no proof. Runciman however was almost certainly acting on the advice of his permanent officials, men who had to deal with new problems in the industry, though mining expertise was largely confined to a different department, the Home Office with its inspectorates. When the message from Cardiff reached Whitehall there was a feeling that the miners had gone too far and a letter was written to them saying as much, but in as suave a manner as possible, by the Secretary of the Board of Trade. This was Hubert Llewellyn Smith who, in the 'eighties had busied himself in social investigation, had with Vaughan Nash written *The Story of the Dockers' Strike* and had been linked up with Miss Beatrice Potter in such matters. Once he became a civil servant (in 1892) he steered very clear of any kind of socialist, as Beatrice Webb recounts in her Diary where she tells of how he had sheered off from any connection with them.

Llewellyn Smith's letter of 25th August, with impeccable logic, reviewed the decisions made, pointedly reminded the miners that the "reference to the President was expressly inserted during the Cardiff conference at the request of your Executive" and furthermore that at the hearing on August 17th, before Mr. Runciman, both sides pledged themselves to accept his decision on points referred as final and binding." Runciman's award of August 21st, covered such questions which "must now be considered as closed, and cannot be reopened. I am accordingly to express the Ministers' regret that they do not feel able, consistently with the terms of July 20th, to discuss with a deputation any matter which has been put before Mr. Runciman as the agreed referee, and which was dealt with in his award."

As the Council heard this letter from "Your obedient servant, H. Llewellyn Smith" it was reported that the Llanhilleth, Arrael Griffin, Cwmtillery and Rose Heyworth Powell Tillery Collieries were "on stop, consequent upon the refusal of the stokers to work under the award of Mr. Runciman". Thereupon it was resolved, firstly: "That the deputation proceed to London", where they would interview the three Ministers and would claim "their right to make public use of the Notes of Proceedings before Mr. Runciman" (27 viii 1915). Secondly, in the case of Abertillery they telegraphed the following resolution to the district secretary:

"That inasmuch as the matter at present in dispute is of a general character applicable to workmen employed at all the collieries, which is being dealt with by the Council, and is to be considered at a conference on Tuesday next, the Council urge upon all workmen that sectional stoppages of collieries is very detrimental to the efforts made to secure a satisfactory settlement; and that no stoppage should take place that has not been authorised by a decision of the whole coalfield".

By the following Tuesday the delegates assembled in Cardiff were in an angry mood. When they heard that the General Secretary had telegraphed from London asking for postponement until the morrow, and that their executive council proposed to "accept the recommendation to adjourn until tomorrow, and advise the coalfield to continue working," there was an immediate amendment: "That we instruct the coalfield to 'down tools' tomorrow, and to remain idle until the agreement be settled" (31 viii 1915). On a card vote the amendment was defeated but by a very small majority, viz 1,244 to 1,128. It was an index of the

F

high feeling in the coalfield. On the next day the delegates learned that it had been too late to alter the principal agreement which embodied Runciman's award of 20th August; but that their deputation to the Government had secured a supplementary agreement which "notwithstanding anything to the contrary in the Principal Agreement" reversed Runciman's decision completely. This, signed by all the members of the Board, is an unusual document.[1]

3 COMPULSION, MILITARY OR INDUSTRIAL

Up till the autumn of 1915 there had been no opportunity for "a voice from the coal mines" to be uttered in a national trade union assembly, no congress or conference to discuss the rights and wrongs of the European war in relation to the standpoint of international socialism. At last, in September, 1915, when the opportunity came at the Bristol Trades Union Congress it was clear that the delegates had long ago made up their minds as between "pro-war" and "anti-war" and that new issues had come to the fore. Thus a resolution in full support of the war effort was carried at the Congress with almost complete unanimity (only seven dissentients out of 610 accredited delegates) : but on conscription the formal unanimity hid divergencies of outlook.

Speaking for the miners Robert Smillie, himself regarded as "anti-war", demanded trade union action to prevent any measure of compulsion being operated and though other speakers were less forthright, the total impression amongst the miners was that conscription had been killed.[2] A month later the same questions arose at the MFGB Annual Conference which began by placing on record "its deep regret at the death of Mr. Keir Hardie" who was one of their members "through his local branch in Ayrshire" and recognising that "the labour movement generally has suffered a severe loss". There in the Mechanics' Institute in Nottingham the forty delegates from South Wales could hear from their president's address what precise political conclusions he drew when avowing himself "a pacifist" and always "a bitter opponent of militarism and war." Smillie said : "I feel even as a pacifist that it would be too much to expect our country in view of the sacrifices in blood and in treasure which we are making, to lower itself unless it is beaten down to the ground, to lower itself to even negotiate peace terms so long as the enemy is not on their own soil, but on the soil of France and Flanders" (5 x 1915).

But the most fervently uttered portion of his speech dealt with not only military but industrial conscription, for which the campaign, already

[1]This 3rd September document appears as an illustration in this history.

[2]After the great debate with its overwhelming support for his speech Smillie was standing by the author in the corridor and said to him with a joyful countenance, "After that, if they try it on, we'll stop the bloody wheels."

agitated in an angry debate in the House of Commons in the last week of July, had continued unremittingly. So with renewed passion Smillie exhorted the delegates on this question. He asked : "Do you think it is to secure men for the Army ? If you do you are sadly mistaken, the conscription campaign has behind it more than that. It has behind it conscription of industries, workshops, mines and railways in this country. It has behind it the desire to set up what our lads believe they are fighting against, to establish here militarism as existed in Germany.

"If we had the industrial militarism some people hope for we should have trials of our industrial classes and civilian classes behind closed doors without any opportunity being given to us to see and know what is going on. This should have our strongest opposition.

"I deny, and will fight as bitterly as I possibly can, the right of one class to conscript in the industrial movement my class, or to conscript for military purposes my class until they have first conscripted the land of the country and the capital of the country and put everything into it. These people talk of sacrifices; these people whose sacrifice is the giving away in income tax a very small moiety of their income, they speak of the working classes as not having sacrificed. Where is the home where the lads have gone away, or the father has gone away, that there is not a thousand-fold more sacrifice than any wealth can give ? Now when the bread winner goes away, or the lads leave father and mother and go to the front they are sacrificing their all, their life" (5 x 1915).

Robert Smillie's address met with a rapturous greeting from Winstone of South Wales, moving that the Conference "extend to the Chairman its hearty thanks" for his "eloquent and instructive address" and also "hopes that he may long be spared to carry on his good work in the interests of this Federation". But that same afternoon a jarring note was struck when the Conference reached item No. 18 on its agenda as follows :

"That no guarantees or agreements be entered into between the Executive Council and the Government or any other body where questions of principle are involved before the matter has been decided by a National Conference called for the purpose." *South Wales.*

The resolution as moved by Frank Hodges[1] who for two years had been agent for the Garw Valley, implied a repudiation of the MFGB Executive Committee's decision on Sunday June 27th and was felt to

[1]Frank Hodges, once a student at Ruskin College, Oxford, had written in the *Plebs* magazine about a visit he had paid to Laura, daughter of Karl Marx. Hodges was a keen supporter of the war effort and, with his forensic style of speaking, was much in demand for meetings inside South Wales and as spokesman at national conferences. Indeed he was for a time their "favourite son."

Amongst keen socialists, however, there was some doubts about "Frankie" who was said to be a self-seeker and overkeen on making money, as was recounted to General Secretary David Francis and to the author by Alf Palfreman who told how Frank Hodges had agreed to speak at their branch of the Independent Labour Party on "The Life of Karl Marx." He made a remarkable speech, and then charged them £3 as expenses in strong contrast to George Lansbury, who, coming from London, had asked "Could you afford 5/- ?"

be a motion of censure on Smillie and his colleagues. The mover concluded: "You cannot bind us in South Wales not to have a strike if the circumstances of our relationship with our owners compel us to have a strike, and you cannot do that with any of the other districts who were not disposed to striking as South Wales, and in moving the resolution I should like it to be understood that we repudiate the decision of the Executive Council and that we refuse to be bound by it, on the grounds that you have no constitutional or democratic authority for entering into that undertaking with the Government. I move that resolution."

This speech roused great anger in the Conference and was answered first by Stephen Walsh, M.P., and secondly by the Chairman, each of whom gave a very full account of the negotiations in the last days of June with Lloyd George and their endeavours to prevent the miners from coming under the Munitions Act. The debate which followed was very tense. When a Yorkshireman asked: "Supposing this resolution is carried, will it not mean a virtual repudiation to the pledge which we have given ?" Hodges replied: "We want a repudiation of the decision of the Executive." Immediately before adjournment James Doonan from Scotland said "We are not satisfied with the attitude of South Wales on that question" and, after hearing the pacific utterance of Vernon Hartshorn pertinently asked "which of these two voices is the real position of South Wales ?" Next afternoon, on the resumption of debate delegates became impatient at what they thought to be unnecessary speeches from South Wales and James Robson of Durham complained: "It has been Wales first from beginning to end; and it seems to me that this is a Welsh Federation and not a British Federation". Finally, the Chairman said "We have had it stated here last night that South Wales had agreed to withdraw their resolution unconditionally"—whereupon response came from Winstone, withdrawing it.

So no decision on the matter was taken, but it revealed not only a division inside the ranks of South Wales delegates, but also a certain impatience in some of the other miners' associations with the standpoint and behaviour of the South Wales delegates. This did not trouble those in the Welsh delegation who held the same views as Noah Rees about many miners' leaders in Scotland and England as "citizens first and trade unionists some way after."

4 THE TRIPLE INDUSTRIAL ALLIANCE

Draft proposals dated 4th June 1914 for a joint scheme between miners, railwaymen and transport workers "for offensive and defensive purposes" were put from the chair by Robert Smillie. He recalled the Scarborough decision,[1] on the initiative of South Wales, in this matter. These the MFGB Executive Committee had begun to carry out "in rather a modest way" by inviting "the representatives of the Railway Servants and the Transport Workers' Federation to a meeting" in April 1914 from which, after "a very considerable amount of discussion" in June 1914, the three Executives drew up the draft. "These proposals" Smillie said "are modest in the extreme: there is nothing revolutionary about them but merely an endeavour to link up three great organisations", every one of which suffered if there were a dispute in connection with any of the other two. He explained in detail:

"If the transport workers had a serious strike at the docks, the railwaymen and the miners have to stand idly by whilst they fight it out. If the railway servants have a dispute a large section of the miners have to stand idly by whilst the dispute is settled. If the miners strike that immediately affects the railway workers and transport workers: and from that point of view we ought to set up a joint link and try to bring us more closely together if the necessity arose."

The resolution for acceptance of the proposals for co-operative action on a common programme, moved by John Robertson of Scotland and seconded by James Winstone, was carried unanimously. Thereafter, at a national joint conference of miners, railwaymen and transport workers on Thursday, 9th December, 1915, the constitution of the new alliance was finally ratified.[2]

A further proposal from South Wales moved by Vernon Hartshorn that the resolutions of past years should be gathered together in a national programme to be pushed through by action of the new Triple Alliance[3] met with immediate resistance from the Scottish delegates. The fears that Smillie had anticipated and sought to still by his opening remarks on the Triple Alliance discussion were roused when Hartshorn said that "it was only when this Federation applied the industrial pressure to the political machine" that they had succeeded in getting granted a Minimum Wage Act. At this point James Doonan rose and said: "On behalf of Scotland I have to move the rejection of this resolution" and then in his speech put the following argument:

"Now what is the procedure in respect to Bills or Amendments to Bills or Acts of Parliament which has been followed?

"We pass our resolutions showing the amendments necessary, created

[1]"That the Executive Committee of the Miners' Federation be requested to approach the Executive Committees of other big Trade Unions with a view to co-operative action and the support of each others' demands" (9 x 1913).

[2]For the nine clauses of the Constitution see *The Miners : Years of Struggle.*

[3]"That this Conference instructs the Executive Council to prepare a national programme to include amendments of the Minimum Wage Act, Compensation Act, Eight Hours Act (to include surfacemen) and the Mines Act. The Council in debating the new Bills to have regard to suggestions received from various districts, and also decisions of National Conferences, and to submit the Bills to a further Special National Conference called for the purpose with the object of making them a programme to be submitted to the joint body of Railwaymen, Transport Workers and Miners for action" (7 x 1915).

by our experience of the working of the several Acts. We pass resolutions at the Trades Union Congress, and they are brought by the Labour Party and Parliamentary Committee before probably a Minister of the Crown with a view to having legislation brought forward and these amendments incorporated.

"Now, what we propose in this resolution is this: to alter that position, and to simply set up this arrangement, that if the three bodies are agreed, certain amendments of the law are necessary, they will meet together and formulate proposals, and place the matter before a Minister of the Crown, and if they do not take action in the way we desire, then we shall use our Industrial Organisation for the purpose of forcing the hands of the Government.

"That is a vital principle which is sought to be established, underlying these proposals. It is a principle which we ought to seriously consider, and I suggest that this is a matter of such vital importance we ought not to agree to it at the present moment."

But the motion from South Wales was seconded on behalf of the Lancashire and Cheshire Miners' Federation (an earlier adherent to the Labour Party than any other miners' association) by Steve Walsh, M.P., and there was very little further discussion: and the Cardiff resolution was carried. In the sequel the Triple Industrial Alliance dealt with a whole variety of subjects. G. D. H. Cole wrote:

"The Triple Alliance pressed throughout the war period for the increase of old age pensions to a more reasonable sum. It also took an active part in the successful opposition offered to the Government plan for the introduction of foreign, especially Chinese, labour in order to deal with the shortage of workers due to enlistment. It was active in pressing the Labour demands in respect of after-war policy upon the Government, and was recognised as one of the most influential organisations in the Labour world."

5 INTER-UNION RELATIONS

For well over two centuries of trade unionism, growth was slow and fitful while its extent was narrow enough, taking in for the most part only the skilled men within a few trades.[1] From 1889, the year of the Miners' Federation of Great Britain, the scope widened to take in new grades so that numbers doubled within a decade, and touched two millions by 1900, two-and-a-half millions by 1910. With the upward leap to four millions on the eve of the 1914-18 war and with the great strikes, "the industrial unrest" of 1910 to 1914, there were signs of a qualitative change—a new zeal in the rank-and-file and growing evidence of "class consciousness". In the coal mines, sections hitherto unorganised, including some of the craftsmen, began to join unions. But with this came difficulties of inter-union relations and sources of friction at their frontiers.

[1]"History of Trade Unionism, 1666-1920" by Sidney and Beatrice Webb.

In the autumn of 1915, an example of this emerged in South Wales. It followed upon September's heated debates in the Bristol Trades Union Congress, where the larger issue of industrial unionism had arisen from a miners' motion for the bigger associations to have additional representation on the Congress Parliamentary Committee. By November the MFGB Executive Committee, having considered letters received from craft unions, had expressed "its willingness to meet the Executive Committee of both those bodies at separate times" (10 xi 1915).

This was after George Barker had told of having been "constantly in conflict with Enginemen's and Surfacemen's Associations", until recently, when "some 1,200 of these men had come over *en bloc* to the Federation bringing their own Agents (William Woosnam and William Davies) with them"; and of how the South Wales Miners' Federation had been trying to carry out the four-year-old Southport resolution of the Miners' Federation of Great Britain, since they believed in "one union for one industry, as did the founders of the Miners' Federation" (10 xi 1915).

The dozen representatives of the Enginemen's Societies, bidden to the Westminster Palace Hotel a month later to table their complaints, found themselves rebuked by Smillie and other miners' leaders for having divulged to the Press their differences; but, having admitted their fault, were then reassured to learn that no hasty steps would be taken to carry out the Southport resolution that "all workmen employed in and about collieries should belong to the same organisation" (4 x 1911).

On the same day, but in a very different atmosphere, there took place a fully recorded encounter[1] with another union.

The two powerful trade union bodies were very different in their origins, history and structure. Each was self-sufficient, each recked little enough of the opinion of the others. The Amalgamated Society of Engineers had earlier in the century seceded "in high dudgeon" from the Trades Union Congress, while the Miners' Federation had stood aloof from the Labour Representation Committee which other unions were joining, maintaining for many years its own Parliamentary representation. But now new circumstances had led as we have seen to the Triple Industrial Alliance. In the Amalgamated Society of Engineers, too, there was a break with the tradition, signalised by their chief spokesman, F. S. Button, and by W. H. Hutchinson, for many years a member of the Labour Party Executive Committee, while General Secretary Robert Young in the previous year had responded to Beatrice Webb's invitation for a week's discussion on control of industry and questions of industrial

[1]Minutes of Proceedings at a Joint Conference between the Executive of the Miners' Federation of Great Britain and Representatives of the Council of the Amalgamated Society of Engineers, held at the Westminster Palace Hotel, London S.W., on Wednesday, December 8th, 1915. Mr. Robert Smillie in the Chair. (T. Ashton, Junr. Trades Union Printer (48 hours) Toxteth Street, Nr. Openshaw, Manchester).

unionism under her new Fabian Research Department. Indeed their whole representation on this occasion stemmed from the "revolution in the A.S.E." of 1912 when the offices in Peckham Road had been barred against extruded executive members. For some nine months the A.S.E. had had thrust upon it problems for whose solution there was nothing to help in the sixty-odd years' history of the Society. But with the help of the Fabian Research Department, and its memorandum of a thousand cases of penalties (including imprisonment) imposed on munition workers throughout Great Britain, they had put up a formidable case to the Minister of Munitions. Lloyd George had to yield to this reasoned remonstrance by the Society and, on 9th December, 1915, before the Munitions of War Act was six months old, to present an amending Bill to Parliament.

F. S. Button began their conference very disarmingly by saying "We know that in the past (and we are first to agree) the Amalgamated Society of Engineers have not always supported the miners in their just claims for better conditions and increases in wages" (8 xii 1915).

After this placatory remark Button went on to say that they felt it possible "for some arrangement to be made between the Federation and ourselves whereby our own membership will be safeguarded and yet, at the same time, give you that control of your industry which I think we are prepared to concede". He added :

"We believe that occupational control in the mines is a principle which can be established with far greater justification than in the case of any other industry in the country . . . and because of that, Mr. Chairman, we are keenly anxious to meet you in the most fraternal spirit possible."

After this auspicious opening by F. S. Button, the Chairman said :

"We do not want to conceal the fact that there have been unions organised during the past few years whom we have not the slightest sympathy with, because we feel that they are to a greater or less degree bogus organisations which did not require to exist . . . . Sometimes half a dozen labourers on the pit bank of the colliery, if called out, may stop a colliery employing one thousand men . . . . If they were stopped the Miners' Union would have to support one thousand men in a quarrel in which only six persons were engaged, and the miners would have no control or say in the matter at all."

Then Smillie made it clear that the Miners' Federation had "no rivalries" as against the Amalgamated Society of Engineers, saying "Your union is an old-established union, and it provides many benefits for its members, for which of course they pay, which the miners, as an organisation, do not."

The miners fully recognised "the terrible injustice it might be" to any person, paying in for years, if he were forced to leave the A.S.E. and lose superannuation allowance, the benefits "which he had honestly looked forward to": and consequently it could be taken for granted that "we have never made any attempt anywhere to force members to leave another union." This Smillie then amplified in the following statement:

"We feel that something must be done to get all craft workers in a cognate industry into closer touch with each other, either into one organisation, or if that is not considered by organised labour to be the best method, then it is the duty of organised labour to meet and calmly deliberate on the question, without injury to any other organisation, if it can be avoided, and try to strengthen the whole."

After considerable further amicable discussion, Button in his final statement broke new ground, saying: "Not only from the point of view of the interests of our own members, but from the point of view of the ideal of the organisation which you have sketched, we have a right to our place in the sun, and it may be that the Triple Alliance sooner or later may see their way clear to invite the engineers to come in." Apart from the stressing that they must absolutely safeguard the interests of their own members, the representative of the A.S.E. stated their willingness "any time and every time" to meet to endeavour to find a common basis for any work since they felt sure "as my colleagues also have said, that it is better for us to link up together if we are going to fight the common enemy". Button compared the Triple Alliance and the Amalgamated Society of Engineers as being four fingers "each doing its own particular work which the others cannot do for it, and yet linking up in a fist for the purposes of offence and defence."[1]

The Joint Conference concluded with Smillie saying: "I should like to thank you, gentlemen, for the very fair way in which you have put your views before us today. I remember the Amalgamated Society for many years back in the early days, and it struck me just now that I remember the time when a meeting such as this was not possible. I remember the time when your society would not have thought of meeting us on a matter of this kind; and it certainly shows, I think, a very great and sensible advance to see two executives such as this meeting round a table and talking as we have talked to each other today."

6 THE MERTHYR TYDFIL BY-ELECTION

James Keir Hardie, Member of Parliament since 1900 for the double-barrelled constituency of Merthyr Tydfil, died on 26th September,

[1]The engineers had called in to the Fabian Research Department on their way to meet the miners' leaders: and the author can remember with what keen interest the research staff (then mostly also guild socialists) heard of this first approach from the great craft union, even if severely limited, in the statement of F. S. Button, that "I am prepared to concede to the Miners' Federation what I am not prepared to concede to the Railways or the dockers."

1915. Described by Engels as "a super-cunning Scot whose demagogic tricks are not to be trusted for a minute"[1] Hardie had come to be looked upon as a founding father both of the Socialist International (1889-1914) and of the Labour Party : and so he bore an increasingly hallowed name within the Labour movement. But from 1910 onwards it was clear that he did not have the support of the younger miners who had begun to follow the banner of Marxism, at any rate in the valleys of Glamorgan : and the last months of his life were scarcely happy as he witnessed the triumph of "evil forces" alike in Parliament and in his own constituency. As early as 6th August, 1914, at the peace meeting called in Aberdare he had been howled down by angered miners and others with C. B. Stanton the local miners' agent heading them.[2]

The opposition between what was vaguely classed as the pro-war and anti-war elements within the South Wales Miners' Federation now came to a head in the November by-election. On 1st October, 1915, the Executive Council, after a vote of sympathy with the relatives of the late Member of Parliament, decided "to nominate a candidate for the above vacancy, under the Miners' Federation Parliamentary Representation Constitution", and to invite miners' lodges in the Borough of Merthyr Tydfil to send in nominations for a ballot.

On 18th October, the sub-committee to handle the arrangements for the by-election reported to the Executive Council as follows :

	Votes
Charles Butt Stanton, miners' agent, Aberdare	2,699
James Winstone, miners' agent, Pontnewynydd	2,641
John Williams, miners' agent, Merthyr	2,508
Robert Smillie, President, Miners' Federation of Great Britain	1,816
Enoch Morrel, miners' agent, Troedyrhiw	1,623

The highest three then went to second ballot, with the result that President James Winstone came first and was duly put forward as Labour candidate : and, under the terms of the electoral truce then in force, should then have been elected without opposition from the Liberal or Tory parties. Stanton thereupon resigned as miners' agent and

[1]Letter to F. A. Sorge, 10 xi 1894.

[2]Ted Stonelake, secretary to Keir Hardie in the constituency through four general elections, at the age of 85 recalled that famous meeting.

"Keir Hardie was a good speaker but quite like a child : he had little grasp of human nature. Again and again I had noticed this. So when I met Hardie that day and heard the usual question from him 'What is the feeling here ?' I replied : 'The people have gone mad' and I told Hardie they were all speaking of the German invasion of Belgium. But Hardie could not take it in.

"On the way to the Market Hall (holds about two thousand) I saw the thugs that C. B. Stanton had brought along. I shut my teeth like a gin-trap and went on to the hall where it was soon obvious that those who wanted to break up the meeting were organised in four gangs. I spoke first, for about ten minutes. Then Keir Hardie got a storm of interruptions : but he faced them and spoke for about twenty minutes, before it was impossible to go on. It broke his heart. It was little more than a year after that he died." (Interview 22 ix 1958).

ran under the heading of "Independent Labour". James Winstone, although his sentiments on war questions were not always clearly stated (he favoured voluntary recruiting and was against strikes during war-time) was an old member of the Independent Labour Party and had for long been very keen to get into Parliament. But his invitation to Ramsay MacDonald and F. W. Jowett, both reputed to be of the pacifist minority in Parliament, to speak on his behalf scarcely helped him in his candidature. Stanton, who was said to have had the support of the British Socialist Party, won the election by 10,286 votes to 6,080. Stanton claimed to have been elected as a "patriot" and in the House of Commons immediately took up what was regarded as an extreme jingo attitude. Presently he linked up with a new organisation formed with the stated object of waging the war more effectively than through the policy pursued by Labour Party members. This was the British Workers' National League to which some miners' leaders such as Gilmour of Scotland belonged: and even John Hodge, M.P., adhered to it for a time until Arthur Henderson, as Secretary of the Labour Party, warned that they would have to choose between membership of the Labour Party and of this new war-time "circus". C. B. Stanton, however, could not be offered this choice: he had made himself an outcast from the South Wales Miners' Federation and from the Labour Movement. At the end of the war, in opposition to the Rev. T. E. Nicholas,[1] the Labour candidate, Stanton stood for Aberdare as candidate of the (Coalition) National Democratic Party. He was returned with an overwhelming majority: but was unlucky in his subsequent electoral career, even when he stood as a Liberal candidate.

7 FOR CONSCRIPTION OR AGAINST?

From the beginning of the year 1916 the attention of the South Wales Miners' Federation's membership, conference and Executive Council was to be concentrated on an issue that lay outside the familiar questions of wages, hours and conditions. Conscription, the liability of every male of military age to undertake service in the armed forces, a feature of most countries of Europe, had never been imposed in Great Britain where the huge Royal Navy was relied upon as the main arm of offence or defence. A small professional and long-service army, designed mainly for use overseas, much of it to garrison and police India and elsewhere within the British Empire, was considered, with its reserve, to be a sufficient supplement to the Senior Service. Neverthe-

[1] T. E. Nicholas (1879-1971), famous Welsh bard and fighter for peace before the First World War; foundation member of the Communist Party. In April, 1912, his article in "The Leek" in support of the miners' strike stressed that strike action alone was not enough and that the working class must fight for socialism.

less advocates of conscription were increasingly active from the Boer War (1899-1902) onwards. Their advocacy had produced a counter-affirmation against conscription : and throughout the people as a whole, though hardly in favour of voluntary enlistment (for soldiering was looked down upon in Britain, as in China, as an occupation of a very low type) this attitude was widespread.

When war broke out in August, 1914, Field Marshal Lord Kitchener of Khartoum and the Cabinet avoided the dislocating conscription for which clubmen in Pall Mall were clamouring, and in its stead set afoot a system of voluntary enlistment. Everywhere throughout the country could be seen a glaring poster bearing a photograph of Lord Kitchener whose bulbous eyes followed the beholder as he read the caption "Kitchener Wants You". The result was remarkable. Within less than six months a million men had voluntarily enlisted.

When the summer of 1915 was reached the inflow of voluntary recruits was no longer able to cope with the ever-increasing demand for more "cannon fodder", as pacifist and anti-war speakers described the young men in uniform, and there came a newspaper campaign for compulsory military service. This aroused keen opposition by those who believed conscription to be precisely one of the features of German militarism that the war was being fought to prevent. In September, 1915, the Bristol Trades Union Congress was unanimous in its protest against any proposals for conscription, "which always proves a burden to the workers". It seemed to many in 1915 to be "the servile state" foretold by Hilaire Belloc in 1912—far though it was from Belloc's intention to link slavery with conscription.

In these conditions the Cabinet had to move warily. Step by step means were found to wear down the opposition or to divide its forces. The first notable public step was the appointment of Lord Derby, of the family of Stanley, a leading figure of the landed aristocracy who on 6th October, 1915, introduced a recruiting scheme as a half-way step towards it. When this scheme was set afoot the Miners' Federation of Great Britain at once found its fears of conscription reinforced. Their fear was that there would be an attempt to carry on industry under a semi-military discipline : and this or any other attempt to interfere with the civil rights of the colliers they were determined not to tolerate. From the Home Secretary, Sir John Simon, they got an undertaking on 19th November, 1915, that miners attesting under the Derby Scheme would still retain their full civil rights. Meantime Colliery Recruiting Courts were set up under the Derby Scheme to prevent further over-enlistment of miners.

Throughout October and November, 1915, the campaign for compulsion mounted higher until it became clear that new conscriptionist legislation was in the offing. Consequently on 30th December, 1915, the South Wales Miners' Federation Executive Council passed the following resolution to be sent to members of the Cabinet :

"That this Council, representing practically the whole of the workmen employed in the South Wales coalfield, strongly resent the sinister efforts that are in operation by certain party politicians and a section of the Press, to impose upon the people of this country a system of compulsory military service, and desire the officials of the Miners' Federation of Great Britain to at once call a national conference to again enter the protest of the miners of the country against any legislation that may be proposed for this purpose" (30 xii 1915).

These forebodings turned out to be justified. A Military Service Bill was introduced in Parliament on Wednesday, 5th January, 1916. That same day the Executive Council resolved "to continue our uncompromising hostility to the action of the Government in attempting to pass a measure for enforcing compulsory military service." They convened a Special Conference for the next Wednesday with a view of "confirming our decision to continue to oppose to the uttermost extent this interference with the civil rights of the people" (5 i 1916).

By a week later much had happened. On 6th January a Labour and Trade Union conference in London had advised the Labour Party in parliament to oppose the Military Service Bill. The three Labour Ministers (including the SWMF President Brace) now felt it necessary to table their resignations from the Government. An anxious meeting with the Prime Minister followed: and on 12th January the three withdrew their resignations, while the second reading of the Military Service Bill was carried in the House of Commons by 431 votes to 39. That same day in the Cory Hall in Cardiff 281 delegates representing 133,340 workmen, heard James Winstone, acting-president, deliver his address, after which a large number of resolutions were submitted and there was long discussion. Finally on a show of hands the following decisions were taken:

"Against the Compulsory Service Bill by 211 to 35, being a six to one majority.

"For down tools policy if Bill passes by 162 to 83, or nearly a two to one majority.

"For taking a ballot before 'down tools' by 127 to 109, being a majority of 18" (12 i 1916).

What lay behind this overwhelmingly strong rejection of the Conscription Bill by the South Wales miners? Not all the coalfields had shared their opinion. When reports were given at a Miners' Federation of Great Britain special conference in Westminster on Thursday, 13th January, it turned out that there were nearly 40,000 (Nottinghamshire, Leicestershire and Forest of Dean) in favour of the Bill while four other small districts were described as neutral. The larger districts were against it: and, taken all over, the reports from districts showed ten miners against the Bill for one miner either in favour of it or neutral. Within this overwhelming majority against conscription, however, there were different degrees of opposition, as was soon to be seen.

The Cabinet itself had not been unanimous. Sir John Simon had resigned rather than continue as Home Secretary in a Government "guilty" of bringing in conscription. It seems to have been the last time that Sir John Simon took such a strong principled stand on any political matter: for while his tender conscience may have troubled him privately thereafter, it was never again on public exhibition. His place was taken by Herbert Samuel, who together with Premier Asquith met the miners on 21st January 1916. To this meeting in 10 Downing Street the miners came to suggest an increase in the payment to old age pensioners. Their suggestion was well enough received (but without anything definite being decided) by the Prime Minister who himself then raised the question of military service and asked Herbert Samuel to give an explanation. Robert Smillie was not in the position to put forward any view on behalf of the miners as the Miners' Federation had taken no decision. Consequently Smillie could only put forward various points in relation to the effect on the work of the Mines Organisation Committee if recruitment of miners continued at the existing rate and if the special recruiting for the purpose of tunnelling were to constitute a particularly heavy draft on the available manpower. Smillie said: "We recognise that the work of the Tunnelling Corps at the front must go on" (21 i 1916).

Neither the attitude of the South Wales miners nor that of the other Mining Conferences was able to prevent the passage through Parliament of the Bill, which became an Act on 27th January. Its passage was facilitated by provisions which had the effect of dividing the forces opposed to conscription : this Military Service (No. 2) Act was to apply to single men only. Plastered over Britain was the recruiting slogan : "Will you march, too, or wait to March Two?" For the Act was to become effective on 2nd March, 1916, from which date all sound men liable to military service would be called up: they would be "deemed to have been enlisted and transferred to the reserve".

When it came to the miners' national conference in the second week of February 1916, at the King's Arms Hotel in Lancaster, the South Wales delegates alone voted for their own resolution which instructed the MFGB Executive Committee to arrange for a ballot vote of the workmen to be taken "For or Against the repeal of the Military Service Act". The Durham resolution ran: "That this conference adheres to the finding of the Labour Party conference held at Bristol (26th to 28th January) namely to offer no opposition to the Military Service Act 1916". Finally, after considerable discussion, Northumberland put its resolution: "That this conference expresses its opposition to the spirit of conscription and determines to exercise a vigilant scrutiny of any proposed extension of the Military Service (No. 2) Act." This was carried by 368,000 votes to 349,000 cast for the Durham resolution.

South Wales had been defeated but not convinced. Very soon delegates made it clear that they intended something more drastic than "vigilant scrutiny" against the extension of conscription. For the moment, however, the matter had to be left over for a couple of months until their annual conference on 17th April. There, in Cardiff, the proposition to disagree with the national conference resolution was carried by 153 votes to 101 and, on a card vote, by 1,579 votes to 1,225. Following this another long discussion ensued and the following resolution was passed:

"That this conference reaffirms its opposition to compulsory military service and demands the Government to repeal the Act now in operation, that steps be taken to get this adopted as a national policy by the miners and the trade union movement as a whole, and that in the event of the Government proceeding with the suggested extension of the scope of the present Act, a coalfield conference be immediately called to consider the situation" (17 iv 1916).

What then had been the reasons for the greater strength of the anti-conscription agitation in South Wales? One who was part of it put forward later his view of Federation leaders that "in practically all cases their opposition was of the pacifist type", while amongst the working miners the propaganda of the Socialist Labour Party was "fast creating an active rank and file movement with a definite working-class view of war", a view "anticipated in Will Hay's pamphlet" and solidly held in the Unofficial Reform movement. This was Ness Edwards, who wrote:

"This clarification of thought in regard to the war now began to find expression in the Executive meetings, especially in regard to conscription. To carry on an agitation against conscription was not of necessity, according to the views of many of the leaders, to be in opposition to the War. It was an easy attitude to adopt among the miners, and found many adherents in the organisation, especially among those who believed in the War but preferred that others should do the fighting. The cowards and the courageous, the pacifist and the class conscious, all coalesced in this anti-conscription agitation."[1]

Other factors, too, were coming into play. As war disasters cumulated towards the end of 1915, moves were made to suppress opposition to Government measures. When the London evening newspaper *The Globe* printed what was regarded as a Cabinet secret about the decision of Lord Kitchener to withdraw troops from Gallipoli the military authorities sent soldiers to smash up the types in the printing works, just off Fleet Street. When Lloyd George on Christmas Day 1915, spoke to Clyde workers in St. Andrew's Hall in Glasgow, he got a poor reception and a still worse reception at his meeting at Parkhead Forge. But when the weekly newspaper *Forward* on 3rd January reported fully this meeting at which Lloyd George had such a rough heckling from the shop stewards, headed by William Gallacher, it was suppressed by Government order for four weeks. On 3rd February *The Clyde Worker*,

[1] Ness Edwards: *History of the South Wales Miners' Federation.* (Lawrence and Wishart 1938).

organ of the Clyde Workers Committee of which the chairman was William Gallacher, and *The Socialist*, organ of the Socialist Labour Party, were both suppressed. Four days later William Gallacher, John McLean and two shop stewards were arrested in Glasgow. All this was followed closely by the miners of South Wales and had a challenging effect upon them.

8 NON-UNIONISM IN ABEYANCE

Non-unionism in the South Wales coalfield constituted a problem of long standing. The Monmouthshire and South Wales Coal Owners' Association had not only extinguished the trade unionism of 1875 in the coalfield but for a quarter of a century under the lead of Sir William Lewis had successfully obstructed the effective formation of a union able to negotiate through a Conciliation Board. When eventually the Conciliation Board was formed in 1903 the employers, many of them sharing "Lewis's extreme hostility to trade unionism", were loath to concede full recognition of the trade union.[1] Hence the wording of the opening paragraphs by which particular individuals are named as representatives either of the owners of a set of collieries or of the workmen thereat employed so that the Wages Agreement itself is between those persons on each side and not, as might have been expected from the pattern of other large coalfields (and even in the neighbouring small Forest of Dean), between the employers' association and the trade union. This non-recognition attitude persisted in South Wales for over another decade, and it remained sufficiently clear to all seeking employment that trade unionism was not favoured.

On the other hand in the valleys there was to a greater extent than in most other coalfields a readiness to drop out of regular payment of trade union contributions. These contributions were not high. They brought in less per member than in most other coalfields, and to such an extent that any unusual expenditure, such as on dispute pay, had to be made by calling a levy on the members of the union. Neither wages nor hours nor other conditions, but non-unionism was the proximate cause of most disputes.[2]

After the national minimum wage strike of 1912 many efforts were made by means of Show Card days to bring it to an end. In the second year of the war the same problem was still there. With the depletion of what may be called the established labour force by massive voluntary enlistment tens of thosuands from areas of Wales and England in which trade unionism had been a feeble growth sought employment in the mines. There were sporadic strikes, as we have seen in Chapter

[1]Clegg, Fox and Thompson. *A History of British Trade Unions Since* 1889 (Oxford University Press page 231).

[2]See also *South Wales Miners Glowyr De Cymru* Chapter XII.

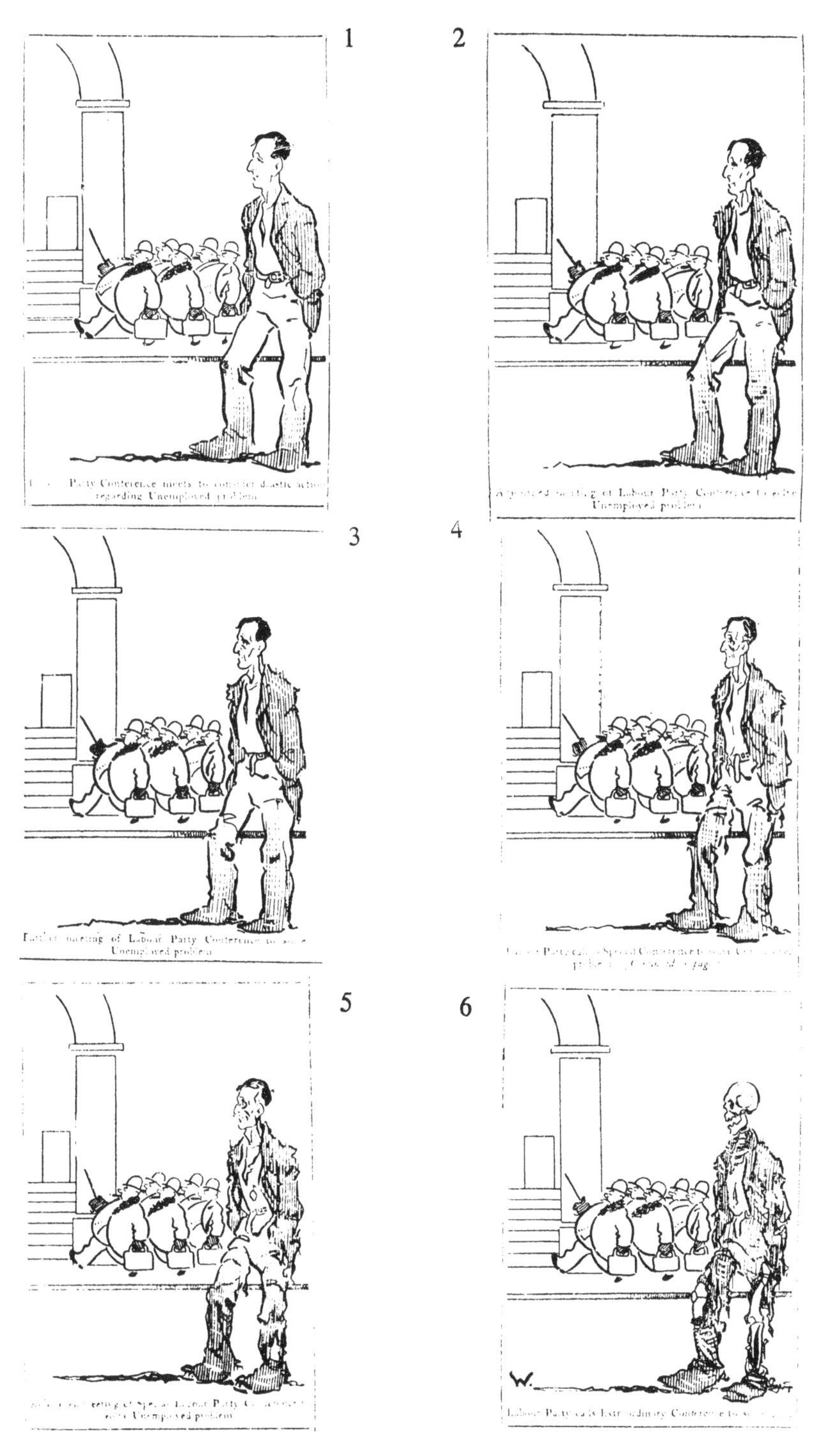

6 COMMENT ON INACTION OF LABOUR CONFERENCES
(Reproduced from *The Communist* March 5, 1921)

DOWLAIS DISTRICT S.W.M.F.

Is there to be a Non-Unionist Strike?

Are the Non-Unionists, now only 5 per cent of the Men employed, going to bring about a Strike at the Dowlais Collieries ?

Will 200 Non-Members render idle indefinitely over 4,000 other Workmen ?

Will the few Mechanical Workers and Craftsmen still outside the Federation, continue in their Sectional Policy, and not only bring about the stoppage of thousands of Workers, but perpetuate the scandalously low wages which the Mechanical Workers and Craftsmen have always paid for their Sectionalism ?

Unless a 100 per cent Membership of the Federation will have been achieved by Saturday, May 26th, all the Dowlais Collieries will be on stop.

DEMONSTRATIONS.

DOWLAIS, Next Tuesday, May 22nd,

At 10-30 a.m. at the ODDFELLOWS Hall.

FOCHRIW, Next Tuesday, May 22nd,

At 10-30 a.m. at the Fochriw Square.

BEDLINOG, Next Wednesday, May 23rd,

At 10-30 a.m., Near the Gosen Hall.

SPEAKERS: Messrs.

JOHN JAMES, Miners' Agent, Cwmgorse.
A. J. COOK, „ „ Rhondda Valley.
NOAH ABLETT, „ „ Merthyr.
WILLIAM HOPKINS, Mechanical Agent.
S. O. DAVIES, B.A., Miners' Agent, Dowlais.

From the above Meetings, Demonstrations will be formed, and will proceed to the houses of all Non-Unionists.

All Members of the Federation, who are anxious to avoid a stoppage, are urged to be present at the above Demonstrations.

Devote ONE MORNING from your three days Holidays to your own Cause, and establish once again that POWER which alone can RAISE you above the present day conditions of slavery.

18/5/23. BY ORDER, DISTRICT MEETING.

WALSH PRINTER DOWLAIS

7 BACK TO THE UNIONS CAMPAIGN, 1923

II, from the spring of 1915 onwards. Already by an Executive Council meeting of 1st March, 1915, resolutions were received from the Pontypridd and Rhondda District on the question of advisability of "Show Card in April next". On the 12th March, 1915, a letter was received from the Cwm Cynon Lodge protesting against the Council's non-fulfilment of their promise that "before another agreement be ratified a clause must be inserted" making trade unionism a condition of employment. By 1st April, 1915, the General Secretary reported a stoppage of the Cyfarthfa Collieries to the Executive Council, which decided to raise the matter at the next meeting of the Conciliation Board. The result was that on 31st May, 1915, the following proposal for dealing with the non-unionist question was elaborated and sent to the Coal Owners' Secretary:

"That the Owners be requested to agree that the Workmen be given all the facilities necessary at the Collieries for ascertaining whether any Workmen are employed who are not members of the Federation, and that joint action be taken by the Management and the Officials of the Federation Branch to ensure that no Workmen shall be employed in and about the Collieries who are not members of the Federation.

"The Workmen's Representatives agree that this undertaking on behalf of the Employers is to be without prejudice, and intended solely for the purpose of preventing any stoppages of Collieries during the continuation of the War" (31 v 1915).

On Wednesday, 9th June, the matter was again discussed and it was resolved as follows:

"That the following proposals for dealing with this matter be forwarded to the Owners' Secretary:

'1. That the Secretary or other appointed representative of the Federation Lodge at each Colliery shall be supplied from the Colliery Offices with a list of the names of all Workmen at present employed at the Colliery.

'2. Any Workmen who are not members of the Federation shall be jointly informed by the Colliery Officials and the representatives of the Federation that for the purpose of preventing stoppages of the Collieries during the continuance of the War, the Colliery Owners' and Workmen's representatives have agreed upon the necessity for every Workman to become a member of the Federation.

'3. That in future all Workmen given employment at the Collieries shall be informed by the Colliery Officials before they start that they are expected to become members of the Federation, and the Colliery Official shall supply the Federation Representative with a weekly list of all Workmen given employment.

'4. If it is found that, notwithstanding the foregoing joint effort to prevent disputes over this matter, there are Workmen who jeopardise the regular working of the Colliery by refusing to comply with the arrangement, the Officials of the Colliery and the Representatives of the Federation shall endeavour to get a settlement before Notices of a Stoppage are given" (9 vi 1915).

Nothing came of these proposals nor was there any indication that the owners would abandon their intransigent attitude or accept the recommendation of the Coal Mines Organisation Committee (May 1915) for cooperation with the representatives of the workmen to end stoppages on non-unionism.

No sooner were the troubles of that summer ended by the signature on 3rd September, 1915, of the new agreement for a Conciliation Board than the non-unionism question arose again. On the 7th September 3,000 miners at Tylorstown in the Rhondda ceased work and six days later, on the same non-unionism question, about 1,000 men were idle at Ynyshir. Here, however, the issue was complicated by a question of transfer of members of the Enginemen and Stokers' Association to the SWMF, and it was not until a week had passed that the strike was settled. At the end of September 2,000 miners ceased work at Cwmaman Colliery, Aberdare, and did not return to work until the 4th October.

Similarly at the end of November, 2,000 men ceased work at Abergorky Collieries, Treorchy, and did not resume work until 4th December.

In the early weeks of 1916, however, the problem and the strikes that took place began to become a major issue. The miners in the Merthyr Tydfil and Dowlais areas, the former of which included the Cyfarthfa Collieries, stated they would strike unless non-unionists were removed or had joined the Federation. The matter came up at the Council meeting in Cardiff on the 7th March, 1916. A deputation attended and explained to the Council as follows:

"About 12 months ago they stopped work to deal with this matter, but upon an appeal from the General Secretary, after having been idle for two days, we were well on the way to getting all the men in. The General Secretary then informed us that there was every possibility that an arrangement would be made to prevent these stoppages, and we returned to work, but nothing was done. A fortnight ago we tendered 14 days notice again to deal with the matter. Failing to get the matter settled, Mr. Brace, M.P., attended some meetings and met the Manager, Mr. Howell Jones, after which a meeting was held at Merthyr on Sunday night, when Mr. Brace pressed upon us to see Mr. Howell Jones again, stating he was confident that an agreement could be arrived at, but we failed and decided to stop. But upon a communication from the General Secretary, they again refrained from stopping, although in consequence of what transpired last year they were very reluctant to do so. The notices have been deferred for a fortnight, but they were instructed to inform the Council that unless the non-unionist question is settled they would be compelled to stop. The total number employed was about 2,000; there were 113 non-unionists, and 200 in arrears."

The General Secretary read correspondence with Sir G. R. Askwith, Board of Trade, upon this matter, who invited the Council to send a deputation to see him.

By the next day trouble had spread to other districts. So Sir

George Askwith undertook on 8th March to be the mediator between the owners and the miners. After a week a settlement was reached: the owners, "without prejudice to their position after the war" gave reluctant agreement to the miners' demand, namely, that membership of a recognised trade union must be a condition of employment for the period of the war. The agreement, provisional on 16th March, was finally signed on the 18th April, 1916.

The July 1915 settlement followed by the September new agreement had in it other seeds of future trouble between the owners and the miners. In the spring of 1916 the chief question at issue was the rate at which payment should be made for the Sunday night shift. This, it was held by the men, was an optional shift and where it was worked should consist of six hours only, any time worked beyond these six hours to be paid for as overtime. The owners' contention was that the shift was compulsory and that the full hours must be worked without any question of overtime payment. A crisis developed when the workmen at the Albion Colliery refused to work the shift unless on payment of overtime for more than six hours. Thereupon the coal-owners took the case into Court. The stipendiary magistrate found against the workmen and by his decision they were compelled to work the full eight hours without overtime payment. The miners' view, that their demand was in accord with the agreement of 1915, came up before the Executive Council which unanimously decided to submit a resolution to a forthcoming special conference. At the conference held two days later the resolution as recommended was unanimously carried as follows:

"That this conference regards the action of the coalowners in taking proceedings against the night-men at the Albion Colliery for not working the Sunday night shift, and the threat to take proceedings against workmen at other collieries in respect of the same matter as a violation of the spirit and intention of the Conciliation Board Agreement, as the representatives of the Government by altering the provision of the 1910 agreement dealing with the subject, made it clear that additional payment was intended for working a Sunday night shift of eight hours, and that the Executive Council be instructed to inform the Coalowners' Association that the workmen insist that the shift, when worked, should either be one of six hours, or if eight hours are worked, additional payment shall be made therefor, and that failing a satisfactory settlement being forthwith arrived at, a further conference be called for dealing with the matter" (31 i 1916).

A less vital but still important point of difference as to the interpretation of the 1915 agreement was the question of the bonus to be paid to ostlers and the rate of pay for craft workers on the surface of pits. On this last the same special conference resolved: "That the Council also press for a revision of the rates of surface craftsmen" and further resolved that in the case of ostlers the Council should "press the matter of the payment of the bonus turn to these workmen."

By the 21st March these grievances had assumed serious proportions and a strike was threatened. By a narrow majority of 9 to 8 the Executive Council had decided on 7th March to bring the matter before the Government before calling a conference which would give strike notice on these questions of Sunday night shift, ostlers' bonus turn, craftsmen's rates. Once more Walter Runciman was asked for a further interpretation of the meaning of the agreement that he had drafted. At first Runciman would not intervene. But two days later, on 23rd March, he said he would nominate a conciliator. On 24th March he nominated Judge O'Connor to be the conciliator between owners and the workmen on these disputes.

It was, however, not until three months later, namely on 19th June, 1916, that Judge O'Connor issued his award on the matters referred to him on 24th March. His appointment, however, had staved off the threatened strike. On the whole his award was favourable to the miners both on the question of the Sunday night shift and on the ostlers. But the rates to surface craftsmen still fell considerably below those demanded by the South Wales Miners' Federation.

9 CONCILIATION BOARD TROUBLES

General rates of wages and their determination under the Conciliation Board continued to be a source of difficulty and trouble throughout the year 1916. It will be recalled that under the old conciliation agreement, which expired on 30th June, 1915, after more than five years currency, there had been a maximum fixed of 60 per cent above the standard of December, 1879. This maximum had been reached on 1st June, 1913. Thus in the two years that followed there was no possibility of change although the price of coal was tending to rise up to August, 1914, and thereafter, as we have seen, rose quite considerably. The main war-time feature, however, was the special rise in general prices, bringing the Prime Minister's 5th May award for an immediate advance of wages, followed a week later by the award of Earl St. Aldwyn that the war bonus in South Wales should be 17½ per cent on the standard rate of wages. By the agreement after the July strike, wages were fixed at 18⅓ per cent above the new standard, included in which percentage was the war bonus of 17½ per cent of 12th May. Wages remained at this level from 15th July to 20th August.[1]

That year, in December, 1915, saw the end of the chairmanship of Earl St. Aldwyn, who died in the next April, twelve years to a day since he was first appointed Independent Chairman and forty-eight years since he was a member of the first "ministry of Mr. Disraeli". The secretary of the coalowners' side of the Conciliation Board, Gascoyne Dalziel, who had taken it over from his father, the original secretary

[1]For further awards see Appendix to this Chapter.

of the Coalowners' Association when it was founded half a century earlier, also sent in his resignation : he was succeeded by Finlay Gibson. The chairman, F. L. Davies, offered his resignation but was persuaded by his fellow coalowners after some months to withdraw it. Thus there were at any rate on the side of the coalowners and of the independent chairmanship considerable changes in personnel at the opening of the year 1916.

The Board of Conciliation for the Coal Trade of Monmouthshire and South Wales, as formally re-established on 2nd September, 1915, had its own rules of procedure. Under these it was laid down that should there be a desire by either party to vary the rates of wages the Board would meet on the 10th day of the months of February, May, August and November: and notice of such meeting by either party should be given by the Secretary of either side ten days before the 10th of any such month. On 1st February, 1916, came the usual day of claims for an adjustment of wages. The workmen's side of the Board made application for an advance of 5 per cent while at the same time the coalowners applied for a reduction of 3¾ per cent. The miners' claim was based on a rise in the selling price of coal. The owners' claim was on the ground that costs of production, in their view, had risen more than proportionately to the price of coal. In the constitution of the Conciliation Board attention was directed to the selling price of coal as the main but not necessarily the sole factor to be taken into account in determining wage rates. There was now a new chairman of the Conciliation Board, who, when the Board failed to agree, had to adjudicate. Lord Muir-Mackenzie[1] assumed office on 7th February and gave his decision on the 21st February : he rejected both the owners' claim for a reduction and the miners' claim for an advance. This meant that wages would remain at the existing level for another three months. It was not a decision that pleased the miners.

On 1st May each party made application to the Conciliation Board —the owners for a reduction of 7½ per cent in the standard rate on the new 1915 standard, the mineworkers for an advance of 15 per cent. By the 10th May the parties failed to agree and the new independent chairman, Lord Muir-Mackenzie had once more to adjudicate.

[1]Kenneth Augustus Muir-Mackenzie, born in 1845, was the fourth son of Sir John William Pitt Muir-Mackenzie, second baronet of Delvine near Dunkeld in Perthshire. The new chairman therefore came of a sufficiently ancient lineage. He was educated at Charterhouse and Balliol and at the age of 28 became a Barrister of Lincoln's Inn; and then was Clerk of the Crown in Chancery for 35 years from 1880 to 1915, when a barony was bestowed upon him. In his 71st year he entered for the first time into the hurly-burly of industrial relations when he became independent chairman of the Conciliation Board. Nine years later, he was made by Ramsay MacDonald into a Lord-in-Waiting, which office has been described as "almost the lowest form of governmental life". In the second administration of Ramsay MacDonald, beginning in June, 1929, the now 84-year-old peer was once more given the post of Lord-in-Waiting until his death on 22nd May, 1930.

Before the adjourned meeting of the Board could be held in his presence, Lord Muir-Mackenzie was ill-judged enough to send an epistle to both owners and men in which he put down his views as to the proper basis for concluding the disputed wage. This caused immediate trouble.

Actually his previous award given on 21st February had by no means pleased the South Wales Miners Executive Council but they realised they had to deal with a tyro at the business compared to their previous chairman. Some seven weeks later, on 11th April at the Executive Council, there was a strong expression of opinion. The award on the general wage rate and the question of fixing an equivalent was discussed and the following resolution was adopted :

"Having been invited by Lord Muir-Mackenzie to express our desire in respect to the continuance of his services as independent chairman to the Conciliation Board, we are of the opinion that it will be a great inconvenience to the Board to have to make another appointment at the present time. We recognise the difficulties he had to contend with in arriving at his first decision, which is not satisfactory to the workmen, and express the opinion that it should not form a basis for future decisions when the whole matter of the relation of the cost of production to wages will again be laid before him" (11 iv 1916).

Again, a week later on reassembly of the adjourned annual conference, the matter came up. Under the heading "General Wage Rate" there was a discussion and the following resolution was adopted :

"That this conference expresses its profound dissatisfaction with the recent wage awards of Lord St. Aldwyn and Lord Muir-Mackenzie, which means that too much consideration has been paid to the increased cost of production in fixing the general wage rate, and that in the opinion of this conference the next wage award should restore to the workmen the old basis of Sir David Dale's Award on the equivalent selling price, as arrived at by him in 1903" (18 iv 1916).

At the Council meeting a fortnight later there was a discussion on the general wage rate and the following resolution was carried by 16 votes to 6 :

"That the Council decide that the owners be informed that we consider that the present method of arriving at decisions for the regulation of the General Wage Rate for this coalfield is in an unsatisfactory condition, and that steps should at once be taken to secure a settlement of the equivalent selling price to the minimum wages under the agreement. Pending this, an application for an advance in wages shall have reference only to the present increase in the selling prices, without any committal by the Council to the acceptance of the position created by previous decisions since the 1915 agreement has been in operation. Therefore, an application be made, with the foregoing proviso, for an advance of 15 per cent" (1 v 1916).

This, it will be noted, was before any question could have come up at the Conciliation Board. Three weeks later, after the Conciliation Board had met and failed to agree, there came a letter from Lord Muir-

Mackenzie in which he indicated that a temporary equivalent should be fixed for considering the applications of both the owners and workmen for a change in the general wage rate. Thereupon the Executive Council "having carefully considered the letter of Lord Muir-Mackenzie, sent to the Joint Secretaries of the Conciliation Board and dated the 15th instant", expressed its regret "that his Lordship should have given an opinion upon the applications under consideration by the Board, before having the matters discussed under his presidency" gave their opinion that "having done this renders it impossible for him to adjudicate upon the applications" (22 v 1916). This protest they sent to Lord Muir-Mackenzie, the Coal Owners' Secretary, and the President of the Board of Trade, whom they asked to meet a deputation comprised of the whole Council. The result was immediate. Three days later they met Walter Runciman who suggested he should convene a meeting of the Conciliation Board to discuss the matter further. Back at the Westminster Palace Hotel, the Executive Council mulled over this proposal and over the communication received that same day from Lord Muir-Mackenzie resigning his position. Finally, they resolved to request the President of the Board of Trade "to use his good offices to bring about an early meeting before 2nd of June of the Conciliation Board, with himself or some other member of the Government presiding over our deliberations, for the purpose of dealing with the workmen's application for 15 per cent advance in wages, based on the increased selling price of coal" (25 v 1916).

At a further meeting with Runciman it was arranged that a meeting of the Conciliation Board should be held on the next Monday and that Sir George Askwith, Chief Industrial Commissioner, should "keep in touch with the proceedings thereat." Why did the Government take this step? In no uncertain terms the Executive Council had told Runciman that unless the wage advance of 15 per cent were granted there would be a strike of the coalfield.

When on 29th May the Conciliation Board met and failed to reach a settlement the three officials (plus Vernon Hartshorn) were sent to London to see Sir George Askwith, they had several interviews with him on 30th and 31st May and again on 1st June. The terms of settlement thereafter were drawn up. These conceded the increase of 15 per cent and at the Executive Council on 3rd June were unanimously accepted.

The owners were furious. At first they declared they would not pay the advance. Three days later, on 5th June, they swallowed their objections and agreed (but under protest) to pay the 15 per cent. The owners' argument was that the miners had broken the Conciliation Board agreement in that they had not agreed to the appointment of a successor to Lord Muir-Mackenzie until after their wage demand had been complied with. The miners on the other hand knew that it might be a very long time before agreement could be reached on the successor.

The miners' argument on the matter was that it was useless to agree to matters going before the independent chairman in view of the difference in the Board as to how the agreement of the previous July should be interpreted. However, after the 15 per cent had been granted they were willing to go on to the appointment of a chairman. The two sides could not agree on a nomination. So finally under the constitution of the Board it was referred to the outside authority in accordance with Clause 4 of the agreement, namely, "when and so often as the office of chairman becomes vacant the Board shall endeavour to elect a chairman and should they have failed to agree will ask the Lord Chief Justice of England for the time being or, in case of his refusal, the Speaker of the House of Commons to nominate one." June passed by and then some weeks of July. Finally, on 18th July, 1916, Lord Reading appointed Sir William Pickford, a Lord Justice of Appeal, to be the independent chairman.

10 WAR NEEDS CURTAIL MINERS' HOLIDAYS

The discussion which raged in the Merthyr Tydfil constituency in the weeks before the by-election of 26th November, 1915, had its diminishing echoes through the valleys for another five months, when a more insistent sound broke in upon the debates between the "pro-war" and the "anti-war" groupings of the miners. This was the Easter Rising that began on 24th April when the Sinn Fein organisation headed by Patrick Pearse and others, together with the Irish Citizen Army headed by James Connolly, proclaimed the Republic of Ireland. This event, its suppression and the subsequent executions day after day of its captured leaders made an impact on Europe, even with the largest portions of the continent now involved in war: it affected the people of the United States of America and it had a pervasive influence in the British coalfields where many collier families were of Irish descent. In South Wales feeling of sympathy of one small nationality for another could easily be aroused by such an event.

That Eastertide in South Wales the resistance to conscription, much more strongly felt than in other coalfields, had been mounting when the operation of the Military Service Act brought the call up in April of attested married men of the age groups 27 to 35. In the summer months of 1916, and then as the Battle of the Somme from 1st July onwards was grinding out each day its meal of casualties, there was the growth of a sombre mood in those Welsh mining families who had "boys in the trenches" (and this was nearly all of them) and an unassuaged irritation against the coalowners which was now beginning to extend to civil and military officials. By mid-July there came the request from the Admiralty "that no holidays be taken." The Executive Council decided to call a conference on Tuesday, August 1st, "to consider the question of holidays", and to apply to the coalowners "that additional payment shall be made for working the holidays" (17 vii 1916). It was then found in that meeting that the owners had refused to grant any additional payment for working the holidays : and the General Secretary was instructed to inform the Government of their decision. The South Wales coalowners having been given permission to increase the price of coal for home consumption, on the 31st July made an offer. They would give an extra 1/- per day for one week and boys under 18 years of age 6d. a day as an inducement to work over the August holidays. The next day was Tuesday, 1st August, and the special conference in the Cory Hall was addressed by James Winstone, who said he would not be doing his duty to "the Federation, the country and their kith and kin" if he did not press upon them the great responsibility that rested upon the 268 delegates. He appealed to them to accept the recommendation of the Council "to refrain from taking any holidays next week". Thereafter there was a long discussion. Finally, after several rounds of voting, it was decided by a small majority for a two days holiday "viz : Monday and Tuesday, the 7th and 8th August" (1 viii 1916).

Two days later, a telegram, this time from the Home Secretary Herbert Samuel, was read to the hastily summoned meeting of the Executive Council :

"In view of the absolute necessity of maintaining the supply of coal, the Government have requested the South Wales mine owners to keep their pits open the whole of next week. The Government feel confident that the patriotism of the miners will induce them to forego all the holidays and to work continuously in the national cause" (3 viii 1916).

Once more, as on the outbreak of war in 1914, Admiralty representative Jenkins attended the Council meeting and gave detailed information "respecting the urgent need for coal and the prejudicial effect the taking of holidays at this time would have." A long discussion at the Council resulted first in the calling of a special conference for Saturday, 5th August, "to reconsider the decision for taking two days holiday" and secondly in the decision to issue that day a manifesto to their members through the press. This brought the desired result.

On Saturday, 5th August, the resolution of the previous Tuesday was rescinded by a large majority, and a roll call taken on the proposition "that holidays be suspended," resulted in 2,131 For and 892 Against. This discussion and the subsequent troubles on the Conciliation Board was noticed in Whitehall where the situation on both western and eastern fronts, together with their experiences of the past, taught them to heed danger signals from the coalfield.

11 CONCILIATION COLLAPSES : STATE INTERVENES

The owners had put in their demand on 1st August for a decrease of the 15 per cent while the miners' demand was for an increase of 12½ per cent. The Board of Conciliation could not agree on 10th

August on either application and so decided to ask the independent chairman, Sir William Pickford, to attend the next meeting on 24th August. On 31st August, he gave his casting vote against the applications of both the workmen and the owners, for advance and reduction respectively in the general wage rate, so that wages remained at 40-5/6ths per cent above the new 1915 standard. Pickford had repeated the procedure of his predecessor which had lost his predecessor the esteem of the miners. The rejection was bound to lead to trouble : and indeed soon had this effect in the coalfield. Some five weeks later the Executive Council seeing that "the cost of production is an important factor under the present Agreement in determining the General Wage Rate", decided to approach the owners' representatives forthwith "with a view to a Joint Audit being conducted for the purpose of ascertaining the cost of production, and that terms of reference for this purpose be mutually agreed upon, that the results of these Audits be conveyed to the respective parties at the same time as the ascertained price of Large and Small Coal" (5 x 1916).

The owners refused completely to accept this demand for a joint audit. Almost for the first time since the beginning of the war the newspaper Press now commented unfavourably upon the behaviour of the coal owners of South Wales. *The Times* denounced them for their attitude nor did most other newspapers see any reason to support them.

At a special conference on 30th October James Winstone in his "President's Address" dealt with high food prices due to freightage charges by shipowners against whom he cited a statement in the *Daily Mail* that "the earnings of the shipowners had increased from £20,000,000 in 1913 to £250,000,000 in 1916." Then an exhaustive report was given of the proceedings of the Conciliation Board in dealing with the general wage rate: the workmen failed to secure the 12½ per cent applied for "notwithstanding that there had been an increase in the average selling price of coal as ascertained by the Joint Auditors of 1/11½d. per ton." Treasurer Alfred Onions, giving the report, continued : "It is inconceivable that the Independent Chairman would have given his decision in face of this increased price if he did not accept the contention of the owners that there had been a further increase in the cost of production, which the Workmen's representatives had no opportunity of testing or examining." The Executive Council, therefore, had been compelled to advise the conference to take the steps set forth in a resolution for dealing with a further application (which had to be made upon the 1st November) "in the hope that a fair and equitable method will be found for settling the points in dispute". The important resolution which embodied this policy is quoted in Appendix II to this chapter.

When this application for 15 per cent was put forward on 1st November the owners applied for a reduction of 10 per cent. The miners' demand for the joint audit of the owners' books was turned down. On the 10th November the Conciliation Board proved unable to agree on either application whereupon the workmen's side stated that they would appeal for Government intervention and would not abide by the casting vote of the independent chairman unless the owners agreed to a joint audit. Strike action would take place if there was a failure to make the required concession.

The fat was in the fire. The coalfield was in a ferment. Controversy raged in the Press and for once it was directed against the owners for their repeated refusal to agree to a joint audit. On 23rd November the South Wales Coalowners' Association issued a statement that it would be prepared to allow an independent auditor access to the books but a joint audit it would not allow: the right of the miners to direct participation in the discovery of the selling price on which their wages largely depended was still repudiated. Next day at the offices of the Board of Trade in London the Executive Council met Sir H. Llewellyn Smith. Through him they informed the Government that unless there were an immediate settlement of their 15 per cent demand (which they refused to allow to be dealt with by the independent chairman) there would be a general stoppage in the coalfield. It would be inevitable. For some days longer the negotiations went on. The South Wales coalowners on 24th November had been also meeting with the officials of the Board of Trade. Finally, on Wednesday, 29th November, the Asquith Coalition Government took a drastic step. Under the Defence of the Realm Act they made a Regulation (9G)[1] enabling the Government to take control of any coal mines; and they immediately applied this to the South Wales coalfield.[2]

At the same time the Board of Trade appointed an interdepartmental committee consisting of Sir Richard Redmayne, H.M. Chief Inspector of Mines, W. F. Marwood of the Board of Trade and W. St. Jenkins of the Admiralty to act in an advisory capacity in the control of the mines. Two days later on 2nd December this committee published its decision conceding the workmen's claim for an advance of 15 per cent. At the same time they appointed a Government auditor to ascertain the

[1]By Order under Regulation (9G) the Board of Trade were empowered to apply "either generally to all coal mines or to coal mines in any special area or in any special coalfields or to any special coal mines". The second clause of Regulation 9G ran:

"2. Any coal mines to which this regulation is so applied shall, by virtue of the order, pass into the possession of the Board of Trade as from the date of the order or from any later date mentioned in the order; and the owner, agent and manager of every such mine, and every officer thereof, and, where the owner of the mine is a Company, every Director of the Company shall comply with the directions of the Board of Trade as to the management and use of the mine, and if he fails to do so he shall be guilty of a summary offence against these regulations."

[2]Also dated 29th November, the Order of the President of the Board of Trade read: "Regulation 9G of the Defence of the Realm (Consolidation) Regulations, 1914, is hereby applied as from the 1st day of December, 1916, until further notice, to the South Wales Coalfield, that is to say, to all coal mines in the counties of Brecon, Carmarthen, Glamorgan, Monmouth, Pembroke and Radnor.—(Sd.) WALTER RUNCIMAN."

relative financial position of profits and wages and the costs of production. The Board of Trade wrote to the owners saying that it would be "glad to receive at the earliest possible date any suggestions which the Association might desire to offer with regard to instructions to be given to the auditor." The same day, 1st December, they told the owners that the 15 per cent would have to be given as they had already intimated to the miners' leaders. The coalfield crisis was over. By invoking the Defence of the Realm Act, the Cabinet had cut the Gordian Knot.

12 LLOYD GEORGE TAKES IN LORD RHONDDA

When in the six counties of the South Wales coalfield, at the stroke of a pen on 29th November, all coal mines did "pass into the possession of the Board of Trade" the news of this extension of State Control reached Cardiff on the same day. A coalition Cabinet, still mainly Liberal, had abandoned a cardinal tenet of *laissez-faire*, of the outlook in which its members had been reared and against which British Socialists had inveighed for thirty years. Yet there was no immediate enthusiasm in the valleys, no rapturous welcome. Surprise there was certainly, and much bewilderment, mingled with some apprehension. The Executive Council of the South Wales Miners' Federation simply did not know what to make of it, nor how to deal with it. Their solicitor, W. P. Nicholas, called in to their meeting on Friday, 1st December, to give them an explanation, seemed equally at a loss; for although he could tell them that the Order had been made under the Defence of the Realm Act dated 27th November, 1914, he "had not for the moment any definite opinion as the question was a difficult one." His suggestion that Counsel's opinion should be taken upon the position was accepted and he was instructed so to do.

Three days later, a special conference in the Cory Hall met to mull over this entirely new and surprising development. Again their solicitor was called in, and he addressed the 294 delegates at length upon the effect of the Order on the contractural obligations of the workmen, whether they were subject to any new penalties and the extent to which the Conciliation Board Agreement was affected. So, with only half a dozen voting against it, it was resolved :

"To authorise the Executive Council to take any steps necessary to ascertain from the Board of Trade the full detail effect of the Order respecting the Government control of the collieries," and "that this matter be raised at the conference of the Miners' Federation of Great Britain on Wednesday next" (4 xii 1916).

The decision to raise the matter at the national conference was not a request for intervention in their industrial relations, already summarily rejected in the summer of 1915. The degree of autonomy then maintained was shown again in this same Special Conference when they rejected the recommendation of the MFGB Southport Conference of

23rd November on Absentee Committees in the words "that this Conference votes against forming Committees to deal with Absenteeism" (4 xii 1916).

Indeed, the setting up and functioning of Pit Committees from South Wales was not very satisfactory for the Government Departments which throughout 1916 had been putting increasing pressure on the Miners' Federation to obtain a greater output. The Southport Conference had been called to strengthen the drive for Pit Committees and to elaborate their rules. Tom Richards, reporting at this MFGB Conference on the 400 collieries in South Wales, at only 200 of which had Pit Committees been set up, said that "at a large number of collieries there are no Committees set up, the argument being used by the workmen that this is the thin end of the wedge to bring in Industrial Conscription; and they have turned a blind side to all we have urged upon them"; and he drew attention also to "a large number of managers who are as indifferent as the workmen, and have not taken steps to get committees set up" (22 xi 1916).[1]

A fortnight later at the MFGB special conference in Central Hall, Westminster, there was a long statement from Vice-President James Winstone. To the 153 delegates and 18 committee members he related how the advance in the price of coal of 2/6½d. per ton by the September quarter had not yielded the 15 per cent increase in the general rate for which they had applied "because the coalowners in the previous application had made the increased cost of production the chief factor, that increased cost of production never having been agreed to by us" (6 xi 1916) and how the conciliation machinery had come to a deadlock. Then they went to consult Sir Hubert Llewellyn Smith at the Board of Trade. Within a week's negotiations "on the last day of the interview we were faced with the question as to whether we were prepared to consider the question of control of the mines" and Sir Hubert had said: "You can discuss the control of the mines on the assumption that your 15 per cent has been granted." The SWMF Executive Council then made the following answer:

"The question of the control of the mines by the Government we say is a national one, and in the opinion of this Council should be dealt with on a national basis, and that this Council without in any way committing itself would be prepared in conjunction with the national organisation to consider any scheme which the Government might think desirable to introduce, subject, of course, to proper safeguards being introduced for the protection of the workmen."

[1]Tom Richards gave details as follows:

"Although there were two hundred Committees forty have been disbanded, and disbanded because the managers' and workmen's representatives on the Committee failed to agree as to what report should be sent in. Our men say it is the fault entirely of the manager, that the officials who represent the company on the Joint Committee refuse to put into the report that absenteeism is being caused through any fault of the management. They say that if some of the best amongst the local workmen who attend work regularly lose a day, the manager puts him down as a man not at work, although they know he was unwell."

There had been no further discussion : and on the next day when the letter came with the sudden announcement of the new Regulation 9G "We were" said Winstone "very apprehensive as to whether we were going to be put, or are going to be put, under the Munitions Act." The same fear possessed the delegates who then reached a decision to leave the matter in the hands of their Executive Committee. As they left London, all aware of a great political upheaval and the sudden fall of the Cabinet, their apprehensions were not lessened.

The State control of the Welsh coalfield had been one of the last deeds of the Asquith coalition Government as it was tottering to its fall. The whole of November, 1916, newspapers headed by the brood of the Harmsworths (*The Times, Daily Mail, Evening News*, etc., etc.) had been pursuing Asquith with such persistency that when the *Evening News* afternoon poster contained only the one word, thrice repeated, "WOBBLE, WOBBLE, WOBBLE" all Londoners knew immediately that it must refer to the once widely-revered Prime Minister. Suddenly on 5th December Asquith resigned : and within some forty hours David Lloyd George was Prime Minister. He had been Chancellor of the Exchequer from 1908 to 1915, Minister of Munitions for twelve months, Secretary of State for War for five months; now he had attained the supreme office in which he felt his talents could best serve his nation, his King and country. It was the culmination of a twelvemonth of recurrent intrigues, reaching a pitch of intensity in the foggy days of November. It may be fittingly termed a *coup d'etat* although it was not carried out by use or show of armed force, not by columns of infantry or the scream of artillery shells, but by the columns of newspaper editorial articles and the screaming of headlines and posters.[1]

When the MFGB Executive Committee met two weeks later in the Imperial Hotel, Russell Square, they were still very troubled. The announcement on 10th December of the new Ministers had intensified their anxieties when they perceived that hardly any of their friends amongst Liberal Ministers had survived from the old coalition and that it was predominantly Conservative in its composition. True, John Hodge, General Secretary of the Steel Smelters, had been made Minister of Labour and G. N. Barnes, formerly General Secretary of the Amalgamated Society of Engineers, had become Minister of Pensions, while Arthur Henderson was now to be one of the new select War Cabinet. Nevertheless the leaders of the miners knew of the discussion between the Executive Committee of the Labour Party and the new Prime Minister when in process of forming his government. Smillie knew that not only Ramsay MacDonald but also Sidney Webb had opposed entry into the new administration : and these were the members of the Labour Party Executive with whom at any rate Smillie and the men from South Wales were most in sympathy. In particular it seemed

[1]The new Government, boosted into power partly by newspaper placards, had used its powers before the year was out to put a stop to all posters, on the ground that paper was becoming too precious to be squandered on placards.

a sinister choice that there should be included in the new Cabinet no other than D. A. Thomas (Lord Rhondda) who only two weeks before had been regarded as the most able and most powerful opponent of the Welsh miners, against whom Vernon Hartshorn (one of the three elected Welshmen on the National Executive) had particularly directed a public attack in the November crisis. D. A. Thomas, indeed, had become at once a symbol of unyielding hostility to the miners, and also the outstanding example of the most rapid growth of monopoly tendencies amongst the coalmining capitalists of South Wales.

David Alfred Thomas was both capitalist and politician. In the former capacity he had remarkable success when he constructed the famous Cambrian Combine and even greater success in the war period. In January, 1916, he had been elevated to the peerage as Lord Rhondda of Llanwern. In July of the year 1916 Lord Rhondda acquired a controlling interest in David Davis and Sons Limited with Messrs. Thomas and Davey to act as Sales Agents. Later that month Mr. F. L. Davis offered (on 12th July) to resign his position as permanent chairman of the coalowners' side of the Conciliation Board, and meantime changes were made in the management of D. Davis and Son Limited. Not only was Lord Rhondda one of the thirty of the owners' representatives on the Board of Conciliation but with half a dozen others he made up the powerful Finance Committee of the Monmouthshire and South Wales Coal Owners' Association. Next, on 7th September, 1916, Lord Rhondda acquired control of North's Navigation Collieries (1889) Limited and Messrs. Lysberg Limited were appointed Sales Agents. On 18th October Lord Rhondda acquired controlling interest in the Gwaun-cae-Gurwen Colliery Company Limited and Messrs. L. Gueret Limited were appointed Sales Agents. By the beginning of December, 1916, Lord Rhondda from his base in the rich seams of smokeless dry steam coal was bestriding the South Wales coalfield like a colossus.

To his fellow members of the National Executive Winstone reported that neither the Welsh officials nor the Executive Council could say anything as to the actual meaning of the control of the Welsh mines. President Smillie then reminded them that on the previous day the new Prime Minister had made a statement that the Government would take over the control of all mines in Great Britain. What might this mean? So "after very lengthy consideration and debate" the following resolution was carried:

"That this Executive Committee views with the utmost concern the declaration by the Prime Minister that the Government contemplate taking control of the whole of the mines in the country, and before any definite action is taken we ask the Prime Minister to grant an interview to this Executive Committee at the earliest possible date" (20 xii 1916).

That interview was immediately granted for the next afternoon. There at No. 10 Downing Street they met not only the new Prime Minister but the new War Cabinet, together with other Ministers, and notably Lord Rhondda. The upshot of this interview was that after their suspicions and fear of compulsion had been repeatedly voiced they were given the needed assurances, both by Lloyd George and by Arthur Henderson. The interview which was lengthy ended with this dialogue:

"**The Prime Minister:**

"It was purely to get complete control of the mines in the United Kingdom, and also get rid of the notion that is in the minds of a good many of the miners—quite legitimately in some cases—that the interests of the nation are being exploited in order that huge profits should be made whilst, on the other hand, they are not getting their fair share. We thought then that the nation should take over the whole thing, and that that would be a guarantee at any rate that that state of things should not continue. It was the situation in South Wales that first of all forced it on us. You pressed us, or someone did, for the extension of that to the rest of the country, and the Government felt very strongly that the coal industry of the country ought to be under the control of the Government at least during the war. I might not disagree to going beyond that; but at any rate sufficient unto the day is the evil thereof.

"**Mr. Arthur Henderson:** Or the good thereof.

"**The Prime Minister:** Or the good thereof. What we are about now is with the object of having complete control of the coal of the country. In regard to the Munitions Act, I can assure you that we have no sinister purpose of that kind in mind, and we never discussed it. The Munitions Act was never discussed in reference to this problem at all, either under the old administration or during this."

Once again Smillie continued to show anxiety—an anxiety in which he reflected the feelings of the miners in their conferences. The Prime Minister then gave once more a firm assurance in the following exchange:

"I can only say this at this stage, that there is no ulterior motive. The main, the dominant motive, is the same in regard to the coal as in regard to shipping, that we should be able to control them for national purposes, whether for the purpose of sending coal to Italy, to France, or to Russia or for retaining it for our own purposes at home. The war is the one thing we have in our minds at the moment in this respect.

"In regard to the cost of living, I hope to a very large extent to be able to keep that down by means of very drastic measures that we are going to take about food control.

"**Mr. Robert Smillie:** You tell us that as a matter of fact there is no idea of extending the Munitions Act to us at all?

"**The Prime Minister:** No; we never even discussed it" (21 xii 1916).

So the discussion ended. But before the representatives of the miners went away Smillie said that it would be "very satisfactory to us" if at the same time the miners could receive the Cabinet's idea on the wage question. On this one of those present asked anxiously "You are not asking for an advance in wages, are you?" Smillie replied in the negative and indicated that at the moment they were more concerned with some means to stop the rise in the cost of living by resisting the increase in prices. The anxious enquirer was Lord Rhondda who, abandoning perforce his many directorships, was now launched on his meteoric career as a cabinet minister.

8 CWMLLYNFELL GLEE PARTY, 1923

9 OPENING OF TALYGARN MINERS' REST HOME BY HERBERT SMITH WITH ENOCH MORRELL (first left) AND TOM RICHARDS (first right)

APPENDIX I

Table showing the variation in wages from July 15, 1915, to November 30, 1918, in the South Wales coalfield.

Period From	To	Wages above the 1915 standard (the 1915 standard is 50% above the old standard (that of 1879))	Wages above the 1879 standard which was the standard used up to July 14, 1915
July 15, 1915	Aug. 20, 1915	18 1/3rd%	72½%
Aug. 21, 1915	Nov. 30, 1915	30 5/6ths%	96¼%
Dec. 1, 1915	May 30, 1916	25 5/6ths%	88¾%
June 1, 1915	Nov. 30, 1916	40 5/6ths%	111¼%
Dec. 1, 1915	—	55 5/6ths%	133¾%

APPENDIX II

RESOLUTION ON JOINT AUDIT, 30th OCTOBER, 1916.

"The Council had before them a report by the Joint Auditors of a further increase in the average Selling Price of Coal for the quarter ending September, of 7d per ton, in addition to the increase shown for the June quarter of 1/11½, a total increase of 2/6½ per ton, for which the Workmen have not been able to secure any advance in wages, while for the whole period of the war the relative position of the Owners and Workmen in relation to the division of the enhanced prices have resulted in the Workmen not receiving wages equivalent to prices in the same proportion as those received under any of the previous Conciliation Board Agreements.

"The Council, assuming that the Independent Chairman in his rejection of the Workmen's application for an increase in wages based upon an increase in the Average Selling Price of Coal of 1/11½ per ton, was influenced by the *ex parte* statement of the Owners alleging an increase in the cost of production. The Council immediately approached the Owners with a request that a Joint Audit of the cost of production should be taken and that the result of such audit should be sent to the respective sides at the same time as the result of the audit on prices; unless this is done the Workmen are placed at a serious disadvantage as compared with the Owners.

"The Owners having again refused this reasonable request of the Workmen, the Council are of the opinion that it is impossible for an Independent Chairman to equitably adjudicate upon the demands for an alteration in the Wage Rate while the Owners use the alleged increase in the cost of production which they refuse to submit for examination, together with the facts that notwithstanding any increase in the cost of production the profits of the Owners are very much higher than the pre-war period.

"The Council now make application for 15 per cent increase in wages, based upon a further increase in the price of coal and consider that in the interval between the application being considered by the

Coal Owners and the date when the change should become operative, the Council should ask the Government to allow them to put before it the inequitable conditions prevailing, with a view of securing that the Workmen shall be assured that the relative position of the Owners and Workmen under the agreements before the War shall be maintained, which relative position the owners have on several occasions stated they desired and would be satisfied with."

CHAPTER FIVE

UNDER STATE CONTROL

1 A BITTER WINTER

The year 1917 opened in darkness and bitter cold all over Europe. It was bad everywhere: worse for "the wretched of the earth": worst of all for the millions of men in arms—among them tens of thousands of enlisted Welsh miners huddled in the lice-ridden trenches of Flanders, or frost-bitten on Russian convoys through the Arctic night. No one could say when the war would end: peace overtures in December had been rejected by the Entente governments; and on 31st January, 1917, Germany announced unrestricted submarine warfare. Diplomatic relations with Germany were severed by the United States of America on 1st February, by China on 13th March, and thereafter by Brazil and other Latin-American countries. What had been mainly a war in Europe and on the fringes of Asia was now to become a world war.

The New World may have been "called in to redress the balance of the Old": but it could not yet make up for the heavy casualties of the Somme battles on the Western Front. The shortage had to be made good before the summer. So the new War Cabinet approved a plan to take from essential industries manpower hitherto exempted, including 20,000 mineworkers: and on 22nd January the new Home Secretary took measures to withdraw certificates of exemption. These brought him an angry telegram from Tom Richards, M.P. In it there was a veiled threat:

"My Executive consider this change as a serious departure from the understanding arrived at between the Miners' Federation and your predecessor in office and they desire to emphatically protest against same and to state that the change will certainly produce stoppages and trouble in this coalfield" (27 i 1917).

After an encounter that weekend with "the Right Hon. W. Abraham, M.P., J. Winstone, V. Hartshorn, G. Barker and the General Secretary," who had been appointed "to wait upon the Home Secretary" by the SWMF Executive Council, the new policy was suspended until 1st February, when Sir George Cave, K.C. (promoted to the Home Office on 10th December) would meet the MFGB Executive Committee. Then Robert Smillie told him of "considerable excitement and considerable ill feeling" aroused in South Wales, while Vernon Hartshorn spoke strongly of "a breach of faith on the part of the Government with the Federation". Sir George Cave explained that his proposals were to take men "from three classes", viz. (1) men who had entered the mines since 14th August, 1915; (2) persistent absentees who lose two or more shifts a week; (3) unskilled surface workers. "As you know", said Sir George, "I am new at this job and I was very anxious to do what could be done, quickly and fairly." He ended somewhat plaintively saying: "Gentlemen, that is a plain statement of what has happened. I am quite sure that you, like all patriotic Englishmen, Scotsmen and Welshmen, will be very anxious to respond to the call of the country."

The five representatives from South Wales, satisfied with assurances (that new schemes of recruiting would have to be agreed with the Miners' Federation) received approval of their report from the SWMF Executive Council on Monday, 5th February. It was far otherwise in the Cory Memorial Hall on Wednesday, 13th February, when the report was given by Vice-President Winstone to a coalfield conference. Suspicions had been aroused: three weeks of discussion in the valleys had followed upon the January intervention of the new Home Secretary, the first Tory to hold that office for over eleven years. A motion to reject the Council's report, put to a card vote, received a three to two majority from the 281 delegates.

The Executive Council, somewhat in a quandary, felt that somehow they must "get the Conference to rescind the decision arrived at": but if they failed in this they would recommend a ballot vote to determine the matter. But they did not fail. The Special Conference on 19th February proved amenable to the facts and arguments put forward. This time the card vote was 1,828 for acceptance of the Council's report and 1,309 against acceptance. The decision of 13th February was thus rescinded.

The State control of coalmines was now extended from South Wales to all coalfields. From the end of February, 1917, main problems, not only of wages and hours, but of food supplies and manpower, had to be solved on a national level between the Government, represented in the first instance by a Coal Controller, and the Miners' Federation of Great Britain.

On all troublous questions the South Wales Miners' Federation therefore operated as part of a larger whole: the history of which has already been dealt with elsewhere and in more than one publication.[1]

In a sense, therefore, on all these main questions there ceases to be any separate history of the South Wales Miners' Federation for some years after the spring of 1917. To avoid needless repetition over this period the narrative must be confined to matters peculiar to South Wales, or where the part significantly differed from the whole, or where the initiative coming from Cardiff and the Valleys has to be accorded its due record.

[1]*The Miners: Years of Struggle, Vol. II of the History of the Miners' Federation of Great Britain* by R. Page Arnot (1953). *Labour in the Coal Mining Industry* by G. D. H. Cole (1923).

2 RECRUITING IN 1917 AND FOOD RATIONING

Questions of call-up and comb-out recurred throughout 1917 and 1918. On 4th April the Coal Controller arranged for the MFGB Executive Committee to be met by the First Sea Lord and the Chief of the Imperial General Staff. These desired the Federation Committee to assist in a scheme for drafting a large number of men from the mines to serve with the Colours. To this, a cool response was given by the South Wales Conference which "after several hours' discussion" decided: "That we do not take any part, as a Federation, in respect to the matter" (16 iv 1971). But South Wales delegates were in the minority at subsequent MFGB Conferences. So the South Wales Executive Council recommended that the decisions arrived at by the Miners' Federation of Great Britain be accepted by the South Wales District.

A card vote at the next Conference (on 8th May), showing 1,641 votes in favour and 1,272 against, accepted the MFGB decision.

On the 20th June the miners' national conference by 114 votes to 17 (these last mainly from South Wales) decided to accept the combing-out scheme devised by the Coal Controller. The coal owners also agreed. So a letter to the coalfields, signed on 14th July on behalf of the Mining Association of Great Britain and the Miners' Federation of Great Britain, dealt with a "new scheme of recruiting". The joint letter began:

> "During the present year the War Cabinet have so far decided to take 40,000 men from the Coal Mines for the Army. Of this number so far only about 19,000 have been found; and it is imperative that the balance amounting to 21,000 should be immediately forthcoming."

It was then proposed that the exemptions of men between 18 and 25 years of age should be withdrawn in enough numbers to make up the quota of recruits wanted.

Immediate opposition developed. On 2nd August the Special Conference at Cardiff rejected the scheme by 236 votes to 25: and by 8th August the scheme was postponed. On 7th September, 1917, an MFGB Special Conference had before it two propositions. The first resolution: "That the MFGB take no part in assisting in the recruitment of miners for the Army", was defeated by 485 votes to 245, the minority made up of Scotland's 90 votes, South Wales's 148 votes with four from Somerset and three from Forest of Dean. From the last-named, G. H. Rowlinson explained he had thought "there would be no trouble" amongst the men he represented: but during the August holidays "there was an influx into my district of other men from some other county, who got amongst our young men and started the flame". In this reference is revealed something of the spread in the coalfields since the spring of widespread longing for peace that had received such an impetus with the outbreak of the Russian Revolution in mid-March of 1917.

When the second resolution: "That the suggested new scheme be not put into operation until all persons of military age who have entered the mines since August, 1914, have been combed out who were not *bona fide* miners prior to August 4th, 1914" (7 ix 1917) was put, and carried, South Wales abstained.

Angry discussions in South Wales resulted by 1,712 votes to 897 in a decision for a strike ballot.[1] Five weeks later on 15th November the majority against "a Down-Tools Policy" was 98,946 against 28,903. On 22nd November the Coal Controller accepted the MFGB standpoint to cancel the exemptions of all "who were not *bona fide* miners prior to 4th August, 1914".

The effect of unrestricted submarine warfare, begun on 1st February, 1917, soon began to be felt: and by the end of that month shipping to a total of 500,000 tons had been sunk by German U-boats. In March 600,000 tons were sunk, in April 870,359 tons, in May nearly 600,000 tons. How serious the food situation could become was signalled by a further rise in food prices as well as by shortages: wheat rose to 90/- a quarter from 80/- in November, 1916, and by 26th March, 1917, the four-pound loaf was double the pre-war (July, 1914) price.

By mid-May, on an initiative taken in the Rhondda Valleys, a Conference in Central Hall, Westminster discussed a resolution from South Wales:

"That in face of the grave shortage of food and the unequal distribution of same the Committee be asked to convene a Special Conference to consider the question of Compulsory Rationing."

Robert Smillie from the chair spoke of the gravity of the food situation saying that "in many of the working-class homes, in the homes of the poorest of the people, there has been considerable difficulty in getting a sufficient supply of food and other commodities".

Speaking for South Wales, James Winstone said: "The Government have already very carefully safeguarded the interests of the profiteers, but have given little or no attention to the interests of the masses of the people." He quoted "a lady who had made suggestions": that the "wealthy classes should select the luxury foods and leave the cheaper foods for the poor, that they should drink coffee and leave tea which is cheaper for the poor, eat the choicer fish and cuts of meat, and let the poor have an ample and therefore cheaper supply of herrings and cheaper cuts of meat." This he quoted "simply for the purpose

[1]BALLOT PAPER (8th October, 1917).

The Special Conference of the South Wales Miners' Federation, at Cardiff, on October 8th, 1917, decided on the following Resolution:

"That the South Wales Miners' Federation take no part in assisting in the Recruitment of Colliery Workers for the Army and Navy.

"Are you in favour of a Down Tools Policy in South Wales in the event of the Government proceeding with their Comb-Out Scheme in the mines?

'Yes. No.' "

of showing really what is in the minds of those who are governing us today and who are preaching food economy to the people."

It was believed there was much hoarding: one delegate said:

"I am one of the newly-elected checkweighmen in Nottinghamshire at the Rufford Colliery. I live close to where Lord Saville lives, and it absolutely stinks with food; they have everything they require, and I am informed that they have never had one ounce of war fare yet. I say we do not want compulsory rationing whilst there are these rich hoarders" (17 v 1917).

After Tom Richards had said that the debate had fully justified South Wales in asking that the Conference be called, it was agreed that before Conference committed itself to the principle, the Executive Committee should approach the Government and ascertain if there is any necessity for compulsory rationing.

But in the afternoon a South Wales delegate said that he was disappointed: he had hoped for something more aggressive and added: "I want to see the whole power of this organisation, and even the Triple Alliance, used to come to some decision on this matter. I do not think that Lord Davenport[1] is the proper man to do this business at all." Finally, William Adamson, having persuaded the conference against any step that might appear critical of the Government (for Adamson was an out-and-out supporter of the war and most influential of the miners' M.P.s in the House of Commons), secured the following resolution:

"That the Executive Committee be instructed to meet the Prime Minister and to point out to him the absolute necessity for the Government taking entire control of the food supplies and fixing prices so as to secure equitable distribution of the same among all classes of people, and at the same time putting a stop to the shameful profiteering which is taking place in the country" (17 v 1917).

The Prime Minister on 24th May met the miners' leaders. He divulged to them facts about the food shortage: and four weeks later, when the miners' conference re-assembled, a report on the situation was given by the President. Steps had been taken for "proper distri-

[1]Lord Devonport, of the grocery firm Kearley and Tonge, had been appointed by Lloyd George on 10th December, 1916, to be the first head of the Food Control. It was not a happy choice. As head of the Port of London Authority in 1911 Devonport had put up a strenuous resistance to the claim for improved wages and conditions: at a great assemblage of London dockers on Tower Hill, Ben Tillett fell upon his knees and put up a prayer: "God strike Lord Devonport dead!" While this utterance was remembered for years afterwards few would recall Hillaire Belloc's satiric lines:

"The grocer Hudson Kearley? He,
When purchasing his Barony,
Was offered, so we understand,
The title of Lord Sugar-Sand:
Alternatively, might have been
Lord Overweight of Margarine.
But being of the nobler sort
He chose the style of Devonport
And where the dockers faint and die
Is worshipped to idolatry."

bution" of sugar: maximum prices had been fixed for grain, potatoes and milk: and there was to be a new Food Controller. The Prime Minister's decision to get rid of Lord Devonport, at one time his own Parliamentary Secretary at the Board of Trade, and to appoint in his place Lord Rhondda, formerly D. A. Thomas, gratified the miners.

Robert Smillie, for once praising a capitalist Minister, said: "The new Controller, Lord Rhondda, is prepared to fight the profiteers, and he is a fighter if he makes up his mind." It was then agreed to call attention to the "continuous exploitation of the people's food by profiteers" and to urge the Food Controller "to take drastic measures to prevent, . . . this serious evil" (20 vi 1917).

3 TRIPLE ALLIANCE AND INDUSTRIAL COMPULSION

In the meantime a new factor in world affairs had come into play: and it was not long before the effect of it was felt amongst the coal miners of Great Britain. The Russian Revolution, from the abdication in the second week of March of Nicholas II, Tsar of all the Russias, had an immense and immediate impact throughout the globe. In Britain, where there had been rumours circulating of pro-German influences at the Royal Court in Petrograd, the news of the Revolution was given a clamorous welcome in the Press—where the family connection between the Romanovs and the Wettins[1] was recalled only by the *Daily Express* . In Parliament there was a full and formal acceptance. The Conservative leader Bonar Law moved that the House of Commons "tender to the Russian people its heartiest congratulations" (22 iii 1917). But this vote, like the earlier telegram to "Messrs. Kerensky and Chkheidze, the leaders of the Russian Labour Party" sent by a score of Labour Ministers and heads of trade unions was on the explicit assumption, if not the stipulation, that the overthrow of Tsardom would lead to increased vigour in the prosecution of the war: and a veil was drawn over the fact that the Petrograd rising in the second week of March had been under the slogans of "Down with the War", "Down with the Tsar."

The coming into being of a Council (Soviet in Russian) of Workers' and Soldiers' Deputies was sufficiently startling. But that body had handed over to the motley Provisional Government. Nevertheless the Soviet's Order No. 1 of 13th March to give the soldiers civil rights, reached out in every country to "the lower classes" whose aspirations were once voiced by the parties of the Socialist International. In Britain the popular response began when on 31st March there assembled in London's largest hall a Socialist demonstration "to welcome the

[1]Old family name, altered to Windsor in June 1917 by King George V for his House as well as for all British descendants in the male line of his grandmother Queen Victoria.

Russian Revolution". From April onwards the United Socialist Council, comprising two of the three Socialist bodies represented in the British section of the Socialist International, began a joint campaign, following upon their Easter annual conference for an "immediate democratic peace" and in support of the demands put forward by the Russian Councils of Workers' and Soldiers' Deputies. In this the United Socialist Council aroused enmity amongst those in the Labour Party who were committed to support the annexationist war aims of the British Government.

Thus from the late spring of 1917 the Russian Revolution began to exercise a powerful, if indirect, influence upon the members of the South Wales Miners' Federation. With breathlessly rapid development as differences arose between the Soviet in Petrograd and the Provisional Government which it had created (with eager assent of the Entente embassies); and as gulfs opened up between the parties of the Revolution and within the Congress of Soviets, so these were reflected in new signs of cleavage within the British Labour movement. The first public indication of this cleavage within the miners' ranks was seen at the MFGB Special Conference of 17th May in an item minuted under the heading "Industrial Compulsion."

The harmony of the Miners' Associations came to be disturbed when their President, Robert Smillie said, "I have an announcement to make which we want you to accept." The announcement which came from a meeting held the previous day (and called at the instance of the Miners' Federation) ran as follows:

"That this meeting of the three Executive Councils of Mineworkers, Railways Workers, and Transport Workers, constituting the Triple Industrial Alliance observes with misgiving the various signs of attempts to introduce by gradual stages the principle of Industrial Compulsion. It warns the responsible authorities against the dangers of any efforts, open or hidden, to destroy the influence of Trades Unionism by labour conscription, and further declares that for every reason which can be adduced in favour of the conscription of men, ten reasons can be given in favour of the conscription of wealth and property.

"This meeting moreover recommends that a National Conference of Delegates of the three bodies shall be immediately summoned to consider and determine upon such steps as may be necessary to checkmate the attacks upon trade union organisation and influence" (16 v 1917).

This announcement immediately caused some uproar. Jack McGurk of Lancashire protested against "any such conference being called together" and found he had the manifold vocal support of the Scottish delegation whose senior officials were not in agreement with Smillie in his criticism of the Government's conduct of the war.

Mr. Jack McGurk: "I have asked what district of the Miners Federation asked for a Conference of the Triple Alliance. I want a straight answer."

The Chairman: "I understand that the Council of the South Wales Miners' Federation discussed the question of industrial compulsion at great length and also the question of food supplies. The South Wales Miners' Federation, which is an important part of this Federation, sent through their Secretary, Mr. Thomas Richards, a request to call a meeting of the Triple Alliance to discuss this question. It did not initiate from the Executive."

This did not quell suspicions that South Wales, in touch with Smillie, was behind a move to which the MFGB leaders had committed the miners' county associations.[1] For McGurk immediately said:

"In view of the answer, and in view of the fact of certain things taking place in this country, this conference ought to have something to say about this Federation being drawn at the tail of the United Socialist Council. You are bringing this about, or trying to bring it about."

A South Wales delegate rose "to protect the Chairman against the insinuations of Mr. McGurk" who, he sincerely hoped, "will withdraw or be compelled to retire." John Robertson, leading the Scots delegates, deprecated "personal attacks" as "unseemly" and raised the question whether industrial conscription was a matter for the Triple Alliance or the Labour Party or the Trades Union Congress. William Straker of Northumberland, in support of the resolution, asked: "Is the question of industrial conscription greater than the question of food supplies? While we object to the Triple Alliance doing anything regarding industrial conscription, we have the audacity to decide what shall be done on the food question." Jack Lawson of Durham told of "two hundred representatives at our Council on Saturday" whose opinion on industrial conscription was that "the danger is imminent."

Then Sam Roebuck of Yorkshire, equipped with concrete examples, settled the matter when he said that:

"The danger of industrial conscription is not merely menacing or imminent but it is actually with us at the mines, on the railways, and with the transport workers.

"At a large firm in the western part of the country, near to Pontefract Barracks, the surface workers were so depleted that fifty soldiers were sent down from the Pontefract Barracks to fill the places of the men who had been withdrawn from the surface into His Majesty's Forces. They were paid trade union rate of wages. They were working in khaki. They were brought in motor cars, big motor charabancs, from Pontefract Barracks and conveyed back again in the evening. We instantly dealt with this as soon as we got knowledge of it, we did not wait for action with the Triple Alliance or even by this Federation. Yorkshire itself, on the instant, tackled the position and succeeded in

[1]Hugh Murnin from Stirlingshire asked whether such a thing had happened before without the MFGB Conference being consulted. Smillie replied: "We have called such a meeting before, a general Conference of the three Committees under this Constitution when we dealt with the question of the introduction of black labour into this country, and we approached the Prime Minister and we believe we stopped the introduction of black labour into this country" (17 v 1917).

getting these soldiers withdrawn. I think that you will agree that this was industrial conscription or compulsion in its worst possible form."

He gave another example of a colliery in South Yorkshire where a company of engineers were engaged several weeks erecting a saw mill which was "Very much to the dislike of the soldiers, as they themselves were in strong opposition to it but because of their position as soldiers they could not themselves take action; these men were not in receipt of wages at all, but simply were rationed, sometimes with a drink of beer, and that was the end of it. We have succeeded in getting these men withdrawn, and we have now no difficulty in that direction."

Roebuck's arguments were conclusive and the Conference agreed to "take part in the suggested Conference of the Triple Alliance" (17 v 1917).

One month later a fully representative meeting of the Triple Industrial Alliance was held when 280 delegates, representing 1,286,000 organised workers, formally ratified the constitution, and confirmed the resolution against industrial conscription with the following significant addition :

"That in the event of it being proved to the Executive of the Triple Alliance that there is an attempt to introduce industrial compulsion, they be instructed to immediately ballot our people on the question as to what action shall be taken" (20 vi 1917).

This decision upheld the full use of the Triple Industrial Alliance of which Smillie had been the main architect. But the differences within the miners' associations had now become open. There was a growing hostility towards opponents of the war (often labelled as pro-Germans). Some war enthusiasts were prominent in the British Workers' League, set up a few months earlier with the support of famous Socialist names such as R. B. Cunninghame Graham and H. G. Wells, and now equipped with Privy Councillors and Labour Ministers.[1]

The Convention in Leeds on Sunday, 3rd June, 1917, convened by the United Socialist Council (ILP and BSP) and presided over by Robert Smillie (who was also Chairman of the Triple Industrial Alliance), mustered over 1,200 delegates, mostly from union branches. Alarmed, the Home Office prohibited an open-air demonstration. The Russian Revolution and its policy of peace without annexations or indemnities was greeted with enthusiasm and a resolution was passed by the Convention to set up British Councils of Workers' and Soldiers' Delegates. Robert Williams, secretary of the Transport Workers' Federation, seconding the resolution, said it meant "that which is contained in the oft-used phrase from socialist platforms: The

[1]Its president was the Rt. Hon. John Hodge, M.P., Minister of Labour. Its organ was the weekly *British Citizen and Empire Worker*; and amongst the baker's dozen of its vice-presidents six were from the coalfields : Rt. Hon. W. Abraham, M.P.; J. G. Hancock, M.P.; Stephen Walsh, M.P.; David Gilmour, Secretary of the Lanarkshire Miners; James Robson, President of the Durham Miners; and C. B. Stanton, agent for Aberdare (1899-1915), M.P. for Merthyr Tydfil (1915-18), for Aberdare (1919-22).

Dictatorship of the Proletariat". Noah Ablett concluded the discussion with his usual brevity, saying: "So far we have heard ideas we have heard thousands of times before, and with which we all agree. There is no need for further discussion. But I think there should be before us some sort of programme, some sort of practical suggestion of how we are to set up the Councils."

On the ominously-named "Provisional Committee" of the Leeds Convention were included the four ILP Members of Parliament (Anderson, Jowett, MacDonald and Snowden), together with C. G. Ammon; their four opposite numbers of the BSP (Alexander, Fairchild, Fineberg and Quelch); Mrs. Despard of the Women's Freedom League; George Lansbury from the *Herald*; Robert Smillie and Robert Williams, whose names carried a suggestion or perhaps an aura of strong industrial backing.

4 "ARREST OF LABOUR LEADERS"

Under the heading "Arrest of Labour Leaders" the SWMF Executive Council Minutes of 23rd May, 1917, record "a representation of the Sheffield Strike Committee of Munition Workers attended and submitted the particulars of these arrests on 18th May of eight shop stewards." The strike, of 60,000 in Lancashire by 6th May, of 15,000 in Sheffield by 7th May, of 30,000 in Coventry by 8th May, became general in the London district, and then spread to the most important engineering centres in England. The strike, led entirely by shop stewards' committees, had been against the Government's April decision, in breach of previous agreements, to alter the system of Reserved Occupations and to extend to private work the dilution of skilled labour.

The Council gave a sympathetic hearing and in a resolution regretted "the action of the Authorities in arresting the Munition Workers on strike as being subversive of civil rights of the people, and against the best interests of the nation at the present juncture." They instructed the Secretary to communicate with the executives of the trade unions concerned, expressing "our sympathy with any steps they may decide to take in the matter."

Three weeks later a Commission of Inquiry into Industrial Unrest was set up by Premier Lloyd George on 12th June with instructions to its 24 members organised in eight divisions to work at top speed.

By 18th June, the Executive Council had appointed Noah Ablett, Frank Hodges, Enoch Morrell, James Manning and Noah Rees to prepare evidence to be tendered to the Commissioners. This, approved a week later, was put forward by Noah Ablett and Frank Hodges as spokesmen for the Executive Council while S. O. Davies spoke for "the anthracite" and D. R. Grenfell, as agent for the Western District, gave further evidence. By 12th July the three Commissioners for Wales and

Monmouthshire (D. Lleufer Thomas, Vernon Hartshorn and Thomas Evans) were able to sign their report.

A contemporary analysis, in the second number (August 1917 issue) of the monthly circular of the Fabian Research Department singled out the Commissioners for Wales as "much the most thorough with a report which well repays reading." It was more than twice the size of any of the other reports, and as we have seen was accomplished with great speed and fullness. One distinctive passage may here be quoted in full.

POLITICAL.

"The sense of antagonism between Capital and Labour has been considerably deepened during recent years by the propaganda of a small but earnest group of men whose teachings are rapidly permeating the entire trade union movement. Advanced causes feed on discontent, and the indisposition of employers to concede the claims of the workers to a higher standard of life has provided fuel for the propaganda of the Independent Labour Party and, more recently, of the enthusiasts of the Central Labour College movement.

"The influence of the 'advanced' men is growing very rapidly, and there is ground for belief that under their leadership attempts of a drastic character will be made by the working classes as a whole to secure direct control by themselves of their particular industries. Hostility to Capitalism has now become part of the political creed of the majority of Trade Unionists in the mining, if not in other industries, and unless the employers are prepared to meet the men part of the way disaster must overtake the mining industry in the South Wales Coalfield. Nearly all movements initiated by the South Wales Miners' Federation during recent years, consciously or unconsciously, are directed towards the overthrow of the present capitalist system and the establishment of a new industrial order under which the workers will have a greater measure of control over their industry and a larger measure of the produce of their labour.

"Opinions are as yet divided as to whether such overthrow is to be accomplished by political or industrial action or by both. Until recently the political method was most popular, but industrial action is now in the ascendant. This is possibly due to the fact that the miners have been disillusioned by the failure of the Labour Party to bring about a complete change in the industrial fabric during the past ten years in which they have held a number of seats in the House of Commons. The lack of confidence in Government action, moreover, is not confined to the men. The employers are even more emphatic in their condemnation of governmental interference, and the coalowners of South Wales allege that the chief cause of trouble in the Coalfield has been the 'action of the Government in assisting the men to break their agreements'. They further state that the men collectively never broke their agreements until the Government first 'interfered' in 1915.

"We have mentioned earlier that with reference to Trade Union policy in the coalfield there are two distinct and divergent movements—one for political action, the other for industrial unionism, and what is called 'direct action' outside politics. Broadly speaking, there is a corresponding difference as to ultimate objects and ideals :

"(1) The believers in political action have generally looked forward to and advocated State ownership and control of the mines—as indeed also of the railways and land—and ultimately of the means of production generally. This was to be achieved by purchase not by confiscation. A Bill for the nationalisation of the mines was drafted for and introduced into the House of Commons on behalf of the Miners' Federation of Great Britain. In this it was proposed that the interest on the purchase money should be made payable not by the nation at large but by the industry itself. The adherents of this view, once in a considerable majority, may be described as Collectivists or advocates of State Socialism.

"(2) Those who believe in 'direct action' and industrial unionism are opposed to the nationalisation of the mines, and to their control by the State contending that the transfer of ownership from the present owners to the State would not only not improve matters, but actually worsen them by handing over the control to bureaucrats and by dragging the workers into the meshes of the 'Servile State'. They look not so much to the State as to the trade unions, and place more emphasis on voluntarism. They advocate a policy of gradually absorbing the profits of the coalowners and thereby eventually eliminating them, the functions which they have hitherto discharged in managing and controlling the industry to be in time discharged by the miners themselves through their trade union. This school has gained considerable strength of recent years owing to the growing suspicion of Government action, and the belief that the miners can work out their own salvation. Its policy is summed up in the motto 'The Mines for the Miners', as distinct from that of 'The Mines for the Nation' or 'The Land (including the mines) for the People'.

"Here, however, comes a further divergence; one section, Syndicalists who have adopted Industrial Unionism, advocates a very drastic limitation if not the elimination of the political functions of the State, urging that the whole community should be organised industrially as producers, i.e., in trade unions, and not politically as consumers in the State; that the needs of the nation should be considered and the means of supplying them agreed upon in a National Congress of all trade unions—a truly National Trade Union Congress. The other section, whose tenets are those of Guild Socialism, while aiming at the greatest possible freedom for the self-development of each industry by the workmen in that industry exercising complete control over it, nevertheless recognise the need of the State and of co-operation with it in developing the non-industrial life of the nation. In this latter case the ownership of the mines would remain in the State, but it is not clear what the view of the Syndicalist section is in this respect.

"These different schools of thought, and various blends and confusions of them, are found in the Coalfield. It would appear that the policy of the 'Mines for the Miners' (apart from any definite agreement as to the details of putting it into operation) is now so generally accepted by the miners' leaders that its underlying principle governs all proposals and demands put forward on behalf of the men. A particular demand may appear to be fully justified on other grounds, but unless it harmonises with the ultimate ideal or tends to facilitate the realisation of that ideal, it would not be put forward. The owners, conscious of this fact, regard each claim on the part of the workers and each concession made to them as merely a starting point for a further advance towards the ultimate goal of altogether eliminating the owners, who therefore resist each claim all the more strenuously."

5 NEW RULES AND RESOLUTIONS

Meantime for five days in the middle of June the South Wales Miners' Special Conference had worked out a new series of rules, so that the second object of the Federation under rule three became "to secure the entire organisation of all workers employed in and about collieries situated in the South Wales and Monmouthshire coalfield with a view to the complete abolition of capitalism : and that membership of the Federation shall be a condition of employment."

On organisation they added a new rule No. 48 : "The formation of Joint Committees representing groups of Collieries or Collieries owned by the same Company, shall be encouraged by every means possible, the same to be recognised by the District and Executive Council" (15 vi 1917).

At the Glasgow MFGB Annual Conference in the last week of July, a South Wales resolution proposed an immediate application for an advance in the general wage rate "to meet the continued increase that is taking place in the cost of living." For foodstuffs alone the increase was higher than other items as George Barker showed in moving the resolution.[1] This bore hardest on the smaller incomes. In South Wales in July 1914 the collier's average earnings ran at a little over six shillings and eight pence[2] in a nominal eight-hour day, being the same as the minimum charge made by a solicitor for a consultation, which might last as little as eight minutes. George Barker, citing the most recent wage figures, was able to make a telling comparison of them with the swollen profits of colliery companies over a period of three years before the resolution was unanimously adopted.

"That it can be an instruction to the Executive Committee of the Miners' Federation to at once seek for a 25 per cent increase upon present earnings to meet the increased cost of living" (24 vii 1917).

The other main resolution from Cardiff was : "That the time has

[1]"I find that in 1914, before the Declaration of War, bread was selling at 5½d. for a four pound loaf; it is now selling at 11d. Butter was 1s. 3d. per pound; it is now 2s. 3d. Cheese was selling at 8d; it is now 1s. 8d. Beef and mutton (best joints) were selling at 10d; they are now, in the neighbourhood that I come from, selling at 2s a pound. Bacon before the war was 10d; it is now 1s. 6d. Sugar was 2½d.; now, when you can get it at all, it is 5½d. Milk was 4d. a quart; it is now in some districts 6d. a quart.

"Now, if those figures are added up, you would find that these articles could be purchased in 1914 for 5s. 5d.; the same articles now cost 11s. 4½d. These articles have to come into every working man's home every day" (24 vii 1917).

[2]Cmd. 2740 Eighteenth Abstract of Labour Statistics of the United Kingdom.

arrived in the evolution of capitalism when the miners should take steps to abolish piecework and establish uniform rates of wages." It was moved by Frank Hodges with his usual eloquence but with the unusual argument that all wages would soon be down on the minimum.[1] John Robertson, Vice-President of the Scottish Miners, recalling that this matter was not so much a question of wages as a plea for safety, said "It can be proved to the hilt, that the very large proportion of the accidents that happen at the face, happen because the men are working on the piecework system. There is no man in this room who has worked at the coal face as a miner but what has risked his life over and over again in order to obtain a certain piece of coal before he finished his day's work" (24 vii 1917).

There was considerable opposition from Nottingham and from Yorkshire. But when Smillie wound up the debate, he said: "The piecework system is a system which the employers like. Mine owners and managers in this country are very anxious that the piecework system should continue, and in their own interests, because it is best for them." The resolution was carried by 91 votes to 50.[2]

6 A "STOCKHOLM CLEAVAGE"

In the midst of these domestic discussions there had been a shift to the red in the whole spectrum of international relations: and this was to cause more than a surface stirring amongst the miners.

It was not till five months after the Russian Revolution to put an end to the war and to Tsarist rule that a conference of the miners dealt with war or peace aims: and even so, it was only as constituents of a wider conference called by the Labour Party that they considered these questions. An invitation had come from the Petrograd Council of Workmen's and Soldiers' Deputies and from the Dutch-Scandinavian Committee (of "neutral" social parties, claiming to act in place of the shattered International Socialist Bureau) for the British Labour Movement "to attend an international conference at Stockholm commencing on August 15th or thereabout". This call, sent out by the Petrograd Soviet (which then had an anti-Bolshevik majority composed of Mensheviki, Social Revolutionaries, Trudoviki and other socialist and non-socialist sections), had been several times discussed in the War Cabinet. These discussions were followed by the

[1]The minimum was a time rate of 4s. 7d. a shift plus percentage until raised by the new 1915 Standard to 6s. 10½d.

[2]Nothing more was done about it during the war nor indeed after it, nor even after there had been great changes in ownership of the mines. It was not until half a century had passed that a general secretary of the National Union of Mineworkers, elected from South Wales, was able to drive through, with the consent of the National Coal Board, the proposal for the complete abolition of piecework—with the immediate result that the number of strikes was halved in South Wales as well as in other coalfields, and within ten years halved again as was noted in the Donovan Report of the Royal Commission on Trade Unions and Employers' Associations 1965-68 (Cmnd. 3623).

enforced resignation of the Leader of the Labour Party, Arthur Henderson, from the War Cabinet and his replacement by G. N. Barnes.[1]

The majority of miners' delegates having had no means of forming a view were "not in a position to give a vote on this matter until we had heard the information put before us by the Labour Party Executive" (9 viii 1917). The seeming helplessness of the miners' delegates to make up their minds on a burning issue concerned with war and peace was more apparent than real. At a meeting two days earlier of the Executive Committee Robert Smillie had secured the passage of a resolution beginning: "That this Committee do not discuss the matter now, nor give any lead to the Federation Conference to be held on Thursday next" (7 viii 1917). Late on the next day, the miners' national committee, having learned more of what was afoot from their representative on the Labour Party Executive, decided to recommend the conference "not to come to any decision on the matter until the statement from the Labour Party has been given" (8 viii 1917).

Accordingly, the mining delegates after having listened to Arthur Henderson's statement of 10th August, adjourned for their own discussion on the proposition: "That the invitation to the International Conference at Stockholm be accepted on condition that the conference be consultative and not mandatory."

Steven Walsh, M.P., since mid-March a junior Minister, at once attacked the Labour Party Executive Committee saying: "That the attitude of the Executive of the Labour Party was wholly unauthorised and completely opposed to democratic government," and then went on to say:

"I indict at once Mr. Arthur Henderson. He consulted nobody. He never opened his lips either to his colleagues in the House of Commons or members of the Parliamentary Committee . . . Not a single one, not a single person of the party, was taken into Mr. Henderson's confidence before he makes the statement . . . May I say we had

[1] A contemporary and "inside" account by one of the Party leadership runs:

"After the Russian Revolution of March 1917, the Petrograd Workmen's and Soldiers' Council actually issued an invitation for a working-class "International" at Stockholm; and the participation of the British Labour Party in this International Congress, which was not then favoured by Mr. Henderson, received at one time no small support from the Prime Minister, Mr. Lloyd George. In the end the Government despatched Mr. Henderson on an official mission to Petrograd (incidentally empowering him, if he thought fit, to remain there as Ambassador at £8,000 a year).

"A National Conference of the Labour Party in August 1917 approved of participation in such a Congress at Stockholm; but the French and Italian Governments would not hear of it, and Mr. Lloyd George went back on his prior approval, absolutely declining to allow passports to be issued. Amid great excitement, and under circumstances of insult and indignity which created resentment among the British working class, Mr. Henderson felt obliged to tender his resignation of his place in the War Cabinet, in which he was succeeded by Mr. Barnes, who was getting more and more out of sympathy with the majority of the Party." *History of Trade Unionism*, 1666-1920, by Sidney and Beatrice Webb.

this matter before our Lancashire and Cheshire Federation only a week ago, and by over 150 to seven, after a very full discussion, we carried it to prosecute the war, in conjunction with our Allies, to an honourable result, to an honourable conclusion" (9 viii 1917).

Steve Walsh's speech revealed to the delegates that the quarrel amongst the half dozen Labour chiefs who held ministerial posts had become so bitter as to manifest itself in an attack on the leader of the Labour Party.

James Winstone speaking "on behalf of a united Executive Council" from the South Wales coalfield moved in favour of going to the Stockholm Conference, saying: "The vote given here this morning will be the turning point one way or another, therefore, it does seem to me that we are holding not only the destiny of this country, but I believe the destiny of the whole civilised world in the hollow of our hands." This was seconded by William Carter from Nottinghamshire, a member of the Labour Party Executive.

When the vote was taken the resolution No. 1 to attend Stockholm was carried by 547 votes against 184. Steve Walsh and the other M.P.s who followed the Prime Minister rather than the Labour Party Executive Committee had only been able to muster nine odd votes in addition to the 175 votes of Yorkshire and Lancashire.

The weekend of 11th and 12th August, 1917, following the Labour Conference marked the spectacular resignation of Arthur Henderson, or rather his extrusion from the War Cabinet. Ten days later at a second Labour Party Special Conference the feeling in favour of Stockholm had considerably diminished. Those other Labour Ministers who had remained in the Coalition Government really were casting their weight against Stockholm, following the lead of Prime Minister Lloyd George. At the Miners' Conference a vote was taken and this time the vote was against Stockholm. Those who were in favour of attending numbered 360, those against attendance numbered 376.

7 WAGES NEGOTIATIONS

At the July MFGB Annual Conference in Glasgow, the demand put forward from South Wales on 30th April (as well as from Durham and Northumberland) for an advance in the general wage rate had been carried and put into shape as an instruction to the Executive Committee.

A fortnight later the Executive Committee decided that "early application" be made to the Coal Controller, Guy Calthrop.

On Thursday, 29th August, Calthrop raised a question as to what were the classes of "workmen in and about the collieries" to whom the advance would apply. That same afternoon he was informed "that the advance would apply to coal miners, iron stone miners, clay miners, gannister miners, lime stone quarrymen, and all colliery surface workers, members of the Federation." Two weeks later Guy Calthrop set forth the Government's conclusion in favour of a flat rate payment all round, and made the following offer: "A special advance in the shape of a war wage of 1s. a day to men over 18 and 6d. a day to youths under 18 for every day that a man works, or for every day any pit is stopped by the management (other than on recognised holidays, Sundays, stop days, etc.)" (12 ix 1917).

That afternoon the miners' leaders told him that the offer was "quite inadequate". The Coal Controller, after considerable discussion, improved the offer to 1s. 3d. a day for those over 16, 7½d. for those under 16. That was "as far as his powers would allow him to go." This improved offer if accepted would begin as and from Monday, 17th September.

On 13th September the miners' committee, having accepted the principle of the flat rate advance instead of a percentage advance (which principle was also accepted by 126 votes to 16 when it came to the opening day of the Conference on 26th September) had asked for an advance of 1s. 8d. and 10d. per day in place of 1s. 3d. and 7½d. On Thursday, 27th September, the Conference accepted 1s. 6d. for adults and 9d. per day for juniors under 16. It was the first "war wage" advance wrung out of the Government during the period of their control of the coalfields. There was no stoppage except in one small coalfield for a day or two. It was a settlement that lasted for fully nine months.

8 MASSIVE RECRUITMENT FOR THE ARMY

The new year, 1918, had scarcely begun before the MFGB Executive Committee were asked to meet at the Ministry of National Service, Sir Auckland Geddes, M.P., who had become Minister after Premier Lloyd George had sacked Neville Chamberlain in mid-August 1917. Auckland Geddes asked for 50,000 men from the mines.

Frequent consultation and prolonged discussions in the coalfield ensued. At a national conference on 31st January no decision was reached. When it came to the Westminster MFGB Special Conference on the 27th February there was a very lengthy, wide ranging discussion in which South Wales speakers such as Winstone, Barker, Hodges and Richards were very prominent. A South Wales resolution was carried by 398,000 votes to 326,000 in the following terms:

"That this Conference decides that a ballot of all its members shall be taken and that the form of the ballot paper shall be:

(1) Shall the MFGB agree to the withdrawal of 50,000 from the mines for military service?

(2) If so, shall the Federation machine be used for the purpose of finding the required number?"

The Government, however, could not wait. On 8th March, 1918, the Ministry announced the issue of an Order withdrawing exemption of younger unmarried miners in certain classes. The military situation had become serious on the Western Front with the expectation of a massive German offensive. By the 20th March the ballot figures showed a relatively small majority against the comb-out (219,000 for and 248,000 against) and a resolution was carried unanimously "That in view of the ballot not showing a two thirds majority, we recommend the Conference to advise the men not to resist the taking out of 50,000 men from the mines to the army." It was Friday, 22nd March: and on that day the great German offensive had been launched.

Two months later another conference (held at the Toplady Hall, Whitefield Institute, Tottenham Court Road, on Wednesday, 15th May, 1918) allowed Guy Calthrop to address them on the exact position and needs of the country. The National Service Department would ask for yet a further 50,000 recruits. The February call-up of 50,000 with the reduction in total output had brought about rationing of coal. The miners asked whether, to avoid wrecking the industry, it would be possible for miners in the Forces to be returned. Calthrop indicated it was going to be a razor's edge situation and that the Ministry "issued very distinct instructions to the Regional Officers when the colliery managers advise him that the quota is complete for that mine and have still men coming from that mine to volunteer, they shall use every persuasive means in their power to get the men to go back to the mine".

Negotiations followed. In June the additional number to be taken was limited to 25,000 while 25,000 miners already in the Forces who were no longer "A1" would be returned as soon as possible. It had become clear that it would be impossible to take many more men from the coal mining industry without disabling it and causing it to fail to yield the required minimum amount of coal necessary. Consequently from summer 1918 up to the end of the war the demand was for as many miners as possible as the military could spare should be brought back into the mines.

9 ELECTORAL PLANS AND DEMOCRATIC PRINCIPLES

Out of the travail, confusion and quarrels within the Labour movement in early autumn of 1917 there gradually emerged a new prospect for the future. Eight "Allied Socialist" parties (apart from the Bolsheviks who would not attend) had failed to agree on the conditions for holding an international conference. But now on the Labour Party Executive Committee, where once the ILP representatives had played a major role, the Fabian Society representative became the Lord of the

Ascendant. Together with Arthur Henderson and others Sidney Webb worked out the shape of things to come. The Labour Party was to be transformed from a federal body into a national political party with a Socialist programme and an individual membership.[1]

In South Wales the Executive Council and delegate conferences plunged readily into the new prospects, while some of them, on the other hand, hoped the grand result would be achieved by the direct action of industrial unions such as they believed the South Wales Miners' Federation to be.

This distinction was emphasised after the Second Congress of Soviets had come to power in the "Great October Socialist Revolution" in Russia when Lenin's draft Decree on Peace was passed and broadcast throughout the world. Thereafter those who had been in the Unofficial Reform Committee movement supported recognition of the Soviet Government and full solidarity with the workers, soldiers and peasants of what had been the great wartime ally of the British Empire.

Much of the winter 1917/18 was spent on political plans and preparation for electoral struggles. In addition to their four parliamentary seats, all attained in the Lib-Lab days, they would now oust the Liberal holders of many other seats in the coalfield. From 7th December, 1917, when Arthur Henderson visited the Executive Council the electoral work and preliminary ballots for candidatures went briskly ahead: and, a year later, the miners' candidates won in eight out of ten seats contested.

The same procedure, repeated in many subsequent contests after December, 1918 (five General Elections in less than ten years!) opened up for many the prospects of a political career. Once elected a checkweighman of a pit (often combined with the post of lodge secretary or with membership of the lodge committee) a miner would have a good chance of moving upwards as delegate to the monthly meeting of the valley or district, of becoming a district committee man and, always by ballot vote, of becoming also a district official. There too, when an agency fell vacant he could be put up for it. The ballotting "conducted upon the Exhaustive Vote Principle", might run to several rounds month by month: but in April 1921 the Rhondda District meeting resolved by 21 votes to nine "that all future Ballots taken by the District shall be on the Alternative Vote Principle". At a third level, apart from being chosen as lodge delegate to a coalfield conference, he might become a member of the Executive Council whilst still remaining Agent, or, in a few cases, checkweighman.

[1]The object of the Labour Party up to 1918 had been "to organise and maintain in Parliament and in the country a political Labour Party." Under the new constitution adopted in 1918 the chief object ran: "To secure for the producers by hand and by brain the full fruits of their industry, and the most equitable distribution thereof that may be possible upon the basis of common ownership of the means of production and the best obtainable system of popular administration and control of each industry and service."

At the same time on a parallel ladder there was the Labour representation upon such public bodies as the Board of Guardians and/or the Urban District Council. Then would come election to the County Council and, finally, its Chairmanship or a Mayoralty. Similarly there was election in the local Co-operative Society and finally to the Co-operative Union Conference. There were the innumerable other local activities—religious, cultural, sporting, friendly society—in each of which it was not unusual to find a miners' leader playing his part also, often by elective process. Finally, there was the ascent to Olympus, first to Parliament and, thence, in later years to a ministerial post.[1]

These elective processes were in the sharpest contrast with the other side of their life, the part dominated by the owners of the coal industry, where within the pit there was nothing but orders from above and choices from above of who should give the orders. But it was not only the elective post but also the policies which were fully subject to the democratic process within the Union from Lodge through District up to the Executive Council and Coalfield Conference in Cardiff, and thence to the National Executive and National Conference. All matters of policy went to and from the branch. How jealously these democratic rights were guarded may be instanced. In 1918, after the 19th December Special Conference at Cardiff, on the agenda of No. 1 Rhondda District there appeared a month later a protest, moved by Standard Lodge:

"Fod y Cyfarfod Dosbarthol hwn yn protestio yn erbyn gweithrediad anghyfansoddiadol y Pwyllgor Gweithredol yn Nghynadledd ddiweddar Caerdydd, yn tynu allan Benderfyniadau o berthynas i faterion nad oedd ar y Rhaglen, ac ar y rhai nad oedd y Mwnwyr wedi cael ymgynghori arnynt, ac yn gosod y cyfryw o flaen y Gynadledd er eu mabwysiadu; ac yn y dyfodol nad oes unrhyw fater Politicaidd neu Lafurawl i gael delio ag ef mewn Cynadledd oddieithr fod y cyfryw fater wedi bod o dan ystyriaeth y Cyfrinfaoedd, er galluogi y Cynrychiolwyr i gael eu hyfforddi pa fodd i weithredu."[2]

Three months earlier the current of opinion was clarified within the Executive Council when a deputation from an Unofficial Reform Committee Conference asked to be received. It was carried by 15 votes to

[1]To find a parallel to these elective stages it might be necessary to go outside the organised working class and, indeed, to go back into antiquity—not that of the ancient Hebrews in which their Chapel-bred leaders had been deeply versed—but to the processes of the Roman Republic of over two thousand years ago, where the *cursus honorum* or course of honours ran by the suffrages of the people ran from Quaestor up to Consul. Within the trade union, however, it was not solely at stated intervals but a continuous process.

[2]"That this District meeting protests against the unconstitutional action of the Business Committee at the recent Cardiff Conference, in drafting Resolutions in respect of matters not inserted on the Agenda, and upon which the general body of miners have not been consulted, and submitting such for adoption by the Conference, and that in future no matter, Political or Industrial, shall be dealt with at Conferences, unless such matter has been submitted for consideration to the Lodge, to enable Delegates being furnished with proper mandates" (21 i 1919).

eight out of 30 Council members present, and only after a long discussion, "that the deputation be not received as they are not representative of the Federation" (5 iv 1918). At the same time, however, the Executive Council would defend "the militants". That same day the Home Secretary refused to receive a deputation on the prosecution of A. J. Cook, whom the solicitor, W. P. Nicholas, was then instructed to defend: and a month later, at the instance of the Clydach Vale Lodge, W. H. Mainwaring asked that the Council should take some steps to secure the quashing of the sentence passed upon him under the Defence of the Realm Act. This was part of the repression in 1918, particularly against Marxists whose anti-war standpoint was beginning to be distinguished by the Home Office from that of the pacifists. In the case of Mainwaring it was agreed that the General Secretary on behalf of the Council should sign a petition that was then being prepared. On 25th May a further letter was to be sent to the Home Secretary asking for the "release of Mr. Cook". When the Home Secretary refused it was resolved that the "General Secretary write the Home Secretary expressing the strong resentment of the Council at this decision, and ask for a re-consideration" (1 vi 1918).

The next day the SWMF Annual Conference took the matter further in a general resolution:

"That this Federation strongly protests against the prosecution by the Government under the Defence of the Realm Act, such prosecutions being opposed to democratic freedom and the liberty of the individual; also to the intrusion of the police at meetings of public and of private character; and, further, we resolve to use the industrial power of our organisation to demand the restoration of our lost liberty" (3 vii 1918).

Yet another electoral process was tried out in that year 1918. Thomas Ashton had intimated his intention of resigning his position as part-time Secretary of the Miners' Federation of Great Britain, whereupon the Conference decided on two full-time officials, a President and a Secretary, "instead of merely spare-time men such as we have had up to the present" (9 vii 1918).

There was keen competition for national posts. Before this matter went to the preliminary ballot the Executive Council, having made their standpoint clear in April, took the unusual course of giving a recommendation, namely, "that the General Secretary prepare a leaflet of instructions to the workmen upon the method of voting, and also a recommendation by the Council of the candidature of Mr. Frank Hodges for the position of Secretary" (24 x 1918). The voting was not minuted. The Council meeting had included Noah Ablett, George Barker and William John who, as well as Hodges, were amongst the six candidates. This makes it the more remarkable that the matter was not left to an uninstructed free vote. The voting was as follows:

VOTING ON SWMF NOMINEE FOR THE SECRETARYSHIP

	1st Count	2nd Count	3rd Count	4th Count
F. Hodges	16,185	23,491	28,276	31,189
N. Ablett	14,793	19,852	23,848	26,176
G. Barker	10,238	12,532	15,463	
Wm. John	8,263	10,482		
Mardy Jones	5,023	7,716		
W. L. Cook	3,982			

(2 xi 1918).

This table gives a very useful indication of how in the valleys they esteemed those members of the Executive Council who sought their suffrages. When it came to the national election, which was conducted for the first time on the transferable vote system, Hodges came top of eight candidates, each major coalfield having put forward a nominee. He maintained this lead and on the fifth count was elected by 151,813 votes over Robson of Durham who had 94,239 votes.

For the Presidency Robert Smillie was supported. He was opposed only by J. G. Hancock, M.P., Lib-Lab, and was elected by 290,756 votes to 90,882.

The selection by ballot of a South Wales nominee for the MFGB Treasurership was another indication of how the political wind was blowing. There were six counts for five candidates. Hartshorn from the beginning topped the count with Onions second and Winstone third. This indication that the Acting-President of the South Wales Miners had lost ground may have been partly due to the fact, that as a member of the ILP Winstone had against him the current feeling caused by the pacifist "Bermondsey resolution" at their 1917 Conference. Certainly at this time the ILP leaders had lost a great deal of esteem. An example of this was found in the Scottish coalfield where Ramsay MacDonald, in what was to be claimed as a mining constituency, had intervened on behalf of a Liberal pacifist, Arthur Ponsonby, and had had a motion of censure passed against him.[1]

10 A "WORKERS' CONTROL" RESOLUTION

On 25th March the Executive Council set up a sub-committee to consider proposals to be put forward to the MFGB Annual Conference. Messrs. Hartshorn, Powell, Lucas, John and Hodges were appointed. They elaborated a series of far-reaching proposals concerned not only

[1]Letter from Arthur Henderson to Thomas Ashton enclosed the resolution of censure of the Executive Committee of the Labour Party passed on 30th May, 1918:

"The Executive accepts the position that Mr. MacDonald had no intention of breaking either the letter or the spirit of the Constitution; views with satisfaction his statement that his action was inexpedient; but expresses the opinion that his action was at variance with the spirit of the Constitution" (30 v 1918).

with the perennial problems of wages and hours, safety and compensation, housing and education, but also with an endeavour to work out a complete change in the administration of the industry, as well as in its ownership. This was a big new departure: and it is significant that of the resolutions that the South Wales Miners tabled at the July MFGB Annual Conference at Southport the most important of them was unanimously accepted.

Nationalisation of Mines. That in the opinion of this Conference the time has arrived in the history of the Coal Mining Industry, when it is clearly in the national interests to transfer the entire industry from Private Ownership and Control to State Ownership with joint control and administration by the Workmen and the State. In pursuance of this opinion, the National Executive be instructed to immediately reconsider the Draft Bill for the Nationalisation of the Mines (as agreed upon at the Swansea Conference, 1912, and subsequently amended by the Executive Committee and the Labour Party) in the light of the newer phases of development in the industry, so as to make provision for the aforesaid joint control and administration when the measure becomes law. Further, a Conference be called at an early date to receive a report from the Executive Committee upon the Draft Proposals, and to determine the best means of co-operating with the National Labour Party to ensure the passage of a new Bill into law" (10 vii 1918).

The resolution on the nationalisation of mines was taken as first business and was moved for the South Wales Miners by James Winstone, and supported by speakers from Yorkshire and Durham. Then Frank Hodges from South Wales said:

"The principal point to me in this resolution is one that has not yet been elaborated, that is the question of control. For the last two or three years a new movement has sprung up in the labour world which deals with the question of joint control of the industry by representatives from the side which represents, for the most part, the consumer and representatives of the workmen who are producers. Nationalisation in the old sense is no longer attractive. As a matter of fact you can have nationalisation but still be in no better position than you are now under private ownership. That is the experience of institutions which have been State owned and State controlled for many years."

Frank Hodges then developed the argument on control, saying:

"Now, is it any good to have these mines nationalised unless we are going to exercise some form of control as producers? If not, the whole tendency will be towards the power of bureaucracy. We shall be given no status at all in the industry, except to be the mere producers, as we have been in the past years. Under State ownership the workmen should be desirous of having something more than the mere question of wages or the mere consideration of employment; the workmen should have some directive power in the industry in which they are engaged."

His last point was:

"Finally, this Federation may have to embrace within its four walls every man engaged in the industry, whether he be a collier producing coal or whether he be a colliery manager. Under an effective system of control we must make provision for every man in the country, whether manual worker or brain worker."

This standpoint, which by another speaker in a later debate was described as "Guildist" was thought by Frank Hodges to be distinctive, for he ended with the phrase:

"I hold these views, and unless they are accompanied by an effective form of working class control, I do not believe that nationalisation will do any good for anybody."

11 THE FINAL MONTHS OF THE WAR

By mid-summer, 1918, the enemy's spring offensives on the Eastern Front and on the Western Front had reached and passed their climax. In the East the imposed Peace of Brest Litovsk had been signed at the beginning of March: in the West the German and Austrian offensives had come to a standstill by the third week of June: and one month later the German retreat across the Marne began. In the first week of August, 1918, British troops were landed in the North and in the South of Russia, at Archangel on the White Sea and at Baku on the Caspian Sea. On the 6th August the British Government issued a "Declaration to Russian Peoples", stating that they had "no intention of interfering in Russian politics". The actions of the British military authorities and their support of anti-Soviet forces spoke otherwise. It is doubtful if the statement was swallowed anywhere—save in the House of Commons. It was not readily accepted in the Rhondda, where for the Monthly Meeting of September, the Standard Lodge put forward a resolution:

7.—Bydd Cyfrinfa y Standard yn cynyg.—"Fod y Cyfarfod hwn yn protestio yn gryf yn erbyn y Cyfryngiad Arfogol yn Rwsia, mewn gwrthwynebiad i ddymuniadau cyhoeddedig Llywodraeth y Soviet, ac mewn gwrthwynebiad uniongyrchol i ddadganiad yn ffafr hunan-benderfyniad yr holl Genedloedd. Y mae y Cyfarfod hwn yn credu y byddai dymchweliad gweinyddiaeth y Soviet yn drychineb i symudiadau Llafurawl drwy yr holl fyd, ac yn agored i'w gamesbonio fel tystiolaeth o fwriad y Llywodraethau i wneyd Rhyfel ar y Dosbarthiadau Gweithiol. Y mae yn galw ar y Llywodraeth Bryndeinig i roddi fyny ei gwladlywiaeth bresenol o berthynas i Rwsia, ac i gynyg i Rwsia y cynorthwy celfyddydol a threfniadol sydd yn angenrheidiol er ei hadwneuthuriad."[1]

[1]"That this Meeting strongly protests against the Armed Intervention in Russia, in opposition to the declared wishes of the Soviet Government, and in direct contradiction of the Allies' pronouncement in favour of the self-determination of all Nations. This meeting believes that the overthrow of the Soviet Administration would be a disaster to the Organised Labour Movement throughout the world, and could only be construed as evidence of the intention of the Governments to make War on the Working Classes. It calls on the British Government to abandon its present policy with regard to Russia, and to offer to Russia the technical and economic aid required for her reconstruction."

In the District Committee on 9th September there was a difference of opinion on the question which led to the Standard Lodge resolution being deferred to the October Monthly Meeting, at which it was carried.

By September Allied offensives had developed not only in Flanders and North Italy but in Palestine against the Turks and Macedonia against the Bulgarians. By the first week of October the German and Austro-Hungarian Governments had sent Notes to President Woodrow Wilson proposing an armistice. Before mid-November the Red Flag had been hoisted on all German warships at Kiel, revolution had broken out in Berlin, the Kaiser Wilhelm II had abdicated, to be followed three days later by the Emperor Karl of Austria. On 11th November hostilities on the Western Front ceased at 11 a.m.

That same week James Winstone submitted the following resolution to a Special Conference in Cardiff. It was unanimously adopted by the whole of the delegates standing:

"That this Conference of South Wales Miners' Delegates place on record our high appreciation and heartfelt gratitude to those brave comrades who have fought in the Great War, and our sincere sympathy with the relations of those killed.

"We further join with the Men and Women of all countries in Europe struggling for Freedom, and pledge ourselves not to abate our energies until the profound general causes of war have been removed and a just and enduring Peace arranged by and between the Democracies of the Countries involved in the war" (16 xi 1918).

This utterance was in strong contrast to the demands of the Conservatives and Coalition Liberals in the campaign for the mid-December General Election with their insistence on "Hang the Kaiser !" and (in the words of a Tory Minister) "Squeeze Germany like a lemon—until the pips squeak."

But for the South Wales miners the war was over. The questions that had been thought out for over a year would now come to the fore. There would be gains and losses. But few, other than the bereaved families, dwelt upon the losses that exceeded all that was recorded of previous wars.[1] The Prime Minister and those with him who were issuing a false prospectus of land and homes "fit for heroes to live in" as well as clamouring for Queen Victoria's grandson to be put to death by hanging swept the polls. They received nearly five and half million votes against less than two and a half million for Labour, one and a quarter million for the Liberals, a quarter million for Irish Nationalists and nearly half a million for Sinn Fein. The Coalition representation in the Commons was over five hundred seats out of 707.

[1]The strength of the British Empire armies by November 1918 was 193,192 officers; 5,144,841 other ranks. Total casualties (approximately) were: killed (including missing) 46,000 officers; 960,000 other ranks. Allied casualties (French and Russian together) ran into well over three million killed. The United States army had approximately 35.000 killed.

APPENDIX

Excerpts from *Industrial Unionism and the Mining Industry.*

The Report of Vernon Hartshorn and his two fellow-commissioners in July 1917 failed to dispel the fog that for six years had hung around the word "syndicalism". An attempt to sort out the various socialist standpoints appeared that same year in a polemical book[1] (excerpts from which are given below) which sought to show that trade unionism in general and the MFGB in particular had failed, in that their "bases, structure, object and policy" were all wrong. It also put the case (together with "the arrangement of industries", 30 in all) as argued by Daniel De Leon in the United States.

Against Tom Mann, whose militant agitation had played so big a role in 1910/11/12, the polemic descended into scurrility: Mann had stolen the thunder of the sect.

★ ★ ★

On the front page of its Party-owned organ, *The Socialist*, in the October issue of 1905, under the heading "The Press in the Class Struggle", there appeared the following declaration:

"We, the National Executive Committee of the Socialist Labour Party of Great Britain, hail with unqualified approval the formation of the Industrial Workers of the World at Chicago, 27th June, 1905, and pledge ourselves to work incessantly for the formation and success of the British wing of that movement in place of the British so-called Trade Unions, based as these are on capitalist principles."

★ ★ ★

The Socialist Labour Party alone owns its own Press.

★ ★ ★

The founder of the I.L.P. (Keir Hardie) wrote in the *Labour Leader* of 2nd and 9th September, 1904, "An Indictment of the Class War", in which he denied that principle and also the theories of Marx and Engels upon which modern Socialism is based. In his election address issued to Merthyr Tydfil Electors, in 1900, he said:

"I first learned my socialism in the New Testament, where I still find my chief inspiration".

★ ★ ★

The 1917 Conference of the I.L.P. ruled out also a motion to propagate Industrial Unionism, while Mr. Bruce Glazier, writing on the first anniversary of James Connolly's death, made it plain that the I.L.P. viewed with great sorrow the advance of Ireland's Socialist Martyr from Reformism to Revolutionary Unionism and Revolutionary

[1]"Industrial Unionism and the Mining Industry" by George Harvey (Student of Ruskin College, Oxford in 1908. Editor of *The Socialist*, 1911-12) published by the author at Miners Hall, Wardley Colliery, Pelaw-on-Tyne.

Political action. On all sides Revolution is debarred; I.L.P.ism stands for Capitalism, State-Ownership pure and simple, hence the attitude of its **privately-owned** official organ.

As with the I.L.P. and *Labour Leader*, so with "Justice" and the Social Democratic Federation. That body expelled from its ranks members who sympathised with **Industrial** Unionism, and threatened others who might go that way. To the end of its existence it abhorred Industrial Unionism, remaining a pure and simple political reform organisation. It opened its privately-owned organ *Justice* to opponents of Revolutionary Unionism.

★ ★ ★

The Clarion is another privately-owned **Socialist** opponent of Industrial Unionism.

★ ★ ★

The prosecution of Syndicalists in 1912 drew a great deal of attention to the doctrines of Syndicalism. The Capitalist Press, ever desirous of confusing the working class, set out to educate the workers along the usual line. Thus anything was trotted out as Syndicalism. Industrial Unionism was said to be Syndicalism, extreme Socialism was said to be Syndicalism, Socialists were described as Syndicalists. Consequently few people are clear on the difference between Syndicalism and Industrial Unionism.

★ ★ ★

What is Syndicalism? How came it to be advocated in England? These are interesting questions.

"Syndicat" is the French word for the English "Union".

The term "Syndicat" up to 1895, stood in France, for Unions which were of the type of our pure and simple Trade Unions. After that date the term "Syndicalism" gained ground. It originated from the policy which came into prominence at that time. This policy was a departure from the old orthodox policy. It substituted "Revolutionary Trade Union Action" for "Reformist Action", "Direct Action" for "Political Action". It advocated the General Strike and Sabotage, and when the Revolution was accomplished, production was to be controlled by Syndicats or Trade Unions.[1]

[1]Syndicalism rejects the centralisation of power and centralisation of funds. True, there are Federations of **Syndicats**, but they have no central power. The local **Syndicats** have full autonomy. Thus the central power is practically nil. We know how local-self-glorification and local fighting funds have proved useless in Britain, but in France the position is even worse. Syndicalism is not even so advanced as our **Trade** Unionism and therefore cannot even expand to fight the masters let alone burst the shell of capitalism. Its schemes are wild and **erratic**, and marked by lack of method. In a modern capitalistic State, Syndicalism can only be the means to one end—working class degradation.

What is "Direct Action ?" **Direct Action** was first named in France. From France it spread to other countries.

Sabotage is putting the machinery on strike, through temporarily disabling it. If the Syndicalist is a railroader, he cuts wires, puts cement in switches, signals, etc., runs locomotives into pits and tries to disorganise the railroad system. If he is a machinist, he oftentimes hides, steals, or **destroys** some small indispensable machine part which is difficult to replace.—Earl C. Ford and W. Z. Foster, in a pamphlet published by the Mother Earth (Anarchist) Publishing Co.

* * *

That is Anarchism pure and simple, and the idea that **local** unions shall carry on production when the revolution is accomplished is an idea in accordance more with the times of Jesus than with modern times. Such an idea, with its repudiation of a directing central authority and organic connection in Unionism, is Anarchist Communism—the contrary of Industrial Democracy as understood by students of sociology from the socialist standpoint.

* * *

How came Syndicalism to England? In 1909 Tom Mann left Australia for Britain and, after a trip to Paris, came back to England, to advocate **Syndicalism. Industrial Unionism** was good enough for him in Australia and South Africa, but in Britain it was not popular at all. His trip to Paris brought him into contact with revolutionary Trade Unionism called Syndicalism. There he found the Confederation Generale du Travail or General Confederation of Labour, which is composed of National Federations and Trade Councils—National and Local Sections. Their policy of Direct Action and the General Strike, and their anti-political character, being summed up as "Syndicalism", Tom Mann hit upon the idea of Industrial "Syndicalism". At the Conference which he held in Manchester on 26th November, 1910, he told the Delegates "We must use a word understood on the Continent as we are internationalists, and—**Syndicalism** is the word.

At this Conference the following resolution was carried:

"That whereas the sectionalism that characterises the Trades Union Movement of today is utterly incapable of effectively fighting the Capitalist Class and securing the economic freedom of the workers, this Conference declares that the time is now ripe for the industrial organisation of all workers on the basis of class, and not trade or craft, and that we hereby agree to form a Syndicalist Educational League to propagate the principles of Syndicalism throughout the British Isles, with a view to merging all existing unions into one compact organisation for each industry, including all labourers of every industry, in the same organisation with skilled workers."

So that is how Syndicalism came to Britain—to suit the interests of one who seems to be a professional showman, and one feels sorry that the miners should pay handsomely to Mann, and people like him, to speak to them at their Annual Picnics, where the most learned and capable men and women of the working class movement alone should exercise that privilege. No wonder the workers are confused.

Industrial Unionism versus Guild Socialism. One of the latest middle-class theories to be developed is that of National Guildism, or "Guild Socialism".

The National Guildsmen came mainly from the Fabian Society, being a reaction against the spoon-ladled political Collectivism of the Webbs, and also of the Labour Party. They discovered what the S.L.P. discovered a decade before, viz.: lack of revolutionary aim and methods in Trade Unionism. They also discovered, likewise late in the day—that Abolition of the Wages System should be the objective.

As an Industrial Unionist, as one of the advocates of the theory in its fight for establishment in Britain, as one familiar with its literature from the early days, it does seem to me that Guild Socialism is simply Industrial Unionism half digested by a middle-class Socialist mind and thrown back to "the public" mixed up with all the silly nonsense of State and Municipal Socialism which has ever dominated the "middle-class" drawing-room Socialist.

CHAPTER SIX

THE SPIRIT OF REVOLUTION

1 THE MINERS MILITANT

As the wars of intervention in Russia were gaining momentum the great war of the British Empire and its Allies against the central empires came to a sudden end.[1] The sailors of the High Seas Fleet at Kiel hoisted the Red Flag and the rulers of Germany fled helter-skelter. While the British military chiefs were working out their plans for a far-off victory in the late summer of 1919, the enemy had collapsed : the morale of the troops, complained the Prussian generals, was undermined by a year of Bolshevik revolutionary propaganda. With the cease-fire on 11th November, 1918, there came in Britain an indescribable surge of relief from what they had endured of the horror and agony of over fifty months—an emotional tide, "the tide of victory". It was to be canalised by Prime Minister Lloyd George, "the man who won the war," into a mid-December General Election which hurled his motley coalition government into four years of office.

But the tide of revolution soon caught up with the tide of victory. The whole of Europe, confided Lloyd George to the Allies in March 1919, was "filled with the spirit of revolution" : and, he added, "the whole existing order in its political, social and economic aspects is questioned by the masses of the population from one end of Europe to the other."[2] From one end of the immensely swollen British Empire to the other there was anger and revolt, from Ireland, "the oldest colony" to the "great dependencies" of Egypt and India.

Ill-conceived schemes for demobilisation of the five million in the British Empire armies in January 1919 sparked off fifty mutinies—"a convulsion of indiscipline" amongst the soldiers—and brought from the coal-pits the claim for "full maintenance at Trade Union rates of

[1] **Cardinal Dates in Autumn 1918.**

October 14th —Invading British forces (which by 4th August had landed at Vladivostok on the Pacific—as also at Archangel in the North and Baku on the Caspian) reach Irkutsk on Lake Baikal.

October 29th —Mutiny began in the German Navy.

October 30th —The Ottoman Empire signed an armistice.

October 31st —Revolution broke out in Vienna and Budapest.

November 4th —Red Flag hoisted on all German warships at Kiel.

November 9th —Abdication of the Kaiser Wilhelm in Berlin: Republic proclaimed.

[2] *Impact of the Russian Revolution* by R. Page Arnot, p.150.

wages for mineworkers unemployed through demobilisation." Workers' and soldiers' delegates were seen to be of one accord.

The "spirit of revolution" was abroad in the coalfields where "the whole existing order" and not only the private ownership of mines and minerals was being questioned. The miners, confronted directly by the British Government, caught sight of new horizons : they began to have a heightened consciousness, beyond the ordinary reach of their trade union outlook, that theirs was a common struggle with the workers in every capitalist country and with subject peoples. There was an accession of international solidarity against the governments and the ruling circles of imperialism.

The miners of South Wales shared this mood : they would not put up with half-measures. The Executive Council on December 30, 1918, pressed for the national programme demands on shorter hours and on nationalisation of mines to be included with the demobilisation claim : while at the mid-January national conference their vote was cast for a fifty per cent increase in wages instead of the thirty per cent for which Thomas Ashton had asked the Coal Controller in the last days of December 1918. At Southport on 14th and 15th January, 1919, the proposal from South Wales to incorporate the hours and nationalisation portions of the national programme with the demobilisation demand was adopted and elaborated in great detail. On 16th January the delegates from Lancashire and South Wales insisted on an advance of 50 per cent on current rates (exclusive of the three shillings war wage) and carried their opposition to a card vote against the Executive Committee's proposal for 30 per cent.

On Thursday, 30th January, the first item on the agenda of the MFGB Executive Committee was "Disorder and unofficial strikes in Lanarkshire". Jacob Tonnor gave a report of these happenings, "of men prevented from attending their work by massed pickets", and that "the whole County is now idle". He appealed to the Executive "to issue a special manifesto to Scotland" to urge the men to remain at their work. Letters were then read from the Lancashire and Cheshire Miners' Federation, the South Wales Miners' Federation and the Nottinghamshire Miners' Association on Wages and Policy, and were treated "as matters of urgency" by the Executive Committee. They resolved :

"In view of the serious unrest at present existing in the mining districts regarding the wages question, we are desirous of having a reply by Monday next, 3rd February, at latest."

On Friday, 31st January, 1919, a conference was held at the Ministry of Labour between ten representatives of various Government Departments and the sixteen representatives of the Miners' Federation of Great Britain. The miners' proposals had reached a Cabinet that, beset with mutinies and "lightning strikes" and threats of stoppage, was anxiously seeking to cope with this "Bolshevist menace," which had rendered some of its members well-nigh distracted.[1] So the Ministers decided to play for time. They asked that the miners, already impatient at the delay and subjected since mid-January to a hostile Press campaign, wait yet another ten days for an answer. The leaders, inured to Government tactics, took it calmly enough and that day passed a resolution urging miners "who have struck work in order to realise more speedily the resolutions as passed at the Southport Conference" to continue working "until a National Conference decides otherwise." (31 i 1919).

But the men in the pits were set on edge by this further delay. Consequently when the Cabinet, after "very anxious consideration," gave its reply on Monday, 10th February, and this considered reply amounted to an offer of 1/- a day and the promise of a Committee of Inquiry, there was an outburst of wrath.

On Tuesday, 11th February, the House of Commons was commanded by the King "to attend His Majesty immediately in the House of Peers" after which the new Parliament settled down to business with debate in each House upon "His Majesty's Gracious Speech from the Throne." First came the Rt. Hon. William Adamson, for many years secretary of the Fife and Kinross Miners' Association and now the newly-elected leader of the Labour Party in Parliament. He devoted a great part of his speech to "the Labour unrest". He declared himself and the Labour Party to be firmly opposed to "the spirit of revolution" saying, "As a constitutionalist, I speak for a party that will not give encouragement either to revolution or to unofficial action in the Labour movement."

This statement was gratefully received by the Prime Minister who said, "I am very glad to hear from the right hon. Gentleman of his intention to support the Government in every honest endeavour they may make to deal with the social difficulties of today: we can claim no more". Lloyd George, hurriedly back from the meeting of all the Allied and Associated Powers in Paris, then told the Commons the reason for his post-haste:

"Every morning before I went to the Peace Conference I had messages from London about a strike, and when I returned in the evening about another strike, trade union leaders thrown over, and bargains repudiated. I do not mind saying it, I think it would have been to the advantage of the Peace Conference had I been able to remain there for a few days longer."

Lloyd George then began an attack on the miners by suggesting that their demands would mean "four shillings a ton on coal" and that such increases "may deprive us of hundreds of millions of trade in all parts of the world", which in turn meant "throwing hundreds of thousands of men out of work". He equated the internal strike threats, especially those "with ulterior motives, to hold up and to overthrow

[1]See Appendix I to this Chapter "Hysteria in the Cabinet."

the existing order", with the struggle just concluded against the external enemy :

"May I say, in all solemnity, on behalf of the Government, we are determined to fight Prussianism in the industrial world as we fought it on the Continent of Europe with the whole might of the nation."

In his peroration he called on "all classes of the community" to rally with the same spirit "they have exhibited in the face of an equally great menace" and thundered that "no section of the community, however powerful it may be, can or will be allowed to hold up the whole nation."

On Wednesday, 12th February, seven-score miners' delegates found themselves once more in Southport, this time at the Temperance Institute. The Conference had been transferred from London because of the underground railways ("the workers were on strike") and the likelihood of a London blackout by the Electrical Trades Union.

Smillie first explained how, at a meeting in Whitehall on 10th February, the Minister of Labour had made a short statement to the Executive Committee, "a statement brimming over with sympathy for our class, and emphasising the importance of our class", and that he then "read to us the document now in your hands". The opinion of the Executive was that "it is a very cleverly prepared document. It is not merely clever but it goes the length of being a cunning statement intended for public consumption; intended to be used by the Press; and intended to influence the general public of this country against our class".

This immediately introduced a serious atmosphere into the Conference. Smillie then said, "It was ill-advised on the part of the Prime Minister to speak as he spoke last night. He was not speaking to the House of Commons so much as he was speaking to this Federation. He was actually going the length of threatening this Conference . . . I told him two and a half years ago, that no threats that he or the Government might make would intimidate this Miners' Federation of ours, and none of us here will in any way, I think, be guided by what he said last night but will be guided by the best interests of our own class, and the best interests of the nation."

The threat had the reverse effect.

Conference rejected the terms offered by the Government "as being no answer to our claims" and took the decision that a national ballot vote be taken. On the next day, they accepted the Executive's recommendation : "We therefore strongly urge the members to vote in favour of a national stoppage until our demands are conceded."

In his closing remarks Robert Smillie said :

"If we have to fight we will be absolutely united together as brothers, and there will be no quarrelling amongst ourselves of any kind, and that we will let every class of the community know how the miners can conduct industrial warfare should it be necessary to do so."

A ballot paper with the fourfold claim was drawn up immediately as follows:

The Strike Ballot (to be returned by the 22nd February). 1. Application for 30 per cent increase in wages. 2. Six-hour day. 3. Full maintenance at trade union rates of wages for mineworkers unemployed through demobilisation. 4. Nationalisation of mines. 5. The Government having failed to grant any of the above proposals are you in favour of a national strike to secure that? Yes. No. Place a cross opposite Yes or No in the space provided for the purpose.

For four weeks the demands had met with a hostile Press but now the strike recommendation was met by such a torrent of intemperate abuse reinforced by daily Government advertisements that the miners' leaders were impelled to make public their reply.[1] The Government's efforts were seconded by C. B. Stanton, M.P., and others of the National Democratic Labour Party saying that "a stoppage of work now could help Germany," telling the miners to stay underground, and "still bidding crouch whom the rest bade aspire."

The result of the ballot vote was sufficiently startling; nearly a six to one majority in favour of a strike. The figures were: for a stoppage, 615,164: against stoppage, 105,082; majority for stoppage, 510,082. There were some anomalous features in these results. Whereas amongst the 19 Districts the majorities for stoppage had run from 10 to 1 in Yorkshire, to 11 to 1 in Lancashire, 12 to 1 in Nottinghamshire, they leaped up to 17 to 1 in the case of the Midland Federation (with 52,599 votes to 3,021); in the case of South Wales the majority was much less overwhelming and was little more than 3 to 1 (with 117,302 votes to 38,261).

Whatever was it that brought about this anomalous result?

The vote was to take place in the South Wales coalfield on Wednesday, 19th February. On Monday, 17th, Tom Richards, M.P., General Secretary of the SWMF, gave an interview to the *South Wales Daily News*, which set down his response to the question "How should the miners vote, Mr. Richards?"

"Most emphatically I say they should vote against the strike. I consider that the decision of the Conference in submitting such grave issues to ballot without proper time being secured for their consideration to be altogether unwarranted. For this reason (besides others I might

[1]"To this ballot paper Sir Robert Horne objected in a letter addressed to Robert Smillie but published in the Press before Mr. Smillie had even received it. This made it appear as though the Government were getting at any pretext to discredit the Miners' Federation. This intention became perfectly plain a few days later when the Government, at the cost of thousands of pounds of public money, inserted advertisements in most of the newspapers urging the miners to vote against the advice of the Conference. A fortnight later, Mr. Smillie elicited the information that Government Departments had supplied the newspapers with alleged 'facts' as to the effect on industry of the miners' proposals"—Official Reply to the Government's Proposals signed by Robert Smillie and Frank Hodges (13 ii 1919).

advance) I have no hesitation in advising every miner who attaches any importance to my advice to vote against it.

"I do this as a believer in the justice of their claims, and as an advocate who will not be content until their dreams are realised."

This advice was heeded throughout the coalfield : hence the relatively low majority for a strike, something unexampled in South Wales.

The *Western Mail* headlined "Leaders Oppose Strike" and "Older Workers' Indictment of Young Irresponsibles," added : "It may be confidently stated that the majority of the members of the Executive Council of the SWMF entertained the same views as the General Secretary." Meantime at a mass meeting held by the Merthyr Tydfil District of the SWMF at the Olympia Rink, the miners' agent, Noah Ablett, said he was very distressed and sorry to find "the apostle of constitutionalism —the one man who of all men had always been preaching throughout a lifetime that whatever was determined in a democratic manner, whatever men's views might be individually, if they were to be strong as an organisation they must go together—was the first to 'break out' at a most critical time in the history of the Federation. (Shame). Today the Press was full of paid advertsiments—paid for 'by your money'— to convince you that you are wrong" (18 ii 1919).

A motion by Idris Davies to ask that Richards tender his resignation was spoken against by Ablett, who asked them to defer action "pending a personal explanation by Mr. Richards." A month later the Executive Council, having received several letters protesting against the action of the General Secretary "in relation to the ballot for tendering notices" and asking that he should tender his resignation, resolved :—

"That in the opinion of this Council, after hearing the explanation of Mr. Richards in regard to the interview before the Ballot, the whole matter should drop as we consider his past services to the Federation (better known to the Council than to the rank and file) more than counter-balances anything there may be in this question" (17 iii 1919).

The incident showed the extremely high regard paid by the miners in each coalfield to the advice of their leaders—a matter which was favourably commented on by Smillie and others that same year when they praised the "loyalty" of their followers—almost as though they had been there not by election but by right divine. It also brought out that each coalfield, like each English county, was self-contained, almost a mini-nationality. Within the South Wales coalfield this held true for each valley, so that, to a degree beyond that indicated in the analysis by the Webbs,[1] officials, once elected, were in practice irremovable. Hence it was impossible, with an Executive Council mainly made up of miners' agents, for Ablett or S. O. Davies to realise their dream of a centralised democracy in the coalfield. Equally, only in elections of the three representatives on the Executive Committee of the Miners'

[1]*Industrial Democracy*, by Sidney and Beatrice Webb (1898).

Federation of Great Britain was truly democratic choice made by the coalfield as a whole.

2 LLOYD GEORGE AND THE MINERS

Prime Minister Lloyd George hurried back to London and invited the MFGB Executive Committee to No. 10 Downing Street where on Thursday, 20th February, he combined threats (if the ballot resulted in a decision to strike the whole power of the forces of the State including the control of food supplies would be used against the miners) with promises that (if they would postpone the expiry of strike notices from 15th March to a later date) an immediate inquiry, in which miners could take part, would be set up on Monday, 24th February, and its report would be given to Parliament with great promptitude. That afternoon the Executive Committee convened a Special Conference "to consider the statement of the Prime Minister" (20 ii 1919) : and on the next morning the Prime Minister was to be told "that this Executive has decided to make no recommendation to that Conference".

Leaving the Prime Minister to guess what might happen, the Committee then considered how industrial action might be supplemented by the mining M.P.s urging "the whole of the claims of the miners upon Parliament" when the occasion would arise "on Monday next". They resolved "That we urge the Labour Party very strongly to press upon the Government that the sections dealing with wages and hours should be conceded without waiting for any Committee of Enquiry" (21 ii 1919).

On the Monday, 24th February, when a Bill would be introduced to give special statutory authority to the proposed Coal Industry Commission, their own mining M.P., the Rt. Hon. William Adamson, re-elected earlier that month as Labour Party Chairman, would move to omit wages and hours from the Bill and to concede these demands without further delay.

On that weekend, 21st to 24th February, much water flowed under the bridges at Westminster.[1] By Tuesday, 25th February, emboldened

[1]There had been a great deal of bluff in Lloyd George's statement to the miners on the morning of Thursday, 20th February. That evening at the house of a mutual friend Lloyd George met the Webbs and tried "to sound out the other side" as to whether the miners could accept a commission and with what sort of personnel. But in this encounter the Webbs also did some "sounding out". The next day Beatrice Webb wormed out of the Secretary to the War Cabinet, Tom Jones (who was a Fabian Socialist) the proposed names. They turned out to be anti-nationalisers. Smillie was informed of Lloyd George's proposed tricks. He knew that a strike under the conditions of that spring would have won all the miners' demands. He knew also that Lloyd George was bluffing: but he recoiled from the suffering that he knew would be entailed by the strike. The sort of 50/50 Commission the miners' stipulated would, it seemed to him, have avoided the suffering and gained aims the miners sought. It was a way out of the impasse. By Saturday the 22nd the points had been worked out between Sidney Webb and Smillie. The two had worked together closely on the war time War Emergency Workers' National Committee.

by the overwhelming ballot vote for stoppage, the miners' committee decided to recommend to the Conference on the morrow "that if we secure the right to nominate one half of the members of the proposed Commission we do form part thereof". Then if the Government were to accept this stipulation the strike would be postponed for a single week from the Ides of March.

A South Wales delegate immediately moved that the conference take no part in the proposed Commission. Noah Ablett briefly took the same standpoint. Then S. O. Davies said "The ballot has gone overwhelmingly along the lines we recommended from the last Southport Conference; and today we are seeking ways and means to undermine that ballot". On Lloyd George, S. O. Davies said : "While this same gentlemen was making his speech when meeting the Executive, expressing his sympathy and grave concern as regards the condition of the miners, I at any rate as a coalminer cannot forget the fact that he was the very man responsible for what happened on the Clyde the other day. I hold him as head of the Government responsible. I hold him, the man who is attempting to foist this Commission upon us, responsible for the tactics used; the machine guns, bared bayonets, on the Clyde.[1] I do not think we should accept gifts from the Greeks".

But after a moving appeal by Robert Smillie it was carried "That providing the Government agree to this Federation having the right of appointment or approval of half the Commission, this Conference agrees to take part in this Commission". The vote was 779 *nem con.*

Would the Prime Minister and the Government accept the stipulation of the miners ? Robert Smillie said : "I think it ought to be a clear yes or no. There ought to be no higgling or quibbling about this. We ought to be able to get a yes or no from the Prime Minister whether we have the right to appoint or approve of half the Commission."

The Prime Minister was given ten minutes by Smillie to reach a decision. Lloyd George yielded to the ultimatum. The strike notices were postponed to 22nd March. The composition of the Commission was finally reached about 1st March with Mr. Justice Sankey in the Chair.[2]

Much was done to impress the miners and the public with the importance and thoroughness of this Commission which occupied the King's Robing Room in the Palace of Westminster, while the pro-

[1]The reference was to the reading of the Riot Act in Glasgow and arrest of Gallacher and Shinwell on 31st January as planned in the War Cabinet that same week.

[2]John Sankey (1866-1948); created Viscount Sankey of Moreton in 1932; Lancing College and Jesus College, Oxford; called to Bar and Middle Temple, 1892; K.C. 1909, Judge of the King's Bench Division, 1914-28; Lord Chancellor, 1929-35; Hon. Freeman of the City of Cardiff, 1934.

ceedings not merely secured but maintained a prominence as front page news day after day.[1]

The witnesses for the Miners' Federation were Straker from Northumberland on nationalisation; Robertson from Scotland on standard of life (housing, health, education and accidents); Potts of Yorkshire on hours and output; Hartshorn from South Wales on wages.

In the course of his evidence Vernon Hartshorn had said:

"As I say there, even if such figures as I put in prove to be inaccurate, and even if the other side can prove that on the question of the standard of living, or the cost of living, wages have kept pace with the increase in the cost, yet the miners still say that the pre-war standard of living was so inadequate that they must insist upon a substantial advance in wages.

"I think in considering this demand the general conditions of the miner's life and the nature of his employment must be taken into account. If you take the ordinary working day of any miner (I have in mind a representative case in my own district) the colliery starts winding coal at 7 in the morning. The men have to be down somewhere between 6 and 7 o'clock—say an average of half-past-six. They come up between 3 and 4—say an average of half-past-three. So that we get the miner in his pit clothes from about 5 in the morning until, say, half-past-three when he ascends the pit, and by the time he gets home and has his food and a bath and gets out of his pit clothes again, it is half-past-four. Of course I think that a miner is at work all the time he is in his pit clothes. A man has to leave his bed in the cold winter mornings and come down into a cheerless kitchen without any fire. He cannot take his clothes up to his bedroom, but he has to come down to change, and the moment he gets his pit clothes on he cannot move from chair to chair or room to room. Every movement he makes leaves its mark and it is the same when he comes home.

"The collier's work is done in the bowels of the earth in the darkness. During the whole of the winter months a miner never gets more than one or two hours of daylight on any day except Sunday. I know from personal experience, having worked at the coal face

[1]A third of a century later, the publication of *Beatrice Webb's Diaries*, disclosed much that happened behind the scenes and also raised the curtain on the public scene in her entry of the next month:

"March 12th—I looked in at the Coal Commission this afternoon. It was a scene of strange contrasts. The Robing Room of the House of Lords is appropriately decorated with highly ornate frescoes of faded and sentimental pomp. But today it is serving as the crowded stage—crowded by an audience of all the interests in a mood of exasperated anxiety—for a body calling itself a Royal Commission on the Mining Industry, but in its proceedings far more like a revolutionary tribunal, sitting in judgment on the capitalist owners and organisers of the nation's industries until the 20th of March.

"The ostensible business of the Commission is to examine and report on the miners' claim for a rise in wages and a reduction of hours; but owing to the superior skill of the miners' representatives it has become a State trial of the coal owners and royalty owners conducted on behalf of the producers and consumers of the product, culminating in the question 'Why not nationalise the industry'?"

myself for about twelve years, that it is a very arduous occupation and very laborious. I know when I was a growing lad it was quite a common thing for me, after I got home in the night and after getting my food, to lie down on the hearthstone in front of the fire, feeling too tired and stiff and lifeless to get a bath and rest. In the morning, when I was hauled out of bed, I felt it was like going to the gallows to get up at all. I think that is the common experience of the miner, having regard to the nature of his occupation."

On 20th March those three Reports were presented to Parliament, Bonar Law announced that the Government had adopted the Sankey Report "in spirit and in letter." He also saw fit to say that if a strike took place "the Government would use all the resources of the State without hesitation", a threat at once resented by the Labour Members in Parliament and by the delegates to the Conference meeting.[1]

When the 177 delegates (with no fewer than 45 delegates from South Wales including six M.P.s and the whole of its Executive Council) assembled in the Central Hall, Westminster, they were given an adequate summary of the Interim Reports published the previous day.

Robert Smillie succinctly explained the provisions of the Report signed by the Chairman and three other Commissioners (always referred to as "the Sankey Report"). After considerable discussion and questioning, especially from South Wales, Hodges read the following letter addressed to the Secretary of the Miners' Federation from 11 Downing Street, Whitehall, S.W.1., and dated 21st March, 1919:

"Dear Sir,

Speaking in the House of Commons last night I made a statement with regard to the Government's policy in connection with the Report of the Coal Industry Commission. I have pleasure in confirming, as I understand you wish me to do, my statement that the Government are prepared to carry out in the spirit and in the letter the recommendations of Mr. Justice Sankey's Report.

Yours faithfully,

A. BONAR LAW".

At the adjourned Conference of 26th March, 1919, the President of South Wales, the Right Hon. William Brace, one of the six Members of Parliament in their delegation of 45, moved to take a ballot of the men on the question of the acceptance or non-acceptance of the terms and was seconded by Tom Greenall of Lancashire. Smillie had said from the Chair: "If you agree to take a ballot, the Executive asks you to strongly recommend the men to ballot in favour of a settlement on the lines indicated". Noah Ablett of South Wales moved "that this Conference do not recommend the men to accept the terms which have been gained by the Executive Committee from the Government". He said: "I do not deny that an advancement has been made but the

[1]See *The Miners : Years of Struggle*, Ch. VII.

advance is nothing like worthy of the movement. What have we got? I do not see why we should wait four months before the 7 hours comes into operation, and that we ought not to wait two years for the six-hour day; because, after all, even at the end of two years, there is no certainty that we shall get it then".

On a vote there were 126 for recommending acceptance of the terms and 37 against.

When the result of the MFGB ballot[1] was declared on 15th April it showed a majority in each of the 19 districts and a nine to one majority overall—693,084 votes for acceptance of the Government's terms and only 76,992 against. So the MFGB Special Conference meeting the next day ordered the withdrawal of the strike notices.

The miners and the whole trade union movement were clear upon the point that the Government had pledged itself to the ending of the private ownership of coal mines. The tension was loosened. The Government had weathered the crisis.

3 SANKEY COMMISSION—SECOND STAGE

On Wednesday, 23rd April, the second stage of the Royal Commission began. During the next two months evidence was taken on 28 days. One hundred and sixteen witnesses were examined and a total of 28,408 questions were put to them. Expert economists were taken

[1]The following is the form of the ballot paper:

Miners' Federation of Great Britain.

Ballot

The Government, as the result of the Coal Industry Commission having offered:

Hours.

1. A reduction of one hour per day in the hours of underground work from 16th July, 1919, and, "subject to the economic position of the industry at the end of 1920", a further reduction of one hour from 13th July, 1921.

Surface Workers' Hours.

2. Forty-six-and-a-half working hours per week, exclusive of meal times, from 16th July, 1919.

Wages.

3. An increase of 2s. per day worked to adult colliery workers and 1s per day worked for colliery workers under 16 years of age employed in coal mines or at the pit heads of coal mines.

(The above to apply as and from 9th January, 1919).

Nationalisation.

In view of the statement in the report of the Chairman of the Commission that "the present system of ownership stands condemned" and that "the colliery worker shall in the future have an effective voice in the direction of the mines", the Government have decided that the Commission must report on the question of nationalisation of the mining industry on 20th May, 1919.

Are you in favour of accepting the above terms? Yes........... No...........

Please put your "X" opposite "Yes" or "No" in the space provided for the purpose.

first, to be followed by owners of mineral royalties, Home Office officials, witnesses as to the working of nationalisation abroad or in the Colonies, technicians, coal owners, coal miners, miners' wives, industrial consumers, managers, expert administrators and sundry others. Of all the matters considered those that attracted greatest public interest were the examination of the royalty owners and, private ownership of the mines having already been condemned, the positive proposals put forward for nationalisation and workers' control.

There was some consternation when Robert Smillie on the 25th April asked that royalty-owning members of the House of Lords be summoned before the Commission, which had power to command attendance. So from 7th May onwards each was examined by the Chairman on the *precis* of his evidence to be submitted. Thereafter cross-examination by members of the Commission was conducted mainly by Robert Smillie and the two other officials of the Miners' Federation with resulting headlines in the newspapers. Foremost in public interest was the evidence of the Most Noble Alan Ian Percy, eighth Duke of Northumberland, with 244,500 acres of proved mineral rights, followed by Charles Stewart Henry Vane-Tempest Stewart, seventh Marquis of Londonderry, and other great coalowners of the North-East coast.

Next came a series of South Wales owners of whom the first was the Most Hon. John Marquess of Bute and Earl of Dumfries.

A very searching cross-examination by Robert Smillie made it seem that these noblemen were "in the dock", for they were treated as though their mere possession of land was in itself reprehensible. It was suggested that their ancestors had acquired land by methods repugnant to fair dealing.

The Marquess of Bute owned 128.582 acres with an output of coal and other minerals averaging 3,241.962 tons per annum, with a sliding scale royalty of 1/6d per ton for one seventh and for the rest of his property fixed royalties[1] of over 6d a ton.

As "nature of roots of title to mineral properties" the first two of twenty-nine properties listed were granted in 1547 and 1550 by King Edward VI (then between ten and fourteen years of age) to Sir William Herbert for quelling "the Rebels in the West parts of this our kingdom of England". In cross-examination it was put to the Marquess:

"In effect the conclusion is generally held in South Wales by those best able to judge that the Executor of the Will of King Henry VIII appropriated for himself, under the signature of the King, who was then ten years of age, all the Lordships of Miskin, Glynrhondda, Llantrisant, Pentyrch and Clun and about 30 more in addition in Monmouthshire and Breconshire. Are you aware of that?"

John, Marquess of Bute, answered "No. I am not aware of that".

[1]Average income from mineral royalties and wayleaves over the period of six years from the time of the Minimum Wage Strike of 1912 was as follows: from royalties £109,277; from wayleaves £6,495.

Frank Hodges, continuing cross-examination, quoted from the *South Wales Daily News* a nine-year-old statement: "For 300 years the industrial classes over a vast territory in South Wales have paid enormous revenues into the pockets of those who have inherited that property. Literally, millions of money for agricultural rents, mineral royalties, ground rents, etc., have been paid and received as the outcome of this gigantic fraud" (1 vi 1912).

As a matter of fact, Sir William Herbert had owned the whole of Cardiff with property that extended from Chepstow to Swansea including "all that valuable mineral property of the Rhonddas and Glyn Neath right down to Neath".

The Right Hon. Courtney Charles Evan Lord Tredegar began the *precis* of his evidence:

"My estates in which there are minerals are situate in the Counties of Monmouth, Glamorgan and Brecon, and my residences are at Tredegar Park in Monmouthshire and Ruperra Castle in Glamorganshire".

Lord Tredegar who succeeded on the death of his uncle in 1913 said:

"The approximate area of my estates in the above three counties is 32,000 acres in Monmouthshire, 7,000 acres in Glamorganshire and 43,000 acres in Breconshire, most of which consists of waste or common lands of the Lordship of Brecon. Of these areas only about 12,500 acres in Monmouthshire, 2,500 in Glamorganshire, and 3,800 acres in Breconshire contain coal. The average annual income received by me in respect of royalties and dead rents on coal for the six years ending 31st December, 1918, after allowing for concessions, were £74,397 and average receipt in respect of wayleaves were £9,430. The coal output of the six years up to 31st December, 1918, was 3,564,500 tons with an average royalty in that period of one thousandth of a penny less than fivepence per imperial ton".

Now, one of the features of Lord Tredegar's evidence which had been looked forward to with lively anticipation by many of the South Wales miners is what would be disclosed about the famous Golden Mile. Resentful of references made to this property in the first stage of the Commission, Lord Tredegar put the following points in his evidence: "Questions have been asked before this Commission by I believe Mr. Smillie and Mr. Tawney with regard to my Tredegar Park Mile Railway. Every statement contained in those questions is incorrect and misleading and founded on entire misapprehension of the facts. No wayleave whatever is charged on traffic passing over the Tredegar Park Mile Railway."

He explained that he was simply in the position of a statutory railway company, that the railway was his and, he said, "I am simply entitled, under various Acts of Parliament, to charge the company using my railway road tolls on the same basis as any other railway company."

This sounded very much better than "wayleaves" until the detail of the amount received was gone into by the Commission. When Robert Smillie took up the cross-examination he asked the question: "Let us see how far they are misleading ?" and went on to elicit further particulars and made it clear that the amount per annum received was £19,000.

"That is less than half the sum that was reported ?"

"Precisely : less than half the sum."

"Do you know what it cost to lay that six miles of railway ?"

"I think I can give it to you. I think it cost £40,000."

"£19,000 a year would be a very fair return surely; or at least a non-fair return on £40,000 ?"

"I quite agree, a fair return."

"You agree ?"

"Yes, I do."

Lord Tredegar had of course much larger resources than that and, as we have seen, this was only a little over one third of his total income. This discussion of the "golden mile" and the way in which the Tredegar family had been able to get so much out of one mile of railway was greeted with the utmost interest in South Wales.

4 IN PLACE OF PRIVATE ENTERPRISE

Damning evidence had been given before the Commission by their own Assessor, Sir Richard Redmayne, K.C.B., H.M. Chief Inspector of Mines, Head of the Production Department of the Controller of Coal Mines, who gave as an opinion "generally accepted" that "The present system of individual ownership of collieries is extravagant and wasteful, whether viewed from the point of view of the coal mining industry as a whole or from the national point of view" : and he listed the advantages of a system of collective production. Such a system could only be carried out by a great coal trust or by a series of trusts or by nationalisation. Sir Richard Redmayne, fearing bureaucracy, was in favour of a Coal Trust.

The evidence on this central question was followed up by scores of witnesses beginning with "scientific economists." There was conflict of ideologies and of interests. A series of professors of political economy were whistled up. Many members of the Fabian Society came to give reasons against private and for public ownership of coal mines. Amongst them was Sidney Webb, himself a Commissioner and for a quarter of a century one of the leading figures of the Socialist International (1889-1914). In his *precis* he amplified what he had written in 1916 on "Nationalisation of the Coal Supply" as part of a Fabian Research Department study[1] and indeed presented the classic Socialist indictment of private enterprise and arguments not only for unification but also against British coal trusts, in favour of public ownership. He said : "A single monopolist concern, having its tentacles in every constituency in the Kingdom, with a million families on its payroll, would be far too powerful a Leviathan to be dragged with a hook by the Home Office."

The cut and thrust of this debate in public about their own future was closely followed by the South Wales miners. Their daily interest was intensified when it came to a discussion of the principles underlying the MFGB resolution (10th July, 1918) for transferring "the entire industry from private ownership and control to State ownership, with joint control and administration by the workers and the State." On this the first witness was G. D. H. Cole, a Fellow of Magdalen College, Oxford; Honorary Secretary of the Labour Research Department; Executive Member of the National Guilds League. Asked about "Guild Socialist" and "a Miners' Guild", Cole gave an explanation :

"Guild Socialism is the name of a school of thought which holds that it is necessary that public ownership should be assumed over the various industries. It holds at the same time that the right way of administering these industries is not through bureaucratic State departments, but through associations which we call Guilds, including the whole necessary working personnel of each industry; that is to say, including not only the manual working elements, but including also the managerial elements, and in fact every person who is necessary to the complete carrying on of the industry or service."

Stating the case for direct participation in control from the standpoint of the worker himself, Cole put forward some general propositions, as follows : "Human freedom, where it exists, is not a name, but a living reality. It implies, not the absence of discipline or restraint, but the imposition of the necessary discipline or restraint either by the individual himself, or by some group of which he forms, and feels himself to form, a part. A democratic or 'free' system of government is one in which every individual not only has a share or vote, but also feels that his share or vote is of some effect by virtue of his community with his fellow-sharers or fellow-voters."

He then went on to say that "This principle of freedom" should apply to industrial organisation which forms in a modern community "so important and so insistent a part in a man's life," and explained how it would apply, stating : "If, then, a man must receive orders, he must, if he is to be free, feel that these orders come from himself, or from some group of which he feels himself to be a part, or from some person whose right to give orders is recognised and sustained by himself and

[1] *How to Pay for the War* (Allen & Unwin) 1916.

by such a group. This means that free industrial organisation must be built up on the co-operation, and not merely on the acquiescence, of the ordinary man from the individual in the pit up to the larger units."

Cole's *precis* was amplified in the examination from a member of the Commission, R. H. Tawney, an old friend who held a similar standpoint. The result was a sort of duet played in front of the public and other members of the Commission. This effect was repeated in the cross-examination by Frank Hodges, described at a Miners' Conference the previous year as a Guild Socialist.

But if evidence of this kind gratified many in the South Wales coalfield where, as we have seen in the Report on Industrial Unrest in summer 1917, the earlier Socialist tenets rife in the old British Sections of the Socialist International were yielding ground to Industrial Unionism on the one hand and Guild Socialism on the other, it was the reverse with some others who were very upset by the proceedings before the Royal Commission.

The mineowners were opposed, as always, to nationalisation : but the new proposals for joint control left them completely aghast and horrified. The Rt. Hon. Baron Gainford of Headlam, vice-chairman of Pease and Partners Limited and for ten years a Minister of the Crown in the Liberal administrations, gave evidence with the authority of the Mining Association of Great Britain on whose Executive Council he had sat for many years. He was opposed to nationalisation and he was also opposed to joint control. A very carefully drawn up anti-nationalisation statement was made by him. He complained that half of the Commissioners put questions which "appear to disclose, in the minds of all of them, a preconceived and settled opinion in favour of the nationalisation of every industry."[1] This he was convinced would be disastrous "to the whole nation and spell ruin to the workers themselves." With great emphasis he said : "I am authorised to say, on behalf of the Mining Association, that if owners are not to be left complete executive control, they will decline to accept the responsibility of carrying on the industry, and though they regard nationalisation as disastrous to the country, they feel they would, in such event, be driven to the only alternative—nationalisation on fair terms" (20 v 1919).

5 SOUTH WALES CONFERENCES

Beyond the dramatic events on a national and international scale of which they were part, the miners in South Wales found the first weeks of 1919 had passed with relative smoothness. The first Special Conference on 25th January, with the Rt. Hon William Brace back in

[1]See Appendix II to this Chapter.

the Chair after nearly five years of office in Coalition Governments, was entirely concerned with the problems of their demobilised soldiers. In February the Executive Council met in new permanent offices within St. Andrew's Crescent, Cardiff, where they were to be for a half-century.

On 23rd February the death of Guy Calthrop, the Coal Controller, was noted with regret; and in the coalfield the miners were voting for a strike. By March the atmosphere in the Conferences showed signs of change. At the end of the month a significant decision came at the second Special Conference with 286 delegates representing 150,867 members; by 186 votes to 100 the workmen were "strongly recommended" to vote "No" to the Government's offer in the ballot.

The workmen, however, paid little heed to the Conference recommendation. Instead they followed the advice in the printed leaflet signed by the national officials, Smillie and Hodges. A bird in the hand was worth two in the bush. By a seven to one majority in South Wales they voted for acceptance of "the Sankey Award."

Throughout the summer of 1919 members of the South Wales Miners' Federation were seen to be taking an enhanced interest in all social and political questions. Problems of local government, for example, came to the fore. The Executive Council proposed that the National body should press the Government through the Labour Party "to demand payment for Local Government Members on the same principle as Members of Parliament" (3 v 1919). On the same day Oliver Harris, J. D. Morgan and V. Hartshorn, M.P., were appointed to attend a three-day Conference called by the Labour Research Department "upon the reorganisation of Local Government, to be held in London on 15th, 16th and 17th May".

It was natural for the Executive Council in Cardiff to decide to participate. At the Conference attended by 320 delegates, the concluding address, on the basis of his local Government experience and previous writings on the subject, was given by George Bernard Shaw, then Chairman of the Labour Research Department. From this time onwards for a number of years the communication between the miners' associations and the Labour Research Department became close and frequent.

The 31st March Conference in Cardiff had resolved "that we call upon the Government to immediately release all conscientious objectors": and in mid-May the Council was asked from Mardy Colliery to take steps "to secure the release of Mr. Arthur Horner who was now in prison as a conscientious objector and who had been appointed Checkweigher at the Mardy Colliery". It was decided that the officials see the Home Secretary and the War Office on this matter. The sequel was Horner's release and installation as checkweigher at Mardy.

When the SWMF Annual Conference was held at the Cory Memorial Hall from 16th to 21st June, 1919, an indication of the as yet meagre support for the "younger militants", who had suffered from the attention of the police, was shown in the election of officers:

President:

Right Hon. W. Brace, M.P.	...	177 votes
Mr. W. H. Mainwaring ...	...	61 votes

Vice-President:

Alderman J. Winstone, J.P.	...	227 votes
Mr. A. J. Cook	...	24 votes

General Treasurer:

Alderman Alfred Onions, M.P.	...	173 votes
Mr. Noah Tromans ...	...	71 votes

A very considerable body of resolutions was prepared and passed dealing with amendments to the Coal Mines Acts, particularly on Safety; Compensation; Pensions; Allowances and Health; Wages details and, under the heading *Constitution, Rules and Procedure*, "that one recognised Union shall be for the whole of the Mining Industry, viz., the Miners' Federation, and this shall be immediately enforced".

Under *Policy* the Conference viewed with great concern "the progressive introduction of machine productive methods into the Coalfield, the more so because of its attendant evils of increasing the already dangerous character of our calling. We also declare our deep conviction that only under a system of National ownership of the Mines of our Country with joint control can the obvious advantages of machine production be obtained both for the miners and the Nation. We therefor reaffirm our strong determination to press forward the National programme with this end in view, believing it to be in the best interests of the community and secure at the same time the welfare and safety of the miners".

The keen realisation of the importance of a Labour paper was shown in the resolutions as follows:

"That we urge upon the Coalfield the necessity of supporting the *Daily Herald*, both morally and financially.

"That a South Wales edition of the *Daily Herald* be asked for; that if necessary the proprietors be subsidised by the South Wales Miners' Federation for this purpose".

Finally, on the question which had first been raised in the Rhondda District, of the attack on the Workers' Republic of Russia the resolution showed a significant development in political understanding. Already at the end of March the Special Conference, with a threat to take "a week's holiday" had called upon the Government "immediately to withdraw all British troops from Russia, and to take the necessary steps to induce the Allied Powers to do likewise" (31 iii 1919). Now they proposed stronger measures:

"This Conference of the South Wales Miners' Federation strongly condemns the continual efforts of the Allied capitalist nations to crush the Soviet Government of Russia, in face of the repeated denial by responsible Statesmen of any such intention on their part and the united protest of the organised workers of this and every other country.

"We welcome the expression of working class loyalty displayed by the French and Italian workers, and appeal to the organised and unorganised workers of this country to join them in their efforts to save the workers' Republic.

"As a first step to this end we instruct our representatives on the MFGB to at once give a lead through the medium of the Triple Alliance for a general national stoppage within 14 days unless the Military and Naval interference with Russia is brought to an end and the troops, etc., withdrawn" (20 vi 1919).

"We further protest against the continuance of the present policy as applied to Ireland, India, Poland, and other countries, together with the repressive measures generally adopted to prevent free expression of the workers' aspirations for self-government and economic freedom".

"That this Conference enters its emphatic protest against the continual increase in the cost of food, clothing, boots, etc., and the profiteering arising therefrom, and demands that the British Miners' Executive urge upon the Triple Alliance to take steps to bring about an immediate remedy; also that the Blockade be immediately abolished to permit food to be sent to the starving peoples of Europe" (21 vi 1919).

6 "DECEIVED, BETRAYED, DUPED"

No sooner had the Coal Industry Commission sent in its reports on 20th June, 1919, with majority recommendations for nationalisation than the counter-campaign, which had begun in mid-April once the strike menace had been removed, was greatly intensified. Before the end of June a formidable number of members of the House of Commons had sent in a round robin to the Prime Minister in which they announced that they would fight against nationalisation.

Not only coalowners but the Chambers of Commerce throughout the country with one accord had sent in to Sir John Sankey anti-nationalisation resolutions. From mid-June onwards this campaign, both publicly and behind the scenes, was further stepped up. Capitalists in "mass meetings" were addressed by Lord Inchcape, the shipping monopolist; by Lord Leverhulme, the head of Unilever and by the chiefs of other great monopolies who thus gave unmistakable warning of their deep hostility to any scheme of public ownership. Under this menace the Government forbore to take any step but, for week after week, like Brer Fox, they "lay low and said nuffin" : or, as it was put in Parliament, "the matter remained under consideration."

But while the employers campaigned, with their ready access to the millionnaire newspapers (several to be owned by coal and iron magnates from South Wales) the Miners' Federation initiated no campaign. "It was generally believed amongst the miners that the coal mines of this country would be nationalised . . . and that nationalisation would be realised within a reasonable time"—stated Robert Smillie a year later at Royal Leamington Spa in his last presidential address. So, in a trustful mood, they were simply awaiting the decision of the Government, as week after week passed by, though at their Keswick Annual Conference they "noted the political and industrial pressure now being brought to bear upon the Government with a view to getting it to ignore the recommendations of the Coal Industry Commission" (15 vii 1919).

On 18th August, at the end of the Parliamentary session, Lloyd George announced the Government's intention not to accept the finding of the Commission majority in favour of nationalisation : but "that unification should be promoted by amalgamation in defined areas." In this statement the Government, as it seemed to the miners, broke its pledged word. In the debate that followed Vernon Hartshorn, M.P. for Ogmore, put the matter very strongly : "We did not ask for a Commission. We accepted it. We gave evidence before it.

"Why was the Commission set up ? Was it a huge game of bluff ? Was it never intended that if the reports favoured nationalisation we were to get it ? Why was the question sent at all to the Commission ? That is the kind of question the miners of this country will ask, and they will say, 'We have been deceived, betrayed, duped' " (18 viii 1919).

A fortnight later a national MFGB Conference met "to consider the refusal of the Government to accept the Majority Report of the Coal Industry Commission for the Nationalisation of the Coal Mining Industry". William Brace, M.P., moved a resolution (which was carried unanimously) to invite the Trades Union Congress to declare for action "to secure that the Government shall adopt the Majority Report of the Commission" (3 ix 1919).

Seven days later Congress instructed the Parliamentary Committee "to immediately interview the Prime Minister to insist upon the Government adopting the Report." If, however, the Government was still refusing, a Special Congress was to decide on the action to be taken "to compel the Government to accept the Majority Report of the Commission" (10 ix 1919).

In the event, no less than two gatherings of a Special Trades Union Congress were needed, one in December and one in the spring of 1920. In addition the Triple Alliance had postponed taking its own ballot vote on direct action in support of the miners pending the Special TUC. During the long wait for these deliberations to mature, feeling in the Welsh coalfield built up against the Government and its policy on more than one count. At the District Meeting of 22nd September, after hearing reports on the MFGB and Triple Alliance Conferences on the Government's refusal to accept nationalisation, it was resolved :

"That Monday, 6th October, be taken as a holiday, for the purpose of holding demonstration meetings in the District, the object being :

A. To protest against the British Government's intervention in

Russia, and demand immediate withdrawal of troops from Russia and Ireland.

B. Protest against the Government in refusing to carry out its pledges re conscription, and demand total abolishment of the Military Service Act.

C. Demand that the abatement for income tax purposes be increased to £250 per annum with full allowance for dependants, clothes, tools, etc.

D. Protest against the action of the Government in refusing to recognise and accept the Majority Report of the Sankey Coal Commission on Nationalisation of the Mines."

They then decided "That this District provides for one in every ten of its members a copy of 'Further Facts from the Coal Commission'."

At the Special Trades Union Congress, held in December, industrial action, to the disgust of Smillie and the Welsh leaders, was ruled out. Instead an educational campaign was launched to be run by "The Mines for the Nation" Committee representing the Parliamentary Committee of the TUC, the MFGB, the Labour Party and the Co-operative Union Limited. Numerous meetings were held and material for the campaign was widely circulated.

7 INTERNAL MATTERS

After the midsummer conference of 1919, prolonged to six days by its plenitude of resolutions (none of which reappeared on the agenda of the Keswick MFGB Annual Conference in mid-July)[1] attention within the South Wales coalfield had been bent on national policy.

During these autumn and winter months of 1919-20 the matters before the Council were largely those of particular pits or groups of pits. There were some internal changes. At a Special Conference in Cardiff it is minuted: "The General Secretary, the Rt. Hon. Thomas Richards, M.P., having conveyed to the Conference his desire to relinquish either the position of Member of Parliament or General Secretaryship of the Federation the Conference passed a unanimous request to the General Secretary to retain his position as Secretary. Mr. Richards thanked the Conference for the confidence they had expressed in him and stated it was also his own desire to remain their Secretary" (8 xi 1919). Six weeks later his salary was set at £750 per annum, a sum increased to £800 in the following July.

The Council was now very fully representative with some 33 members, amongst them the four office bearers. The Honorary President, the Rt. Hon. William Abraham, M.P., intimated that he was

[1]The only proposition from South Wales was to urge upon the Government to take over "under State control the whole of the establishment's institutions and workshops now in existence for the benefit of the blind."

"desirous of relinquishing his parliamentary duties," and it was agreed upon the request of the Rhondda District, "that Mabon be given a retiring pension.[1]

In 1920 the first item minuted was: "Mr. A. J. Cook was welcomed as a new member of the Council" (16 i 1920). Cook, now miners' agent for the Rhondda No. 1 District, had come first in a contest of many candidates. On 14th April, 1919, the District Meeting of the Rhondda had resolved to have a second agent. Ten days later the District Committee proposed that the appointment be made by a ballot of the members "on the Exhaustive Vote principle" and that nominations (from the three dozen Rhondda lodges) be confined to "Members of the No. 1 Rhondda District". This would have ruled out Arthur James Cook of the housecoal pit at Trehafod, one of the seventeen lodges of the Pontypridd and Rhondda District. The attempted restriction was questioned at the 12th May District Meeting which then on 2nd June decided by 23 votes to 5 that the applications for the position of Agent should be "left open to the South Wales Coalfield."

Applications rolled in with 25 candidates. The District meeting resolved that eight applicants outside the Rhondda No. 1 and Pontypridd No. 2 Districts "be struck out, leaving 17 names to be proceeded with to a Ballot": and this ballot was duly held on 3rd and 4th September.

The subsequent District Meeting of 22nd September had a crowded agenda, covering a score of important items, local, national and international. For example, after correspondence had been read two members of the Executive Council gave a detailed report of work done at the Executive Council, the Joint Board and Disputes Meetings during the month. Reports were also given of the MFGB Conference in London on Nationalisation and on the Conference of the Triple Industrial Alliance on the postponement of the "Ballot vote re direct action".

After this on Item 12 they resolved "That we accept the report and result of the first round of District Miners' Agent ballot, and that the fourth highest be included in the second round, the District officials to make the necessary arrangements."

In the first round ballot Noah Rees had 5,184 votes while A. J. Cook

[1] **Statistical Department.**
A development in that year in addition to the installation (after 23 years) of Tom Richards as Full-Time Secretary was the decision to have a Statistical Department with a Full-Time Secretary in charge of it. So in the summer after the report from the sub-committee it was resolved by the Executive Council: "That Mr. Oliver Harris be appointed and the salary be £350 per annum." It was further resolved "that the Statistical Secretary shall be under the control and direction of the General Secretary and any information required by Council members must be applied for through the General Secretary." And further an application was received from James Griffiths, a student at the Labour College "for leave of absence in order to further his candidature for the post of Assistant Miners' Agent in the Anthracite District."

had 4,353 votes in a total poll of 30,230[1]. At the second round ballot, held on 15th and 16th October, 1919, Cook of Trehafod had 11,890 against 9,337 for Noah Rees of Cambrian, 7,418 for Rhys Evans of Abergorchy, and 6,536 for Tom Smith of the Naval Pit, the last three being members of the SWMF Executive Council. The total poll was 35,719. At the third round ballot taken on 12th and 13th November, 1919, Cook came first with 14,598 votes, Noah Rees second with 12,114 votes, Rhys Evans of Abergorchy came third with 7,921 votes on a poll which was a few hundred less than in the second ballot.

The final round ballot for the District Miners' Agent taken on 26th and 27th November, 1919, resulted as follows:

A. J. Cook of Trehafod	...	18,230 votes
Noah Rees of Cambrian	...	17,531 votes

The poll was the highest—over 35,936 votes out of a total membership in the books of just over 39,000. The keenness of the contest in four successive ballots and the size of the poll contrasts with the comparative apathy of the electorate outside industrial democracy in the sphere of bourgeois democracy as laid down by Act of Parliament.

On the 11th March, 1920, the adjourned Special Trades Union Congress reassembled at the request of the miners to decide what should be done next to compel the Government to nationalise the mines. The great propaganda campaign "The Mines for the Nation" had failed to rouse the needed support.

At the opening it was clear that the miners themselves were divided. Their own (MFGB Executive Committee of 9th January) resolution had been "whether we should propose a general trade union strike."

When the 299 delegates from the South Wales miners (representing 201,892 members) assembled for a decision on the Nationalisation of Mines, the President, Rt. Hon. William Brace, M.P., in the Chair, suggested that a long discussion was unnecessary "as the delegates had their instructions." To the proposal "that the delegates to the MFGB Conference vote in favour of the proposal for a trade union strike to enforce the nationalisation of mines", an amendment was moved "that we do not support the proposal for a trade union strike but continue the propaganda for securing the nationalisation of mines by political action." On a card vote 3,487 voted for the proposition and only 610 for the amendment (8 iii 1920). It was a five to one majority. But overall it was only a three to two majority in the British coalfields, Yorkshire and Durham being against it.

At the Special Trades Union Congress there was no doubt as to the lack of enthusiasm for strike action. An overwhelming vote of

[1]Amongst the 17 candidates for the position of District Miners' Agent were the names of many then or afterwards to be well known such as Dai Lloyd Davies of Maerdy (the sponsor of Arthur Horner), G. H. Hall of Penrhiwceiber, W. F. Hay of Standard.

the Special Trades Union Congress (3.732,000 against 1,050,000) decided against a general strike and in favour of intensive policital propaganda "in preparation for the General Election." The miners were indignant. They knew that a General Election was not in sight and as an immediate aim nationalisation would have to be shelved. At the MFGB Annual Conference in Leamington Spa, it was resolved unanimously:

"This Conference views with regret the failure of the Government to introduce legislation for the purpose of nationalising the mining industry, and reiterates its conviction that this industry will never be placed upon a satisfactory basis in the interests of the community until it is publicly owned and worked between representatives of the State and the technical and manual workers engaged in it and resolves to continue to educate and organise working class opinion until the Government are compelled to bring about this fundamental change in the ownership and management of the industry" (8 vii 1920).

A quarter of a century was to pass before the miners were again within measurable reach of their goal of nationalisation.

8 CLEAVAGE IN THE MINING CAMP

With the spring of 1920 a cleavage in the mining camp was manifest both in conferences and in ballot votes. Diversities there had always been in the coalfields, from South Wales (now with one-fifth of British output and with a union of over 200,000 in January, 1921, out of a total paid-up British membership of 957,000) to the lesser coalfields such as Bristol which had little over 2,000 members. For generations the miners' associations in England had county and local officers who adhered to Primitive Methodism or other Protestant Dissent from the State-established Church of England. In Wales, right up to the days of A. J. Cook and A. L. Horner, few agents had not been local preachers or to the fore "in the chapel." Non-conformity, to a greater extent than in most English coalfields, was shot through with a firm adherence to Liberalism and to the Liberal Party up to the earlier twentieth century. In addition, the sentiment of nationality was infused alike into their nonconformity and their Liberalism and even into their trade unionism.

All had been welded together by their Great Strike of 1912. Thereafter they pursued common aims, and the twenty constituent parts seemed to be coming closer within the Miners' Federation of Great Britain. Moreover, with the Socialist Robert Smillie as President, the miners had acquired for their democratic policies a guidance that had been sorely lacking for nearly nine years.

With the outbreak of the War of Empires in August, 1914, the old Lib-Lab dominance had prevailed within the counsels of the Miners' Federation; the Liberal Government's war policy had triumphed while the miners voluntarily enlisted in the armed forces to an extent that depleted the mines of essential manpower. Only in South Wales had there been a short-lived attempt from an anti-war standpoint to carry out the opposition enjoined upon all working-class organisations by the resolutions of the International Socialist Congress. Elsewhere class consciousness had been hushed and—save for that "still small voice" from the past—the call for "national unity" had prevailed in every industry for over nine months, until the behaviour of the South Wales coalowners in connivance with Liberal ministers had precipitated the coalfield strike of July, 1915.

In that month the South Wales Miners' Federation had separated themselves from the standpoint in other coalfields, had reached a confrontation not only with the private capitalists and the politicians but with their own elected leaders both Lib-Lab and Socialist. In this form the sharp antagonism did not last long. But class consciousness and its democratic striving had been around; and within twenty months was stimulated by the news of revolution in Europe, sparked off by working-class demonstrations against their rulers, responsible for the war and hunger.

By summer 1917, the cleavage in the miners' leadership between the anti-war and the pro-war standpoints had become visible in the Special Conferences of the Labour Party and of the Miners' Federation of Great Britain. Allegations were made that Smillie and his South Wales supporters were in a cabal with the United Socialist Council. From autumn 1917 the situation became more complicated, with incipient further cleavages. On the one hand within the minority there had been discernible a distinction between the standpoint initially voiced by John McLean and James Connolly and what came to be dubbed "the Centrist" tendency initially represented by the ILP leaders. Then in spring 1917 in its Bermondsey Conference the ILP, into which for thirty months there had been a steady infiltration of middle-class and religious personnel and pacifism, adopted, against the advice of its parliamentary leaders, a purely pacifist resolution and so forsook the standpoint of the old Socialist International anti-war resolutions.

On the other hand within the original "pro-war" majority (which had rallied in 1915 to the support of the Asquithite coalition government and then in December 1916 to the Lloyd Georgian coalition) a cleavage, most clearly visible in the Parliamentary Labour Party, opened up in 1917 between those who supported this "knock-out blow" policy of the War Cabinet[1] and those, more numerous in the Executive Committee of the Labour Party, who stood for peace-by-negotiation as afterwards elaborated into a programme by the Henderson-Webb sub-committee.

By 1918 majorities in the coalfields had swung behind the policies of Smillie, who was no longer supported only by the South Wales

[1]Amongst the mining M.P.s Abraham, Brace, Hancock and Walsh with G. N. Barnes as their leader.

Miners' Federation : and the older Lib-Lab leaders still heading the county Miners' Associations, were silenced if not completely won over.

In February 1919 miners in the coalfields, in no mood to accept the hesitancy of their leaders in the MFGB Executive Committee,[1] ballotted for an immediate strike. It was then when Smillie and other leaders recoiled from the prospect that the speakers from South Wales, notably Noah Ablett and S. O. Davies, stiffened up the sinews of the older leaders to the point where Smillie gave a ten minute ultimatum to the Prime Minister of the United Kingdom to accept the conditions on which the miners would play in with the proposed Royal Commission.

A month later, however, when the Sankey Report went to a ballot with the strongest recommendation by Robert Smillie and Frank Hodges for its acceptance and when the South Wales delegate conference advised its rejection, the vote was overwhelmingly in favour of accepting Smillie's advice. Throughout the summer and early autumn of 1919 the quarter-million miners in the South Wales valleys were apparently accepting the advice of their older leaders Brace and Richards together with that of Vernon Hartshorn, M.P., in support of the policy of Smillie.

It was the behaviour of Lloyd George which shattered the plans of the leaders and made it difficult for Smillie to retain his ascendancy in the councils of the Miners' Federation. For when Lloyd George finally announced and confirmed that he would break his government's solemn promise to the miners and when the recourse was had to the special Trades Union Congress in December 1919, Smillie felt that the miners had been thwarted first by Lloyd George, second by the slowness of his allies and third by a Trades Union Congress which preferred words to deeds. Smillie took it very hard; he felt himself to be a defeated man. His health, too, began to give way and in the beginning of February, 1920, he was away ill for two weeks, to be welcomed by the Excutive Committee expressing its delight in having him back again to lead them. Could he still lead them? In the Committee on 25th February there were strong differences of opinion on prices, wages and costs. When the meeting resumed on the 26th Smillie was not there. A letter came from Scotland saying he wished to resign from the Presidency, and returning the cheque for his monthly salary.

At the Special Conference of 10th March, 1920, delegates were curious to know as to what had happened. The explanations given by Frank Hodges were not taken very well by the delegates who had begun to feel that Hodges and Smillie did not get on well together. Vice-president Herbert Smith said : "Mr. Smillie was anxious not to leave this movement until he had achieved what he had propagated all his life—nationalisation", to which James Robson of Durham added :

[1]To the 158 delegates assembled for their Special Conference at the Temperance Institute in Southport Smillie more than once mentioned "the seething discontent which almost overwhelmed our Executive at the last meeting" (12 ii 1919).

"We knew he was suffering from ill-health. The man's nervous system is entirely smashed up, that is my own feeling". Pressure was exerted from the conference to get Smillie to withdraw his resignation. This he did but only after fifteen weeks.

Meantime, the conclusion which Smillie had foreseen and dreaded, namely, that the Trades Union Congress would fold up its tents and steal silently away was abundantly confirmed in March when the adjourned special Trades Union Congress abandoned any possibility not only of industrial action but of anything more than the most general educational campaign in preparation for a far distant general election. It was abandonment of their September 1919 standpoint. It was a retreat.

It was from this moment in the opening months of 1920, that the cleavage can most clearly be seen. South Wales and Lancashire were overwhelmingly for the general trade union strike. Yorkshire and Durham on the eastern side of the island were against. But if the struggle for nationalisation was ended (not to be resumed for another 25 years) the struggle for wages was acute: and became more so, as the cleavage deepened, with South Wales and Lancashire coming out sharply against the majority of the national committee.

9 PRICES AND WAGES

On the 12th March, 1920, the day after "a General Trade Union Strike for the Nationalisation of the Mines" had been rejected by the adjourned Special Trades Union Congress, the MFGB Special Conference moved for an advance in wages, consequent upon the high cost of living on which there had already been many meetings. Negotiations now took place with the Prime Minister. On 29th March having received his "final offer" the MFGB Conference decided to put it to a ballot vote.[1]

The miners in a poll of 820,273, voted in favour of acceptance of the Government offer by a narrow majority of 65,135, but Lanca-

[1]BALLOT

For a Strike.

Are you in favour of a stoppage of work to enforce the claim put forward by the Miners' Federation of Great Britain on behalf of all their members for an advance in wages of 3s. per shift flat rate for all persons over 16 years of age, and 1/6d per shift flat rate for all persons below 16, to commence as and from Monday, 1st March, 1920?

For the Offer of the Government.

Are you in favour of accepting the Government's offer of a 20 per cent advance on gross wages, excluding War wage and Sankey wage, with guaranteed flat rate of 2s per shift advance for persons of 18 years and upwards, 1s per shift for persons between 16 and 18, and 9d per shift for persons below 16, to commence as and from the 12th March, 1920?

Please put your X in the space provided for the purpose, opposite the one which you favour.

shire voted overwhelmingly for a strike by 62,466 to 17,509 (78 per cent to 22 per cent) and South Wales by 116,621 to 47,496 (71 per cent to 29 per cent).

An agreement with the Coal Controller was signed accordingly on 29th April.

Within seventeen days the price of household coal was suddenly raised by 14/2d a ton. The miners' leaders were of the opinion that by this the Cabinet aimed at something more than the creation of prejudice against the miners and that their plan was to place each coalfield and each pit on a profit-making basis: and in this way to meet the wishes of the coalowners for a completely uncontrolled industry.

By the time the MFGB Conference had met on 10th June, 1920, to consider the rise in the price of household coal the cost of living had again leapt upwards. Within three months the general retail price level increased from 130 per cent to 150 per cent. What the British miners had gained after four months of Conferences, prolonged negotiations and ballot votes in April, 1920, had been summarily wiped out. They had to enter on the process again.

In the Library of the Memorial Hall, Farringdon Street, London (where the Labour Party had come into existence just 30 years earlier), business began with a resolution: "That this Conference heartily welcomes Mr. Smillie back again after his illness, and trusts that he will long be spared to continue his work on behalf of the Miners' Federation of Great Britain and workers in general." Then the Executive was instructed "to formulate a claim for a substantial increase in wages, and submit same to a conference at an early date" (10 vi 1920).

At the MFGB Annual Conference in Leamington Spa a month later the wages question was first business. The Executive Committee had been persuaded by Smillie to put forward, as an indivisible demand, the reduction of household coal prices by 14/9d together with an advance in wages of 2/0d a shift.

There was sharp difference of opinion. Frank Varley of Nottingham moved an amendment to delete any reference to domestic coal and to put in the figure of 4/0d instead of 2/0d as the claim. A. J. Cook in seconding was able to quote a South Wales Conference recommendation: "that the delegates representing South Wales at the National Conference shall propose that an advance in wages be demanded commensurate with the ascertained surplus profits of the mining industry" (6 vi 1920).

In a very impassioned speech Cook said: "We were able to convince the men to agree to a flat rate advance commensurate with the rest of the coalfields, but we cannot convince the men on a question of idealism or to try and practise altruism whilst the rest of the Trades Union Congress is using their organisation to increase their wages and increase their standard of living."

At the end of Cook's speech the financial figures showing the position of the industry for quarter ending March, 1920, made it clear that only "four Districts were paying their way."

Every District except Northumberland, Durham, South Wales and Yorkshire had a deficit between price and cost. Hodges said: "You have very wide extremes. You have for example in South Wales a difference between cost and price of 80/7d per ton, that is, on the credit side, whereas you have the other extreme in Cumberland and Westmorland, you have 10/3d a ton less".

Smillie said in an eloquent speech with which he closed the discussion: "We are advised by our Welsh friends who are about the first people in the world whom we would have looked upon as the idealists of the Labour Movement, we are advised to drop idealism and let the bottom dog fight for himself. May I say to my Welsh friends and any others that when we drop the idealism we drop reform" (6 vii 1920).

On a card vote 545 supported the Executive Committee. The 360 votes for the minority were made up of: South Wales 180; Lancashire 80; Northumberland 42; Nottinghamshire 35; North Wales 15; and Leicestershire 8.

Smillie had won over the Executive Committee members including first one and then another of the representatives on it from South Wales. In the second half of 1920 South Wales, once Smillie's most reliable ally, found itself in frequent opposition to the national policy that he had advised and that had been accepted by a majority of the Districts.

The Government's reply was an uncompromising negative. "The view of the Government is that whatever surplus profits are derived from the sale of coal during the next twelve months should go into the Exchequer" (26 viii 1920).

The Special Conference on 12th August decided by 168 votes to 3 for a ballot which on 31st August showed a majority of over two-thirds for strike action.[1] There were 608,782 votes and only 238,865 against, being a strike majority of 367,917. In South Wales there was a 78 per cent majority for a strike; in the Midlands 82 per cent; in Lancashire 90 per cent. The overall percentage was 72 per cent against 28 per

[1]The form of the ballot was as follows:

"In view of the refusal of the Government to concede the claims of the Miners' Federation of Great Britain for a reduction in the price of domestic coal by 14/2d. per ton, and an advance in wages of 2/- per shift for members of 18 years and upwards, 1/- for members from 16 to 18 years, and 9d per shift for boys below 16 years of age, are you in favour of strike action to secure those claims?

For strike action . . .
Against strike action . . .

Please place your cross according to your choice in the space provided for the purpose."

cent. So on 2nd September the MFGB Special Conference agreed that all members of the Federation should hand in notices "so that all members will cease work on 25th September, 1920."

There followed one of the most crowded and dramatic chapters in the history of the Miners' Federation.

10 THE CAULDRON BUBBLES

The story of these three months has already been chronicled.[1] It has been told how the two dozen miners' leaders made their decision to call a special conference in mid-August, and meantime set off to the Lake of Geneva for ten days of the 25th Miners' International Congress. In these ten days that they were away the Government was busy with a thoroughly misleading Press campaign which, owing to the absence abroad of 65 leading miners, had the field of propaganda pretty well to itself and met with no adequate rebuttal.

With the mid-August announcement that there would be a ballot the Government's propaganda against the miners was intensified. In the last week of August the MFGB Executive Committee held meetings where they considered the need of a publicity campaign to put the miners' case before the public. The officials were asked to take the necessary steps and before the end of August the Labour Research Department had been requested to give its aid. On the same 31st August Robert Smillie gave an explanation to the assembled Executive Committees of the Miners' Federation, the Transport Workers' Federation and the National Union of Railwaymen.

On 1st September the three Executives decided in conference: "That this Conference declares that it is satisfied that the miners' claim is based on justice and equity." It was also agreed that a sub-committee should act "as a Press or Publicity Committee." Thereafter the materials prepared by the Labour Research Department were to be issued under authority not of the Miners' Federation only but of the whole Triple Industrial Alliance.[2]

On 2nd September the Miners' Delegate Conference heard the result of the ballot vote. There was a majority of 71¾ per cent for a stoppage. The decision was for a strike on 25th September. Thereupon the President of the Board of Trade invited the miners to come to London where they found little or nothing changed, except that the President had thrown out a vague suggestion that brought up the question of output. Before the middle of the month the Board of Trade published a White Paper.[3] These figures, however sceptically examined, made it

[1]See *The Miners' Years of Struggle*, Chapter 9.

[2]See Appendix III to this Chapter.

[3]Summary of Coal Output, Costs of Production, etc., for Three Months to June 30, 1920, Cd. 949.

clear that it was not possible to continue the miners' claim on the basis of the previous figures discussed in June, and at their Annual Conference in the first week of July. Consequently the miners' leaders altered the policy. In their own words: "The Committee with full deliberation undertook the responsibility of modifying the form of the claims now before the Government, and to decide that, provided the Government accepted such modifications, they would recommend the adoption of the change to a Special Conference to be called for the purpose." But when on 16th and 17th September the MFGB Executive Committee had prolonged conferences with Sir Robert Horne at which the modified claims were put forward these were met by rejection.

For the second time Sir Robert Horne raised the question of output saying: "I for one am prepared to take a totally different view of any wage claim which is based upon output." At a further meeting on Monday, 20th September, the MFGB Executive Committee reaffirmed their refusal to accept an arbitration tribunal on the wages claim.

The Special Delegate Conference beginning Tuesday, 21st September and continuing throughout the week had voiced criticisms of the change of policy on the hitherto generally accepted claim. But there was a cleavage. Lancashire as well as South Wales found themselves in a minority of 73 against 105 for the National Executive Committee.

The MFGB Special Conference met on Thursday, 23rd without an Executive recommendation before it. Robert Smillie had been unable to win a majority in the Executive. He then pleaded that the Conference vote for the acceptance of arbitration, or rather for taking a ballot vote of the men on this proposition. Smillie was at once assailed by old Tom Greenall of Lancashire who was against the suggestion of arbitration. Backing Lancashire were the speakers from South Wales, notably A. J. Cook and Noah Ablett and George Barker. Robson of Durham also argued against taking a ballot. In the vote there was a majority against Smillie's standpoint. He was defeated by 545 votes to 360. The majority against "referring the principle of a tribunal back to the men" was made up of South Wales 180, Durham 126, Scotland 90, Lancashire 80, Derbyshire 49, and smaller Districts (South Derbyshire 8, Somerset 6, Forest of Dean 6, and Kent 2).

Meantime the Prime Minister sent letters in which, while insisting on an arbitration tribunal, he went on to propose the principle of basing increases of wages on increased output.

That evening at the adjourned meeting of the full Triple Alliance there was fierce debate. J. H. Thomas announced that the NUR delegates had decided against coming out on strike on Saturday midnight of 25th September in support of the miners. Miners' delegates were angry and gave full vent to their feelings. Vernon Hartshorn abruptly proposed the immediate dissolution of the Conference: this was seconded by Frank Hodges in a few bitter words. Smillie urged:

"Do not let us begin recriminations." Vernon Hartshorn then gave the argument for the miners' decision to reject the tribunal. He recalled what had happened before the tribunal on the Sankey Commission. He told how the Government had spent "hundreds of thousands of pounds in a Press campaign, by means of which they created an atmosphere in this country against the miners." Then once more he said that they had called in the Press and with the same purpose : "A greater campaign of villainy and perjury as never had been inaugurated, even in the Press, against us. If we allow the Press to defeat us in this campaign, then goodbye to Trade Unionism."

On Friday the miners again interviewed the Prime Minister. As a result the Miners' Executive recommended the suspension of strike notices for a week in order to meet the owners on wages in relation to output. Back at the MFGB Special Conference in the Holborn Hall, the recommendation was accepted by 134 votes to 31, namely : "That this Conference accept the recommendation of the Executive Committee to suspend notices for one week to give the Executive an opportunity of meeting the coalowners" (24 ix 1920).

That evening at the full meeting of the Triple Alliance Conference Smillie reported the suspension of notices. It was received with joy, and indeed relief, by the miners' partners, railwaymen and transport workers, in the Triple Alliance. But Ernest Bevin made a critical speech ending with the words : "By God it has revealed itself to be a paper alliance this week." Ernest Bevin on this occasion was in the right.

The first meeting with the coalowners was held on Saturday, 25th September, but agreement could not easily be reached. This became clear by Wednesday, 29th September, and was so reported to the Government. It was put before the MFGB Special Conference on 30th September which adjourned to 1st October to enable suggestions to be made.

Meantime there came a discussion in Cardiff on 27th September, 1920. The MFGB Committee representatives from South Wales had asked for information respecting the causes of reduced output. It was unanimously resolved thereupon that a resolution be telegraphed to the South Wales representatives on the Miners' Federation of Great Britain Executive Committee. The resolution was as follows :

"This Executive Council having considered the very general protests received from the Districts against committing the workmen in the present negotiations to the future regulation of wages by output, resolves to telegraph this decision, with which the Council are in agreement, to our representatives on the MFGB Committee.

"The Council are unanimously of the opinion that the present demand for the increase in wages should be settled, and that the whole matter of the consolidation of present wages and the methods of regulating future wages shall be the subject of investigation and further consultation with the whole of the workmen".

It was further resolved to call a Coalfield Conference for the next Wednesday to which "the representatives of the MFGB Executive be asked to attend" (27 ix 1920).

Two days later the General Secretary, at a Special Conference in the Co-operative Hall in Cardiff, moved the Council's resolution. Mr. Noah Ablett seconded it and the resolution was carried by a large majority. The Conference had 324 delegates representing 200,988 members, almost the maximum in many years.

A further Special Conference in Cory Hall resolved "That the suspension of the notices be accepted" (2 x 1920).

Two days later the Executive Council meeting resolved "to proceed with the printing and issuing of the ballot papers, together with posters to be put up at the pitheads", and it was also further resolved "that we advise the workmen at the Conference on Wednesday to take part in the ballot, and that we recommend them to vote against the employers' offer". A manifesto was to be issued the next day to the workmen.[1]

At a Council meeting on 16th October, 1920, it was resolved to consider "the advisability of withdrawing the whole of the men from each of the collieries in Great Britain."

Six days later at a coalfield conference in the Cory Hall in Cardiff William Brace from the chair stated that "he was at present against withdrawing all the men from the collieries," and supplemented this statement by a long report of what had taken place in the House of Commons. But there turned out to be a large majority for the principle of withdrawing all men from the collieries and a further resolution was carried:

[1]SOUTH WALES MINERS' FEDERATION.

2 St. Andrew's Crescent,
Cardiff,

5th October, 1920.

TO THE MEMBERS.

The Council has given detailed consideration to the terms offered by the Coalowners for the settlement of the present Wage Dispute, and unanimously recommend the South Wales Members of the Federation to vote solidly against the acceptance of those terms.

While these proposals do not contain the term "Datum Line," the Council will take it that a vote against the Owners' proposals is a vote against the principle of determining Wages by a Datum Line.

We take this opportunity of issuing this Manifesto so that there should be no misconception as to what Owners' terms contain.

We strongly recommend that all members should participate in the ballot.

(Signed) THOMAS RICHARDS,
General Secretary.

NOTE.—The Council have given instructions that no ballot papers are to be given to boys who are not Full Members of the Federation.

10 RELEASE OF ANTHRACITE STRIKERS, 1925
STANLEY EVANS (middle, second row); IANTO EVANS (second left, second row)

11 JACK WILLIAMS (FOREST OF DEAN) AND
NOAH ABLETT (MERTHYR)

"That representation be made to the MFGB Committee to convene a National Conference to be held on October 27th, to consider and determine a policy with reference to the withdrawal of the whole of the men from each of the collieries in Great Britain, and that such policy be put into operation on October 30th, should the strike be not settled before that date" (22 x 1920).

Tom Richards then reported upon the membership and the amount of funds available and suggested several methods of paying strike pay. The following was then adopted: "That the strike pay be at the rate of 12/6d per member per week, and 1/6d for each child to commence next week." There was a further resolution "That no District or Lodge make any supplementary pay from their general funds to the central strike pay." Before the Conference ended they passed a resolution about the unemployed demonstration the previous Monday in London as follows:

"That this Conference strongly condemns the action of the Authorities in brutally battening a peaceful procession of unemployed men and women in London last Monday and calls upon our Members of Parliament to demand an explanation from the Home Office".

Finally standing orders were suspended to call attention to some Press reports of statements made by the Rt. Hon. William Brace, M.P., and Major D. Watts Morgan, M.P. The two of them replied to the observations made. It was clear that the delegates were extremely alert to each detail.

At the Executive Council Meeting on 23rd October instructions were issued as to the workmen to be permitted to work at the collieries.[1]

The MFGB Executive decided to recommend to the Conference on 1st October the taking of a ballot on the terms put forward by the owners. The Executive recommendation was accepted by a large majority, "That notices be suspended for a fortnight until Saturday, October 16th, 1920."

On the back of the ballot paper was printed the owners' offer

[1] **Arrangements for the Employment of Workmen for the Maintenance of the Collieries.**

It has been decided by the Federation Executive Council, and the Enginemen and Stokers, etc., Committee, that the only workmen to be employed during the Strike are the following:

All Winding Enginemen, all Stokers, Fan Compressor and Power House Workmen, Ostlers, Pumpsmen, Banksmen, Hitchers, Loco Men, Lampmen, Ashmen, Pitmen, Unloaders of coal for boilers, Coke Oven and By-Product Workers.

The foregoing grades of workmen to be employed must be rigidly adhered to, and no exceptions to be made without the sanction of the Miners' Agent and District Officials, who shall consider any cases of emergency that may arise.

In event of the District Officials authorising any departure from the list a report of what had been done shall be sent to the General Secretary.

At collieries where there is a Branch of the Enginemen, Stokers and Surface Craftsmen's Association, the Federation Committee should co-operate with the Committee of the Enginemen's Association in carrying out the arrangements.

(Signed) William Hopkins, Thos. Richards, General Secretaries.

signed by their Chairman, Evan Williams. The main clause of this offer was for an advance in wages of 1/- per shift if output in the first fortnight of October were at the rate of 240 million tons per annum; if at the rate of 244 million tons, 1/6d etc. a shift; and 6d a shift for each additional 4 million tons.

The result of the ballot papers was announced to the Special Conference assembled on Thursday, 14th October. Feeling in the coalfields was very strong. The Executive's recommendation was on the result of the ballot which showed a more than 3 to 1 majority against the owners' offer. The majority against was 453,670, or 78 per cent against the offer: while beyond this, South Wales was 88 per cent against it.

The delegate conference endorsed the ballot by 154 to 27 and in favour of the Executive's recommendation: "That in view of the ballot vote the men be advised to allow the notices to expire, and that a cessation of work take place after Saturday, 16th October, 1920".

On the next day, Friday, 15th October, the conference proceedings began with the Chairman reading a letter from Lloyd George which had arrived the previous evening. It was very cleverly written but the delegates realised clearly how the Prime Minister had been playing his hand in such a manner as to break away wherever possible public support for the miners' case. In this knowledge they passed the two-fold resolutions:

1. "That this Conference do not agree to revert back to the previous claim including the 14/2."
2. "That in view of the unsatisfactory reply of the Government to the letter sent yesterday in connection with the claim for 2/-, 1/-, and 9d per day increase in wages, this Conference do now adjourn and that notices finish tomorrow afternoon."

On the next day, Saturday, 16th October, the strike began.

For five days the strike went on. At a debate in the House of Commons on Tuesday, 19th October, the Government showed no willingness to make any concession. On Wednesday, 20th October, the Delegate Conference of the National Union of Railwaymen met to consider what should be their attitude. On Thursday, 21st October, the NUR decided to strike at midnight on Sunday, 24th October if the miners' claims were not granted or negotiations resumed by Saturday the 23rd. This transformed the situation. A conciliatory letter from the Prime Minister reached the MFGB Executive Committee on the morning of Saturday, 23rd October, and it was agreed that the officials meet the Prime Minister on the Sunday at 10 o'clock. That afternoon of Saturday they met the NUR and decided to ask them to postpone the operation of their resolution to take strike action until further notice in view of the fact that negotiations had been resumed with the Government. At 4 o'clock in the afternoon the miners' Executive attended the Special General Meeting of the NUR and stated their position.

Sunday morning, 24th October, and for the next four days negotiations went on. Draft after draft was being discussed at 10 Downing Street: while simultaneously on the other side of Whitehall in Parliament the Government were pushing through the Emergency Powers Bill introduced on 22nd October, a repressive measure already prepared in advance. It was rushed through Parliament in four days and on Wednesday, 27th October, Royal Assent was given. The Emergency Powers Act had become law. It was a measure which gave such drastic powers of suppression and arrest to the King's Ministers and to the Police as had never been known in time of peace.

A Trades Union Congress summoned for the 27th passed a strong protest. On Thursday, 28th October, the MFGB Executive Committee decided by the Chairman's casting vote that a ballot vote of the workmen be taken on Tuesday, 2nd November, as to whether or not they were in favour of the Government terms. The terms, very detailed and elaborate, can be summed up as follows:

1. The advance of 2s a shift was conceded immediately and equated to a figure of output.
2. Additional increases of wages corresponding to further increases of output.
3. The scheme was to continue only until the setting up of a National Wage Board to be negotiated between owners and workmen who were bound to report not later than 31st March.
4. The Government were to guarantee the 2s a shift advance until the end of December in any event and were to guarantee export prices at 72s a ton.

The result of the ballot vote taken on 2nd November on the Government's terms was announced to the National Conference on 3rd November, as follows: For the offer 338,045, against the offer 346,504. Majority against offer 8,459. Thus it was a very narrow majority. Actually most Districts had voted for the offer and the narrow majority against was due to the fact that South Wales had cast a 65 per cent majority against the offer and Lancashire an 83 per cent majority against it: all other Districts had been more or less in favour. The Chairman, citing the rules of the Federation, namely, that "If a ballot vote be taken during the time a strike is in progress a vote of two thirds of those taking part in the ballot shall be necessary to continue the strike". It was decided after much murmuring, particularly from Lancashire and South Wales, that the rule should be carried out by 121 to 46. So it was agreed the Conference declare the strike at an end "in accordance with the rules of the Federation". The men were instructed to return to work the next day. The Datum Line strike was ended.

There was a sequel to the ending of the Datum Line strike. At the Special Conference in the Cory Hall, Cardiff, it is recorded:

"Messrs. Winstone, Hartshorn, Barker and Brace, reported upon the negotiations with the Government, and the receipt of the ultimate terms of a settlement to be submitted to the workmen in the ballot.

"A general discussion ensued upon a proposal that the Conference recommend the workmen to vote against the acceptance of the terms of settlement which was ultimately carried by a large majority" (30 x 1920).

Behind the bald and colourless wording of this minute there is (unrecorded in detail) the story of a fierce struggle. The majority, (amongst whom A. J. Cook, together with Noah Ablett and S. O. Davies, had been the leading spokesmen) had found themselves, to a mounting degree throughout the autumn, in considerable disagreement with their President and the most prominent of their other representatives on the MFGB Executive Committee.

In the first minute of November dealing with the Council meeting following upon the Cory Hall Conference of 30th October, there is recorded the receipt of a resolution from the Rhymney lodges "regarding their confidence in Messrs. Brace and Hartshorn" and "thanking our representatives on the MFGB Committee for the part taken in the recent negotiations". As we have seen, the standpoint of those opposed to Messrs. Brace and Hartshorn carried the Council while their recommendation to vote against the terms was followed in the ballot vote of the South Wales coalfield by a very significant majority.[1]

The climax was not delayed. One side or the other had to give way: and it was reported to the Council meeting on 13th November that Messrs. Brace and Hartshorn had departed as is shown in the minutes as follows:

"The resignation of Mr. Brace, as president of the South Wales Miners' Federation and member of the MFGB Committee, was received, and also the resignation of Mr. Hartshorn, as a member of the Council and member of the MFGB Committee.

"Mr. Brace also resigned his position of Member of Parliament for the Abertillery Division."

Resolved "That the resignation of both Mr. Brace and Mr. Hartshorn be accepted".

Further resolved "That Mr. Richards, General Secretary, and Mr. Noah Ablett fill the positions on the MFGB Committee, until the usual ballot for the members of this Committee be taken next year".

Further, "That Mr. Winstone be appointed President and Mr. Morrell, Vice-President, until the election at the Annual Conference" (13 xi 1920).

[1]Lancashire and South Wales with two other Districts had voted heavily against the offer, Lancashire by a 2 to 1 majority (98,052 against 51,647). Lancashire's majority was 83 per cent against 17 per cent and Nottingham 52 per cent against 48 per cent. These three together with Forest of Dean sufficed to make the ballot vote of the 20 constituents of the Miners' Federation yield a majority (346,504 against 338,045).

But, as we have seen, the majority was not large enough to warrant the continuance of the Datum Line strike.

It was a little over nine years since at the end of the Cambrian Combine Strike the mistrust of the colliers in their leading officials had been so manifestly shown in the elections to the MFGB Executive Committee that Brace had offered his resignation to his District. Then it was not accepted. This time there was, however, to be no going back. Brace departed and at the same time became a Government official in the Conciliation Section of the Ministry of Labour. This acceptance of a Government post and the throwing up of his seat in Parliament provided sensational news not only in South Wales but also in London where parliamentary colleagues of Brace were astonished at his having sacrificed a career with a sure culmination in the first Labour Cabinet. But for Brace himself it was a step that had always seemed possible once he had tasted the experience of almost four years of office in Whitehall from 1915 to 1919.[1]

APPENDIX I

HYSTERIA IN THE WAR CABINET

The Cabinet Papers in the Public Record Office tell something of how these mutinies and strikes affected ruling circles.

On 8th January, 1919, Lloyd George in 10 Downing Street, learned of 1,500 soldiers outside wanting to meet the Prime Minister. The military men present were very troubled about an assembly of "soldiers without officers", one Field Marshal saying that the soldiers' practice "bore a dangerous resemblance to a Soviet" (Pro Cab 23/9 W.C. 522).

Thursday, 30th January: the War Cabinet discussed whether to use soldiers to break strikes, especially in view of the 40-hour strike on the Clyde, and at what moment to arrest "the ringleaders". When it was pointed out that in a railway strike in peacetime a few soldiers had been employed as engine drivers and guards, General Childs said that "a few men had been so employed, and at that time we had a well disciplined and ignorant army whereas now we had an army educated and ill-disciplined". Mr. Churchill said: "The present situation in Glasgow has been brewing for a long time. The disaffected are in a minority and, in my opinion, there will have to be conflict in order to clear the air. We should be careful to have plenty of provocation before taking strong measures . . . In the meantime the Defence of the Realm Act is still in force and some of the leaders of revolt should be seized."

The War Cabinet then took five decisions of which the last was "that the Lord Advocate should examine the legal grounds for the arrest of the ringleaders of the strike should it be found desirable to do so". Apparently it was found desirable for, on the next day, 31st

[1]Twenty-five years later in interviews with the author Brace told how he had been torn in two by feelings of uncertainty. "They had gone wild, Page Arnot. They were wild men, particularly Cook. I knew I was right and I believe I could have defeated them. But then I had the thought that if I turned out to have been wrong, it would be too late for me to lead them back on to where they were before".

January, Gallacher and Shinwell were arrested in George Square, Glasgow, where the authorities "read the Riot Act". The necessary provocation had been carried out.

It was on the same day that the Miners' Executive met the Committee of the Cabinet to discuss the four-fold claim put forward in mid-January.

On Tuesday, 4th February, the War Cabinet minutes show the Home Secretary rather unmanned by the news of a strike on the London "tubes". He urged "that from the War Cabinet there should be a statement to the Press pointing out that these were not bona fide strikers, but a bolshevik attack upon the whole fabric". He considered that "if an announcement on these lines were issued in the Press, the Army would not regard the utilisation of their service as strike-breaking" (Pro Cab 23/9 W.C. 522). It was a prolonged discussion. The views of Bonar Law, leader of the Conservative Party, are as follows: "He thought that the Trade Union organisation was the only thing between us and anarchy, and if the Trade Union organisation was against us the position would be hopeless".

On Wednesday, 5th February, the First Lord of the Admiralty said that "use of Government lorries would be interpreted as a strike-breaking act, and might cause trouble, unless carried out with care and tact. Unless we act soon the situation will become worse and worse each day. There is no doubt that we are up against a Bolshevist movement in London, Glasgow and elsewhere". He had just returned from one of the Naval ports where there had been "a little trouble which was purely of a Bolshevist nature". With regards to electricians in the Army, General Robertson had grave doubts about employing these men. They were waiting to be demobilised, and many were members of the Amalgamated Society of Engineers". Churchill stated with regard to the suggestion to use skilled men from the Air Force that "they are the least disciplined and most trade-unionised of His Majesty's forces: they are not trained soldiers, and are hardly distinguishable from trade unionists". The Minister of Labour (Sir Robert Horne) added that "one favourable feature in the situation was the fact that the Amalgamated Society of Engineers' Executive had met and suspended their District Committees in Glasgow, Belfast and on the Thames for permitting these unauthorised strikes" (Pro. Cab. 23/9 W.C. 527).

APPENDIX II

THE MINERS' BILL (1919)

The evidence from the Miners' Federation of Great Britain was presented on the last week of May, 1919. Henry H. Slesser, Standing Counsel for the Miners' Federation, who had been responsible for the legal drafting of the 1912 Bill,[1] submitted on 23rd May, a draft Parliamentary Bill embodying the changes decided upon at the Miners'

[1]Nationalisation of Coal Mines and Minerals Bill, 1912, published with explanatory notes in July, 1913, as Fabian Tract No. 171, price one penny.

Annual Conference in 1918. This, put in as purely formal evidence of an explanatory kind but without arguments, was then supported on 27th May by William Straker of Northumberland and James Winstone of South Wales. The Bill provided for the nationalisation of all mines and minerals forthwith, and the vesting of all powers in a Mining Council consisting of the Minister of Mines, for the time being, and twenty whole-time members, ten appointed by the Government and ten by the Miners' Federation, each for five years. To avoid bureaucratic running of the mines, District Councils with three-year tenure of office were instituted and Pit Councils with one-year tenure of office, with powers delegated from the Mining Council. The Mining Council was the supreme authority. The scheme expressly contended that there would be no restriction on the miners' right to strike.[1]

APPENDIX III

"FACTS ABOUT THE COAL DISPUTE."

In this pamphlet[2] was set forth the history of coal prices since 1914. There had been eight separate increases and one temporary decrease as follows:

		per ton s.	d.
1915	Standard increase under Limitation of Prices Act ...	4	0
1916	1st June (South Wales and Forest of Dean only) ...	2	6
1917	12th October	2	6
1918	24th June	2	6
1918	8th July	1	6
1919	21st July	6	0
1919	1st December, decrease in household coal ...	10	0
1920	12th May, increase in household coal	14	2
1920	12th May, increase in industrial coal	4	2

An examination of these prices showed that they had never been justified and that the cause was not in increased costs. The real cause was the coalowners' pressure for decontrol, as is clearly shown in a later part of the statement.

The figures were then given in very considerable detail and it was shown that the standard profits allowed to the coalowners under the Finance Acts were far more favourable than the average of those allowed to other industries with the result that an altogether disproportionate amount of profit free of tax was being secured for them.

Arguments were then given for the reduction of coal prices in order to bring about a reduction in the cost of living then shooting up higher

[1] In the nationalisation of the coal mining industry carried through a quarter of a century later the right to strike, though not formally cancelled, was in practice withheld by the agreement between the Union and the Board for compulsory arbitration.

[2] "Facts about the Coal Dispute" (Triple Industrial Alliance, 8 St. Martin's Place, Trafalgar Square, London W.C.2. and Labour Research Department, 34 Eccleston Square, London S.W.1. Price 2d).

from week to week. It was explained that "this circle of high prices, high profits and high taxation is the true vicious circle which the miners are determined to play their part in breaking". It was said "the motive of the Government and the coalowners in objecting so strongly to the miners' attempt to reduce the cost of living is obvious: the Government seek to remove the control at present exercised over the industry and thus to bring about a further increase in prices to the consumer".

The argument was then given for the increase in wages and finally there were considerations on output, a subject which was to come up much more prominently in the later discussions of all parties that autumn. A table of coalowners' profits and of wages were added to the pamphlet.

CHAPTER SEVEN

THE VALLEY OF HUMILIATION

1 UNEMPLOYMENT

In South Wales in the winter of 1920-21 there had been a growing number of miners out of work. On 3rd January, 1921, seven pits of the Main Collieries Company at Neath were rendered idle (3,000 men) "owing to trade depression." Each week applications for out-of-work pay from the districts came up before the Executive Council in Cardiff, until by the end of February, 1921, it was estimated that about 80,000 Welsh colliery workmen were unemployed "through trade depression." A world economic crisis, originating in Japan in the Spring of 1920, had spread to other countries and became manifest in Britain in the autumn. In December, 1920, there were 691,103 out of work in the U.K. or 5.8 per cent of the approximately 12 million persons covered by the Unemployment Insurance Act of 1920.

Although coal mining was less hard hit than several other British industries[1] the exporting districts, such as South Wales, suffered severely enough. In the accounts of the South Wales Miners' Federation the payments to unemployed workmen which had been no less than £29,202 in the year 1920, amounted in 1921 to £216,323. In mid-February the Executive Council, having before it a report on the "high percentage of unemployment in South Wales as compared with the English coal-fields" resolved "to communicate with the MFGB with regard to this matter", and also that the officials should interview the Ministry of Mines. It was further resolved "that the claims for out-of-work pay cannot be met from the money available" (12 ii 1921).

[1] **Percentage Numbers of Insured Workpeople Unemployed (1921-1923 at Quarterly Intervals).**

	All Trades	Coal Miners
March 1921	9.1	2.0
June 1921	18.2	7.0
September 1921	12.5	9.9
December 1921	16.2	11.1
March 1922	14.6	8.1
June 1922	12.8	8.2
September 1922	11.9	6.1
December 1922	12.2	4.6
March 1923	11.1	3.6
June 1923	11.3	2.5
September 1923	11.7	3.1
December 1923	10.6	2.4

(From the 18th and 19th Abstract of Labour Statistics Cmd. 2740. Cmd. 3140).

A special Conference in the Cory Hall with 319 delegates representing 228,098 members resolved on "a levy of 6d. for each day's wages paid be deducted at the colliery offices in support of the unemployed."

Three days later on Tuesday, 22nd February, 1921, the MFGB Special Conference at Central Hall, Westminster, opened with unemployment as the first item on its agenda. George Barker, M.P., at once gave the harrowing picture of the ravages of unemployment; over half the miners in Monmouthshire were under notice. This was "not a matter for either Monmouthshire or South Wales, but for the whole of Britain", said James Winstone, now SWMF President, who then put the South Wales resolution :

"That we recommend, as the Government have refused to put into operation the policy of the Labour Party for dealing with unemployment, measures be taken to get the whole Labour Movement to take drastic action within fourteen days to enforce its policy."

In support of Winstone, A. J. Cook said "I am coming to the conclusion, after the last two months, that all the virtue has gone out of this Federation. It seems to me, looking back and seeing the growth of trade unionism, that with that growth and power there seems to be a lack of fighting spirit . . . "

"I am told by many older men that we must try again constitutional methods, that is Parliament . . . That is why we are getting no further. If we cannot move Parliament to do something we ought to be able to do it ourselves. We have been talking about control of the industry. We have talked about national combination. We have, first of all, to destroy the system, if we have come to the conclusion that there is no solution under this present system" (22 ii 1921).

But Joe Tinker from Lancashire said immediately :

"We cannot support any drastic policy. I am rather surprised at the people from South Wales always advocating the policy of fighting, because when we get to a fight they are not as strong as the leaders are."

This brought Tom Richards to his feet. He said, "I regret the strictures about South Wales and their fighting policy. All I want to say is that you are absolutely wrong. South Wales in my history, and I have been associated with the mining movement as a representative for 35 years, have never been reluctant to enter a fight and never cried out to end it at any time."

After this impassioned utterance, Tom Richards went on to say that unless the situation in South Wales was "taken seriously by the rest of the Federation (and when we do cry out a bit we are not to be criticised like that) then the future of the South Wales Federation and of this Federation is in serious jeopardy." Speaking directly to the 212 union representatives, forty of them from South Wales, Richards continued : "You are not feeling it so acutely, your pits are working regularly, and there are not starving men, women and children—if you had you would begin to cry out yourself." Then he told how in the five weeks ending 5th February, 1921, the number of coal-raising shifts in South Wales had diminished by 3,876 shifts with a loss of output of 1,430,228 tons, a situation that demanded "sympathy and not criticism." Finally, Tom Richards said, "If Mr. Cook's policy were possible I would support it at this moment, but we all know that it is absolutely and entirely impossible and impracticable."

George Spencer, M.P., thought the resolution would end in a fiasco. Hogg of Northumberland held that it would "be a calamity and a disaster" to accept the resolution.

S. O. Davies from South Wales raised the question of the trade depression, saying "Some of us believe that it is the collapse, the irrevocable collapse of the capitalist system . . . this sytem had at least reached the edge of the precipice . . . I think we only have one course to take, it should be to go wholly over the precipice, and then we would have to establish a new economic system."

He was followed by G. H. Jones of the Midland Federation who said: "If you read history you will find no rising has been successful without a discontented army. We have a well clothed army, well fed, who would be willing to do the bidding of the capitalist classes." Jack Hughes strongly supported Winstone and Cook saying "I come from a very large coal mining district, the Cambrian Combine . . . we do not see any other way to save the situation than the one suggested from South Wales."

Another delegate from South Wales, "surprised and distressed at the remarks which have been made from old experienced leaders regarding this proposal for direct action," said "I cannot understand any miners' leader, in whatever capacity he is, running down direct action".

The Chairman, Robert Smillie, then wound up the debate, "I have urged direct action again and again during the last few years. I have always urged it at a time when I felt sure that the needs of the nation itself would make it successful if we tried. I am not of the opinion that the present time is the time for direct action being taken. I believe absolutely that the employers would welcome it . . . What we mean by direct action is a general strike of organised labour in this country. I do not think this is the time to establish a new Labour millenium in this country by a general strike. My heart is sad for the unemployed and their families, and I feel sure that every man in this room feels the same. We would make any personal sacrifice, we would be prepared to make it an order to help the unemployed in any industry or in our own industry, but I do not think we can help along the lines of general action."

The Chairman then put the vote "For the South Wales resolution moved by Mr. Winstone." The result was 51 for, and 106 against.

The next question which came from South Wales was: "Should there be a levy in aid of the unemployed ?" On this Smillie spoke very movingly and, in finally replying, said: "Can we not in a limited way do something in our own ranks? The South Wales miners, probably the most advanced section in this Federation, have recognised to some extent that it is their duty as a local South Wales miners' association to do something to help those who are unemployed. They have decided to levy themselves 6d per day worked" (24 ii 1921).

At the Labour Conference of 27th January, 1921, a policy had been discussed: but later at the adjournment (23rd February) the delegates had been unable to make any advance. It was left to the MFGB Conference (adjourned to 24th February) to see what could be rescued of the items of Labour policy. Robert Smillie,[1] after he had referred to the "sad spectacle that organised labour had to leave that conference practically admitting so far as they were concerned they were powerless to take any action", had then gone on to deliver a speech on unemployment, which it was decided to print off and circulate as a leaflet in the coalfields.

The Miners' National Conference agreed, after a telling speech from Cook ("Voluntary levies are not successful, you must compel the men to pay, and rightly or wrongly the only way to get the money is through the colliery offices"), that a possible solution would be a compulsory levy.

An Executive Committee recommendation, sent out on 3rd March, gave a scheme to deal with unemployment in the coal mines with contribution of 6d for each shift and benefits of £1 per week plus 2/- per dependent child.

Events, however, moved too fast and unemployment spread too rapidly in the coalfields for the raising of levies. At the Annual Conference in the Cooperative Hall in Cardiff a proposal to institute a levy was referred back to the lodges for consideration by 98 against 76. But by the beginning of August, 1921, replies from the lodges on the recommendation of the Annual Conference that a levy of 5 per cent of wages be deducted for the purpose of assisting the unemployed showed 54,350 in favour of the levy and against it 78,800. Thereupon the matter was "referred to the districts to make their own arrangements to endeavour to get the workmen now out absorbed at the collieries and to contribute to the support of those unable to get employment" (4 viii 1921).

Further relations with the unemployed miners now came up in the form of approaches by a local "Unemployed Committee" to the SWMF Executive Council. These form part of the story of the relations which

[1]Earlier that week Smillie had presided for the last time at the MFGB Executive Committee where the first item had been headed "Greeting to a Newly Appointed Member":

"On behalf of the Committee the Chairman welcomed a Mr. A. J. Cook to membership of the Committee and expressed the hope that Mr. Cook's connection with the National Executive would be a long and mutually happy one" (21 ii 1921).

grew up eventually between the Union and the National Unemployed Workers' Committee Movement of which Wal Hannington was the outstanding organiser.

2 A LOCKOUT DECLARED

In the opening month of 1921 wages in the coalfields reached the highest point in the history of the industry. Under the terms of the Agreement with the Government of 28th October, 1920, an output bonus of 3/6d per shift was payable. The average wage per shift worked was 20/3d in January 1921 : in the South Wales coalfield it was 21/6¾d. While owners and miners were still holding joint meetings to discuss an Agreement on the future regulation of wages and conditions the Government suddenly announced that it would end State control of mines five months before the date of 31st August as laid down in the Coal Mines Act of 1920. A Miners' Special Conference unanimously confirmed the protest of their Executive Committee against the proposal of the Government "to decontrol the coal trade", as prejudicial to the interests "both of the coal trade and the nation generally" (24 ii 1921).

The Government for its part, having reached agreement with the owners, rushed ahead with their Decontrol Bill. On 24th March it became an Act of Parliament.

The coalowners soon made it clear that there would be drastic cuts in wages. On 16th March, 1921, notices were posted throughout the coalfields that all contracts of service—including those of the "pump-men and the safety-men" would end on 31st March. The reduction looming ahead would be far beyond expectations.

On 18th March the owners' proposals for future regulation of profits and wages were tabled : and the Miners' National Conference referred to the districts the question whether or not "to temporarily abandon the policy of a National Wages Board and a National Pool" with a view to "a temporary agreement on a district basis." Several of the leaders including the acting-president Herbert Smith and secretary Hodges strongly urged this course. But the South Wales delegates were mandated, by a unanimous resolution at their Special Conference in Cardiff on 23rd March, as were all the larger districts except Northumberland and Yorkshire. The voting was 627 to 241 at the National Conference of 24th March : Smith and Hodges were defeated.

On 29th March the coalowners issued statements of the reduced wages to be paid as from 1st April in the various districts.

At the Board of Trade on 30th March the matter was argued out. The miners were willing to accept some reduction in wages so long as it did not mean a lower standard of living; and to avert this, they asked to get "some financial assistance from the Government". This was rejected immediately. There was bitter argument. Tom Richards said :

"Our men in South Wales, getting on for 300,000 of them, are in a desperate condition. We are in that position because we did not think about the economic profits during the war; you made us subsidise the nation. We say that the Government has scuttled the ship . . . Under ordinary conditions, I am not a fighting man; all my life I have been considered to be much too peaceful; but this situation is desperate . . . It means a reduction of from 45 to 50 per cent" (30 iii 1921).

The miners were angered at what they felt to be a callous attitude, while the miners' wives were even more insistent than the men themselves on making a firm stand.[1]

At the Miners' National Executive that same morning the following resolution was carried by ten to eight:

"That instructions be sent to Districts informing them that all notices should be allowed to expire regardless of occupation in every mine and plant connected with the Federation."

This meant that the enginemen, pumpmen and others concerned with keeping the pit in working order, who had received notices like everybody else, would cease work with everybody else: and this in turn meant that a certain deterioration of the coalowners' property would set in. The coalowners, in declaring their universal lockout, had not assumed that this loss of property through inflow of water would be one of the consequences. They were furious: and the President of the Board of Trade, Sir Robert Horne, who as a former solicitor had an experience which was largely that of protecting property interests, stood completely aghast.

On Thursday, 31st March, 1921, the Government gave up control of the mines: on the same day the notices given by the owners became effective. The next day over one million miners were idle, locked out, standing in the village streets of the mining villages and valleys, gazing at the gaunt and silent machinery on their pithead.

3 A STATE OF EMERGENCY

Meantime a Royal Proclamation had declared the country to be in a "state of emergency". Emergency Regulations followed under the Act. Troops were moved into the coalfields. On Tuesday, 5th April, the War Office cancelled all leave. Troops were brought back from Ireland, where war was being planned against Sinn Fein which, on 7th January, 1919, had summoned their M.P.s to Dublin to be the Dail Eireann. Parks in London and elsewhere were used as armed camps. Day by day, even hour by hour, tension was mounting until on 8th

[1]A month later at a meeting of the Executive Council a large number of resolutions passed by meetings of miners' wives and daughters "urging upon the miners to stand firm, and extending their thanks to the Executive", were received (30 iv 1921).

April Lloyd George told the House of Commons: "I have therefore advised His Majesty that a situation has arisen in which he is justified in sanctioning the issue of a Proclamation calling up the Reserves of the Army and Navy and Air Force." An appeal was to be launched for the enrolment of Special Constables; and furthermore, "a special appeal to patriotic citizens to enlist in an emergency force, the Defence Force." Enlistment was to be for ninety days at the ordinary rates of pay and allowances. Within ten days 80,000 had enlisted—many of them, it is understood, from the ranks of the unemployed.

On Tuesday, 5th April, in the House of Commons, the stage had been set at Question Time. The Secretary for Mines was asked whether steps had been taken to remove pit ponies from the mines and "so save them from starvation or drowning." To this the answer was in the affirmative by the Secretary of Mines who stated: "My information is that at a group of collieries in South Wales 620 horses were below ground yesterday, but the Divisional Inspector of Mines reports that arrangements have been made to withdraw them . . . In the Rhondda Valley there is also some difficulty about getting ponies out". But he added that the Executive of the Miners' Federation was doing all possible to see that all horses were withdrawn.

Question Time was followed by a resolution of "humble thanks" to His Majesty for the Royal Proclamation. Mineowners, headed by Evan Williams, sat in the gallery and heard emotional appeals on behalf of mining property. Colonel Claude Lowther, for example, said it was "a terrible thing to think that at this moment there may be ponies in the mines either drowning bit by bit or gradually starving to death." He said that the miner had been "told by Bolshevik agitators, paid by German gold", that the mineowners wished "to ruin him, to profiteer and to get everything possible out of him." All these humanitarian effusions about the mares and geldings marooned in the bowels of the earth were somwhat spoiled when the Secretary for Mines admitted that Herbert Smith had promised to send a telegram "to any place which I know of if ponies are still below to assist in getting them brought up" : and on the next day, that "no pit ponies have been lost in the mines". It seemed the parliamentary orators had stumbled into a mare's nest.

This did not prevent the Prime Minister at the close of the debate from dwelling upon the susceptibilities of politicians and journalists, perorating: "It is essential that the Miners' Federation should give every facility and assistance to prevent the pits from being destroyed and also to save the lives of these poor dumb animals."

Amid these appeals a multitude of emergency regulations were being published under the Emergency Powers Act. Power was taken to assume possession of any land, buildings, plant, works (including gas, electricity and water undertakings); to regulate and restrict road transport and to take control of vehicles, light railways and canals; to take possession of food and forage; to requisition ships and to give directions as to cargoes; to take possession of coal mines and give directions as to their management and use; to regulate the price and distribution of coal. Moreover, the Postmaster-General was given power to direct that telegraphic messages "of such classes or descriptions as he may prescribe shall not be accepted for transmission." By regulation it was made an offence "to do any act calculated to cause mutiny, sedition, or disaffection among any of His Majesty's Forces, or the police force or the fire brigade, or to impede the distribution of food, fuel or water." Powers to search premises were assumed together with very drastic powers of arrest, so that any police constable might "arrest without warrant" any person "who is guilty or who is suspected of being guilty of an offence." Furthermore, the Secretary of State, a Mayor, a Magistrate or Chief Officer of Police might make an order prohibiting the holding of meetings "when there is reason to apprehend that the assembly will give rise to grave disorder and will thereby cause undue demands on the police or military forces."

At its Monday meeting Rhondda No. 1 District resolved: "That we protest most emphatically against the importation of military units and police into this area, and demand their immediate withdrawal by the authorities" (11 iv 1921).

In South Wales it was believed that much movement of troops was provocative. At the Executive Council "the importation of police and military into the industrial areas" was raised and they resolved to send "a telegram to the Joint Standing Committees of the Counties of Glamorgan, Monmouth, Carmarthen and Brecon protesting against this action and calling for their withdrawal" (12 iv 1921).

In the telegram the Executive Council protested "most emphatically against the importation of police and military forces into industrial areas" where hitherto there had been no sign of disorder of any kind. "We further ask for their immediate withdrawal, as their presence is provocative of trouble, and involves the County in unnecessary expense." To this the Chairman of the Joint Standing Committee for Glamorganshire replied that he disagreed with the statements in the telegram and that while he regretted "the necessity for the importation" the necessity existed and "while it exists these forces must remain."

4 "BLACK FRIDAY"

On Wednesday, 6th April, Lloyd George announced it would be "quite impossible to have negotiations whilst the mines are gradually crumbling owing to the difficulties of keeping them from being flooded."

Next morning, on Thursday, 7th April, the Prime Minister asked that there should be "a truce" in this industrial warfare and that the pumpmen should go back to their work. Herbert Smith as Acting President replied: "We are anxious to save the mines but we are equally

12 ARTHUR HORNER, PRESIDENT SWMF 1936-46

13 S. O. DAVIES, VICE-PRESIDENT SWMF 1924-33

anxious to save women and children, and that appeals more to us than the mines, which are the property of the owners." It was complete deadlock.

But meantime the two partners of the miners in the Triple Alliance had been called into the discussions.

At the beginning of the dispute the miners' leaders had resolved "that we ask the other organisations in the Triple Alliance to take strike action in order to assist the miners in the present crisis" (31 iii 1921).

Decision was taken on Friday, 8th April, for a strike on the railways and in transport as from midnight of Tuesday, 12th April. The two partners of the miners in the Triple Alliance claimed an interest in negotiations: and their deputation went to see the Prime Minister on the morning of Saturday, 9th April, and urged him to break the deadlock. They found the Prime Minister inflexible. Unless the miners would give way on the question of pumpmen, the Government would not agree to reopen negotiations.

Perhaps, suggested Lloyd George, the deputation would use their influence with the miners to remove the deadlock. The deputation consented.

That same day the miners, under pressure from their partners, sent a telegram to all Districts: "A conference with the owners being opened unconditionally, we urge upon all our members to abstain from all action which will interfere with the measures necessary for securing the safety of the mines, or will necessitate the use of force by the Government" (9 iv 1921).

The No. 1 Rhondda District, meeting in the Porth Hotel on Monday, 11th April, resolved "In face of negotiations being reopened between the Owners and Miners Representatives, and the instructions issued by the MFGB, this District advises our men to maintain a united inactivity pending further instructions. We also call upon all trade unionists to stand firm by the miners in refusing to do any Blackleg Labour" (11 iv 1921).

That morning of Saturday, 9th April, Jimmy Thomas had soon been able to reach an understanding with Lloyd George: indeed, Thomas and George had learned to understand one another in the last two years of the war.

The Allies had been successful in their "mediation". The miners' leaders had to give way lest their refusal would furnish a pretext for their Allies to desert them. But their most effective weapon for gaining an early settlement had been stricken from their hands.[1]

[1]"The actual effect of his decision, which was generally observed, was to remove the danger of flooding, and also to eliminate the chief factor which would have necessitated a speedy settlement of the dispute. It is by no means certain, even from a national point of view, that the resumption of work by the safety men was an unmixed blessing."—G. D. H. Cole op. cit. page 207.

Negotiations broke down late on Tuesday, 12th April. The Miners' Executive, meeting that evening decided: "That, having fully considered the terms set forth in writing by the Government, we reject such terms as they offer no solution to the present dispute."

From the Government's point of view however, there was no failure. The two days spent in fruitless negotiations had effected a postponement of the strike notices of the railwaymen and the transport workers: and a strike postponed, it was known, is often half way to no strike at all.

On Wednesday, 13th April, the full Triple Alliance met again. In face of the deadlock the call for a strike was reissued and the date was fixed for two days later at 10 p.m. on Friday, 15th April. Meantime, the two partners of the Triple Alliance were joined by other Unions. The Associated Society of Locomotive Engineers and Firemen would go on strike; and their representatives attended the Triple Alliance meetings. The Executive Committee of the Electrical Trades Union (whose London District Council had decided for strike action) came to consult with the Triple Alliance. So did the Executive of the Post Office Workers. The Railway Clerks Association recommended strike action to its members. The Cooperative Wholesale Society offered its aid in preparations for the strike. On Thursday, 14th April, the National Joint Council of Labour made up of the committees of the Labour Party, the Parliamentary Party and the Trades Union Congress meeting at the House of Commons resolved to support the miners. The issue was widening from a Triple Alliance strike to one that would involve hundreds of thousands of other workers, from a dispute over wages to a gigantic head-on collision.

For two weeks the miners had been locked out. Now, as it seemed, powerful reinforcements were coming up. With such backing it seemed that the miners were bound to win.

On the evening of Thursday, 14th April, at an informal meeting of Members of Parliament, Frank Hodges made what was understood to be an offer to enter into a temporary wage settlement, waiving for the time being the miners' main demands. Lloyd George seized the opportunity. On the morning of Friday, 15th April, the Miners' Executive had before them a letter from the Prime Minister to Frank Hodges asking if they would now meet on the basis of dropping the controversial issues. This proposal was rejected. The Miners' Executive insisted on the two principles of a National Wages Board and a National Pool. Having taken this decision they immediately reported it to their partners. These, after discussing the matter among themselves, sent their leaders to the Miners' Executive asking that "it should reverse its decision and accept the Prime Minister's invitation". This the miners indignantly refused to do and they made it clear that they expected their Allies to come out on strike that evening at 10 p.m. as already fixed.

What happened thereafter may be told in the language of the official History of the Miners' Federation :

"Then their allies went back to Unity House, the headquarters of the National Union of Railwaymen. There the atmosphere was now near to hysteria. Fear that they might wreck their organisations, fear of Lloyd George's cleverness, fear of the forces that would be opposed to them, all these fears oppressed the delegates. In such a mood panic was possible. One or two speeches stampeded the Conference : and within a few minutes J. H. Thomas, unable to disguise his relief, was out speaking to the pressmen who waited at the doors telling them that the strike was cancelled."

The day this decision was taken, in which the Triple Alliance partners decided to call off the strike, came to be known as "Black Friday". Bitter anger was felt throughout the Trade Union Movement.

5 LATER STAGES OF THE STRUGGLE

The withdrawal of the Triple Alliance partners left the miners to struggle alone. Repeated attempts to persuade them to give in and return to work were repeatedly rejected by the miners. After ten weeks of lock-out a National Delegate Conference decided to take a ballot of the miners on the combined terms of the Government and the Mining Association.[1]

There was over a quarter of a million majority for continuing the fight for principle as against the terms of the Government and the owners.

In the MFGB Executive Committee endeavour was made to get other unions affected by wage disputes to meet and take national action with the miners "to secure their mutual demands." The Executive Council, on 21st June, decided that the motion (put forward by Noah Ablett on the National Committee) "for the withdrawal of the safety men be supported." A committee of five was appointed "to consider

[1] Wording was as follows:

(1) Are you in favour of fighting on for the principles of the National Wages Board and the National Pool, with loss of Government subsidy of ten million pounds for wages if no settlement by the 18th June, 1921 ?

(2) Are you in favour of accepting the Government's and the owners' terms as set forth on the back of this ballot paper ?

The result of the ballot was:

For continuing the Fight on principle	435,614
For Government and Owners' Terms	180,724
Being a majority for the Fight	254,890

In the South Wales District the votes recorded were:

For continuing the Fight	110,616
For the Terms	40,909
A majority of	69,707

Two thirds of the miners in the 19 district unions of the MFGB, with a total trade union membership of 957,610, cast their votes; but over three-quarters in South Wales. There the majority was 73 per cent, slightly more than the national average of 71 per cent.

sources from which funds can be raised for the alleviation of distress," following on a report that "the Co-operative Societies and others in the Rhondda and other places would not give further credit to the workmen."

On Friday, 24th June, the National Executive resolved to ask the Government and the owners for a meeting "with a view to negotiating a satisfactory wage agreement, which we can recommend our members to accept."

The National Executive next day wrote to the districts stating "In order that no more suffering should be endured by a continuation of this struggle, we took upon ourselves the freedom to negotiate a wages settlement . . .

"We therefore strongly urge you, with the knowledge of the seriousness of the situation, to accept this agreement, which we have provisionally agreed to today, and authorise your Committee to sign the terms by Friday next."

When the reports came back the four smallest districts, together with Lancashire, were opposed. Other districts were for acceptance. On Friday, 1st July, the Committee authorised the following telegram:

"Overwhelming vote in favour of resumption of work. Workmen to return without delay."

At the Special Conference in Cardiff on 30th June Tom Richards proposed the resolution recommended by the Council: "That this Conference, while strongly condemning the action of the majority of the National Executive in disregarding the recent ballot vote of the workmen, and negotiating terms of settlement without consulting them, feel we have no option, if the Federation is to be preserved, but to accept the terms".

A. J. Cook and Noah Ablett supplemented the report and supported the resolutions. A motion "that the terms be rejected" received 109 votes for the recommendation against 112. It was a narrow majority.

One day later the workmen had to return without delay. The lockout was ended, the miners were defeated, they had come through great tribulation and they were for a period about to enter into the valley of humiliation.

At the MFGB Annual Conference which followed in August there was a survey in retrospect by Vice-President Herbert Smith as acting-President. In this he indicated that the policy of fighting for the National Wages Board and the National Pool had been mistaken. He stood for those (himself and Frank Hodges) who had led a small minority of the Executive and he made references to "disloyal" leaders of the districts. A bitter debate followed. Hodges, in a defensive speech, brought in as relevant Smillie's drive for direct action to nationalise the mines—a suggestion much resented from Durham ("the greatest disloyalty has been on the part of the officials of this Federation"). In South Wales, however, trust continued to be reposed in their new leaders on the National Executive—those who, together with Tom Richards, had taken the place of both William Brace and Vernon Hartshorn.

The terms now accepted were that a temporary scheme, to end on 1st October, was to be succeeded by a permanent scheme wherein a National Board and District members were to be set up. A new District standard rate was to operate. The owners were to have a standard profit of 17 per cent of the standard wages. If there were surplus profits these were to be divided among workmen and owners in the proportion of 83 per cent to wages and 17 per cent to profits. This profit-sharing agreement was to continue until December, 1922.

6 THE TERMS OF SETTLEMENT AND THEIR SEQUEL

The South Wales Miners' Federation emerged from the lockout of 1921 battered and beaten. This severe defeat had been inflicted upon them, so they felt, by the employers and the Coalition government which had devised in advance the strike-breaking machinery of the Emergency Powers Act, so that from the beginning it was "not a fair fight" : and it left in the valleys an abiding hatred for Liberal and Tory politicians alike. Nor was there any tendency towards industrial reconciliation. The Monmouthshire and South Wales Coal Owners' Association made full use of the victory. Wages were brought down with a rush. Within a twelve-month of the beginning of the "permanent period" under the Terms of Settlement[1] the average daily wage of 1921 had been halved. In South Wales the fall was even greater from 21/6¾d per shift in January, 1921, to 9/5½d in October, 1922.

In other matters, too, the owners had proved unaccommodating. Writing for *The Colliery Workers' Magazine* eighteen months later the Rt. Hon. Thomas Richards dismissed as a delusion any notion that the employers could be induced "to relinquish their *hostility* to the Minimum Rate of Wages, the Seven Hours Day, the Subsistence Wage, the Six Turns for Five," or that they would refrain from using every legal opportunity "to raise all manner of technical objections to the payment of Compensation for Injuries and Death." The Terms of the Settlement on 1st July, 1921, "between the Parties and His Majesty's Government as to the wages thereafter to be payable" had set up thirteen District Boards in Great Britain. A Memorandum of Agreement between owners' and workmen's representatives in South Wales (to be placed in a Contract Book at each colliery and to be signed "by each Workman employed thereat") was concluded on 14th November, 1921. The first of its 28 clauses ran as follows:

1. "The Board of Conciliation for the Coal Trade of Monmouthshire and South Wales (hereinafter referred to as 'the Board'), shall be deemed to be the District Board for the said District of South

[1]See *The Miners: Years of Struggle* pp. 333-336 for full text of these terms.

Wales and Monmouth (hereinafter referred to as 'the District') and the Board shall determine the wages to be paid to the Workmen in accordance with the Terms of Settlement, and deal with disputes at the various Collieries of the Owners subject to the conditions hereinafter mentioned."

In this Agreement, signed by thitry representatives[1] of the workmen "who may be members of the South Wales Miners' Federation" and by some twenty representatives of 121 collieries (members of the Coal Owners' Association and covering nine tenths of the total output of the coalfield) the opening sentence of Clause Nine ran : "The wages payable during any period subsequent to the month of September, 1921, shall be the 1915 standard base rates applicable to the different classes of workmen employed plus the percentage upon such rates to be determined by the proceeds of the industry for the district based upon the ascertained results of a previous period to be fixed by the National Board constituted in accordance with the Terms of Settlement and therein referred to as 'The Period of Ascertainment'."

For the next twenty years the "Ascertainments" and their results were a source of controversy and strife in the coalfield.

It was provided that the wages payable "shall in no event be less than the 1915 standard base rates with 28 per cent added thereto." Pieceworkers were also to receive the additional 14.2 per cent consequent upon the reduction of working hours from eight to seven. How this would work out in the Monmouthshire and South Wales coalfield was laid down in general in the agreement under the Terms of Settlement.

More than once in 1922 and in 1923 the South Wales Miners' Conferences voted in their misery to put an end to the Agreement on which the Conciliation Board was hinged; but found themselves in a minority within the Miners' Federation of Great Britain. For what chance was there in the bleak winters of 1921-22 and 1922-23 of anything better ? They could only hope for improvement in the terms themselves. But appeals to the owners were in vain. They appealed on 19th October, 1922, to Lloyd George only to be told that he had that very hour handed in his resignation to the King. They appealed to the new Prime Minister Bonar Law who on 2nd December, 1922, admitted that conditions were "horribly bad" in the coalfields : but could see no way of meeting their appeal except by telling them to hope for better times. Thereafter appeals to the new parliament; either in debate or through a Coal Mines (Minimum Wage) Amendment Bill—tabled on 9th May, 1923—proved also to be in vain.

[1]"**Workmen's Representatives on the Conciliation Board, 1921.**

E. Morrell	S. O. Davies	D. R. Grenfell	Noah Rees
Gwilym Richards	J. D. Morgan	A. J. Cook	George Davies
Thos. Lucas	John James	Vernon Hartshorn	George Daggar
Ben Davies	D. L. Davies	Albert Thomas	Noah Ablett
Owen Powell	William Woosnam	William Dunn	Walter Lewis
Hubert Jenkins	William Hopkins	David Lewis	Thomas Richards,
Arthur Jenkins	John Thomas	John Griffiths	Secretary."
William Jenkins	D. J. Williams	Ted Williams	

For the General Election there was issued on 1st November, 1922, a manifesto[1] "to miners, miners' wives and voters in coalmining districts," signed on behalf of the Miners' Federation of Great Britain by the four national officers.

The result of the General Election of mid-November, 1922, was a Conservative victory with 345 seats in the House of Commons. But the Labour Party with 142 seats doubled its representation. The two wings of the Liberal Party (National Liberal and Liberal) had 116 seats between them. The candidates of the MFGB numbered 53 of whom 42 were successful.

Of the 36 Members of Parliament representing Wales 18 were Labour, 11 Liberal, 6 Conservative and 1 Independent. Of the eighteen Labour representatives ten stood under the auspices of the South Wales Miners' Federation and won every seat contested. Their names were as follows: G. H. Hall, Aberdare; D. R. Grenfell, Gower; W. Jenkins, Neath; Vernon Hartshorn, Ogmore; T. I. Mardy Jones, Pontypridd; D. Watts Morgan, Rhondda (East); W. John, Rhondda (West); Geo. Barker, Abertillery; Chas. Edwards, Bedwellty; Evan Davies, Ebbw Vale.

7 DOWN AND OUT

For many miners the crushing defeat of 1921 seemed irretrievable. The effect was seen in a catastrophic fall in union membership. By the end of 1920 South Wales Miners' Federation membership had risen

[1]The hour has come. Men and women of the coal mines and colliery districts: at last the Coalition Government is dead! You, of all workpeople, who have suffered most at their hands, can now pass judgment upon the political authors of your misery.

You will not forget that they were individually and collectively responsible for supporting a policy which has brought the greatest economic disaster ever known into your lives.

You will remember that Tory and Liberal alike in the Coalition supported the creation of the Sankey Commission, then rejected its principal finding—the nationalisation of the mines. You cannot forget that Liberal and Tory alike combined to decontrol your industry out of due time, and caused you to endure thirteen weeks lock-out, from which you are far from recovery. You cannot forget how Tory and Liberal alike on March 31st, 1921, swept away your wage rate, your flat rate, your Sankey wage as though it were nothing to you . . .

Reparations and Unemployment.

They made the Germans pay, in coal, and destroyed the foundations of our European coal trade. The German miners work overtime in consequence, whilst 75,000 British miners are drawing unemployment pay.

We asked for bread and they gave us a stone.

Men and women, unparalleled poverty is with us now . . . when we ask the coalowners for better wages, they offer us a longer working day, at a time when we can't sell the coal we are producing. When we ask the Government to help us out of the wreckage they have created they offer us their congratulations, that we at least are in an industry that is on an "economic basis." It is "an economic basis", true, but maintained by famine wages.

Vote for Labour, Work for Labour.

to a peak of 197,668. By the end of 1922 there were only 87,080 left in the Union. Frank Hodges, after addressing seven meetings of miners in that bleak winter of 1922-23, registered his impression "of an almost universal spirit of pessimism akin to hopelessness", and in a retrospective article wrote: "There is something mercurial about the Welsh miner, which distinguishes him in a very marked sense from the English or Scottish miner. In bright days he is radiantly happy, electrical, dynamic, with an infectious humour. He is by nature carefree and joyous. In dark and difficult days his cheerfulness quickly and almost completely evaporates. He too quickly slides into the deep shadows of despair. In this gloom his faith in trade unionism falters; his confidence in leaders is shaken; a marked tendency towards the anarchy and indiscipline of the bad old days is thrown up in bold relief. In this darkness any luminous will-o-the-wisp is eagerly chased, and disaster is accumulative in consequence."[1]

This cold analysis with its veiled reference to A. J. Cook as the *ignis fatuus* was hardly welcomed in the valleys.

The distress due to low wages and low employment was made worse by certain coalowners who were singled out for condemnation at a Cardiff Conference. It was stated that active trade unionists were being victimised, former established practices were being disregarded by management, and unjustifiable wage reductions were being enforced.[2] Vernon Hartshorn (President of the South Wales Miners' Federation after the untimely death of J. Winstone) who had earlier been an exponent of the policy of cooperation and conciliation in the coal fields, made a very different speech at the May Day demonstration of 1922. He declared that "he had been right always when he had been fighting and wrong always when he had been trying to bring about a spirit of conciliation."

A delegate conference of the South Wales Federation met in May 1922 to formulate a plan of action and resolved:

"That this Conference, having considered the position relating to the membership of the Federation, resolves that the officials, committeemen, agents, and all members interested in the welfare of the Federation, make every effort to bring to the notice of non-members that, in their own interests, and to secure the protection of united effort, it is imperative that all colliery workmen shall be members of the Federation. Further, that a report be made to the annual conference in June next

[1]*Colliery Workers' Magazine*, Vol. 1, No. 3.

[2]"That this Conference strongly condemns the action of various coalowners in their victimisation of workmen, thus robbing them of their right to earn a livelihood as a punishment for their activities in connection with the Federation. We also strongly protest against the non-observance by the coalowners of the terms of the national agreement entered into at the end of the recent lock-out, disregarding all former practices, customs, and price lists, and the enforcement of unjustifiable reductions in wages. Unless grievances have not been remedied by the date of the annual conference, the notices on the non-Unionist question shall also be used for this purpose" (8 v 1922).

upon the position, and that the lodges be asked to authorise their delegates to the annual conference to decide that if the report be not satisfactory, fourteen days' notice shall be tendered to enforce membership of the Federation" (8 v 1922).

Six weeks later the Delegate Conference at Cardiff decided that they were no longer prepared to tolerate the present conditions. Unanimously they resolved to ask the MFGB to make an immediate application for an increase to 60 per cent above pre-war wages and in the event of failure to secure this from the owners, the MFGB Executive were to take the matter to the Government. On the question of non-unionism it decided to tender 14 days strike notice on 10th July, 1922, with a view to compelling all mineworkers to join the Federation. Resolutions were also passed in support of a six-hour shift, five-day week, a fortnight's holiday a year and the abolition of piecework. But on 11th July it was decided to postpone the strike notices.

In South Wales the miners had been seething with unrest at the presence of so many non-unionists in the coalfield. The owners had contrary to the policy adopted early in 1916, refused to cooperate with the miners in settling this vexed question. The Executive Council again ballotted the lodges on the question of taking strike action to induce non-unionists to join the ranks of the Federation. When the result of the ballot was a large majority in favour of strike action, the Delegate Conference of 30th September decided to give fourteen days strike notice. But four weeks later a Special Conference received the report of the Executive Council on the decision "to terminate contracts on the non-unionist question" which showed that only a small percentage of the members (55,631 or 28 per cent) had tendered notices. The Executive Council submitted that the "general action" methods had not been so effective as the former practice of leaving districts and lodges to adopt their own methods: and recommended therefore the withdrawal of the strike notices with a view to the districts selecting the methods best suited to their peculiar circumstances. So matters wore through the winter of 1922-23.

The non-unionist trouble came to a head in March, 1923, in South Wales. The policy of leaving districts and lodges to adopt their own methods to solve the problem led to a number of strikes at pits. But it was also wider. In the Rhymney Valley 2,000 men came out and only returned to work when the non-unionists joined the Federation and paid up their arrears. At one colliery in Llanelly 100 per cent organisation was achieved after one week's strike. On 5th March some 15,000 to 18,000 miners in the mid-Glamorgan area (Garw, Ogmore, Gilfach and Maesteg Districts) tendered notices on 5th March. On 18th March they fulfilled their notices (with the exception of the Ocean Colliery in Ogmore Vale) and a week thereafter resumed work having brought in many to the Federation. On 19th March 17,000 miners in the Rhondda Valley gave notice to terminate their engagements in a fortnight if non-unionists had not come into the Federation by that time, and by 4th April there were 40,000 idle.

It should be noted the Federation regarded members of the Mechanical and Surface Workers Union as non-unionists. These workers had seceded from the SWMF in August, 1921 : and the dispute centred round the strike of members of the Federation at the Nine Mile Point Colliery. Meantime this "breakaway" union was refused recognition by the Trades Union Congress General Council.

The non-unionist strike at the Nine Mile Point Collieries ended on 23rd April when the Mechanical Workers' Union decided to subscribe, under protest, to the Miners' Federation.

Meantime a test case came before the Pontypool Magistrates on 10th March, when 53 miners at two collieries at Abersychan were summoned for alleged breach of contract by absenting themselves from work between 17th January and 22nd January. The case for the plaintiffs was that on 17th January, 1923, a show of cards had revealed a number of non-unionists : and when the employers refused to help the miners' leaders to get the non-unionists into the Federation, the men had come out on strike without giving a fortnight's notice according to the Conciliation Board Agreement. Tom Richards, in defence, said that the owners had recognised the custom of "show cards" for twenty years and had assisted in getting the men to join the Federation. Two years ago the owners changed their policy, refused to help the Federation, but did not abolish the custom of "show cards." After a six-hours hearing The Bench gave a verdict for the plaintiffs and ordered each of the 53 Defendants to pay the damages claimed, 26/- each, together with costs. A request that payment of the money should be suspended pending an appeal to the High Court decision was disallowed.

By the month of May, 1923, it was reported that the strikes in South Wales against non-unionism had practically come to an end and that the majority of non-unionists had rejoined the Federation. Membership in the Rhondda was increased from 18,000 to over 40,000.

The Monmouthshire and South Wales Coal Owners' Association, having heard the decision of the Prime Minister Bonar Law of "no Government assistance", made a statement in January 1923 to the effect that "the miners must return to the eight-hour shift." The wages structure built up during seven years of war and its aftermath had been dismantled and torn down : and notice was now given that longer hours would be the next objective, as had already been hinted in 1922.

On the other hand, Hodges declared : "When the unemployed are absorbed, when the workmen can work a full week, 287,000 tons will be secured; then the miners will ask that the recommendation of the King's Commissioners shall be translated into law, and a six-hour day established." These were brave words.

8 PARLEYS OVER THE 1921 AGREEMENT

By the late autumn of 1922 the miners had fallen to almost the lowest paid of the big groups of industrial workers.

Table.

Average Wage per Shift in Five Selected Larger Districts.

	June 1914		Dec. 1920		Oct. 1922	
	s.	d.	s.	d.	s.	d.
Scotland	6	8.88	23	6	8	4.8
Northumberland	6	2.17	—		9	10.65
Durham	6	2.55	22	0	8	7.4
Lancashire, Staffs and Cheshire	6	0.33	21	11	9	10.8
South Wales	6	9.22	25	9	8	9.6

(Monthly Circular of the Labour Research Department, November, 1922).

Would a higher price have had any effect ? The miners considered this. They put it before the National Joint Board for the Mining Industry on 5th October, 1922. The miners' representatives asked that wages should be brought to a level to correspond with the cost of living. The owners rejected this proposal but put forward a counter-suggestion, namely, that in the near future it would be necessary to consider a reduction in the minimum "in order to recoup the owners for the arrears of 'standard profits' which had accumulated under the agreement". It was at this time that, turning about every way to find relief, the miners began to discuss an amendment to the Coal Mines Minimum Wage Act of 1912.

At the MFGB Special Conference of March, 1923, a motion to bring to an end the National Wages Agreement proposed by Lancashire and seconded by Vernon Hartshorn, M.P., on behalf of South Wales, was opposed by the Executive Committee, who obtained 438,000 against a minority of 305,000 made up of Durham, South Wales with Forest of Dean, and Lancashire.

Another Special Conference accepted a resolution of the Executive Committee by a majority as follows : "That in view of the arrangements made to facilitate the second reading of the Coal Mines Minimum Wage Act (Amendment) Bill no decision be taken today upon the question of the National Wage Agreement, and that the discussion upon the motion be adjourned until the Annual Conference commencing 10th July, 1922" (30 v 1923). When the Miners' Bill came up for Second Reading on 21st June, 1923, it was defeated in the Commons by 230 votes to 154. Owners, Government and Parliament had now all flatly refused to consider any improvement in miners' wages.

Meantime there had been an improvement in trade.

A rise in export prices resulted from the situation on the Continent of Europe. For the best Admiralty smokeless large coal exported at Cardiff between mid-February and mid-March the f.o.b. price had risen from 29/6d to 38/-d per ton. Union membership, at 200,000 in March, 1921, had sunk to 87,000 by December, 1922, but now rose to 117,500.

At the Folkestone Annual Conference beginning 10th July, 1923, the Lancashire resolution for termination of the agreement was not put to the vote, while a recommendation of the Executive Committee was carried by 479,000 votes to 277,000 against a minority made up of Lancashire, Scotland and South Wales.[1] It ran : "That this Conference take no vote on the question of terminating or continuing the agreement but that the Executive be empowered to submit to the National Board proposals for improving the agreement in certain of its clauses, particularly—

(1) The revision of the ratio of profits and wages;
(2) The revision of the prices minimum in the agreement;
(3) Fuller information as to the other costs;

and report to a later conference" (12 vii 1923).

Representatives of the Mining Association of Great Britain on Thursday, 2nd August, 1923, met the MFGB Executive Committee. The view of the owners did not seem to differ very much from that voiced at the August Assembly of the British Association; that the only thing wrong with the Agreement was the Minimum Wage Clause, which had been "stuck like a ramrod into its delicate mechanism." In much the same terms Colonel Lane Fox, the Secretary for Mines, expressed himself in his second Annual Report, issued on 4th October, 1923, on the same day that the owners again met the MFGB Executive Committee. The coalowners had spent these two months "consulting the Districts." When they met they intimated they were not prepared to make any concessions on the first two points. As regards point 3, however, Evan Williams preserved an open mind and with his fellow owners was prepared to analyse the costs more minutely if any useful purpose would thereby be served.

A further meeting between the two sides on Thursday, 15th November, 1923, resulted in a suggestion by the owners that a joint

[1]There were other matters in which the left-wing outlook of the South Wales miners was shown, sometimes on matters of wording. In the spring of 1923 relations with the Soviet Union had been worsened by the Note of the Secretary of State for Foreign Affairs, the Marquess Curzon, threatening to break off trade, with the effect of a renewed attempt to blockade the Soviet Union. Whereupon the Executive Committee prepared a resolution "That this Conference calls upon the Government to maintain the full trading relations between this country and Russia. The coal trade of this country is directly affected by Russian commerce, and any interference with the existing relations would involve the mining industry of Britain in still further poverty. Whilst we may not approve of the Russian form of government, we must recognise the right of the people of Russia to have any form of government they care to establish. To deny this would be a violation of everything for which democracy stands."

On this A. J. Cook jumped up on behalf of South Wales and said that the words "while we may not approve of the Russian form of government" should be deleted. This was seconded by Noah Ablett and the words were withdrawn.

sub-committee of seven persons from each side should be appointed in order to enquire into the whole working of the wages agreement and also into applications which had been, or would be, put forward by each side for a revision thereof.

9 STRANGE RESULTS OF A GENERAL ELECTION

A new complexion was put upon everything when Prime Minister Stanley Baldwin unexpectedly announced he would ask the King for a dissolution of Parliament. In the General Election of 6th December, 1923, Labour won 191 seats (142 a year earlier); Liberals 159 seats (116 in 1922) and the Conservatives 258 seats (345 a year earlier). Of the 43 mining seats ten were in South Wales.[1] A week later the MFGB Special Conference called on a ballot and recommended to vote against continuance of the Agreement. The ballot showed a nearly four to one majority against continuation. In South Wales (130,000 were for termination and 15,000 against) the majority was 9 to 1, in Lancashire nearly 19 to 1. On 7th January, 1924, a letter beginning: "We the undersigned officers and members of the Executive Committee of the Miners' Federation of Great Britain do hereby tender three months notice," was handed to the Central Committee of the Mining Association of Great Britain. The owners said they would consider their reply: but it was not till six weeks later that they were able to give an answer. By this time a further development brought changes in the personnel of the miners' leadership both in South Wales and in the Miners' Federation of Great Britain.

On 22nd January, Stanley Baldwin handed in his resignation. James Ramsay MacDonald took office, and on the same day the death of Lenin was announced. The thirty members of the SWMF Executive Council, meeting in Cardiff, resolved "That we heartily congratulate Mr. J. R. MacDonald upon being made Prime Minister, and assure him of the loyal support of the South Wales miners" (26 i 1924). They also passed a vote of "condolence with the family and the people of Russia": and five days later in London the first business for the MFGB

[1]**Glamorgan**	Majority
Aberdare—G. H. Hall	5,217
Gower—D. R. Grenfell	2,086
Neath—W. Jenkins	6,434
Ogmore—Vernon Hartshorn	9,843
Pontypridd—T. I. Mardy Jones	6,217
Rhondda (East)—D. Watts Morgan	3,121
Rhondda (West)—W. John	7,011
Monmouth	
Abertillery—Geo. Barker	Unopposed
Bedwellty—Chas. Edwards	7,138
Ebbw Vale—Evan Davies	7,996

Of the 36 Members of Parliament representing Wales, 18 were Labour, 11 Liberals, 6 Conservatives and 1 Independent.

Executive Committee on Thursday, 31st January, was to pass a resolution expressing "Deep sympathy with the Russian people in the loss they have sustained by the death of the President of the People's Commissaries, Nikolai Lenin" (31 i 1924).

Vernon Hartshorn, one of the three mining M.P.s taken into the new Cabinet on 26th January, resigned his Presidency of the South Wales Miners' Federation and was succeeded by Vice-President Enoch Morrell.

At the subsequent meeting in London of the National Committee Steve Walsh who had gone to the War Office resigned as Vice-President : and the Rt. Hon. Thomas Richards was appointed Vice-President in his place. At the same meeting resignation from the Secretaryship of Frank Hodges, who had become Civil Lord of the Admiralty, took immediate effect. Amongst those changes the most significant turned out to be the change of Secretaryship.

The rule of the Miners' Federation, passed in 1918, was that in the event of the Secretary becoming a Member of Parliament, or a paid official of the Government, "he must relinquish his position as a permanent official of the Federation." Frank Hodges, in 1918 the successful candidate from South Wales, had gained an ascendency in the councils of the Federation after the departure of Smillie at the end of February, 1921 : and by 11th April the Executive had placed on record "its high appreciation of the splendid service rendered by the Secretary (Mr. Frank Hodges) to the miners in their struggle for a National Wages Board with a National Profits Pool." Within the week, however, Hodges had belied the trust reposed in him and by his speech at the informal meeting of parliamentarians in the House of Commons had furnished the pretext for the desertion of the miners by their allies.

After the lockout he had continued to win golden opinions particularly from outside the ranks of the Miners' Union, by the summer of 1921 he had ceased to voice radical views. Soon he was known to work in considerable harmony with the coal owners. In South Wales and in Lancashire, too, he had become unpopular largely because of his defence of the 1921 Agreement. Consequently when it was suggested at the Annual Conference in Folkestone that Frank Hodges should be exempt from carrying out the rule about the Secretaryship and a proposal so to alter the rule was made from Somerset and the Midlands it was defeated on a card vote by 520 to 236.

Despite this, Frank Hodges, having had the backing of the Labour Party chiefs (whose yearning to see him in Parliament had been expressed in a deputation in October 1922) and convinced that the rule on Secretaryship would be suspended in his favour, announced in mid-November that he might stand for Parliament. Having secured the sponsorship of the Midland Miners' Federation he was duly elected M.P. for Lichfield three weeks later. Further, when delegates assembled for the MFGB Special Conference they found the Executive Committee had recommended the "continuance of the Secretary's services until Districts have had an opportunity of considering the whole situation arising from the fact that he has been elected to the House of Commons" (14 xii 1923). But then something went wrong with the plan.

"The best laid schemes o' mice and men,
Gang aft agley."

James Robson of Durham rose and said: "An attempt was made at the Annual Conference to alter the rule which failed, and yet Mr. Hodges has run in face of that rule." And so the Durham amendment "That the resignation of the Secretary be accepted at once, but that he be requested to continue his services until the necessary arrangements are made for the appointment of his successor," was carried on a card vote by 401 to 353, the majority being made up of South Wales, Durham, Scotland, Northumberland and Derbyshire.

Just before the vote was taken Hodges asked if he might make a personal statement: he indicated that if the conference rejected the Executive's recommendation he would refuse to give the three months' notice laid down in the rule under which he had been appointed but would resign forthwith. Some people, he said, criticised him "because of my attacks so regularly made in all places against the Communist method of Government. I have tried to establish the fact that the Bolshevik form of Government is no use in Great Britain. I have consistently done that, and I shall continue to do so. I am perfectly sure there are some who are taking this opportunity of trying to dispense with my services because of that, which I think is not as straightforward as it might otherwise have been."

After the vote, Hodges got up to "tender my complete resignation": but in spite of his insistence on leaving immediately it was agreed the Conference should listen to Tom Richards who said: "I say, and say it quite kindly, even if we have to lose the services of Frank Hodges as our Secretary, I think he was ill-advised, knowing the character of the rule, he was ill-advised to do it without further consultation. It is done, but to throw up, make his resignation definite from today, will tell not only against himself but the workmen. It must not be done. The Federation must have time necessary, if it is done, to appoint a successor."

In answer to this plea Frank Hodges said, "I had thought that the debate would be tempered with a little magnanimity and a little 'generosity' but I find this is not so. I was pained beyond words." Finally, he said, "I do accept Mr. Richards' advice" (15 xii 1923). It meant that he would now begin to work out his three months notice.

10 RED INTERNATIONAL OF LABOUR UNIONS

Thirty months earlier, after the ending of the 1921 Lockout, the delegates from the lodges were undismayed and their continuing mood of militancy was voiced at the Annual Conference of the South Wales Miners' Federation when they resolved, by 120 votes to 63, to link up with the most advanced and militant expression of international struggle,[1] viz: "That the Miners' Federation of Great Britain, at the Annual Conference of that body, be urged to affiliate and actively identify itself with the Third International" (23 vii 1921).

An invitation received "from the Provisional International Council of Trade and Industrial Unions" to appoint delegates to attend their International Congress in Moscow on 1st July had been brought up at the Executive Council on 21st June, when it was resolved "That it lie on the table": but from more than one valley delegates attended the Congress.

While the decision of 23rd July came too late to be discussed in the MFGB (Llandudno) Annual Conference of 1921, and had to wait a twelve month till 1922 summer, the subject was kept alive. The Conference discussion had been reported in *The Communist*, a weekly which had become widely known by its mordant comment on what was regarded as the betrayal of the miners on Black Friday.

At the MFGB Blackpool Annual Conference of July, 1922, Resolution No. 2, as printed, ran: "That the Miners' Federation of Great Britain be urged to affiliate and actively identify itself with the Third International." The Agent for the Dowlais District, S. O. Davies, after explaining "a clerical error" in the last two words (which should have been "Red International of Labour Unions") introduced the resolution with a survey of the threatening international situation, and of the International Federation of Trade Unions, which had nothing in its constitution "to meet a situation of this kind, nothing to protect the class which it is supposed to have brought together with a view to meeting this latterday phase of capitalism." S. O. Davies concluded:

[1]This issue harked back for seven years to the collapse of the Second International in 1914 when the *Plebs* magazine, often functioning partly as the organ of the Miners' Unofficial Reform Committee, raised the question of a new International. In 1917 the tenth of Lenin's *April Theses* ran:

"A new International. We must take the initiative in creating a revolutionary International, and internationally directed against the *social chauvinists* and against the 'centre'."

Two years later came the manifesto of the Third (Communist) International. Its third Congress in June 1921 was followed in July by the Congress of the Red International of Labour Unions summoned in opposition to the International Federation of Trade Unions which had no socialist basis.

A British Bureau of this RILU (of which the Forest of Dean miner, Nat Watkins, subsequently became secretary) came into existence in the spring of 1921. Tom Bell, British Representative on the Executive Committee of the Communist International, told of the miners' lockout in a letter to which Lenin replied in a letter reproduced on another page.

"We recommend that we should affiliate with an international class conscious organisation, an international organisation out for struggle; out for fighting capitalism at every point, and not merely out for words" (19 vii 1922).

A. J. Cook seconded in a detailed speech.[1]

Frank Hodges in a very lengthy reply attacked the Red International as having split the French Trade Union Movement and defended the Amsterdam Internationale as "the natural evolution of the Trade Union Movement." Hodges gave details of France saying: "You have the French Trade Union Movement split up, and some are affiliated to it and some not. When it began to operate on the fiery French temperament it split that organisation in twain and destroyed for a generation any effective Trade Union Movement in France. They have a Trades Union Congress in France but look at the membership. The membership of the Trade Union Movement has gone down and down until at this moment the employers can do anything they like. There is no effective resistance—all because of this biting internal canker in French trade unionism. If you want to save British trade unionism, if you want to save us from this kind of thing, you must wash your hands of it, or the blight will come upon us.

"It is very strange that the weakest district in the Federation, from the point of membership, should be putting forward this resolution today. It is the same old cry, when you are weak instead of making yourself strong from within, you go outside and try to get someone else to help you. Instead of wasting the time and thought of your people upon this remote, indefinite and intangible thing, organise the men back into your Union, and then see if you cannot do something without seeking the aid of the Red International."

A vote by Districts showed that all 723 votes to 118 were against South Wales.

S. O. Davies and A. J. Cook were not dismayed but continued the campaign that autumn. A circular from the Red International of Labour Unions whose Secretary was Nathanial Watkins, with National Headquarters at 3 Wellington Street, Strand, London WC2, stated that a Special Conference of Delegates from Trades Union Branches, District Committees and Trades Councils had been convened for Cardiff and District "to discuss matters which are of vital importance to the future of the working class and the Trade Unions in particular," with the following:

1. Wages. No more reductions.

The wages of the workers continue to fall. Within the last eighteen months the organised workers have suffered reductions in wages to the extent of £10,000,000 per week. A resistance to this process of reduction must be made.

[1]See Appendix for A. J. Cook's speech.

2. Hours of Labour. No longer hours.

Attacks on the hours of Labour are proceeding apace and overtime is being worked indiscriminately, although there are still one million and a half unemployed.

3. Organisation of the fighting front.

(a) Local—Reorganise the Trades Councils and bring together the employed and unemployed workers.

(b) National—Reorganise the Trade Unions and the General Council of the Trades Union Congress.

(c) International—The building up of the Red International of Labour Unions and support its struggle against the Amsterdam Internationale.

(d) The Election from the Conference of a Delegate to the Second World Congress of the Red International of Labour Unions to be held in Moscow on 25th October, 1922.

Each branch was invited to send delegates and "so help in this great task of creating the united front against the onslaughts of the employers."

The Minute Book of the Dowlais District contains the following:

Mass Meeting, Oddfellows Hall, Sunday, 15th October, 1922. Mr. Thomas Rees presiding. Mr. S. O. Davies made an apology for the unavoidable absence of Mr. A. J. Cook, Miners' Agent, Rhondda. The meeting then discussed the agenda of the Red International of Labour Unions Conference.

Re District Conference at Cardiff.

Dear Sir and Brother, 13th September, 1922.

Owing to difficulties that have arisen and which up to the present we have not been able to overcome, it is found necessary to postpone the conference called for 16th September until Saturday, 21st October, at 2.30 p.m.

The conference will be held in the Lower Cory Hall, Windsor Street, Cardiff, and S. O. Davies, of the South Wales Miners' Federation will take the Chair.

We therefore again take the opportunity of requesting that the notice of your members be drawn to the important issues that will form the basis of discussion at this conference and trust that as a result the members of your organisation will be represented by two or more delegates.

Wages, hours and the reorganisation of the Trade Union Movement (locally, nationally and internationally) are questions that are of paramount importance in the Labour world at the present time.

In his own Dowlais District the decision was taken to send a delegation to the Second World Congress of the RILU due in the late autumn of 1922. S.O. himself was chosen as the miners' agent to be the District delegate, and obtained long leave of absence for this purpose.

In the Russian Socialist Federal Soviet Republic, where his worth and capabilities were immediately recognised, he was invited to write a textbook on mining. He was equipped for this task both by his technical studies which had brought him a mine manager's certificate and also by his experience in the industry both at the coalface and in dealing with the multifarious problems with which a miners' agent has to be familiar. S.O. for five months was in Russia going to one mining district after another so that he might so compile the text book that it would fit into the special conditions of the old Tsarist coalfields.

APPENDIX I

COOK'S SPEECH ON THE RED INTERNATIONAL OF LABOUR UNIONS (19 vii 1922).

"I rise to second the resolution, and I hope that this Conference will start to propagate this principle. I will attempt to explain what the Red International stands for and what the International you are connected with stands for. I think everyone here will remember, and will realise, especially miners' agents, that during the last eight months they have had their noses to the grindstone, and the insults they have had to contend with in colliery offices which they never dreamed they would have to put up with, and I hope that, as miners' leaders, they will not have to continue to do these things. I want to ask you to consider very seriously today why it is we have had this to do. In the first place, we must try to get as miners' leaders the best for our men, and as a miners' annual conference we must prepare for tomorrow, prepare for the future, and as miners there is no body of men who have more reason to consider the international question than the miners; no body of men are more affected by international relationships than the miners. Today you have heard it stated by everybody else that the miners are suffering because of international complications, because of the Versailles Treaty. We must suffer; we have suffered. You know what excuses we have had from leaders of our trade unions. America is going through a struggle, and we understand that their people are asked to accept a 40 per cent reduction in wages. France is going through a struggle because the employers are asking for a suspension of the eight hours. In Germany they are compelled to make arrangements with regard to wages. Welshmen, Northumbrians, and Scotsmen, while they are going six days a week, do not trouble as to others being brought into competition. We never trouble about the German miners or Indian miners. We have an International Congress. Mr. Smith said something about paying attention to getting closer together with America. Well, it is necessary to consider the conditions of the American miners, the German miners, Indian miners, Australian, Belgian and French, because they directly affect the British miners. The British miners cannot hope to keep the seven hours day and hope for a higher standard of life if they allow the standard of other men to be reduced down to the starvation point. You have the employers' excuses, that in

America they cannot compete with us unless they reduce wages; that you must suspend the eight hours in France because they cannot compete with us. We do not want wages reduced or the eight hours suspended. The circle goes on and the men are the sufferers always. There is no solution by miners' leaders appealing to the Government. What is the International to which we are affiliated? There was an International before the war, the president of it being a Labour patriot who asked men to fight the Germans not realising it was a capitalist war. It broke down because it was fundamentally wrong in principle; it broke down because it limited itself to a national outlook. The president was Jimmy Thomas, a name which no miner can mention without shame. I cannot forget I went through the struggle. As a member of the Executive I saw and heard sufficient, but such cannot be repeated on a public platform, yet this man is president of the new International, the Yellow International—a good name—formed 22nd November, 1920. I have heard that when this Conference was held under the presidency of Mr. Thomas a Canadian asked whether he would be committed to direct action. The Conference laughed, and Thomas said 'No, it is not built for that purpose; go back home and still continue on your limited national outlook.' I stand for the Red International. Why? The district I am agent for sent it forward, not with my propaganda, but after hearing the facts. The duty of an agent is to put the facts. What are the facts? The International to which we are affiliated has failed, and it is better to have no International at all if it fails to function. The men realise that it has failed. You have an organisation to which you pay, and with which you are affiliated, and such is not in a position to take action, as we found out in connection with the Triple Alliance, the great 'Jack Johnson,' when we wanted assistance we found it wanting. Now, did the Yellow International come to our rescue in the strike or lockout which went on for four months? They did not. Your little *Daily Herald* collected more money than all the rest put together. There is great need of an International, and no man in this Conference can stand up and deny that today the mining industry depends absolutely on a closer international relationship than what you have ever had up to now. My district sent this in a democratic way. After being discussed in the branches they sent forward this resolution asking that we sever our connection with the Yellow International and become affiliated with the Red International. I have explained this for fear I might be challenged as to the vote of my district. We sent it forward to the South Wales Delegate Conference, which passed the resolution urging the Miners' Federation of Great Britain to affiliate with the Red International and discontinue our connection with the Yellow International.

"I think it would be better to take a ballot of the lodges and decide whether they are in favour or not, and if they decide in favour of the Red International then we should have the rank and file with us on this matter. In the only place where a ballot has been taken, in Balders Lodge, Durham District, the men decided by a huge majority in favour of the Red International. You have never had a chance with the Yellow International; you have never been consulted. What is the difference between the Red International and the Yellow International? The difference in principle is that the Red International desires to abolish capitalism, but the other simply appeals to it. There are many leaders prepared to do that, but what is oratory without the necessary force behind it? If it is a question of converting capitalism let the men at Oxford and Cambridge do that. We have been for eight months trying to reorganise and get a strong organisation. If it comes to putting a case on behalf of the Federation no man can do it better than Frank Hodges. I have heard him and know, but it is not altogether oratory, it is the power behind the gun. The Red International Trades Union is not connected with the Communist Party. I believe in Communism, although I am not a member of the Communist Party . . . "

"A Delegate : You were kicked out.

"Mr. Cook : I was not kicked out, I resigned. I do not object to you smiling, not a bit. I pin my faith in the Red International Trades Union. What does it stand for? It stands for revolution—some of my friends say blood—no, revolution of thought. You must have a mental revolution, and if there had been a revolution of thought in the coalfield things would have been different. I do not want to fight with guns, bladders are bad enough for me. I believe in the organised might of the working classes. I believe in the workers' might, therefore do not be afraid of a revolution. With regard to the Red Trades Union formed in Russia they have a membership of several millions now, formed with the definite object of preparing for the international overthrow of capital, and if that fails to become operative then we must be prepared to face losses in wages. We have come to the conclusion, rightly or wrongly, that our coal trade and our conditions are determined absolutely by the international conditions. We want not only a minimum wage, but we want a better, a higher, and a fuller measure of living for our people. We have heard a lot about housing; we say that it is all a result of the present system of capitalism. I say that there is a class war, and I want an organisation which is so linked together that it will save us from these difficulties, save us from capitalism as it will be organised in the future; a real organisation with which we can face this class struggle."

CHAPTER EIGHT

A YEAR OF GOOD HOPE

1 PISGAH-SIGHTS IN JANUARY

In January, standing at the portal of the opening year, the miners could look back on a twelvemonth of struggle that had ended in victories with the abolition of the oppressive Wage Agreement in their industry and the electoral success of the Labour Party at the December polling-booths. In the South Wales coalfield, where output and exports had reached their zenith, where in a series of strikes non-unionism had been virtually abolished, the advent of a Labour Government, unprecedented if not wholly unexpected and with the additional grace of their own Vernon Hartshorn in the Cabinet as Postmaster-General, was a cause of great gladness and flung open the doors of hope. At last they were in sight of the Promised Land. Correspondingly, considerable dismay was caused among coal owners, who began to speak softly. Evan Williams, president of The Mining Association of Great Britain, and in South Wales president of the coal owners' representatives on the Board of Conciliation, when meeting the MFGB Executive Committee made a reply that was "couched in the most conciliatory terms."[1]

In February, the lodges, having sent in their nominations for the choice of a coalfield candidate in the contest for the post vacated by Hodges, then carried through a ballot taken on the transferable vote system. There were seven contestants.

W. H. Mainwaring throughout was the favourite until the sixth count when the transfer of Ablett's 29,286 votes brought A. J. Cook out on top—but by a narrow margin. The final figures were : A. J. Cook 50,123; W. H. Mainwaring 49,617; majority 506.

Before the ballot there had been a meeting of the Miners' Minority Movement to discuss candidatures. Arthur L. Horner, checkweigher in Mardy and a well-known Communist, was in the chair. Arthur Horner cast all his influence in favour of the non-Communist, Cook.

[1] In their Report to the Annual Conference the MFGB Executive Committee confessed themselves "greatly influenced by the character of the reply given on behalf of the owners. The almost entirely negative attitude which had been consistently adopted by them at all the numerous meetings of the past two years had disappeared." Somewhat naively the Committee set down their view that "the fact that the owners had allowed nearly two years to elapse before manifesting this new spirit cannot be too strongly deplored. Only after notice to determine the Agreement had actually been tendered and the prospect of a stoppage in the industry had become a possibility no longer to be ignored did the owners recede from the attitude which they had previously consistently taken up from the commencement of 1922."

ELECTION OF SOUTH WALES NOMINEE FOR SECRETARY OF MINERS' FEDERATION OF GREAT BRITAIN

Candidates	1st Count	2nd Count		3rd Count		4th Count		5th Count		6th Count	
		Transfer of D. Lewis Votes	Result	Transfer of S.O.D. Votes	Result	Transfer of T.W. Votes	Result	Transfer of A.J. Votes	Result	Transfer of N.A. Votes	Result
Ablett	19561	+ 487	20048	+ 2225	22273	+ 3223	25496	+ 3790	29286	=29286	
Cook	22150	+ 656	22806	+ 3462	26268	+ 2950	29218	+ 4873	34091	+16032	50123
Davies	14525	+ 414	14938	=14938							
Jenkins	16036	+ 585	16621	+ 2608	19229	+ 2933	22162	=22162			
Lewis	5195	=5195									
Mainwaring	22844	+1239	24083	+ 3036	27119	+ 6273	33392	+ 8773	42165	+ 4752	49617
Williams	15810	+ 799	16609	+ 1635	18244	=18244					
Non-transferable			1015	+ 1972	2987	+ 2595	5852	+ 4726	10578	+ 5802	16380
Total	116120	—	116120	—	116120	—	116120	—	116120	—	116120

Mr. A. J. Cook was accordingly elected.

against Mainwaring who was a member of the Communist Party and much respected as a Marxist lecturer at the Central Labour College.

This choice of a non-Communist by a Movement which was itself led by Communists, was unprecedented: and it was much discussed. Had Horner and other Communists gone against instructions? The matter was considered to be of national importance: and was discussed at Communist Party headquarters where, after a sharp tussle, a majority gave approval to the choice.

At their meeting on 8th March the Executive Council recommended Cook as the South Wales nominee and two days later a coalfield conference "urged the workmen" to support him for the MFGB Secretaryship.

2 A PARLIAMENTARY INTERLUDE

For the election of their national officers the Miners' Federation of Great Britain had adopted the transferable vote system not only as providing several advantages over a system of second and third ballots but as the most democratic method for a big electorate: and, on request, the Proportional Representation Society took charge.[1]

Throughout March, 1924, whilst this electoral process was going forward, and while the owners were spending several days on a joint sub-committee until on March 12th they could give their terms for the new Wages Agreement, the sudden illness of the MFGB President had thrown the chief responsibility upon the newly-installed vice-president.

Next day at the Special Conference in Westminster Tom Richards spoke of himself as "a new and highly nervous chairman." Actually Richards had a long record of over thirty-five years as a miners' official and was also an experienced parliamentarian having sat through seventeen years in the House of Commons. So the Committee "keenly alive to the fact that a Labour Government was in office for the first time in our history," and "exceedingly anxious to give it every opportunity of proving its value to our people," decided to recommend a change of tactics. When Tom Richards from the chair presented the Committee's report and on the next day proposed a resolution it was carried unanimously as follows:

"That this Conference, having regard to the inadequacy of the terms offered by the coalowners, cannot advise their acceptance by the workmen. We, however, urge upon the Government to pass the Minimum Wage Bill to secure for the miners a wage commensurate with the cost

[1]The principle of Proportional Representation in contrast to the single-member constituency system (whereby with a plurality of candidates a small minority could provide an MP) had been widely advocated within the trade union movement, and was actually passed by the House of Commons in the Third Reading of Representation of the People Act of 1918 but was thrown out by the House of Lords.

of living. It is decided that this Conference stand adjourned until March 26th" (14 iii 1924).

That same day the Committee went to the House of Commons to meet the mining Members, as arranged a week earlier, to discuss such questions as nystagmus in mines and unemployment insurance. On arriving at the House of Commons they found not only the mining Members of Parliament assembled to meet them, but in addition the Prime Minister, the Government Chief Whip and the Secretary for Mines with permanent officials of the Mines Department. The Prime Minister and the Government had taken advantage of this opportunity to make a statement on the general situation. Ramsay MacDonald said :

"I very much regret having to report a changed parliamentary situation in respect of the Minimum Wage Bill due to be introduced into the House of Commons by Mr. John Guest on 21st instant. Owing to the time of the year in which the General Election took place and the break in the continuity of parliamentary business caused by the election, and the assumption of office by the Party, the Government on taking up office has found itself in the position in which very little time is afforded us for obtaining from the House the necessary Votes of Supply which are essential before the end of the Government Financial Year on March 31st. The difficulty of time has increased by the obstructionist methods pursued by the other two parties in the House."

The Government had to have more time and they wanted to take from the Private Members the day on which Guest's Minimum Wage Bill would have been introduced. He reminded them there might be a General Election in the near future : "Of course they all hoped and trusted that in such an event the Labour Party would not only consolidate but greatly improve its position in the country. In that event all would be well." Concluding, the Prime Minister said : "In view of all these considerations I trust that the Federation will not put itself into a position of completely closing the door upon an industrial solution of the problem."

The miners were very much taken aback. Their whole calculations had been upset. The meeting was pressed to allow the original arrangement for the Bill to be introduced on 21st March to stand. But an amendment was carried to acquiesce in the Government's proposal "on the understanding that it will itself introduce legislation on similar lines at the earliest possible opportunity."

Emmanuel Shinwell, Secretary for Mines, now took up the running. Was the door closed, by the resolution of 14th March, to obtaining an industrial solution of the wage problem ? Tom Richards told him that the Federation had not closed the door "to any avenue which might provide the miners with wages acceptable to them."

The Committee, realising that "quite clearly the parliamentary weapon is one which cannot be relied upon in the present exigency," had further interviews with the Secretary of Mines on 21st and 22nd March. They continued :

"In the circumstances your Committee, being acutely conscious of its responsibilities towards our vast membership, felt that it could no longer pursue a political solution of the problem, and accepted the suggestions of the Secretary of Mines to arrange a further meeting with the owners as soon as possible."

3 THE COURT OF INQUIRY

On Thursday, 10th April, 1924, the MFGB Executive Committee had before them three reports. The first was the election of the South Wales nominee to be secretary. The second was in a letter from the Trades Union Congress General Council about an inter-union dispute in the South Wales coalfield. The third report submitted was on the ballot vote (ordered by Special Conference of 27th March) which showed a division between big districts such as Lancashire, Scotland and South Wales with two to one majorities against acceptance of the owners' proposals and those like Durham and Northumberland with equally decisive majorities for acceptance. In the total vote the proposals were rejected by 338,650 to 322,392. It was a very small majority. So on the next day the officials reported the result of the ballot and the desirability of a wages inquiry to Emmanuel Shinwell. Thereupon, on 15th April, the Minister of Labour, under the Industrial Courts Act of 1919, appointed a Court of Inquiry. Its terms of reference were "To enquire into and report upon the question of wages in the coal mining industry and the matters in issue between the Mining Association and the Miners' Federation relating thereto."

The members of the Inquiry were Lord Buckmaster,[1] a former Lord Chancellor; Roscoe Brunner[2] and A. G. Cameron, General Secretary of the Amalgamated Society of Woodworkers.

On Monday, 14th April, the new Secretary had assumed office. Arthur Cook made it clear he was entering the MFGB premises at 55 Russell Square as a crusader : and he lost no time in making changes. Finding that his first task was to get ready for the Court of Inquiry he went to the offices of the Labour Research Department whose Chairman since 1920 had been W. H. Hutchinson with G. D. H. Cole as Hon. Secretary (and with which the South Wales Miners' Federation had earlier connections) and since the task of "tabulating the information" was, according to the subsequent Report of the Executive Committee, "beyond the power of the Federation staff in the time

[1]Stanley Owen Buckmaster (1861-1934) Christ Church, Oxford: Liberal MP Cambridge 1906-1910; Keighley 1911-1914; Solicitor-General 1913: as Baron Buckmaster of Cheddington, Lord Chancellor 1915-16.

[2]Roscoe Brunner (1871-1926) Cheltenham and Cambridge; Barrister; a director of Brunner Mond & Co. (soon to be merged in Imperial Chemical Industries Ltd.)

allowed" he requested their help. This was readily given, as is described at the time in the *Monthly Circular*.[1]

In doing this Cook ignored the decision taken three weeks earlier by his own committee (when it seemed that the Prime Minister's withdrawal of facilities for the Minimum Wage Bill might precipitate an industrial dispute) and minuted.[2]

The result was that the MFGB was able to furnish the Court with numerous tables of statistical and other information, no item of which was challenged. What the Mining Association of Great Britain was able to produce was meagre by contrast and, actually, in the course of the Inquiry was subjected to challenge as being inadequate.

For example, in a comparison with wages in other industries the owners made a great point of the fact that mining was an "unsheltered trade," in competition from other countries—wherefore the miners must expect a low wage. Their comparative wages table was immediately challenged by A. G. Cameron, the Assessor: on examination it proved to be calculated in such a way that it was not possible to check the figures: and in the one case where this checking was possible the figure was found to be incorrect. In the five days on which the Court of Inquiry sat between 24th April and 1st May the main witnesses for the Miners' Federation were President, Herbert Smith; General Secretary, A. J. Cook; and Vice-President, Tom Richards.

Tom Richards, on 30th April, presented a case which obviously

[1]"Just before Easter the Department was asked by the Miners' Federation of Great Britain to undertake the gathering of materials and preparing statistics for the Court of Inquiry into mining wages set up by the Minister of Labour. The Inquiry was to begin on Thursday, 24th April; and the task of getting everything ready in five days—onerous at any time—was particularly difficult in view of the Easter holidays, when most of the staff would be normally on holiday, and when all normal sources of information were temporarily unavailable. Miss Olive Budden was given charge of the Easter weekend work, with three of the Labour College students, who readily gave up their Easter holidays in the service of the miners. The work was carried on, working fifteen to sixteen hours per day, and by Easter Tuesday it was possible to furnish the printer with the detailed particulars required. During the week succeeding Easter the secretary was mainly engaged on the work of this Inquiry at the headquarters of the MFGB. By the time this *Monthly Circular* appears much of the work done by the Department will already have been published at the Inquiry. It is understood that there is a project of more extended publication later."

(*Monthly Circular* of the Labour Research Department, Vol. 13, No. 5, May 1924).

[2]"Mr. W. W. Henderson, MP, attended a meeting of the Committee, together with other members of the Publicity Department of the Labour Party, and laid certain proposals before the Committee in connection with publicity work during the crisis. Mr. Henderson also stated that the services of the Labour Party (Publicity Department) would be placed at the disposal of the Federation. It was agreed to accept the offer of the Party, and the following persons were appointed to act in conjunction with the Research Department as a Publicity Committee during the crisis: Mr. Noah Ablett, Mr. J. E. Swan, and Mr. J. Hilton.

"It was further decided that a member of the Labour Publicity Department be permitted to use the offices at Russell Square for the purpose of conducting publicity work. Thursday, 21st March, 1924 (at 55 Russell Square).

impressed the Court and it was afterwards issued as a pamphlet by the South Wales Miners' Federation. Tom Richards with his very long experience and his seventeen years in the House of Commons was particularly effective in putting forward a well-founded case. Moreover, he had long experience of Evan Williams.

The Inquiry resolved itself very largely into an examination of the extremely complicated terms of the 1921 Wages Agreement. The evidence given was found very enlightening by the members of the Court. Their Report[1], published on 8th May, explained as best they could the July 1921 Wages Agreement and how it had operated on rates of wages and conditions of employment; surveyed the negotiations on the matters of dispute; and then put four paragraphs of conclusions, beginning with:

31. That the agreement of 1921 has failed to provide an adequate wage in many of the poorer districts is not really in dispute. The real issue, while primarily exhibited in a request for increased wages, is really far more fundamental. With the merits of this contention for "a full living wage" the Court stated: "We are not concerned. It is a political question." Earlier their Report stated that the miners' representatives had made it clear that they no longer adhered to the proposals which had been the subject of negotiation with the mineowners, but that the claim which they wished the Court to consider was "a living wage, which should not be less than the rates obtaining in 1914, with the local adjustments since made to remove anomalies, plus the increase in the cost of living and the increase of 2/- per shift recommended by the Sankey Commission."

On this the members of the Court could not reach a conclusion: but in their third conclusion they suggested resumption of negotiations between the parties "with a view to a modification of the terms of the agreement of 1921."

The miners' leaders were very disappointed when all they got, apart from public ventilation of their case, from all the Inquiry was that they would have to resume negotiations.

So, as before, a sub-committee was appointed to meet the Mining Association of Great Britain on 13th May. The miners argued that the conclusions of the Report warranted substantially improved offers from the owners, to which the owners replied that the offer already made even at the time it was made "went far beyond the economic capacity of the industry to bear"; that the position had now worsened; but that they would stand by their previous offer "even in the light of the present state of the industry." The sub-committees in their long drawn-out battle met on 15th, 20th, 21st and 22nd May. On 28th May the following resolution was passed for submission to the Special Conference called for 29th May: "The Executive Committee, having exhausted all possible means of negotiations in obtaining the proposed

[1]Report by a Court of Inquiry concerning the wages position in the coal mining industry. Cmd. 2139 of 1924, 6d. net.

terms of settlement,[1] now recommend that the terms be accepted, and the Committee be authorised to enter into and sign our Agreement for twelve months subject to one month's notice by either side."

A special conference of the South Wales Miners' Federation on Monday, 26th May, in the Cory Hall, Cardiff, had been called "to consider the instructions to be given to the South Wales delegation to the National Conference on 29th May, when the acceptance or otherwise of the proposed terms of settlement will be determined". It was attended by 233 delegates, representing 157,327 members. Arthur Horner from Mardy moved that the South Wales delegation at the National Conference be instructed to vote against acceptance of the proposed terms. Noah Ablett, a member of the MFGB Executive, stated that no one would attempt to defend the terms offered—they all agreed that the proposals were quite inadequate—but they must face the fact that the previous terms were rejected by a majority of only 16,000 out of a total of 800,000 votes. There was an evident disinclination of the miners of Great Britain as a whole to take industrial action at the present time. S. O. Davies, soon about to be a South Wales representative on the National Executive, also opposed acceptance, saying that the position of the miners was now much stronger than it would be twelve months hence. On a card vote 65,150 were for the terms and 87,600 against.[2]

To the Special Conference in the Memorial Hall in London the MFGB Executive Committee recommended acceptance of the terms. The South Wales amendment was that the terms be rejected. On a card vote the conference accepted the terms by 473 to 311, with South Wales, Lancashire, Scotland and Leicester in the minority.

So ended, for the time being, the struggle within the British miners which had gone on for some two and a half years, ever since the South Wales Miners' Federation had taken the first steps to put an end to the 1921 Wage Agreement.

4 STRATEGY FOR A COMING CONFLICT

With the acceptance on 29th May of the 1924 Wages Agreement, there was peace in the industry. But the Agreement was only for a twelvemonth. It gave a year's grace to make preparations. Much thinking and discussing went on in the valleys and particularly in the growing Miners' Minority Movement.

[1] *The Miners : Years of Struggle.*

[2] When a month later at the Annual Conference in Cardiff it was proposed by Coegnant Lodge "that our General Secretary, Mr. Tom Richards, be censured for advising the South Wales coalfields to vote in favour of the owners' terms in the recent ballot, and this in spite of being contrary to the decision of the National Conference" (26 vi 1924), there was a long discussion. But the proposition was defeated by a large majority and a vote of confidence in the General Secretary was carried.

The strategy that unfolded was never set out fully in a programme. But its broad content can be summed up as a burning desire for working-class unity—unity in the coalfield, unity in the coalmining industry, unity in all industries, and unity internationally. This began with the effort to build up the Union and to bring back into the fold all waifs and strays.

Much had been accomplished before mid-summer of 1923. Vernon Hartshorn already noted for his methods as agent in Maesteg (where in a drive to end non-unionism, beginning at the head of the valley he would lead a growing number, knocking at doors, interviewing those within, urging them to join the campaign) in his presidential address to the Annual Conference could claim that from March to May membership "had been restored almost to the pre-war position" (18 vi 1923).

Further account was then taken of those who had strayed, and of those other unions that had encroached on their membership, taking advantage of the national lock-out in the coal industry in 1921.

On 10th October, 1923, it was reported to the Trades Union Congress General Council that the National Union of General Workers had so encroached: and, in support of this complaint, the names of nearly 130 workers employed at South Wales collieries as smiths, fitters, stokers, carpenters, strikers, wagon repairers and general labourers, etc., were submitted. The decision, conveyed in a letter from TUC Secretary, Fred Bramley, on 2nd April, 1924, was that men who had been in the South Wales Miners' Federation before the lockout in 1921, were now required to transfer back.[1]

[1]"The findings have been considered by the General Council and ratified by them.

"I have sent a copy of the memorandum to the National Union of General Workers, and have called their attention to paragraph 8 of the memorandum. I have asked that they get in touch with your Federation with a view to effect being given to the decision contained in that clause.—Yours sincerely, Fred Bramley, Secretary."

"THE MINERS' FEDERATION OF GREAT BRITAIN v. THE NATIONAL UNION OF GENERAL WORKERS.

MEMORANDUM OF DISPUTES SUB-COMMITTEE.

"1. On the 10th October, 1923, the Miners' Federation of Great Britain reported to the General Council that the National Union of General Workers had taken advantage of the national lock-out in the coal industry in 1921 to encroach on their membership in the South Wales coalfield.

"2. The hearing of the case was arranged for the 16th November, 1923, but was postponed. The hearing took place on the 19th March, 1924, before Messrs. E. L. Poulton (in the chair), A. G. Walkden, and J. Turner, of the Disputes Committee.

"3. The Miners' Federation representatives stated they insisted that all men employed in or about a colliery and whose wages and conditions are controlled by the Conciliation Board, shall be of the Miners' Federation. They could not recognise the contribution card of the National Union of General Workers as entitling a man to be employed at a colliery without becoming a member of the Miners' Federation.

"4. It emerged during the proceedings that an arrangement exists between the Miners' Federation and the Amalgamated Engineering Union whereby the

A more complicated case arose from a complaint (on 23rd May, 1923) by the Electrical Trades Union that the Miners' Federation in the South Wales coalfield were treating ETU members as non-unionists and threatening to prevent their carrying on their work : and from a later "counter-charge of poaching in 1921" against the ETU. Three specific cases were brought forward by the ETU, while on the other hand the question whether twenty-one men "alleged to have been poached by the ETU" were or were not originally members of the Miners' Federation was in dispute. Here the decision was that men "whose duties were not those of skilled electricians shall be returned to the Miners' Federation."

Another case from South Wales, also raised as a complaint in May, 1923 (but "not proceeded with until twelve months later") was in respect of certain men employed on colliery saddlery work in the Maesteg district. It was discussed in the MFGB *Report of the Executive Committee* for the year ending 30th June, 1925, as :

"Another example of that with which the Federation has continually had to contend with following the stoppage of 1921, namely, the encouragement given by craft unions outside the industry to certain types of workmen to forego their loyalty to the Federation in times of adversity and to seek some special benefit for themselves at the expense of the larger body of our members. During the reorganisation campaign of our South Wales district in 1923, pressure was brought on the men in question to return to their allegiance, and a complaint was subsequently lodged by the Union of Saddlers and General Leather Workers with the Trades Union Congress General Council."

latter pay a capitation fee to the Miners' Federation in respect of AEU members employed in the coalfields.

"5. A list of approximately 130 names of workers employed at South Wales collieries as smiths, fitters, stokers, carpenters, strikers, wagon repairers, and general labourers, etc., was submitted by the Miners' Federation in support of their claim.

"6. The National Union of General Workers stated that many of the men mentioned in the list had belonged to the National Union of General Workers for a number of years, but had been forced to join the Miners' Federation. They had, therefore, returned to the National Union of General Workers after the national lock-out in 1921. In respect to others, the National Union of General Workers asserted they had never been members of the Miners' Federation.

"7. The Miners' Federation representatives contested the accuracy of this statement, but did not deny that it was possible for a man to be a member of the Miners' Federation whilst still retaining his membership of the National Union of General Workers.

"8. After careful consideration of the evidence, the Disputes Sub-Committee decide that those men who were members of the Miners' Federation in 1921 prior to the national lock-out, and who left that Federation to join the National Union of General Workers, shall be required to transfer back to the Miners' Federation.

(Signed) E. L. Poulton, (Chairman).
A. G. Walkden.
J. Turner.

W. M. Citrine (Assistant Secretary).
WMC/EK. 19th March, 1924."

The award in this case was given against the Miners' Federation, whose leaders, "very dissatisfied", did not ask the South Wales Miners' Federation to implement the TUC decision.

The differences of a dozen years or more between the SWMF and other unions had to be brought into the open, focussed in a strong light and the tension in each case relaxed before the strategy of joint activities of unions could effectively be raised. For the coming struggle, it was clear, allies had to be found : and if the brief traditions of the Triple Industrial Alliance from 1914 onwards had been shattered in the early 'twenties, there were potential allies elsewhere. Such reasoning as this lay behind the proposition discussed and carried at the Standard Lodge, one of thirty such in the Rhondda. The membership of the Rhondda in 1924 was around 30,000, or more than double the 14,000 to which it had sunk two years earlier after the defeat and debacle of 1921. The proposition began by ruling out their former allies and proposing an approach to other unions. The wording was :

"That while accepting the principle of solidarity and unity of action amongst all sections of the working-class, we recognise the obvious tendency of Railway, Transport, and other sections of Distributive Workers achieving such striking successes by sectional action; that unity from them which will give any practical aid to a general programme of advance is remote.

"We therefore urge the immediate approach of Engineers, Textile, Building Trades, Iron and Steel, and all other sections of Productive Workers, with the object of forming one big Alliance, to be used for the purpose of presenting simultaneous programmes upon our employers."

Details were then elaborated setting a three months period from midsummer to "sound MFGB and other sections enumerated" to ascertain their respective views upon this project. If then the response was sufficient to warrant going ahead with the project a conference was to be called immediately to establish an Alliance of all those who would attend on the following basis :

1. Alliance for offensive and defensive purposes.

2. Two months be allowed from date of establishing Alliance for the rank and file of each unit comprising Alliance to present programmes of demands upon respective employers.

3. All demands to contain the principle of a real living wage based upon the cost of living, and to be presented simultaneously upon the same day.

4. The demands to be minimum ones, and no compromise to be agreed upon during stage of negotiations without the express sanction of respective rank and file.

5. One month from date of presenting demands be given for negotiations which, if not satisfactory to all, the organisations to be consulted with a view of enforcing them by industrial action.

6. That if proposals be accepted by South Wales, and not by the MFGB, the Conference to decide upon the wisdom or otherwise of proceeding alone as a South Wales section with the other organisations in forming Alliance.—Standard (25 vi 1924).

Clearly it was felt that at any rate in South Wales there was a prospect that the lessons of the inherent weaknesses of the old Triple Alliance had been learned and that necessary steps would be taken and necessary safeguards instituted in the building of any future Alliance. When this was debated at the Annual Conference of the SWMF (Cory Hall, Cardiff, 24th-26th June, 1924) there was a very long discussion. An amendment was submitted by the Coegnant Lodge to delete the whole of the first clause and to substitute the following:

"That in order to establish solidarity and unity of action amongst all sections of the working class, the workers in all industries be organised on regional lines; each region to be afterwards linked up. We therefore urge the immediate approach of all Unions catering for the Productive and Distributive workers with the object of forming one big Alliance to be used for the purpose of presenting simultaneous programmes to our Employers."

In the Colliery Workers' Magazine it was stated:

"The arguments for and against the two propositions were put in speeches of exceptional ability by a number of speakers, and the discussion generally fully maintained the high standard of debate usually attained on matters of this kind at the South Wales Miners' Conferences.

A Card Vote resulted as follows:

For the Standard proposition	...	78,050
For the Coegnant amendment	...	53,250
Majority	...	24,800

"The following amendments to the Standard Lodge proposition were agreed to:

Clause 1. Add 'To be first of all formed locally, everywhere in each District, to be known as Industrial Council.'

Clause 9. Delete 'to,' line 2, substitute 'shall not'.

"The Standard proposition as amended was carried."

This was not the only decision of wide importance either for wage policy or for organisation. For example, there were resolutions carried that any future agreements must have a clause to make membership of the union a condition of employment. Secondly (on the motion of Lady Lewis Lodge) that colliery companies be compelled to recognise any combine committee representing the men at any group of collieries that they controlled. Then there was a decision (on a proposition by the Bute Merthyr Lodge) that in future negotiations the MFGB Committee be not permitted to meet employers either on the question of an agreement or on any other matter "other than in accordance with the demands made by the National Delegate Conference." It was in South Wales nine years before that all the negotiations either with the employers or with the Company had been taken out of the hands of the Union's Executive Council and conducted direct by the Cardiff Delegate Conference.

There were also resolutions (from Seven Sisters and Grosfaen Lodges) demanding that the Labour Government should pass a Bill to amend the Checkweighers' Act, also that the Government should put into operation the provisions of the Holman-Gregory Report, and on this the Mardy Lodge proposed, in order to expedite matters, that the SWMF should "urge the taking of strike action by the MFGB unless the present provisions are so amended by the end of the last parliamentary session in 1924." This was carried by 101 votes to 48.

Finally a motion of censure was carried (proposed by the Tylorstown Lodge) on the National Executive inasmuch as they advised the acceptance of the terms offered by the owners in May "which are not materially better than those rejected by ballot in April" (26 vi 1924).

It was clear that the series of advanced propositions carried constituted this midsummer a whole programme together with the strategy in carrying out that programme. There was however no possibility of this programme being discussed for acceptance or rejection by the other constituents of the Miners' Federation because they were adopted too late for discussion at Swansea on 8th July. It was only a fortnight later and as resolutions had to be in to the Annual National Conference much earlier the South Wales programme could only be discussed in the summer of 1925. But although the various Miners' Associations continued to act in some ways as though they had not been federated nationally, the South Wales programme nevertheless on this occasion had a remarkable effect. Its effect was on A. J. Cook'[1], the new Secretary who in 1924, and for very many months afterwards, still looked to the miners of South Wales and particularly the miners of his own Rhondda Valleys to give him guidance and backing.

[1]From 1924 onwards, if not before, the newspapers personalised union activities into melodrama often with the Union Secretary cast as the villain (or the hero) of the piece. Thereby the journalists ignored the completely democratic structure of the Unions as contrasted with the structure and organisation of the newspapers where there was despotic control, and the journalists had to write (and still have to write) as bidden. In point of fact Cook himself seldom initiated a programme or a policy; his function was that of a populariser, and this function he carried out better than any miners' leader had ever done before. So far from Cook being the sole initiator of the Alliance policy, he had at first been cool towards the idea. When the Amalgamated Engineering Union, amongst whose leaders at the time were W. H. Hutchinson, wrote a letter to the Miners' Federation proposing an Alliance Cook in reply gave his opinion that the miners were likely to prefer to work through established channels and in particular through the TUC.

5 COOK'S CAMPAIGN

Arthur Cook held it to be his duty as national secretary to carry on a wide campaign of agitation within the Miners' Federation. Cook was first and foremost an agitator. He relied on agitation as did his predecessors of over half a century earlier—Alexander McDonald and Tom Halliday.

Every weekend Cook was up and down the coalfields of Britain delivering speeches. His speeches were not so much programmatic as revivalist. He put forward not so much a policy as a recital of grievances. He could tell of the hard lot of the colliers as he himself had suffered it in his twenty-one years of underground toil and had suffered the more because of his protests. In the telling of it he roused his hearers to end it.

Cook very often used to tell the story both of his imprisonment in wartime for strike activities and also of his imprisonment during the 1921 lockout under the "police state" regulations of the Emergency Powers Act: "I was taken in chains to my place of trial and I was seen by everybody in the railway station at Porth standing there in chains." To such a man and such a story as his the miners responded as never before to any of their famous speakers.

Cook came to be a mirror of the coalfield, to reflect the mood of the colliers, to voice what had been brooded over underground for generation after generation.

Cook's campaign, which brought to him a greater trust than had ever been accorded to any miners' leader, was not the product of an individual. Cook was representative of a point of view that was widely held throughout the Miners' Federation of Great Britain and held most intensely and focussed within the South Wales Miners' Federation. The policies that Cook put forward, the aims he set before the miners, the types of argument he used, were common to him and to the foremost representatives in the Cardiff Conferences.

In lodges, valley meetings, coalfield conferences matters were hammered out, policies shaped and definite proposals put forward. This was the powerhouse of industrial democracy with which A. J. Cook's apparently inexhaustible supply of energy was connected.

Cook kept very closely in touch with those who had been responsible within the coalfield for his election as the South Wales candidate, namely, with the old reform committee members, insofar as these and their standpoint was embodied and revitalised in the Miners' Minority Movement. From them he frequently took counsel, in particular from Nat Watkins of the Forest of Dean and from Arthur Horner, the checkweighman at Mardy Colliery, who so often carried advanced propositions within the Cory Hall conferences in Cardiff. On matters of statistical and other information and on questions that lay outside the sphere of his previous experience, Cook turned with increasing frequency to take counsel with the staff and Executive members of the Labour Research Department. To them he had turned in his need to get all ready for the Buckmaster Court of Inquiry in April 1924. This he had done with the full assent and backing of the MFGB Executive Committee who had reason to recall the work done for them during the war and particularly in 1919-1920 on behalf of the miners by the LRD. The resources of the Department from April 1924 onwards were open to the miners' organisations and of this Cook took advantage in weekly and often bi-weekly consultations.

There were others consulted, for Cook was, as Bernard Shaw once wrote of himself, "a crow that followed many ploughs." But these mentioned were perhaps the most significant.

Within the MFGB Executive Cook found that he had the aid of the representatives of South Wales other than Tom Richards. Tom did not actively oppose but took a kindly neutral position and a pleasure that one of the boys from the Rhondda was playing such an active part in all these contests. But Cook had a firm backing through the election in the spring of 1924 to the MFGB Executive Committee not only of President Enoch Morrel but of Noah Ablett, always esteemed the keenest intellect within the Executive Council and S. O. Davies, agent for Dowlais, and Vice-President since 1924 of the SWMF. These together made a pair of keen and quick-witted debaters, clear headed, logical and persuasive, a pair that could not be matched from Yorkshire, Durham, Midlands or Scotland. On the Executive Council also he had the constant support of Jack Williams, formerly of the Garw Valley, who had been chosen to be Secretary of the Forest of Dean Miners' Association. Of the Miners' Minority Movement there were Edmund Collins of Yorkshire, Harry Hicken of Derbyshire, and others throughout the coalfields.

But when all this is said and done the outstanding feature of what had been called Cook's Campaign, that went on for 13 months punctuated by illnesses, breakdowns, and conferences, was the innumerable meetings at which he spoke and put forward the policy that would maintain, if not increase, the miners' standard of living. In the first year, naturally, the audiences were mainly of miners in every coalfield. A. J. Cook had ceased to be "the man from South Wales" in their minds and was the representative of the whole British mining community.

No record, beyond meagre reports in the newspapers, has been kept of these immense gatherings which startled the inhabitants of each coalfield so that the effect of them was communicated throughout the organised workers in each county and locality. To hear A. J. Cook speak there travelled miners on foot, on bicycle, by rail and in busloads. Within the County Palatine of Durham only the famous Annual Gala surpassed these huge meetings in size. Moreover, there were few ceremonial banners, no jollification. The meetings were strictly confined to colliers minding their own business. Although no verbatim records were taken it might be thought that detailed notes would be found in contemporary newspapers. But by some apparent magic, like the spell cast upon the Sleeping Beauty and all her family and attendants in the castle, the newspapers, as though in a trance, ignored these unprecedently large gatherings—except insofar as some phrase taken out of context from a fifty-minute speech would appear good material for a paragraph and, in the hostile newspapers, for horrific headlines.[1]

6 CURRENTS AND EDDIES

Throughout the early part of 1923, the agitation for the Red International of Labour Unions had continued in South Wales, where however it met, inside the Executive Council, with a growing opposition from miners' agents, for whom the attachment to the Labour Party signified an acceptance also of the dominant outlook of the Labour Party leaders. Arthur Henderson was a firm supporter of what had been called the "Berne International" (the old Second International revived) while Clifford Allen favoured the Vienna Union, to which the Independent Labour Party, with a considerable number of supporters in Parliament, adhered. When early in 1923 these two international groupings coalesced at Hamburg, there was at the same time a reinforcement of the Amsterdam Trade Union International and a rally to it amongst several of the South Wales Executive Council.

The editor of *The Colliery Workers' Magazine*, Oliver Harris, announced in the issue of August 1923 that the question of the Red International would be submitted to a ballot, and that the magazine would publish two articles "to state the main arguments for and against the South Wales Miners' Federation affiliating with the Red International." John Thomas, B.A., Miners' Agent, Anthracite District, examined the arguments:

"(1) Why the Yellow International has been no good to the miners;
(2) Why the Red International is the only International worth while to the miners."

[1]Cook had an undoubted flair for publicity: he could coin a phrase that was bound to "hit the headlines" and that left fellow-agitators toiling far behind. Himself a "fellow-traveller" of the communists, he was far ahead of any of them alike in his popular appeal and in drawing the fire of "the class enemy."

In the call for unity and vigilance sent to the conference of the National Minority Movement, Cook turned on his detractors and made the declaration that "I am proud to be a disciple of Karl Marx and a humble follower of Lenin" (25 i 1925). This "drew the fire of the enemy" with a vengeance: and not only in Fleet Street but all over Europe and North America the phrase became almost a theme song of the capitalist Press.

Of all this Cook was well aware. He used eagerly to scan the newspaper columns, and read aloud with relish their attacks upon him, while to anyone present he would recall what Keir Hardie had said in Merthyr: "So long as the newspapers attack me I know I am on the right track." Correspondingly he would exhibit some chagrin if on any day there had been no editorial or no news item about himself.

To this, in the same number, Arthur Jenkins, Miners' Agent, Eastern Valleys District, replied with a survey of the international organisations since the First International but devoted most of the ample space given to him to a denunciation of the Red International.

The ballot was not taken. The agitation for and against continued. With the advent of a Labour Government in January 1924 it might seem that the "Red International" might have been dropped, but it was not so. On the contrary, when it came to the SWMF Annual Conference in the Cory Hall, June 24th to 28th, 1924, there were amongst the multitude of resolutions some of special significance. In the contest for the Vice-Presidency, S. O. Davies on a card vote received 1,726 votes against 999 for Arthur Jenkins: and, of the twelve general resolutions, the seventh ran: "We desire the affiliation of the Trades Union Congress with the Red International of Labour Unions." In the same year, 1924, a leaflet was signed by five of the 21 miners' agents, and three checkweighmen, and was widely circulated, giving "six reasons why we should vote for affiliation."[1]

It should not be thought that the standpoints of the majority of the South Wales miners carried everything before them within the Federation of Great Britain. Acclamation at titanic gatherings, however heartening, and however much the effect began to show itself in resolutions from lodge and district meeting, did not sweep everything before it. On the contrary, it created a steadily growing cleavage of opinion. So long as Frank Hodges, working in considerable harmony with the employers, had been able both in the Executive Committee and in the national conference to quell the 1921-1923 murmurs of revolt from South Wales and Lancashire, so long the differences were resolved in favour of the right-wing sections. But now (as a result of South Wales' persistent pressure) the ballot vote of 10th January, 1924, which alarmed the

[1] Affiliation of the SWMF to the Red International of Labour Unions. Six reasons why we should vote for affiliation.

1. Because the present International disorganisation suits the coal owners. Says Sir Samuel Instone, colliery proprietor and air line chief: "The thing that makes me most happy is the possibility of an American coal strike on September 1st. At the moment the masters refuse to recognise the Unions. It is the aftermath of the last strike, and if a deadlock comes about, America will be forced to buy coal from this country—and we have plenty to sell."

2. Because, in the best interests of the **whole** of the mining community, the Red International of Labour Unions works most effectively for National and International Working Class Solidarity, as the best possible means of securing better working conditions, a higher standard of living, the shortening of the hours of labour under the capitalist system, and **finally** the ABOLITION of this system of ruthless exploitation. This final objective being in accord with the Rules and Constitution of the SWMF.

3. BLACK FRIDAY MUST NEVER BE REPEATED. The Red International is the only organisation which has a clearly defined policy and the necessary international machinery established to prevent such calamities as the betrayal of the British miners in 1921 (which cost the British miners £160,000,000 per year in wages), and the American miners in 1922 and 1923.

4. Remember that 1,250,000 tons of Belgian, French, German and American coal, hewn and shipped by organised labour, was imported into this country

employers showed that a new situation was developing, while the choice of Cook as Secretary was followed by a conscious and rapidly growing movement towards the left stimulated by his campaign. No counter-campaign was set afoot but on the MFGB Executive Committee the older trade union officials, brought up in a different atmosphere, began to evince signs of discomfort. As Cook in his speeches called more and more openly for revolutionary change that would benefit the miners—he alarmed not only the newspaper owners. Many in all three parties, Liberal, Labour and Conservative, dreaded any revival of the untamed revolutionary spirit of the working class that had shown itself in the revolutionary year 1919 as well as earlier. They in turn privately exercised what influence they could to induce the established officials to make some stand against the gospel of the apostle from South Wales. As the situation began to be more and more tense these were stimulated, often from outside, to make some protest. Some occurred inside the Executive Committee. But it was in the conference of August 1925 that George Spencer, MP, complained about Cook's revolutionary speeches, as follows:

"Mr. G. A. Spencer, MP (Notts) : I would like to ask the platform whether they endorse what Mr. Cook has been saying Sunday after Sunday with regard to a revolution. The language which has been used is going to break this Federation. I shall myself protest against it outside. It does not make for unity" (19 viii 1925).

As the conference concluded Vice-President Tom Richards made these remarks:

"The Secretary is in a devilish bad temper. I say to him, don't let little things irritate you. Cook is not a revolutionary, but let me

to defeat us in our struggle against the enforcement of the intolerable conditions imposed upon us by the British coal owners.

5. Remember that 2,000,000 tons of British coal were shipped to America to break the miners' strike there in 1923, whilst coal produced by us was sent to France and Germany to defeat the miners in those countries in their struggle to prevent such degradation as was imposed on us in 1921.

6. South Wales miners supply the foreign markets with the largest of their coal output, and we are as a consequence particularly affected by conditions obtaining in the foreign coalfields. Without contact with a definitely Militant International Organisation, we cannot hope to maintain even the present miserable conditions. These FACTS prove the weakness of existing International organisations. Prepare for the coming struggles by linking up with the Red International of Labour Unions, which stands for real international working class solidarity against international blacklegging. The miners of South Wales have always been in the vanguard of the British Working Class Movement. You were pioneers when you led the fight for a minimum wage for miners, when you stood for compensation for those injured and killed in the industry, when you initiated the Movement for Independent Working Class Education. **Be pioneers now by deciding to affiliate to the only real live International—the Red International of Labour Unions.**

(Signed) Noah Ablett, Miners' Agent. Gwilym Richards, Mines Examiner.
A. J. Cook, Miners' Agent. John Thomas, Miners' Agent.
S. O. Davies, Miners' Agent. Tom Thomas, Checkweigher.
A. Horner, Checkweigher. Ted Williams, Miners' Agent.
S. Jones, Checkweigher.

say this, that great credit is due to Cook for the work he has done during these negotiations. I don't agree with lots of things he says. I tell him privately and publicly, but let us give credit when it is due. Cook has done a great deal of spade work in connection with the Trade Union in getting unanimity, but in his propaganda, he has done a lot of things I don't agree with. He is, however, getting worn out with these long negotiations."

Meantime throughout the coalfields the desire to end their hard lot was expressed in successive district and national conferences. But the means towards this was to be sought not only within the coalmining industry. On the necessity of unity, of and within all trade unions and other working-class bodies, Cook hammered unceasingly, untiringly. It was a principle in the Miners' Minority Movement of which he had been a most ardent supporter. A strength of feeling was aroused on this question of unity which provided the drive to overcome all the obstacles showing that when an idea gets spread amongst the masses to a sufficient extent it then becomes a material force.

By the end of 1924 the MFGB Executive was officially sounding several other unions with a view to the formation of an industrial alliance. This was to be on a wider scale than the old Triple Industrial Alliance, to be better prepared and worked out in order to meet eventualities. Again from spring of 1924 there went on for nearly two years a drive for international trade union unity while at the same time, on the miners' initiative, both within and without the framework of the TUC General Council, measures for effective unity of action were being discussed or worked out. On the international field a two-pronged campaign was proceeding: one within the International Federation of Trade Unions as also within the Miners' International; the other was the proposal for joint working between the British and Soviet Trade Unions as a preliminary to the creation of an all-embracing trade union international.

To this, however, opposition was developing rapidly in the Miners' International, in the group around Frank Hodges who, after his brief spell of glory as Civil Lord of the Admiralty, had been looking for a job and was given for the time being the International Secretaryship of the miners. Within the wider scope of the Trade Union International the Dutch, German and, very largely, the French trade union leaders were strongly opposed to the new drive proceeding from the British Trades Union Congress.

The dismissal of the Labour Government in the autumn of 1924 did nothing to damp these two campaigns. On the contrary, so strongly was it felt that the voting at the General Election had been swayed by a forgery (the Red Letter) that the new Baldwin Government were regarded as having acquired office on false pretences. With this general feeling in the Labour Movement it is not surprising that some of the trade union leaders were ready to use all the industrial strength their members could command to maintain the standard of living of the working class as a whole. Thus the Conservative victory actually gave an impetus to the campaign for unity in the struggle against the employers.

That a struggle was approaching was by this time common knowledge. A big change had come over the international situation which had been so favourable in 1923 to the British coal trade. The change was particularly serious in the world market for coal but extended more widely. Besides these there were political and financial changes in international affairs which were to affect the miners, the coal industry and the miners' standard of life and, finally, changes initiated by the British Government. To all of these we must now turn.

7 SOUTH WALES COAL TRADE

In the summer and autumn of 1924 the coal trade in South Wales entered a difficult period as demand for coal from abroad fell away. Collieries closed, rendering large numbers of workmen idle and many others were working short time. Tonnage output fell from 4,188,878 in April to 4,123,621 in May, and to 3,424,563 in June. By 25th August there were nearly 100,000 unemployed in the British coalfields, thirty thousand of them in South Wales.

Some South Wales coal owners thought all this was due to the New Wages Agreement and began to talk of longer hours and lower wages as the way out of the depression. These suggestions were repudiated in the editorial columns of *The Colliery Workers' Magazine*, which, now in its second year, was each month vigorously contending for the SWMF standpoint, industrial and political.

The Hull Trades Union Congress of September 1924 was hailed as "the most hopeful held for some years". The "United Front" policy had been adopted by a large majority "and, for the first time, we are glad to note the vote of the Miners' Federation was cast in favour of this proposal."

Throughout the autumn of 1924 the economic position of the coal industry had continued to worsen. The deterioration was sufficiently marked for the coal owners on 28th November, 1924, to send a letter to the miners inviting them to a joint meeting "in view of the extremely serious position of the coal industry at the present time." There was hesitation before the miners decided to take the offer at its face value and have a joint inquiry. After a preliminary meeting held on 29th January with about twenty present on each side they met again on Thursday, 19th February, when Evan Williams made a plea for each side having a correct and clear realisation of the situation before any proposals were made. He began by dealing with unemployment in the mining industry which had shrunk from 1,193,700 men working in

May to 1,137,000 in December, a decrease of 56,700 within eight months with "a total of 111 pits closed during that time", 35 in South Wales.

Further meetings were held in March and April of the Joint Sub-Committee appointed to investigate "The Economic Position of the Coal Industry".[1] On this the Miners' Federation of Great Britain submitted a statement in eighty closely-printed pages, complete with a series of appendices giving detailed figures. The scope and tenor of this statement is indicated in its introduction which ran as follows:

The coal mining industry of Great Britain, under its present ownership and management, is faced, we are told, with a position of crisis. Various causes are assigned for this, both by the owners and by independent economists. These causes may be summed up under three headings:

(1) The continued crisis in capitalist production resulting from the war, varying in intensity from country to country, and having as one of its effects a general shrinkage in world consumption of coal to which shrinkage the general low level of the purchasing power of the working class is contributory;

(2) The increased industrialisation and development of other countries such as America, South Africa, India and France, thus raising new and formidable competitors to British capitalism.

(3) The progressive development of sources of power alternative to black coal, particularly oil (either in the form of oil bunkers or Diesel engines) and hydro-electric power.

As far as the British coal trade is concerned all these causes, besides others that may be adduced, are being focussed by the owners on the question of PRICE. No matter what the degree of under-consumption is, no matter how much the facilities for oil burning, etc., are developed, it is, they say, the present high price of British coal to the consumer which is the root of the matter. Viewed simply from the standpoint

[1] At one of these joint meetings in March 1925 between the owners' and the miners' representatives: the Rt. Hon. Lord Gainford, Vice-Chairman of the Mining Association of Great Britain, who had taken a considerable part in the discussion, was, with another owners' official, amongst the last to leave. Cook, being last to leave on the workmen's side, presently found himself in conversation with Lord Gainford, one of the well-known big firms of Liberal coalowners in the North of England, Pease and Partners. As it was related within the same week, the following episode occurred: Cook was approached by Lord Gainford who said words to this effect:

"You must know that the desperate position of the industry demands a return to the eight hour day. Now you are the only man who could persuade the workmen to accept this necessary reform. If you could undertake this it would be of great benefit to all. Of course, it might result in you having to go through a very bad time but we can assure you that we would not allow one who would have been a benefactor to the industry to suffer for his courage and statesmanship."

Lord Gainford then indicated that shares and stocks amounting to about £20,000 would be made available "together with a suitable, well-equipped cottage or small house."

To his auditor, who was rather aghast on hearing this story, Cook added that "Nothing can be said. It would be his word and that of the others in the room against mine. I was alone with them."

of the coal trade, the problem according to them is one of cutting prices.

The owners, we understand, have in mind the facile solution of cutting miners' wages, either by direct lowering of wages or lengthening of the working day, or both, and thereby reaching 'a competitive level.'

To this outlook on the part of the owners the reply of the miners' representatives is threefold :

First—That the crisis in the world's coal trade is greater than can be solved by any facile lowering of price.

Second—That, in any case, whether the price of coal to the consumer is lowered or not, the living wage of the miners (together with hours and conditions) must be untouchable; that the present wage is not a living wage; and no question other than that of raising the present wage to meet the rise in the cost of living can be entertained.

Third—That, if the owners pin their faith to a lowering of price, the miners are prepared to examine where and how the present organisations of the industry, both in finance, production and distribution, is placing a burden on the price of coal which could be and ought to be shifted, and that the waste and parasitic growth of profits in recent years are choking the industry.

Finally, while the miners realised they could not under these conditions discuss nationalisation, nevertheless, short of nationalisation, the miners held that the question of price was much affected by the number of existing factors. For example, they challenged the efficiency and economy of the administration of collieries and stated their wish to examine, jointly with the owners, such matters as "the amount of directors' fees" and "multiplicity of directorships and consequently of the fees taken."

The coalowners for the purpose of the joint inquiry also submitted a statement and a dozen tables dealing with employment; British exports and Continental imports, together with production of oil for ships bunkers and other such details. They supplemented these by another dozen giving the results of colliery working in Germany, France and the USA. They produced statements showing pre-war and contemporary transport charges on coal from collieries for shipment and charges incurred at the Bristol Channel ports.

They were able to show that in 1925 the total charge on coal for export now stood at 3/2½d per ton, an increase on pre-war charges of exactly 100 per cent. Similarly, the charges on the vessel had gone up from 9¼d to 1/3½d, or a total increase of 68 per cent. The two together made an increase of 89 per cent. Exactly the same figure was reached with slightly varied coal cargo destined for northern and Continental ports, the same figure of 89 per cent total increase in pre-war charges per ton. Finally, a table showed that the increase on pitwood imported through Bristol Channel ports to the colliery had also risen steeply from 3/5¼d to 6/0½d making an increase on imported pit wood pre-war costs per ton of 2/6¼d or 73 per cent. This example dealt with the discharge of a cargo of over 2,000 tons of pitwood.[1]

With this difference in emphasis upon the subjects put forward for joint inquiry the factual materials found and furnished by each side were correspondingly different. What purported to be a dispassionate inquiry into the economic position of the coal industry early took on the appearance of preliminary manoeuvres for position between two antagonistic sets of interests. By the beginning of May it seemed abundantly clear to the workmen's side that the owners for the time being had given up the hope of getting agreement for an increase of hours and were now more likely to seek to prove a case for reduction of wages when the twelve months ran out.

By the month of May, 1925, there was some restiveness in the coalfields as to what might emerge from this unprecedented joint inquiry. It seemed necessary to have a clear statement of the subjects that had been under discussion and the standpoint thereon of the Miners' Federation, together with an answer, explicit or implicit, to the contentions put forward by the owners. The case of the owners was buttressed by figures which seemed to show that a rapidly worsening position of the British coal industry particularly in exports could be met with only by a reduction of costs. The owners in the winter and early spring had pinned their faith to the possibility of persuading the other side that the situation demanded a return to the nine-hour day.

On the other hand the miners in their conferences and discussions were pinning their faith to the possibility of getting an increase in wages as a result of a new agreement when the existing agreement expired at the end of June. The Miners' Federation of Great Britain, which had accepted this invitation of the coalowners to a round table conference, also decided to invite the Districts to consider whether they were in favour of ending the present existing wages agreement concluded 18th June, 1924, and to submit proposals to a national conference on 26th February. Accordingly a Special Conference of the South Wales Miners' Federation was held at Cardiff on Saturday, 21st February, 1925. The Executive Council recommended the present form of wages agreement to be continued subject to a series of nine amendments. These amendments would increase both the minimum percentages and the subsistence rates. After the matter had been thrashed out in considerable detail the Conference discussed the fundamental question as to whether the agreement should be amended or ended. Arthur Horner of Mardy proposed that South Wales should declare in favour of ending the present

[1]The output figure for South Wales and Monmouth had gone down very steeply from 54.2 million tons in 1923 to 51 million tons in 1924 and 44.8 million tons in 1925. Similarly the number of men involved by the 35 pits closed within eight months was, in the case of South Wales, 25,000. Moreover, there had been not merely a drop in exports of coal but a rapid drop in export prices, though this did not affect the Bristol Channel ports as severely as those of the North East and Scotland. For there were parts of the Welsh coal exports which no Continental country could do without, particularly the Welsh steam coal, smokeless and anthracite.

form of agreement. This was seconded by Jack Jones of the Garw Valley. After a further lengthy discussion the Council's recommendation was carried by a show of hands, but when a card vote was demanded the majority for ending the agreement was 70,200 and for the Executive Council's recommendation 61,450—a majority of 8,750.

At the MFGB Conference held four days later at Blackpool the very many proposals made from the Districts were tabled for discussion.

At a further South Wales Miners' Federation Special Conference, held in Cardiff on Saturday, 4th April, the proposals made by the various Districts of the MFGB to amend the existing agreement were under discussion. The most important point was whether the present existing method of regulating wages upon the principle of district products should be substituted for that of regulating wages by the cost of living. A vote was taken. The following resolution was unanimously adopted:

"That the minimum rate of wages payable shall be those obtaining in 1914 plus the cost of living percentage as published by the Board of Trade from time to time."

After discussion of the various demands from the other Districts it was decided that the South Wales delegates at the next national conference should support the following proposals:

"Steps be taken to reinstitute the Sankey Award of 2/- to raise the general standard.

"Night workers to be paid at the rate of 1 and 1/5th turns for each shift.

"Membership to be a condition of employment.

"Weekly wage and two weeks holiday a year" (4 iv 1925).

At the MFGB Special Conference, held on 20th May, 1925, in the Free Library of Blackpool, when delegates had been furnished first with the appendices of 18th March-16th April of the Joint Sub-Committee, and when Cook had reported, "Now, in conjunction with the Labour Research Department,[1] we have also prepared our own separate statement, and it will be necessary for me to refer to this at different stages", James Robson of Durham said, "I have never seen in my time figures so searching or so helpful, not only dealing with the economic position so far as our country is concerned, but its comparison with the whole world, and fairly indicating the position in which we find ourselves."

[1]To meet the need for speedy delivery the Labour Research Department set up a team (made up of Page Arnot, Clemens Dutt and two Labour College students from the South Wales Miners' Federation, Bert Williams and W. H. Williams) who worked throughout the Whitsun vacation. W. H. Williams was to be Secretary of the Labour Research Department from 1930 to 1945 when he took charge of research and then of industrial relations in the staff of the National Union of Mineworkers.

The Executive Committee unanimously proposed acceptance of the investigations, as reported by Cook, and their further continuance. An amendment was moved by Jack McGurk instructing the Executive at once to draft proposals for a new Wages Agreement. In the discussion Tom Greenall, M.P., cited a letter from the Lancashire and Cheshire Miners' Federation (sent by Thomas Ashton as Secretary) stating "it was considered that these joint meetings were useless" : and he upbraided Cook for making speeches in Lancashire that did not accord with his report. The amendment, supported by South Wales and Forest of Dean, was rejected by 571,000 to 280,000 on a vote by districts.

On 18th June the owners intimated to the workmen's representatives their intention to terminate "the present Wages Agreement, and further, that in their view a return to the eight-hour day was essential". Whereupon at the MFGB Executive Committee it was resolved "that at the next meeting of the Sub-Committee, after hearing the proposals of the owners, the workmen's representatives intimate to them that the workmen will not agree to longer hours or lower wages, but will press for increased wages which shall be at least commensurate with the increase in the cost of living" (19 vi 1925).

The gauntlet had been thrown down and had been taken up. The gauge of battle was there. It meant a stiff struggle in the days ahead.

8 NAILING THE UNION JACK TO THE GOLD STANDARD

It was on 28th April, 1925, that Winston Churchill, then Chancellor of the Exchequer, announced the resumption of the Gold Standard for the pound sterling. Churchill, at first reluctant to yield to the City's pressure, exercised through "the High Priest of the Golden Calf" Montagu Norman (Governor of the Bank of England) and such Treasury officials, had called in for discussion J. M. Keynes and Reginald McKenna. These two made clear the strong arguments against a return to the Gold Standard, and that many exporting interests were opposed to it. Churchill, however, was overborne by his official advisers. So he turned down the unofficial pundits, whom he had summoned to sustain his rather feeble footing in economics and finance, and announced the departure from a decade of managed currency to "enable the pound sterling to look the dollar in the face" as though he were nailing the Union Jack to the Gold Standard. J. M. Keynes thereupon issued *The Economic Consequences of Mr. Churchill*, in which he predicted an economic upheaval, especially in the export trades; that the fall in exports would "produce an atmosphere favourable to the reduction of wages"; and that "by means of the restriction of credit by the Bank of England you can deliberately intensify unemployment to any required degree, until wages *do* fall". So the decision to force up the exchange with the Yankee dollar, then on gold, from $4.40 to the old pre-1914 parity of $4.86 to the pound, meant a crisis in the export trade, with less employment and lower wages in every industry : and amongst the first, Keynes stated, would be the coal mining industry. These predicted effects were soon made visible.

On 18th June the owners had told the miners of their intention. Whereupon on 24th June the miners' leaders decided to place their case before "the entire political and industrial Labour Movement". On 30th June, A. J. Cook received by hand the notice of termination.[1]

Events that followed in quick succession make up the history of South Wales mining that summer as part of the total mining situation as well as the background to whatever was separately stirring in each district. Chronicled in detail elsewhere[2] they may conveniently be presented here in the form of diary and of documentation.

1st July : The Central Committee of the Mining Association formulated under nine headings their proposals for a new agreement.

3rd July : Delegate Conference took decision unanimously to resist the owners' proposals; to urge the Districts not to depart from the National settlement; to accept nothing less than a wage to meet the increased cost of living; to reject any proposal for an eight-hour day; decisions set forth in a letter from A. J. Cook which concluded :

"Further, we repeat our demand that the mineworkers are entitled to a wage rate not less than is necessary to meet the increase in the cost of living, and we urge all our districts to resist any offers which entail a departure from a national settlement."

4th July : Plans for "the New Consolidated Industrial Alliance" were considered by Joint Committee of the miners, transport workers, electricians, engineers and shipbuilders, the proposed alliance to include some fifty unions with no less than two-and-a-half million members.

7th & 8th July : The Executive Committee of the Miners' International, meeting in London, considered the position not only in Britain but also in France, Germany and Belgium : and decided to meet again in Paris on 28th July to decide the form of international action if need be.

[1]"The Mining Association of Great Britain, General Buildings, Aldwych, London, W.C.2.

Notice to Terminate Agreement of 18th June, 1924.

"We, the undersigned, President and Secretary respectively of the Mining Association of Great Britain, do hereby tender one month's notice on behalf of the members of the said Association to the Miners' Federation of Great Britain to terminate the National Wages Agreement entered into between the parties above mentioned on 18th June, 1924. The commencement of such aforesaid notice to date as and from midnight of this day, 30th June, 1925, and to terminate at midnight of Friday, 31st July, 1925.

"For and on behalf of the Mining Association of Great Britain,

EVAN WILLIAMS President.

30th June, 1925. W. A. LEE, Secretary."

[2]*Miners in Crisis and War*. Chapter XI.

A letter then came to Herbert Smith from Evan Williams[1] to which, on the same day, a reply[2] went with a snub for Evan Williams administered by Herbert Smith.

9th July : The Government intervened : W. C. Bridgeman, First Lord of the Admiralty, accompanied by Sir Arthur Steel-Maitland (Minister of Labour) met the Central Committee of the Mining Association. Thereafter, from the Carlton Club, headquarters of Toryism in Pall Mall, S.W.1, Bridgeman sent a letter which got a reply on the same day.[3]

10th July : MFGB Executive Committee meet TUC General Council.

11th July : Press statement issued by General Council of the Trades Union Congress appealing to the whole organised Trade Union Move-

[1]"Herbert Smith, Esq., J.P., Miners' Federation of Great Britain, 55 Russell Square, W.C.1.

"Dear Mr. Herbert Smith—I am very concerned to think that, so far as one can judge from Mr. Cook's letter of the 3rd inst. to Mr. Lee, your Executive does not contemplate taking any step towards meeting the representatives of the Mining Association until, at any rate, after your Annual Conference next week. Even if you have not formulated any definite policy for dealing with the present deplorable situation in the industry to enable it to establish itself upon a sound economic basis for the future it seems to me that an interchange of views upon the proposals which the Mining Association has put forward and upon your reply to them would be of value.

"The Owners' Sub-Committee which sat with your members to make the joint inquiry will be in London tomorrow, and would be prepared to meet you at any time. It is those who are engaged in the industry who will, after all, have to settle with each other in the end, and we should not lose any of the time left between this and the end of the month in getting to grips with a problem which I think you will admit is the most difficult that we have ever had to tackle.

7th July, 1925. Yours sincerely, Evan Williams."

[2]"Dear Mr. Williams—I received your letter by hand this morning, and in reply I have to say that I cannot see what good purpose would be served by our Sub-Committee meeting your Sub-Committee on the proposals that you have submitted, as our Conference has already indicated that there is no room for negotiations in those proposals. In addition, the duties of our Sub-Committee are now at an end.

"My Committee is meeting on Friday next, and if you have any further communication to make kindly address it to Mr. Cook and it will be placed before it.

7th July, 1925. Yours faithfully, Herbert Smith."

[3]"Dear Mr. Smith—I have seen Mr. Evan Williams and conveyed to him the decision at which you arrived this morning.

"He desires me to say that while he cannot assent to the proposal that the notice to terminate the Agreement should be withdrawn, he would recommend his Association to meet your Federation in conference on an open situation, taking up the discussions at the point where they were suspended.

"You may prefer to consider this matter at your conference next week and to defer any reply till then.

"If so, please let me know as soon as possible at the Mines Department.

10th July, 1925. Yours truly, W. C. Bridgeman."

"Dear Mr. Bridgeman—In answering your letter which was forwarded to Mr. Smith, our President, I beg to inform you that I placed same before my Committee and they regret to learn that the coal owners have refused our reasonable request.

10th July, 1925. Yours faithfully, A. J. Cook, Secretary."

14 LEAGUE AGAINST IMPERIALISM CONFERENCE AT FRANKFURT, 1929
GROUP INCLUDES A. J. COOK (MFGB); S. O. DAVIES (SWMF)

15 1926 MINERS' LOCKOUT : DYFFRYN SOUP KITCHEN AT GELLI

ment to aid the miners.[1] Ministry of Labour intimated that the Minister had "decided to appoint a Court of Inquiry under the Industrial Courts Act 1919 to Inquire into the Causes and Circumstances of the Dispute."

13th July : Letter from Ministry of Labour intimating constitution of Court of Inquiry; inviting Federation to participate and giving names: The Right Hon. H. P. MacMillan, K.C. (Chairman); W. Sherwood; Sir Josiah C. Stamp, G.B.E.

15th July : Telegram from Cook to Minister of Labour :

"Miners' Federation Annual Conference, sitting Scarborough today, decided mineworkers can accept no Court of Inquiry that has for its object the ascertainment of whether mineworkers' wages can be reduced or their hours extended, but it repeats its willingness to meet the coal-owners in open conference as soon as they have withdrawn their proposals."

16th July : Telegram from Minister of Labour re Court of Inquiry :

"In reply to your telegram, the decision of the Conference appears to be based upon a misapprehension as to the objects of the Court of Inquiry. The Court of Inquiry has been set up to inquire into the cause and circumstances of the threatened dispute in the coalmining industry, with a view to the presentation of a report to Parliament, so that the facts and circumstances surrounding the threatened dispute may be made known. Trust, therefore, that the miners' representative will attend the meeting of the Court, which has been fixed for tomorrow (Friday) morning."

17th July : Further invitation from Ministry of Labour enclosing formal request from Chairman of the Court to give evidence. To this request answer was made by Cook : "I refer you to the resolution passed unanimously by the Miners' Conference last week." Court of Inquiry adjourned until Monday, 20th July, in the hope that the miners would attend.

Second plenary meeting of proposed Industrial Alliance heard statement by Ernest Bevin, who had acted as Secretary of the Sub-Committee, and unanimously accepted the draft constitution for consideration by the unions concerned.[2]

[1]See Appendix to this Chapter.

[2]The temper of the assembly and the occasion of its meeting constituted a powerful moral support for the miners. This impression was strengthened by the uncompromising wording of the more important provisions:

"To create by means of an alliance of the specified organisations, a means of mutual support, to assist any or all of the allied organisations, in defending the hours of labour and wage standards, and securing advancement of the standard of living, or to take action to secure acceptance of, or to defend, any principle of an industrial character which may be deemed vital by the allied organisations.

"The conditions of membership of this Alliance shall involve the allied organisations in definitely undertaking, notwithstanding anything in their agreements or constitutions to the contrary, to act as directed by the General Conference of the Alliance."

20th July: Court of Inquiry entered on its inquiry; heard case put by one party to the dispute, the Mining Association.

23rd July: Special Committee of Seven (George Hicks elected Chairman) met MFGB Executive Committee and thereafter decided that the Prime Minister should be approached to bring about an unconditional conference between miners and mine owners.

9 SEVEN DAYS TO RED FRIDAY

24th July: Special Trades Union Congress in Central Hall, Westminster, on the subject of Unemployment received statement submitted by Executive Committee of Miners' Federation, headed "Joint Investigation into the Economic Position of the Mining Industry.[1]

The MFGB Executive Committee passed a resolution instructing their twenty districts as to action in the event of notices not being suspended: and making "arrangements for the minimum number of workmen necessary to secure the safety of the mines and feeding of ponies to continue at work."[2]

[1] It began: "Fellow Trade Unionists, the inquiry conducted by the representatives of the mine owners and yourselves into the economic position of the mining industry was abruptly concluded by the mine owners, as a consequence of our refusal to agree with them upon the necessary remedial measures for lifting the industry out of its present deplorable position. Our own views as to the causes of the present position of the industry, have been set forth in a separate document, entitled, 'The Economic Position of the Coal Industry', which contains a clear summary of the economic position and copies of which are available to the trade union movement."

It concluded "We may say that the mineworkers most earnestly desire a peaceful settlement of the present dispute. They realise fully the disastrous consequences, not only to themselves but to their fellow Trade Unionists, of a stoppage of work in the mines at the present time. At the same time they are confident that their fellow workers will not expect them to accept degrading conditions of employment, or to assent to the retrograde step of reverting to the eight hour day.

"It is possible that the lock-out notices may be postponed; they may even be withdrawn indefinitely. If so, so much the better. We feel bound to say, however, that the mineowners are perhaps the most obstinate set of employers in this country, and present indications seem to point to their having made up their minds to force the lock-out irrespective of the consequences. We hope our worst fears may not be realised, but we must make our calculations, and we must ask our fellow Trade Unionists to make theirs on the basis of a million-and-a-quarter mineworkers being locked out in ten days' time.

"It is not for the Miners' Federation to lay down what action it considers Congress should take. As one of the constituent bodies of the Trades Union Congress, it considers it sufficient to set the facts before the Congress and to indicate the probability of the miners requiring its early and substantial help. It feels assured that such assistance will be readily forthcoming, and on this occasion, if a lock-out matures, it will not be left to a section to fight alone, but the struggle will be taken up, and the issue joined, by the whole Trade Union Movement" (22 vii 1925).

[2] "The Executive Committee recommends that the necessary safety men be allowed to continue working, providing that the rates of wages and conditions of employment are not less favourable than those obtaining in July, and that it be left to districts to agree as to the number of men required to carry on the work, i.e., enginemen, pumpmen, ostlers (for feeding of ponies), coking plants, boiler firemen, and other necessary work. It is understood that there shall be no production of coal or coke."

25th July : TUC Special Committee met the transport and railway unions and secured their agreement not to handle coal if lockout took place.

27th July : The Prime Minister, Stanley Baldwin, who now took charge, heard TUC deputation urge postponement of notices and withdrawal of proposals.

28th July : The Prime Minister met mineowners who remained obdurate; miners' representatives met in Paris with representatives of International Miners' Federation and International Transport Workers' Federation; embargo on international movements of coal was decided upon in the event of a stoppage. Report issued of Court of Inquiry; *The Times* approved its criticism of owners.[1]

29th July : Central Committee of Mining Association published furious attack on Report of Court of Inquiry. Three times over the Prime Minister met the parties to the dispute, one after another, and also the Special Committee of the TUC General Council. In the course of these meetings Baldwin stated definitely that no subsidy would be given to relieve the situation.

30th July : All day meetings and discussions went on; meetings of the Cabinet, meetings of the trade unions, meetings of the Prime Minister with owners and with miners. In the morning the Prime Minister presented the Executive Committee with a document[2] in which he sought to "summarise the negotiations" as far as they had gone and state "the present position as I see it."

In reply the same day the Executive Committee, having given "very careful consideration" to the document, pointed out the weaknesses in its argument and expressed its disappointment.[3]

Special Conference of Trade Union Executives comprising a thousand delegates met in the Central Hall to receive statement from the miners and report of Special Committee. The miners reported a

[1]The Court in its unanimous report delivered some rather severe strictures on the case and the standpoint of the Mining Association. Sir Josiah Stamp, in his separate "Addendum to Paragraph 14," criticised the Government for its insistence upon going back to the Gold Standard, a measure which, he wrote. "would cut out the margin of profit on exports unless we were prepared to reduce the cost of industry at home, **including wages**. in accordance and simultaneously therewith."

[2]The document concluded in two sentences : "I told you yesterday, and I must repeat it today, that the Government are not prepared to give a subsidy to the industry.

"I should like you to consider again your position in reference to the point which I have made as to your inability so far to indicate a readiness temporarily to make a readjustment of conditions as some contribution towards meeting the difficult situation with which the industry is confronted."

[3]"In conclusion we desire to express our disappointment that you have not been able yourself to offer any practical contribution, apart from the suggestion of lower wages and longer hours, towards meeting the present economic position of the mining industry, which, admittedly, is playing such a great part in the operation of the various industries of the country and the economic life of the nation."

statement made to them by Baldwin that very morning to the effect that not only must the miners accept a reduction in wages but that, "all workers of this country have got to take reductions in wages to help put industry on its feet."

Conference of Trade Union Executives approved report of Special Committee and empowered it to give financial support and to issue strike orders. That evening instructions were issued to all members of the railway and transport unions to stop movements of coal. The embargo instructions were specific.[1]

At 10.30 p.m. Prime Minister told miners that the Government were prepared to have a very full inquiry and that, for nine months, there would be a subsidy to the industry.

31st July : Statement by Ministry of Labour.[2] Telegram at 4 p.m. to constituents of Miners' Federation ran : "Notices suspended Stop Work as usual Stop Cook Secretary."

At the eleventh hour the Baldwin-Churchill Government had given way. They had yielded to the threat delivered by the TUC General Council. Indeed "Red Friday", as it was named, became a red-letter day in the Labour calendar.

[1]"Railways : 1. Wagons containing coal must not be attached to any train after midnight on Friday, July 31st, and after this time wagons of coal must not be supplied to any industrial or commercial concerns or be put on the tip roads at docks for the coaling of ships.

2. All coal en route at midnight on Friday to be worked forward to the next siding suitable for storing it.

3. Any coal either in wagons or stock at a depot mav be utilised at that depot for the purpose of coaling engines for passengers and goods trains, but must not be moved from that depot to another.

"Docks, Wharves, Etc. : Coal Exports—All tippers and trimmers will cease work at the end of the second shift on July 31st.

Coal Imports.—On no account may import coal be handled from July 31st.

General.—A general stoppage of men handling coal on other classes of tonnage on Friday, July 31st, midnight.

"Waterways and Locks : All men on canals, waterways, etc., engaged in carrying coal will cease Friday midnight, with the exception of men who have coal en route, who will be allowed to take it to destination and tie up. Safety men for pumping, etc., will be permitted to work for safety purposes only.

"Road Transport : All men engaged in delivering coal to commercial and industrial concerns will cease Friday midnight, July 31st. Men delivering for domestic purposes will cease at 12 noon, Saturday, August 1st.

"Local Committees : For the purpose of carrying out these instructions, the members of the organisations herein concerned shall, from each district, establish small sub-committees so as to co-ordinate policy in giving effect to same."

[2]"The Prime Minister announced that in the circumstances the Government were prepared to render assistance to the industry until the spring, by which time the inquiry would be completed."

10 THE AFTERMATH OF RED FRIDAY

Ministers of the Crown spent a sad Bank Holiday in humiliation after their defeat of 31st July, Red Friday; but brooding over the possibilities of a day that would come when the tables would be turned : and their first steps thereto were decided on 5th August.

On the previous day (4th August) the Government had submitted to Parliament "an explanatory memorandum of the terms of settlement of the dispute in the coalmining industry" (Cmd 2488), dealing first with the nature of the dispute and then with the nature of the settlement, under which latter heading they told of "a full inquiry" over many months and in the meantime that :

"The Government have agreed to assist the industry by filling the gap that lies between the level of wages, provided by the minimum provisions of the National Wages Agreement of 1924, and the lower level of wages which would result from the colliery owners' proposals of 1st July last."

By granting the subsidy the Government had decided in favour of the coalowners in that they accepted as a basis the claims objected to by the Court of Inquiry in its strictures, and unfavourably regarded even by the Press namely, the terms put forward by the owners on 1st July. On the other hand the miners, whose intention had been to press for a revision of the agreement such as would provide them with a living wage, were to have no concession towards their standpoint. The owners had every reason to be pleased with the terms of the subsidy given by the Government.

The events of Red Friday, the delay in reaching the climax (due to the Government's belief that the TUC would not move) had profoundly stirred the people of Britain, as well as the parties to the dispute and their respective allies. There was prolonged debate on Thursday, 6th August, in Parliament. There were repercussions abroad as well as in every kind of public gathering throughout the autumn months.

The coalowners had best reason to be satisfied : the Government in their subsidy had conceded the extravagant claims of 1st July.

The miners, however, were not at all so pleased. In their Special Conference on Wednesday, 19th August, in the Kingsway Hall, Herbert Smith told delegates that "we have no need to glorify about a victory : it is only an armistice," and he went on to say that it would depend largely "how we stand between now and 1st May next year as an organisation in respect of unity as to what will be the ultimate results."

Amongst the politicians outside parliament there was fury that the Tory Government had sustained such a severe defeat at the hands of the trade union movement. Openly Red-baiting ministers made many speeches to placate their followers and keep the near-fascist sections under control.

In the debate in the House of Commons, Lloyd George, having attacked both Baldwin and Churchill on "the precipitate acceptance of the Gold Standard" and taunted them about Red Friday that "the voice that compels them is the voice of Mr. Cook", turned upon the talkative Joynson-Hicks saying, "the Home Secretary has been delivering a great many speeches recently[1] about the Red Peril : it really is no use barking at the Red Flag every time it cracks in the wind, whilst his chief is engaged in humbly gilding the flagstaff—and with Standard Gold. Really it is very sad to see the Chancellor of the Exchequer assisting in that operation. He was very eager to fight Reds on the Volga. I am very sorry to see him running away from them on the Thames and leaving his purse behind" (6 viii 1925).

Lloyd George did not fail in his excoriating remarks (and that it had this effect was shown by poor Mr. Baldwin's complaint to the Cabinet Secretary that "Lloyd George's speech was poisonous") to taunt Ramsay MacDonald, still the leader of the Labour Party, "for having been pretty soundly birched in private . . . his seat must be getting rather uneasy". The reference was clear to all his auditors.

On Bank Holiday Monday, 3rd August, Ramsay MacDonald, the Leader of the Labour Party, speaking at an ILP Summer School at Dunmow had said :

"The Government has simply handed over the appearance, at any rate, of victory, to the very forces that sane, well-considered, thoroughly well-examined Socialism feels to be probably the greatest enemy. If the Government had fought their policy out, one would have respected it. It just suddenly doubled up. The consequence has been to increase the power and the prestige of those who do not believe in political action."

The comment of the Treasurer of the SWMF, Oliver Harris, was as follows :

"This speech was hailed by the Capitalist Press as a 'sane' and 'strong' pronouncement. He attempted to give a lame explanation the following day, but the explanation did not alter the view expressed in the sentences quoted. He apparently regards men like Herbert Smith and Tom Richards as 'enemies of sane, well-considered, thoroughly well examined Socialism' . . .

"No one questions Mr. MacDonald's honesty, and he has a perfect right to express his views, but the Labour Party, if it is to render any useful service to the workers in the critical days ahead, must have a man of a different calibre at its head. Ramsay MacDonald is rapidly becoming the 'Old Man of the Sea' of the Party; the poor record of his Government, the bungling over the 'Red Letter' and now his criticism of the successful policy of organised Labour in defence of the miners makes it imperative that the leadership should be invested in a person

[1]For example Joynson-Hicks at Northampton :

"The danger was not over: sooner or later this question had to be fought out by the people of the land: was England to be governed by Parliament and by the Cabinet or by a handful of trade union leaders?" (2 viii 1925).

more in sympathy with the spirit of the times, and the growing strength of the Trade Unions."

The South Wales Miners' Federation (and to some extent the Miners' Federation of Great Britain) had earlier in the year come to reckon amongst their opponents the old ILP leaders who had held high office in the nine-month Government of 1924. The editorial in the April issue of their Journal began :

"The Miners' Federation Executive have very properly expressed their strong resentment at the action of Mr. Philip Snowden in attacking in the columns of the Anti-Labour Press the Secretary of the MFGB. Whatever opinions may be held as to the relative abilities of Mr. Cook and Mr. Hodges it is nothing less than a traitorous action on the part of anyone who professes Labour sympathies to attempt to deride one of the chief officials of an Organisation, especially when that Organisation is engaged in important negotiations on behalf of its members for improved conditions.

"If Snowden is not prepared to assist the miners he should at least have the decency not to join their enemies and make the fight more difficult. It is time to protest against the superior airs assumed by the so-called 'intellectuals' of the Labour Movement, who so often exhibit such a singular lack of ordinary intelligence. If the attitude of these people towards the progressive section of the Labour Movement and of the Trade Unions is maintained, it can only lead to that disruption which has reduced the Continental parties to such a sorry plight."

The *Colliery Workers' Magazine* had caught sight of the cloven hoof : they had made their prophesy of danger to the Labour Party—to be fulfilled six years later when "that disruption" was engineered by Snowden and MacDonald.

On the day after the great debate in the House of Commons on Thursday, 6th August, 1925, "Mr. Speaker adjourned the House without question put until Monday, 16th November, pursuant to the Resolution of this day". The Government had over fourteen weeks unhampered by parliamentary duties or criticisms, in which to concentrate on preparedness.

APPENDIX

PRESS STATEMENT ISSUED BY THE GENERAL COUNCIL OF THE TRADES UNION CONGRESS

"The General Council are emphatically convinced that the action of the Mining Association in giving notice to terminate the existing agreement is directly responsible for precipitating the crisis, particularly at a time when a Joint Committee of the mineowners and the workers was still investigating proposed remedies for the trade depression in the coalfields.

"The terms put forward by the Mining Association for a revised agreement propose drastic reductions in the already meagre wages paid to the miners, abolish the principle of the minimum wage, destroy the principle of national agreements, make the national unification of the industry an impossibility, and would, if carried to their logical conclusion, eventually lead to settlements between individual companies and their workers and cause chaos within the industry.

"The General Council appreciate to the full the fact that no self-respecting body of organised workers could negotiate on such terms, and they completely endorse the refusal of the Miners' Federation to meet the owners until the proposals have been withdrawn.

"The General Council particularly approve of the steadfast opposition of the Miners' Federation to any proposals for a lengthened working day, and deplore the misrepresentation which has led the public to assume that the seven-hour day represents the actual length of the miners' time underground. All those connected with the industry are aware that, in addition to the seven hours actually spent at the coal face, the time occupied in lowering and raising the miners to the surface and travelling underground makes the working day in reality equivalent, on the average, to more than eight hours per day.

"The General Council are confident they will have the backing of the whole organised Trade Union Movement in placing themselves without qualification and unreservedly at the disposal of the Miners' Federation to assist the Federation in any way possible.

"A Committee, consisting of Mr. J. Bromley, M.P., Mr. A. Hayday, M.P., Mr. G. Hicks, Mr. J. Marchbank, Mr. E. L. Poulton, Mr. Ben Tillett, Mr. A. G. Walkden, together with Mr. A. B. Swales (Chairman) and Mr. W. M. Citrine (Assistant Secretary), has been appointed to maintain continuous contact with the negotiations now taking place, and with power to summon the full General Council in the event of the necessity arising" (11 vii 1925).

CHAPTER NINE

RIOTOUS ASSEMBLY IN THE ANTHRACITE

1 RATIONALISATION IN THE ANTHRACITE

Meantime, from the early spring of 1925 there had been developing a special crisis in West Wales. The Anthracite district, which with an output in 1925 of five-and-a-half million tons had hitherto played a relatively small part, now came to the fore. Just as the Cambrian combine had been formed in the first decade of the century, so by the third decade both capitalist and trade union combines were found in the Anthracite. If Sir George Elliot had been the leading proponent of capitalist combination in 1893 in the coal trade; and if Lord Rhondda had built wide combines in the first and second decades; then in the third decade a leading figure of the great international trusts built up a virtual monopoly in the Anthracite. His name was Alfred Moritz Mond.

To Mond and his fellow manipulators of stocks and shares the Anthracite presented an opportunity to apply the ideas of "rationalisation of industry."[1] The pits were small, numerous and close to one another. Markets were developing in Europe and in North America.

The first step to "rationalisation" was to be amalgamation. Amalgamated Anthracite Collieries Ltd. (Chairman, the Rt. Hon. Sir Alfred Mond, Bt., M.P.) came into existence in 1923. It absorbed first the Cleeves Western Valleys Anthracite Collieries Ltd., which owned the Gellyceidrim Collieries Co. Ltd. The Amalgamated then swallowed the Gurnos Anthracite Collieries Ltd., from 1921 in control of the Ynis-cedwin Anthracite Collieries Ltd. : while its Managing Director, Thomas Cook, received over 7,500 ordinary shares "as remuneration for his services in connection with the negotiations for the purchase of the shares in the Cleeves and Gurnos Companies."

But there was a rival. United Anthracite Collieries Ltd., grouping in 1924 Great Mountain Collieries., Pontyberem Anthracite Colliery, New Dynant Anthracite Colliery (1914) Ltd., and Ammanford Colliery Co. Ltd., had an output of 600,000 tons of the highest quality of anthra-

[1] Mond's arguments were that rationalisation would eliminate competition, pool financial resources, pool wagons, reduce overhead charges, provide joint power plant, allocate coal reserves, open the way to standardised qualities, stabilised prices and new markets, reduce selling costs and develop sales. Emphasis on reduced costs (with the usual sequel in reduced wages) was basic to rationalisation, which finally would put the magnates of each such industry into an exceptionally powerful bargaining position.

cite coal.[1] Output rose to one million tons with the acquisition in the next two years of :—Carway Collieries Ltd., Caerbryn Anthracite Colliery Co. Ltd., Gwendraeth Valley Anthracite Collieries Ltd., New Rhos Anthracite Collieries Ltd., Pentremawr Colliery Co. Ltd.

Within a few months thereafter the two giants were fused into one combine, with a capitalisation of forty-five shillings per ton of output (compared with an average of twenty shillings a ton for the whole colliery industry)—a burden of over-capitalisation inevitably to be reflected in attempts to reduce costs. With a myriad of miners winning over two million tons from a score of pits Mond's amalgamated combine held 40 per cent of the total Welsh production of anthracite.[2]

Other amalgamations followed Mond's example. Sir Beddoe Rees, M.P., formed the Welsh Anthracite Collieries Ltd.[3] The Guest Keen and Nettlefolds—Llewellyn—Buckland group were also in the Anthracite.[4]

Outside the combines were a number of independents, such as the private non-limited concern of Evans Bevan owned by Evan Evans Bevan and producing from its seven pits at Seven Sisters and Onllwyn over half-a-million tons of anthracite yearly.[5]

[1]The price paid for the Great Mountain and Ammanford concerns was one-and-a-half million pounds for two colliery companies whose issued capital together was only £275,010 so that the purchase averaged nearly £6 for each single share. John Waddell and the two Daniels, of the new United Anthracite Collieries directorate, owned the Ammanford company while John Waddell was heavily interested in the Great Mountain concern. A fourth director, Sir Hector McNeal, received £75,000 United shares from the Great Mountain company "in consideration of the services rendered in connection with the formation of the United Anthracite."

[2]"Since 1915 the companies now embraced in the Amalgamated combine have made profits totalling the enormous sum of £3,698,441 or an average of over £300,000 each year, equivalent, on a mean output during that period of one-and-a-half million tons, to four shillings a ton net profit." Monthly Circular of Labour Research Department Vol. XVII. No. 6.

[3]Combined in Welsh Anthracite Collieries, Ltd., were the following concerns:

Company absorbed	Annual Output tons (x)
Llwynllafrod Anthracite Collieries Ltd.	90,000
Ystalyfera Collieries Ltd.	20,000
Abercrave Collieries Co.	90,000
International Collieries Co.	90,000
Trimsaran Co. Ltd.	90,000
Varteg Anthracite Collieries Ltd.	sinking
Gwaunclawdd Abercrave Collieries Co. Ltd.	60,000
New Cwmmawr } from Ashburnam Cwm Capel } Collieries Ltd.	30,000

(x) 1926-27: some estimated.

[4]There they linked together the 300,000 tons yearly output from the three pits of Gwaun-Cae-Gurwen Colliery Ltd., with £700,000 of capital and 400,000 tons yearly from the two Glyn Neath pits of the Vale of Neath Colliery Co. Ltd., the 200,000 tons of the Rock Colliery Ltd., and the Ynisarwed Collieries Co Ltd., and the grouping thus controlled an output of 900,000 tons a year or 16 per cent of the total Welsh Anthacite production.

[5]*The Industrial & Social History of Seven Sisters* by Chris Evans (Cymric Federation Press. 1964).

The process of amalgamation was to move very fast. The Llewellyn-Buckland pits were purchased by the Mond group, which thus raised its output to 70 per cent of the total Welsh production and then continued further.

Behind these amalgamations was the towering figure of the son of Dr. Ludwig Mond (F.R.S.) begotten at Farnworth, near Widnes in Lancashire, and educated at Cheltenham, Cambridge and Edinburgh, whence he moved from being a barrister of the Inner Temple (on the North Wales and Cheshire Circuit) to a series of activities in various fields, one of which was the applied science of heavy chemicals, wherein he was to become the architect of multi-national companies, such as Imperial Chemical Industries Ltd. and the International Mond Nickel Company. By 1906, Alfred, born in 1868, had become Liberal M.P. for Chester whence he moved to Swansea from 1910 to 1923 and thence (still in the Anthracite Belt) to Carmarthen from 1924 to 1928, when he left the House of Commons and entered the House of Peers as Lord Melchett. In the Coalition Government of December 1916 Mond became one of Lloyd George's "clutch of tycoons" as First Commissioner of Works[1] whence he moved (on 1st April, 1921) into the Cabinet as Minister of Health in place of his jettisoned fellow-Liberal, Christopher Addison.[2]

In 1913 there had been over a hundred independent concerns in Welsh anthracite, producing 4,833,000 tons. Fifteen years later, of the total output of 5,575,000 tons, 80 per cent were advertised as produced by the Amalgamated Anthracite—which was, wrote the *Colliery Guardian*, "a great feather in the cap of Lord Melchett, who has never disguised his purpose of establishing complete unanimity among home producers as a step towards an international understanding."

[1]Mond's attempt to administer the Ancient Monuments Act came into collision with Niall Diarmid Campbell, 10th Duke of Argyll, 44th Knight of Lochow, and in his Celtic title the MacCailean Mhor: Hereditary High Sheriff of Argyll; Admiral of the Western Coast and Isles; Keeper of the Great Seal of Scotland and of the Castles of Dunstaffnage, Dunoon and Tarbert. The impoverished Chief of Clan Campbell wrote that "If Sir Alfred Mond or his understudy Sir Lionel Earle present themselves outside the wall of Dunstaffnage Castle, His Grace has given the most direct instructions to his kinsmen and vassals to clap them immediately into the dungeon."

The threat was effective, the Commissioner of Works did not trespass.

It was otherwise in the confrontation later between this great monopolist, who abandoned the Liberal Party in January 1926, and the Trades Union Congress chairman, Sir Ben Turner, each a former Minister of the Crown. So there was to be born the Mond/Turner Plan for class collaboration, initiated in the year after the General Strike, and usually known as "Mondism".

[2]Christopher Addison, M.D. (1869-1951) born in Hogsthorpe Lincs; Anatomist and professional politician. Served as Liberal in seven ministerial jobs, as Labour in five ministries. From 1945-51 Leader of the House of Lords, which he had entered 8 years earlier to become in 1945 Viscount Addison of Stallingborough, and Knight of the Garter in 1946.

2 THE ANTHRACITE DISPUTE

The strikes in the West of the coalfield in 1925 arose from the refusal by the management, in a single pit, to abide by the old customs. The pit was Ammanford No. 1 at the head of the Amman Valley, on the edge of the coalfield, where a new manager, Price Davies, had been put in by the United Anthracite. After months of local strife trouble developed at the end of April 1925 with the victimisation of one of the men named Wilson. Wilson worked with a "butty" who desired his own son to work with him in a particular working place. Wilson agreed to the change on condition that it be ratified by a general meeting of the workers according to long-standing custom. On the following day the son began work. As no ratification to the proposal had come from the men, Wilson refused to start in another place, but went to his old place, thus "defying" the orders of the management. Wilson was sacked.

In the same pit where, from 7th May to 26th May, 115 men had been given notices to end contracts due to "the unremunerative nature of the working places", the workmen disputed the method of withdrawal and demanded the application of the Seniority Rule, namely, that the last man to be employed be the first to be withdrawn. The management refused.

The following resolution was passed at a mass meeting held at the Ammanford Park:

"That this meeting of the Amalgamated Anthracite Collieries (Mond group) protest against the action of the Mine Owners in placing pressure upon the Workers and attempting to again reduce their standard of living, and call upon the Trades Union Congress General Council to press for unity of all classes of workers internationally" (25 v 1925).

At the mid-June Executive Council meeting in Cardiff, John James of Cwmgorse, miners' agent in the Anthracite, reported that strike notices had been handed in at Ammanford: and by 29th June not only that the Ammanford workers were on strike but that notices were to be tendered throughout the district, while the Combine Committee comprising the representatives from the lodges under the United Anthracite Collieries Ltd., declared for a strike ballot to be taken to support the Ammanford No. 1 Lodge in their struggle. Half a year later at a Special Conference of the South Wales Miners' Federation, John James, telling of the circumstances which had led to the strike and its consequences, stated:

"For thirty years the relationship between the Anthracite workmen and the employers in the Ammanford area has been of the most amicable nature, and in that period it was very seldom indeed that the miners' agent was called upon to intervene in any dispute between the management and the men. Since the establishment of the combines however, the whole atmosphere has been changed. The official staff seem to concentrate their efforts and time, not upon the proper management of the collieries, but upon the pilfering of the miners' wages and interference with the customs and practices, to the observance of which the workmen are entitled. This went on until the workmen became exasperated; and it is no wonder that some small excesses have been committed" (2 i 1926).

In its issue of Tuesday, 7th July, 1925, the *South Wales Daily Post* under the headlines "Alarm at Ammanford" and "Expiring Notices: Demand for Ballot" stated that there was a further meeting of the Ammanford strikers and picketing was to be resumed that night; also that the Firemen's Union refused to support the miners—although the miners had helped them in a dispute previously. It continued: "There is a growing feeling of uneasiness over the approaching termination of notices in the other collieries, and a demand for a ballot. The men's leaders are more convinced than ever that the reported finding of explosive at No. 1 colliery was a hoax."

Two days later the *South Wales Daily Post* stated that in the Swansea Valley men were said to be wavering: and that there had been a five hour sitting of the general meeting of the Anthracite District Committee at Swansea.

At the meeting on Saturday, 11th July, the mandates were declared: for strike action 9,918; against strike action 5,795; not represented 1,399. When this result was made known, 2,006 "were prepared to fall in with the majority". Thus a down-tools policy, a general strike of the Anthracite miners, began on Monday, 13th July, as duly reported a week later by John James to the Executive Council at its meeting in Cardiff.[1]

Next day at a mass meeting held at Cwmamman it became known that a few collieries in the Neath Valley had disregarded the mandate to strike. At six o'clock a resolution was put to the mass meeting and carried unanimously that a demonstration proceed that night to meet those going to work the following morning.

The scene was vividly described by Evan (Ianto) Evans,[2] one of

[1]For much of what follows in this section on the anthracite dispute the author is indebted to Hywel Francis (of the University College of Swansea) whose painstaking researches have brought to light much that was obscured in the garbled and often police-inspired reports of the Welsh Press. See in particular his *Disturbances in the South Wales Coalfield* 1925-1936, a paper given by Hywel Francis at a Conference on 20th century Welsh History in Gregynog, Newtown, Montgomeryshire, on 14th November, 1972; and afterwards published in part in *Llafur*, The Journal of the Society for the Study of Welsh Labour History, Vol. 1, No. 2, May 1973 (Special Number, 75th Anniversary of the South Wales Miners' Federation).

[2]E. J. Ianto Evans, unofficial leader at Ammanford in 1925 and later an initial member of the new "laymen's" SWMF Executive Council (set up in 1933) and continuously thereto re-elected for 18 years, wrote the following autobiographical note in response to a request from the author:

31st July, 1962. 16 Betws Road, Betws, Ammanford, Carms.

R. Page Arnot, 46 Byne Road, London S.E.26.

Dear Robin,

History of South Wales Miners.

Yours of the 30th inst. to hand and note contents. I was born on the 20th

the unofficial leaders, who told the story :

"A mass meeting was arranged on the second day of the strike on the Glanamman football ground, and it was a glorious sight, thousands of workers being present. By this time news had come through that these two collieries were working. Eventually a letter from a contact in the Dulais Valley was handed up to the Chairman, Comrade Arthur Thomas, with the information regarding the position, after which he called a Party member up to the platform to move a resolution that a demonstration proceed that night to meet these workmen going to work the following morning . . . The resolution was unanimously carried and a rush was made to Ammanford to get a crowd together, as no prior arrangements had been made.

"That night about 400 strikers left Ammanford at 10.40, led by the Ammanford band, and proceeded up the valley, where they picked up the Cwmamman section, headed by their band, then to Gwaun-cae-Gurwen and Brynamman, with another band each. Through the Swansea Valley the crowd gathered like a snowball and by the time the procession reached Ystradgynlais Common it was from 15,000 to 20,000 strong. They continued to march through the night until they got to Crynant in the Dulais Valley, 21 miles from Ammanford.

"The demonstrators succeeded in stopping all the pits in the Dulais

March, 1890, the 8th of 13 children, 8 sons and 5 daughters, of which 3 brothers now remain; the eldest being in the middle 80's, the other 79 this month, and myself, 72. My mother died at the early age of 40 when I was 10 years old (with 4 additional children younger than myself) which was not surprising having regard to the terrible burden she had borne throughout her all too brief existence. Although she died when I was only a child, I still cherish sweet memories of her superb intelligence and sterling character. It indicates very vividly the terrific struggle to obtain a bare existence a mere seven decades ago.

I began to work as a part-timer at the age of eight-and-a-half. My father and two elder brothers were limestone quarrymen. Outside the normal shift hours boring by sledge and drill was carried on. I helped in this at that early age going up for several hours in the morning even before dawn. All this was at the village called Trefil, near Tredegar, in Monmouthshire, in a quarry owned by the Ebbw Vale Steel, Iron and Coal Company.

I left school after passing the so-called Labour Examination in June, 1902, when I started work full-time as a borer, boring with a metal instrument about 5 feet in length called a churn, with two sharpened ends. This was used for boring holes from 9 feet to 12 feet in depth for blasting large limestone rock. The wage for this arduous work was the princely sum of two shillings per day.

During the period of my part-time employment which, even then was theoretically, at least, illegal, my father was threatened with prosecution for my lack of attendance at school, due to my part-time work.

I worked as a borer until I was between 15 and 16 years of age, when I went to work with my father until I reached the age of 19, when I became a fully fledged quarryman, with a place of my own, on piecework. My father was a staunch Trade Unionist, and saw to it that we were all initiated as members, immediately the first pay day materialised, he, at that time being recognised as the leading official of the local Lodge or Branch. I took over the Chairmanship of the Branch from him between the age of 20 and 21.

I then went down the pits—into Pochin Pit owned by the Tredegar Iron and Coal Company. Later I worked in a place called Tytrist, which in the Welsh language means "the sad house." After a matter of weeks there I worked for a short period on the surface at Whitworth Colliery, and later (during 1911) underground at the same colliery, where I was employed as a shift leader in a hard heading, driving through rock, for the princely wage of 5/6 per shift.

Valley. A skirmish occurred when they met the workmen's train from Neath at Crynant. At this point the police made an appearance but were many times outnumbered. As an eye-witness said, 'The police were a sight for the gods. About 20 had arrived on the scene by now, quaking in their boots, absolutely cringing and begging the crowd to go away'" (15 vii 1925).

Two days later a demonstration of strikers about 700 strong wended their way from Onllwyn to the Rock Colliery—the remaining colliery at work—they were met by a posse of police. The five hundred men at the Rock Colliery struck work immediately.

The demonstrators were asked to disperse but (according to a participant, Dick Beamish) they refused. A baton charge was ordered and "a riot ensued for about fifteen minutes. There were sixteen casualties, including P.C. Bryn Phillips of Port Talbot, a boxer and international rugby forward, who was rather badly mauled" (17 vii 1925).

Now there began discussions about the withdrawal of safety men on the ground that this was the best method of bringing the dispute to an end. Consequently, at an adjourned meeting, and by a vote of 44 lodges to 16, it was decided to begin the withdrawal of safety men.

I returned to work in the quarry at Trefil towards the end of 1911 and became Chairman again. I remained there until the final slam between the boss (who, incidentally, was my cousin) in the middle of December 1912 in a dispute over a miserable shift payment—4/6 nett—which he refused to agree to because it was a Saturday short shift. I packed it in and left home on 29th December, 1912, and started work at Ammanford the following day. It was at the Tir-y-dail Colliery, which in the Welsh language means "Land of Leaves".

★ ★ ★

I remember very well the first strike of 1898. It was a "beautiful summer." I remember also the communal bakehouse, the ten huge tin loaves. It was my business to fetch three to four gallons of water from a spring. The spring ran near a river. In that river there was often adult baptism, total immersion. The last time that this occurred, when fifteen were baptised at once, there was snow on the ground. I myself was religious in my early twenties.

In September, 1914, I was not only religious but patriotic. I joined up, qualifying for first aid and consequently joining the Royal Army Medical Corps. I was at the Dardanelles in 1915. At the beginning of 1916 I was on the Struma front near Salonica. Then I contracted jaundice and was three months in Egypt. From there, in 1917, I was on the Palestine front and in 1918 I was posted to Ramallah, near Jerusalem. I came back from the war in February, 1919, and was elected to the Lodge Committee where from 1922-1927 I was Chairman. In 1924 I also became Chairman of the Anthracite District. On 24th September, 1927, the pit packed up. Until the beginning of February, 1928, I was unemployed. Then I procured work at the Cross Hands Colliery, but within five weeks there was a heavy withdrawal due to depression. Once more I became unemployed and remained so until 1st January, 1929, when I returned to Cross Hands Colliery and within five weeks I was elected Chairman of the Lodge. The membership of the lodge at that time was approximately 120, out of a total eligible personnel of approximately 900. Within six months the lodge was a closed shop—100 per cent organised.

Incidentally within a fortnight of my temporary withdrawal from the Cross Hands Colliery, I was on my way to the 4th RILU Congress, where among other things I had the very great pleasure of making my first happy contact with you, and spending many pleasant hours in your delightful company. As ever, E. J. (Ianto) Evans.

From the end of July onwards until 6th August the town of Ammanford and some surrounding villages were under virtual control of the strike committee. On 28th July there was trouble simultaneously at three collieries: Gelliceidrim Colliery was rushed by a crowd of miners; at Saron Colliery shots were fired, a man in the colliery yard was hit by a bullet and a quantity of explosives were discharged; at Park Colliery explosives were discharged and telephone wires were cut. Extra police brought in seemed inadequate. According to the *South Wales Daily Post* "Extra police protection will probably be needed for the men to remain at work," and owners appealed to the Chief Constables of Carmarthen, Glamorgan and Brecon.

Two days later, on Thursday, 30th July, there were disturbances at Ammanford No. 2 Colliery where there was a baton charge, at Bettws and at Llandebie Colliery. Evan Llewellyn, aged 50, (later sentenced to 17 months imprisonment for having incited riotous behaviour) was reported to have said:

"I don't care a ——— if there are 20 police. I will stand in front of all their bullets. We want to stop everyone going to work. They are not going to work while we are starving. What are the police anyway? If they obstruct you, fight them."

But the "Battle of Ammanford" fell upon Wednesday, 5th August, when as (Ianto) Evans recalled:

"Crowds of workers lined the streets demanding that a march be made to Ammanford No. 2 Colliery . . . where an electrician had sneaked in on the pillion of a motorcycle . . . The police were concealed inside the colliery premises ready and waiting. Nothing daunted the crowd, (they) marched up and demanded that this man be removed. The deputy chief constable led a force of police to the attack and was promptly laid out. Then the fun started."

Some 200 Glamorgan police, brought to Gwaun-Cae-Gurwen, were rushed to the scene. But the strike committee, already well informed, had sent a motor-cyclist to Bridgend to reconnoitre police movements. When the police, travelling in 12 to 14 buses along the Neath-Ammanford road, reached at Pontaman an embankment on either side of the road boulders and stones showered down. All the buses were wrecked and every window smashed. The police re-formed and, as eye-witnesses recalled, "began to baton all the local people in sight, most of whom were innocent bystanders . . . The battle raged from 10.30 p.m. until 3 a.m. with heavy casualties on both sides. But casualties among the police were the heavier."

★ ★ ★

On the next afternoon, one of the Home Secretary's close supporters, Colonel Gretton (Chairman of Bass's Brewery Company), asked him "whether his attention has been called to the serious rioting at Ammanford Colliery, South Wales, last night; and what steps he proposes to

16 CWMPARC GONDOLIERS JAZZ BAND (1926 LOCKOUT)

17 POLICE IMPORTED FROM ENGLAND GUARDING PIT HEAD AND COLLIERY MANAGERS DURING THE 1926 LOCKOUT

take to maintain law and order ?" After an interjection by the irrepressible Jack Jones, ("Send them down some Bass's beer; that will quieten them.") Sir William Joynson-Hicks replied: "Yes, Sir, I have been in daily telephonic touch with the chief constable, and have this morning received from him a report regarding last night's disturbance. It appears that a body of some hundreds of strikers, many of whom were unconnected with the pit in question, armed with staves and other weapons, approached the pit and, in spite of the endeavours of the deputy chief constable to persuade them to disperse, made a determined attack on the police on duty. When the deputy chief constable, and the inspector and sergeant in charge of the men, had all been somewhat seriously injured, the police were forced to retreat to the colliery offices; but the reinforcements which were standing ready and had in the meantime been summoned, were able shortly before midnight, to clear the colliery premises and disperse the rioters. Some damage was done on the colliery premises, but the safety men remained at work. The chief constable of the county is responsible for the measures for maintaining order in the district. I understand that no further disturbances are anticipated at present, but that, as a precautionary measure, the chief constable has taken steps to augment the police at his disposal by obtaining assistance from another force."

★ ★ ★

By 20th July the owners had made an offer that they hoped would end the strike. The District Meeting was adjourned until 1st August when a vote of 13,274 to 3,839 rejected the terms offered. Subsequently it was decided "that the Executive Council of the South Wales Miners be consulted, but that the District Meeting control the dispute."

On 6th August, 1925, a very full meeting of the Executive Council, with 36 present, met in Cardiff to hear a report from Tom Richards on "Red Friday," the day when the Trades Union Congress and Miners' Federation prevailed over the Government. They also heard a deputation (D. B. Lewis and T. Gibbon Davies) from the Ammanford Combine Committee (United Anthracite Collieries Ltd.). The sequel was that on 12th August the Anthracite District delegates at Swansea decided to reconsider the owners' proposals for a settlement of the strike. On Friday, 14th August, the Executive Council, after hearing a report on the steps taken from the President and Secretary resolved to take over the District with power to settle.

When a representative of the Executive Council met the owners a basis for negotiations was agreed upon as follows: (1) Resumption of work; (2) Wages and other terms prevailing before the stoppage to be continued; (3) All workmen to be reinstated upon the undertaking being given to preserve the agreement for tendering notices in future; (4) No proceedings to be taken for alleged breach of contract; (5) An endeavour to be made to find employment for the workmen of Ammanford No. 1 Colliery in other pits of the United Anthracite Collieries Co. Ltd.

On 24th August Ammanford miners, having been on strike for nine weeks, accepted the tentative agreement arrived at by 21st August between their leaders and the coal owners and agreed to resume work immediately. On Ammanford No. 1 Pit the company had stated: "That due to the colliery being unremunerative for some time past it left the Company no alternative but to close the colliery."

★ ★ ★

From these trade union negotiations and from the scenes of strife in the high summer of 1925, with their inspired immediate repercussions in Westminster (which were to have their sequel in West Wales before mid-winter) we must now turn to activities on a national and international scale which bore a close relation to the fortunes of the South Wales miners.

3 "LOOKING OVER JORDAN"

Joy over "Red Friday" was not fully shared by South Wales miners, whose own demands for an improved Wage Agreement had not been met. Nor had the Government's interpretation of the terms of the settlement been at all to their liking, as was made clear at the MFGB Special Conference of 19th August, 1925.

On the other hand satisfaction could be felt that the broad lines of their strategy, popularised by Cook's agitation, had reached a stage that seemed to give good augury for the crucial nine months that now lay ahead. Looking back over the previous nine months, from the formation in November 1924 of the second Baldwin administration, through the rapid worsening of the coal trade[1] they could note the growth of resistance to these adverse conditions, not only in their own ranks but in the working class, both nationally and internationally.

Internationally there had been remarkable changes particularly since the Hull Trades Union Congress in September; followed in November 1924 by a British fraternal delegation attending the Sixth All-Russian Trades Union Congress in Moscow.[2]

A three-day conference in London, representing over six million

[1]From 2.1 per cent unemployed in March 1924 to 11.8 per cent in March 1925 and 25 per cent in June 1925—in contrast to a general figure overall insured workpeople of 9.8 per cent in March 1924 in those later months of 11.1 per cent and 11.9 per cent respectively.

[2]Early in 1925 *The Official Report of the British Trades Union Delegation to Russia and the Caucusus in November and December* 1924, was welcomed in the trade union movement as a clear exposition of the political conditions, social and industrial, and also the truth after seven years of falsehoods.

Russian trade unionists and over five million British, had issued a joint declaration beginning :

"The Joint Conference affirms that national and international unity must be recognised as the first essential condition to enable the Trade Union Movement to defend effectively the present position of the workers against attack and to achieve the social and political aims of organised Labour, as set forth in the declarations made by the workers of many countries" (8 iv 1925).

As a result of the discussions it was agreed that joint efforts would be made "to induce the Amsterdam International, in all goodwill, to agree to a free unconditional and immediate conference with representatives of the Russian trade union movement" (8 iv 1925).

Already, however, the British Report had been subjected on the Continent to attacks from the leading trade union officials, who treated its authors as "bolshevists" and "communists" In fact none of the delegation of seven, nor their advisory delegation, were members of the Communist Party. Many of them had been and continued to be outspoken opponents of Communist theory. The delegation consisted of : A. A. Purcell (Chairman): Herbert Smith, J.P.; Ben Tillett; John Turner; John Bromley, M.P.: Alan A. H. Findlay, and Fred Bramley.

Purcell, together with another of the five British members of the new "Anglo-Russian Joint Advisory Council", took on responsibility for a publication *Trade Union Unity*, a monthly magazine of international trade unionism, of which the first number appeared in April 1925.[1]

Within the wide range of British unions the international development provided suitable hatching ground for the proposed Trade Union Alliance, for which the initial suggestions had come from the Amalgamated Engineering Union.[2] This proposed alliance had gone steadily ahead to provide what it was hoped would be "a steel framework of unions within the wider and lesser association of the annual trade union congress, and go beyond the scope of the old Triple Industrial Alliance."

In all this, the South Wales miners, as is evinced in utterances and publications, gained a heightened consciousness as part of the working

[1]The Editorial Board of *Trade Union Unity* consisted of : A. A. Purcell, President International Federation of Trade Unions; Edo Fimmen, Secretary of the International Transport Workers' Federation; George Hicks, E.C. Member of IFTU. The Editorial Secretary was R. Page Arnot, followed by G. Allen Hutt. It was published from 162 Buckingham Palace Road, the address of the Labour Research Department.

[2]"That realising the poverty-stricken condition of the engineering workers and the futility of securing any substantial relief by means of negotiations with the employers, instructs the Executive Council to approach the Miners' Federation, N.U.R., Transport Workers, and other unions as may be deemed necessary, with a definite proposal for the formation of an offensive alliance against the employers concerned, and to call upon the allied unions to prepare a combined movement for the purpose of securing adequate wages and tolerable conditions of labour for all workers involved" (National Committee of Amalgamated Engineering Union in York, 27th to 31st May, 1924).

class nationally and internationally. Within the labour movement they could descry with a sharper vision the distinction, somewhat blurred in the honeymoon weeks of the first Labour Government, between the Left and the Right. With the collapse of the MacDonald administration, the rose-coloured spectacles were cast aside: and leading trade unionists regarded MacDonald, bamboozled by the intrigue of the *Daily Mail* and some disreputable members of the Foreign Office staff into acceptance of the "Zinoviev Letter"—a forgery exposed at the time in public utterance by Sidney Webb—as a liability rather than the asset they once thought him to be. Cook and others wished to raise the question of MacDonald's leadership.[1] But many even of those now coming to share the verdict of Lenin[2] felt that it was a case of "least said, soonest mended"; and that any action would now only be self-injurious to the party. A sequel was that Philip Snowden and others of his persuasion now rallied to support MacDonald, whom they personally detested, against the developing trade union struggle of the miners and workers in other sections of industry.

There was also a much keener appreciation of the importance of propaganda. This was regularly noted by *The Colliery Workers' Magazine*, where the editorial notes and comments voiced the prevailing mood and outlook within the SWMF. Already in the spring 1925, it is stated:

"The great need of the Labour Movement is a big Press that will reach the homes of the workers instead of the daily and weekly dope that is streaming forth from the capitalist newspapers that are now being bought by the million by the workers of this country. It does seem strange that millions of electors will vote for the Labour Candidate every time, but who go to the anti-Labour Press for their daily news. There was a time when this could not be avoided because we had no Press of our own, but there is no excuse now, and every worker should make it a point to buy a Labour paper first and the capitalist paper should come second."

It is then noted:

"The Labour Press has received great accession of strength during the last few weeks through the starting of two new weekly publications, *The Sunday Worker* and *Lansbury's Labour Weekly*. Both of them express the Left-wing point of view and are consequently doubly welcome, and we hope that the readers of the *Colliery Workers' Magazine* will give them their hearty support.

[1]"Ramsay MacDonald is rapidly becoming the 'Old Man of the Sea' of the Party; the poor record of his Government, the bungling over the 'Red Letter' and now his criticism of the successful policy of organised Labour in defence of the miners makes it imperative that the leadership should be invested in a person more in sympathy with the spirit of the times, and the growing strength of the Trade Unions."

[2]Lenin's article, written in reply to one by MacDonald in *L'Humanite* of Mid-April 1919 stated: "Ramsay MacDonald's article is the best example that could be given of that smooth, melodious, banal, and socialist-seeming phraseology which serves in all developed capitalist countries to camouflage the policy of the bourgeoisie inside the Labour Movement."

"*The Daily Herald* is the smartest morning paper on the market, its news is ample and pungent, its articles are bright and witty, and its literary features from a working-class point of view are such that they cannot be found in any other daily paper, and its circulation should be a couple of millions at least instead of less than half-a-million that is now sold."

The *Sunday Worker* was the first Sunday newspaper to voice the trade union struggle. At first edited by William Paul, and afterwards by Walter Holmes, the *Sunday Worker* announced on its front page an article by Cook, and thereafter week by week in practically every number, there was either an article by Cook, or a fairly detailed report with such headings as "Fighting Speech by A. J. Cook."

To those from South Wales, who year after year attended the Trades Union Congress, that summer and autumn had given great hopes of trade union solidarity. Only four years earlier disillusion after "Black Friday" had demoralised the ranks of trade unionism to its nadir at the Plymouth Congress.[1] "Red Friday" now would raise it to its zenith at Scarborough. The Scarborough Trades Union Congress was welcomed in the *Colliery Workers' Magazine* with extensive quotations. The speech of the Congress Chairman, Alonzo B. Swales, brought the sound of victory when he said:

"This movement of ours has learned many lessons during these years of reaction engineered by the employers, and one of the lessons is that a militant and progressive policy, consistently and steadily pursued, is the only policy that will unify, consolidate and inspire our rank and file . . . and this policy renders necessary a greater degree of Trade Union unity."

The magazine regarded the speeches generally as "of a high level", but "perhaps the most sensational was the speech of Fred Bramley, the Secretary, on our relations with Russia".[2]

To all these developments, welcomed by the South Wales miners, there now set in counter-tendencies. At the same time the dominant sections of the Labour Party made a counter-attack at their Liverpool Annual Conference. Conference voted down all amendments whether

[1]"At the Plymouth Congress we had an exhibition of internal strife, a thoroughly unwholesome Congress in every way, set off by the bright spot of Edo Fimmen's plea for International Unity." A. A. Purcell, September, 1925.

[2]"The Revolution has revealed the interesting fact that you can cut off the heads of kings, you can abolish royal families, you can imprison your Emperors—as they have done in Austria and in Germany—you can promote world wars leading to universal devastation and destruction and universal slaughter, and you can be forgiven and accepted into the comity of nations. You can change your political institutions as you will and all is well, but if you disturb the landed interests of a country, and abolish the exploitation of the wage-earner, deal with the factory exploiter and get rid of the privilege, property and power possessed by a minority, then you will have to face what Russia is now facing—isolation, boycott and international persecution. Russia, from our point of view, is a nation at bay. Its economic system is controlled by the working class movement of Russia. We consider it our duty to stand by the working class movement of Russia."

Communist or not which questioned the policy indicated by the Executive. For example, Ernest Bevin moved :

"That, in view of the experience of the recent Labour Government, it is inadvisable that the Labour Party should again accept office whilst having a minority of members in the House of Commons" (30 ix 1925).

The Conference followed the lead given by Thomas and MacDonald, and turned down Bevin's resolution by 2,587,000 to 512,000.

Communist membership of Local Labour Parties was excluded by a vote of 2,870,000 to 321,000. A further resolution, carried by 2,692,000 to 488,000, was to deprive the trade unions of their hitherto unchallenged right to elect from their own ranks whoever they might choose as delegates to National or Labour Party conferences or meetings.

The Labour Party Conference was followed by the arrest in mid-October of twelve leading Communists.

4 UNEMPLOYMENT

Particularly through the summer and autumn of 1925 the effects of the resumption of the "Gold Standard" were shown in figures and watched with some anxiety in South Wales where employment had been going from bad to worse. On 24th August, 1925, there were, out of 11,500,000 persons insured, 1,440,628 out of work or 12½ per cent : but out of a million and a quarter insured miners there were 279,781 unemployed or 22 per cent; in South Wales mining it was 25 per cent. In a few other industries it was higher; in steel smelting nearly 26 per cent; in shipbuilding and ship repairing 33.5 per cent.

Thousands removed from the register of unemployed as no longer entitled to benefit were forced on to the poor law relief. There the number of persons in receipt of relief increased by nearly a quarter of a million, from 1,046,750 to 1,270,179, in October 1925 compared with October 1924.

Poor relief as a duty in all parishes, set up by the great Poor Law of Queen Elizabeth in 1601 and largely transferred to elected Boards of Guardians set up by Act of 1834, had always operated unevenly : after the War of Empires (1914-18) the "Poplar" agitation headed by George Lansbury brought a measure of equalisation of the Poor Law Rates in London. Outside the Metropolitan area there was no such equalisation—whence came an insistent demand for the cost of administration of the Poor Law and of allocating relief to fall upon the national Exchequer rather than upon the localities. A table of the ten labour Exchanges with the highest percentage of unemployment on 26th October, 1925, begins with Bargoed in South Wales with 64.7 per cent.[1] All were from the North-East or South Wales coalfields. By contrast the ten "lowest" exchanges, each with less than 2 per cent unemployed were all of them in the Home Counties or East Midlands. In any casual survey of the British condition, London and South East England often took on the similitude of a swollen spider, sucking its sustenance from the provincial towns and countryside.

As early as the first onset of unemployment after the War there had sprung up under the leadership of Wal Hannington, an unemployed engineer, what became known as the National Unemployed Workers' Committee Movement. This in its opening period was favourably regarded in Trade Union circles. But in the South Wales Miners' Federation from December 1920 there had been a different view as to how the unemployed should be organised.

The Annual Conference heard a deputation from the South Wales area of the National Unemployed Workers' Committee Movement Messrs. Reed (Blaina), Jones (Cambrian) and Thomas (Standard) addressed the Conference and appealed for the co-operation of the Federation in organising the unemployed into a separate organisation, and for financial assistance to enable them to carry on their work.

"After the deputation had retired, the Conference discussed the application, and the officials stated that they had used the power and finances of the Federation to the utmost extent on behalf of their unemployed members: and they felt that the interest of the unemployed miners could be served much better by the South Wales Miners' Federation than by a separate organisation of their own."

The Conference endorsed this policy by a large majority; and "in

[1]**A TABLE OF CONTRASTS**

Employment Exchanges	Percentage Unemployed
Bargoed	64.7
Jarrow	56.0
Abertillery	54.6
Tonypandy	53.6
Merthyr Tydfil	52.2
Mountain Ash	51.2
Willington Quay	44.9
Bishop Auckland	44.0
Crumlin	42.0
Dowlais	41.6

On the other hand the ten exchanges with the lowest percentage were:

Employment Exchanges	Percentage Unemployed
Mansfield	1.9
Watford	1.9
Oxford	1.9
Peterborough	1.8
Braintree	1.7
Chelmsford	1.7
Redhill and Reigate	1.7
Romford	1.7
Newark	1.3
High Wycombe	1.0

view of the needs of our own members" it was decided that no financial grant could be made.[1]

At the Annual MFGB Conference at Scarborough in mid-July Noah Tromans moved the following resolution submitted by the SWMF Executive Council and it was unanimously resolved :

"That this Conference views with grave concern the frequent disasters involving serious loss of life arising from inundations of water from disused colliery workings, and instructs the Executive Committee to examine the whole question with a view to seeking such amendments of the Coal Mines Act as will mitigate the dangers to which the workmen are at present exposed."

5 STRIKE-BREAKING ORGANISATIONS

When the decision was taken by the TUC Committee to put an embargo on all movements of coal in answer to the coalowners' threat of a lock-out, the effect on the government was immediate. The Prime Minister told his Cabinet (on Thursday, 30th July) of the conversations that he, together with the Minister of Labour and the First Lord of the Admiralty had been carrying on for two days with the parties concerned. The Cabinet had a long and anxious discussion, at the end of which they concluded that it would be worse to have a stoppage of production and transport of coal than to come to the assistance of the mining industry with a nine months' subsidy.

So the Prime Minister, who had declared that there would be no subsidy, had then said that a subsidy would be available. That evening Baldwin had found himself bitterly upbraided by the coalowners' Chairman, Evan Williams, who said in effect: so you have decided to pay Danegelt in face of all the warnings of a thousand years of British history. Nor were the miners so very pleased. But the trade union movement as a whole regarded it as a resounding victory over the Government, and the sound of this victory was still heard a month later at the Trades Union Congress. Throughout the labour movement it was heralded as Red Friday.

"Red Friday" brought consternation to the ruling circles. They had not been ready for it. At the cost of a heavy subsidy, yielding to the owners their claims far beyond what the Macmillan Court of Inquiry of mid-July had considered reasonable or just, the Cabinet had brought a nine-months' truce.

[1]This decision led to a sharp discussion between Vice-President S. O. Davies and Wal Hannington, the organiser of the unemployed in the columns of the *Sunday Worker* (13/20 ix 1925). The Vice-President had defended the carrying through in the Dowlais Valley of his union's policy (as decided and blessed by Bob Smillie in winter 1920) to shoulder responsibility for their own unemployed members. The inability of other unions to carry out a similar policy made possible the growth of the National Unemployed Workers' Committee which Hannington defended in principle.

The General Council in its Report for the forthcoming September Trades Union Congress stated: "The settlement was regarded by the capitalist press as a humiliating defeat of the government by the organised workers". The newspapers had greeted the Government announcement with concentrated fury.

On 5th August the Government, who shared these feelings of rage and humiliation, began their plans for the future "in the event of a strike". Then, one week after the Labour Party Conference ban on the Communists, the Cabinet considered plans for espionage upon the Communists and for the recording of their speeches. These bore fruit and by mid-October the Cabinet learned that spies had gathered evidence which might justify arrest and prosecution of leading Communists "on a charge of sedition". Mindful of what had happened to Sir Patrick Hastings, the previous Attorney General, (whose hasty action in the Campbell case had not had the wholehearted concurrence of the Government) this Attorney General wanted to consult the Government as to whether they thought there was anything which might render a prosecution undesirable; there was no such objection in the view of the Cabinet.

Accordingly twelve leading Communists were arrested and put on trial. The Cabinet were surprised that many outstanding Liberal and Labour leaders (including Bernard Shaw) came forward to give bail, demonstrating an objection to the trial; while they were disagreeably surprised to find an adverse reaction inside the Conservative Party. At a meeting in his constituency, Home Secretary Joynson-Hicks, unaware that the Press was present, sought to reassure his supporters by stating that "we shall give them six months": thereby tearing to pieces the constitutional assumption of a complete separation between the Government and the Judiciary.

Government preparations for the end of "an armistice of nine months" included arrangements of all kinds, some to come into force with the proclamation of an emergency under the Emergency Powers Act of 1920; some with the armed forces; some with local authorities; and some with strike-breaking organisations: and of these last some dated from 1919 when strikes and army mutinies had alarmed the Government. After the railway strike it was announced, on 7th October, 1919, that the Home Secretary had also been building up "a purely civilian organisation" made up of "well-disposed citizens". Local authorities were asked to form "Citizen Guards" to co-operate in maintaining order. This, however, was only the preliminary to other organisations promoted through ex-officers, retired diplomats and former civil servants.

The announcement was made on 25th September, 1925, of the Organisation for the Maintenance of Supplies (President Lord Hardinge of Penshurst, ex-Viceroy of India) with a Central Council made up largely of Admirals of the Fleet and Major-Generals, with a statement beginning, "a movement is being organised to take advantage of a trade dispute, in order to promote a general strike": and to combat this the OMS had been formed. When most newspapers had given it a cool reception it was hastily divulged, after a week, that the OMS had been stimulated by the Home Secretary.

The National Citizens Union (previously the Middle Classes Union) intimated that it had provided "several thousand volunteers during the railway strike in October 1919"; had been thanked by the Government at the time of the 1921 coal lockout and was now going to work in connection with the OMS. The British Empire Union, founded in 1915 for the purpose of an anti-aliens campaign, also publicly announced an intention to co-operate. In emulation of Italian Fascists and their march on Rome in Autumn 1922; in August 1923 the British Fascisti Ltd. was formed for "militant defence of His Majesty The King and Empire." Its circular stated that "should revolution or a general strike be threatened the men's units will most certainly co-operate whole-heartedly, etc., etc., in strike-breaking." The chiefs of this organisation were Brigadier-Generals, Rear-Admirals, and such like. Chief Constables in certain places, notably in Liverpool and Wolverhampton, showed a disposition to enrol these or other local fascists in the Special Constabulary. In that autumn of 1925 the Monmouthshire County Council was asked permission by the Chief Constable "to order 100 uniforms for Special Constables, *for use next year.*"

There were a number of lesser organisations such as the National Guard one of whose founders, a Colonel Fitzjohn, stated that "in the event of a mining dispute the National Guard would be prepared to instal men for pumping operations to prevent the destruction of property."

Earlier that year, however, in January 1925 the railway companies invited employees to join the Transportation Branch of the Army Supplementary Reserve. The War Office provided that railway general managers should nominate the commanding officers and select the men who would be directed to go to the recruiting offices. These recruits would be liable to serve in any part of the world on mobilisation and to be called up by proclamation, and would also be legally liable to be called out in aid of the civil power. The formation of this Supplementary Reserve had been authorised in August 1924 by a Royal Warrant prepared by Mr. Stephen Walsh, the miner who was Secretary for War in the Labour Government.

Thus a series of organisations with Government backing were all directed towards the suppression of any organised resistance by Labour against "wage cuts all round", divulged by Baldwin in the summer to be the official policy. *The Times*, in a leading article on 1st October, 1919, had stated the position quite frankly about "Labour Volunteers" who, it argued, were necessary to form a civil army "for the specific object of defeating attempts by organised labour to hold the State to ransom." But it also argued that "it would certainly be preferable" for such an army to be "organised by private associations."

So now in Autumn 1925 these various "private associations" had been set up to play a part in the preparation of the breaking of a strike by the Government.

The Special Constabulary.

Under the Special Constables Act of 1831 power to appoint Special Constables had been vested in the authorities, particularly Magistrates, if they were satisfied by the oaths of any "credible witness" that any "tumult, riot or felony" had taken place or might reasonably be apprehended. Any householder could be so nominated in writing by two or more Magistrates.[1]

These events were watched with great anxiety in South Wales. Attention was called to the fact that a group of fascists and their activities were being winked at by the authorities. While the strike-breaking preparations of the Government caused apprehension as to the future, particular incidents aroused public attention and discussion. In South Wales, as well as in London, there was very strong feeling manifested about the *Daily Herald's* "Van Case". On 17th October the newspaper van carrying 8,000 copies of the *Daily Herald* was, in the elegant phrase of a later period, hi-jacked, and the driver on his way from Fleet Street to Euston to catch the trains was kidnapped. The persons responsible, avowing themselves to be members of the British Fascisti Ltd., were charged with larceny for stealing 8,000 copies as well as a van. They came up for trial at the Mansion House were remanded and, on the case being further considered, the charge of theft was dropped. The defendants were told by the Magistrate that his advice to them was that they should join the Special Constables.

This incident followed a case in Merseyside, stated to be the headquarters of the British Fascisti Ltd., where Harry Pollitt, Secretary of the Minority Movement, on his way to a meeting was kidnapped by fascists. At the trial, the jury, almost entirely middle-class, refused to convict. This, and the *Daily Herald* incident, spread a feeling that it was no longer only the Government and the authorities as well as the coal owners but that the upper and middle classes generally were bent on provoking a class war with organised labour.

[1]It will be remembered that in the 1860's Karl Marx was somewhat perturbed at the idea that he might be put in the position of being enrolled as a Special Constable. In the 1921 mining lockout a great number were so nominated. The Chief Inspector of Police in his report published in 1922 opined that the chief use of the Special Constabulary was during a strike. In West Sussex the Special Constables enabled the Police Authority to lend nearly half the regular force. In September 1922 the police in England and Wales, not including London, amounted to 60,709 and their first reserves to 7,385, but Special Constables amounted to 110,984. Similarly, in Scotland in December 1921 the police total was 6,500, while the number of Special Constables was 13,669.

6 "VENGEANCE?"

On Tuesday, 1st December, 1925, 167 members of the South Wales Miners' Federation stood in the dock at the County Town of Carmarthen, charged with "Riotous Assembly."

At the opening of the Assize Court on that 1st day of December "a fanfare of trumpets gives the signal of the return of the judge from St. Peter's Church." When the court opened the judge then gave his charge to the Grand Jury. He referred to the heavy calendar of alleged offences. Eight cases were of the ordinary type of felony. The other 167 were miners. The *Sunday Worker* in its detailed report told how the Grand Jury had as its foreman "Colonel F. Dudley Williams-Drummond, C.B.E., while on it there sat two colonels, three majors, a captain, a knight, a parson and an agent for a local owner." The first batch were tried on Wednesday, 2nd December, thus:

> "On 29th July, 1925, in the County of Carmarthen, unlawfully and riotously assembling to disturb the peace and then did make a great riot and disturbance, to the terror of His Majesty's subjects."

Out of this first batch of 19 the prosecution offered no case against eight, while seven of the remaining 11 were found not guilty. The main police witness, under cross examination, admitted that when 150 people assembled outside the manager's house that morning, "no violence was used by a single member of the huge crowd."

The trial went on day after day to deal with groups out of the 167. In most cases the prosecution broke down, or the verdict was not guilty, though in nearly all cases the judge had summed up against the defendants. As they were taken from Carmarthen Assizes to the jail at Swansea they were put in chains and handcuffs—a sight causing much hostile comment against the authorities. In the case of one prisoner after another, policemen called to the witness box had to state that they were "good and respectable persons." The trial went on throughout December until just before Christmas.

Out of the 167 brought to the Assizes, 117 either had the charges against them withdrawn, were found not guilty, or were bound over to keep the peace. On the remaining 50 the sentences varied from 12 months imprisonment down to a couple of weeks. In the words of the South Wales correspondent of the *Sunday Worker*:

> "A number of leaders (including Alderman David Daniel Davies, J.P.) were sentenced at Cardiff before Judge Greer proceeded to Carmarthen on 1st December. In the case of the colliery 'riot', one of the most serious charges brought against 25 miners was that they formed part of a nocturnal procession of 500 people, who sang 'Aberystwyth', the thrilling favourite hymn of all Welsh men and women. The chief witness for the prosecution, Police Constable Hugh Thomas, told the Court that the singing of the hymn had terrified

him. At the request of Sir Patrick Hastings (Counsel for the Defendants) the first verse was read to the judge:

> 'What have I in world so fair
> But oppression grim and care ?
> Cruel wrong and tyranny
> Night and day do follow me.'

"The prosecutor, Lord Halsbury, asked the constable whether by the singing of this hymn the miners meant that their oppressors were the people they were fighting. The constable said 'Yes'."

After the Assizes an agitation developed for the release of the prisoners and against the severity of the sentences. Among the South Wales miners it was held that an acute stage of class struggle was maturing in Britain and not only in the coal mining industry. In the current usage of popular speakers, it was commonly spoken of as class war: and in this class war, hostilities, they believed, had already broken out. An armistice may have been concluded on the last day of July: but in the view of many Welsh miners the truce had been repeatedly broken by the behaviour of the authorities.

Amongst these "breaches of the truce" they regarded the arrest in October and State trial in November 1925 of twelve leading Communists on the time-honoured charge of "conspiracy to utter a seditious libel" including "the publishing of writings of Mr. Lenin." Against this the MFGB Executive[1] had immediately uttered a unanimous protest. Still closer to their own experience, they regarded the quite unusual arraignment of 193 anthracite miners at Cardiff and Carmarthen also as a "breach of the truce" a demonstration of force intended to intimidate and, finally, as a vengeful act of the mineowners with their allies in the local and the itinerant magistracy. Accordingly, a SWMF Special Conference held at Cardiff on Saturday, 2nd January, 1926 (Chairman, Vice-President S. O. Davies) was devoted to the question of imprisoned anthracite miners and Communists. W. H. Mainwaring, chief agent of the Rhondda, submitted the recommendation of the Executive Council:

"To protest against the unduly severe sentences passed upon the members of the Federation implicated in the prosecutions in the anthracite area. Further, that we join the Trades Union Congress General Council and the Labour Party in pressing upon the Home Secretary the consideration of these sentences, with a view to the immediate release of these workmen, believing that the period of imprisonment they have borne more than vindicates any breach of the law they were pronounced guilty of."

Mainwaring then urged the delegates to learn the lessons of "the

[1] "This Committee unanimously protests against the altogether unwarrantable and severe sentences inflicted upon the officials of the Communist Party, considering that the whole proceedings were influenced at every stage by political bias. We unite with the other Trade Unions in demanding their immediate release and the prevention of this attempt to interfere with the freedom of the Press, free speech, and personal liberty of opinion" (27 xi 1925).

class administration as indicated in the prosecution and imprisonment of the Communist leaders." The Executive Council's further resolution unanimously endorsed both the resolution passed by the MFGB Committee and "the great number of resolutions received from the Lodges, protesting against the sentences passed upon the Communist leaders." For several months afterwards protests were carried through in various centres.

Herbert Smith and A. J. Cook, together with George Lansbury and Alex. Gossip, strove for the release of the prisoners as did the organisation set up in 1925 on an international scale called the International Class War Prisoners' Aid. This held conferences from time to time and, apart from raising funds to support the victims of Italian fascism or those who suffered casualty in the class war in any part of the world, they served also as a further focus of support for those who in Great Britain had been sent to prison. Unforgotten, from the point of view of the South Wales miners, was the casting of a medal which was distributed to the anthracite miners who had undergone trial and imprisonment at the Assizes. By this badge the International Class War Prisoners' Aid were reverting to a practice of the earlier 19th century when political trials were a frequent feature of the struggle for liberty of the Press and free speech.

In South Wales miners continued to support and to be supported by the International Class War Prisoners' Aid (with Bob Lovell as British Secretary) right up to its World Congress which was presided over by Engel's friend Clara Zetkin in 1932, a few weeks before she uttered the last speech against Fascism delivered in the German Reichstag—before it was burned down by the Nazis.

7 AT THE THRESHOLD OF THE YEAR 1926

In the mining community amid an atmosphere of fears and hopes there was a heightened awareness that measurable objective factors had to be balanced against subjective factors actual or potential. It was a situation that would become more and more tense.

What were the factors that had to be taken into account? The market had shrunk. Exports, three-fifths of South Wales' total output, had shrunk from over 30 million tons in 1923 down to 21 million tons in 1925. Prices too had come down with a rush from the "zenith" price of 1920 ("soaking the foreign customer") till they were now little more than a quarter of what they had been.[1]

[1]Average declared value F.O.B. per ton of coal exported.

Year	From United Kingdom	From Cardiff
1920	79/11d	83/4d
1921	34/8d	36/6d
1922	22/7d	23/9d
1923	25/2d	26/3d
1924	23/5d	24/9d
1925	19/10d	22/6d

The proceeds of the South Wales mining industry, as defined in the Wage Agreement of 1921, had fallen also from £50 million in 1923 to £45 million in 1924, to £37 million in 1925 converting the positive trading balance of the first two years into a loss of £3.4 million in 1925, a loss that was worsening in each successive month of ascertainment until by March, 1926, it was at rate of loss approaching £7 million per annum.

The coal crisis had reached a greater depth in these months of subsidy : hence the dread of what monstrous birth might emerge from the womb of time when the nine-month subsidy came to an end. Already before summer 1925 the owners had made clear their demand for lower wages and longer hours as the only logical outcome of the market conditions.

But this notion of the impersonal, unpredictable, immeasurable play of market forces as demanding emphatically and inexorably a change only in workers' conditions and not a change in the structure, organisation and functioning of the capitalist-owned industry had ceased to be accepted in South Wales. The lock-out of 1921 might do away with the Sankey war wage but all the efforts of the Samuel Commission could not destroy the enlightenment brought by the Sankey Report.

Besides this the mineworkers knew well that there was no such thing as the "free play of mysterious, unpredictable market forces". In the five years of State intervention that had disappeared together with the "immutable laws" of political economy and the "imprescriptible rights" of private enterprise. State intervention had brought out also the Dawes Plan which enabled German Reparations Coal to ruin their Italian market in 1925. It was State intervention, by Churchill's budgetary leap onto the Gold Standard, which had wrecked the whole export trade.

If the ship of State could be set on a course which had seemed to wreck trade prospects, then it could equally well be set on a different course—even without a complete upheaval in the historically developed social system. It was a matter of policy, as capitalist economist J. M. Keynes had explained, for the benefit of Treasury officials swayed by the gold-mongers of the City of London, when Chancellor Winston Churchill yielded to the policy enunciated by the Governor of the Bank of England, Montagu Norman, whom Lloyd George had dubbed "the High Priest of the Golden Calf". If the State could intervene detrimentally to the interests of industry and trade then it could also intervene in a different manner. But could it be made to do so ?

This question for the South Wales miners brought in the calculus of class forces, of employers' associations and trade unions, of political parties and, finally, of such imponderables as mass agitation and, should need arise, of mass action if and when a growingly critical situation reached the flashpoint.

In South Wales they were very clear about their opponents. First came their age-long antagonists, the royalty owners and the coal-owners. They had endeavoured through the winter of 1924-25 to convince the coalowners with arguments that were finally set forth in "The Economic Position of the Coal Industry" of May, 1925. But they had spoken, as it seemed, to deaf ears. The fact was that whatever might be the general interests of the country's economy, or of the British coal industry, the Monmouthshire and South Wales Coal Owners' Association had not been formed to express these interests. The Associated Owners had been banded together "for mutual protection". Protection against what? Not against domestic or foreign competitors, nor against Government policy, but simply for the purpose "of resisting the men seeking an advance in wages". Consequently, within its narrowly defined objects, the South Wales Coal Owners' Association could be the most powerful of any coalfield in the country. It was limited, local, and extremely effective. So this employers' association was unlike the South Wales Miners' Federation which for a quarter of a century had sought to have its interests furthered and safe-guarded by mining Members of Parliament chosen by themselves.

In the second place, behind the coal owners, covertly or openly (and very openly in the crisis of 1925 and thereafter) stood the Baldwin administration in which they had the highest degree of mistrust as well as a belief that it held its position through the Zinoviev Letter Forgery and was elected to Parliament under false pretences.

Thirdly, the miners' mistrust in the Government naturally extended to its emanation the four Royal Commissioners and the whole apparatus of the Royal Commission on the Coal Industry intended to be "a commission to end all commissions" and in particular to give the quietus to "the Sankey Circus", that is, to the Coal Industry Commission of 1919.[1]

Fourthly, during the last few months of 1925 they were aware of the Organisation for the Maintenance of Supply and the various other

[1] In the month of January, 1926, the Royal Commission on the Coal Industry appointed on 5th September, was busily at work. As to the purpose of this Commission, there was a clear apprehension amongst the miners. According to the views expressed by the Treasurer of the South Wales Miners' Federation, the Government in making its selection of four persons with Sir Herbert Samuel as Chairman was "no doubt guided by the desire to secure a report that would justify an attack on the working men's wages, and an extension of the hours of labour."

The Coal Crisis: Facts from the Samuel Commission 1925-1926, with a foreword by Herbert Smith, published by the Labour Research Department, made the statement: "The Government, of course, represented this Commission as an impartial body. It is true it is not directly representative of the Mining Association but it is difficult to imagine any small body of persons more completely representative of capitalist interests and more completely trained in approaching matters from the capitalist standpoint." The Royal Commission thus composed took evidence in public between 15th October, 1925, and 14th January, 1926. The report itself was completed at the end of the first week in March and published within a day or two. It contained a survey and some 300 pages buttressed with three volumes of evidence and statistical material and into it were dovetailed a number of recommendations.

strike-breaking bodies that were being drilled, organised and made ready to be used against the miners and against trade unions generally.

These seemed to make up the sum of their opponents, a formidable enough array.

To some extent it was felt that the international bankers in whose interests the Dawes Plan (as well as in the interests of the governments behind them) had been drawn up, the international oil trusts and to some extent other international organisations were to be counted as their opponents. But these latter were remote adversaries, were the lion in the desert compared to the more formidable predators directly threatening to defeat their unions and to devour their standard of living.

On the assumption that the policies put forward originally in South Wales from 1922 to 1924 and then spread through all the coalfields by Arthur Cook, as chief officer of the Miners' Federation, would be maintained, the miners made their reckoning in their lodges, districts and frequent national conferences. Who would be on their side ? Who, amid falling exports and unemployment mounting to an average level of nearly 20 per cent of insured persons, would be ready to sustain the miners' resistance and give full backing to Cook's slogan : "Not a Minute on the Day, Not a Penny off the Pay."

First and foremost were the other trade unionists with interests related to their own. To enlist potential allies had been the object set out in June 1924 by the Amalgamated Engineering Union : and in July by the mineworkers : and after a meeting on 4th June, 1925, of the unions concerned, the Constitution of Industrial Alliance had been drawn up in July and adopted in November 1925. But the ballots for final ratification after the November Conference were tardy in coming through, so much so that in the spring of 1926 the miners felt that they must now chiefly repose confidence in the larger organisation, namely, the Trades Union Congress, which had been so effective in the crisis of "Red Friday."

Before the publication of the Samuel Report in mid-March the TUC Industrial Committee in Joint Meeting with the MFGB representatives had, on 19th February, uttered a declaration, reiterated on 26th February that :

"The attitude of the Trade Union Movement was made perfectly clear last July, namely, that it would stand firmly and unitedly against any attempt further to degrade the standard of life in the coalfields. There was to be no reduction in wages, no increase in working hours, and no interference with the principle of National Agreement. This is the position of the Trade Union Movement today."

This, "sent to all the affiliated Trade Unions" was bound to hearten the miners in their hopes for the coming weeks of crisis and tension, provided always that their allies would stand firm. Nevertheless the absence of preparedness in such bleak and startling contrast to the Government's completest degree of preparedness, was bound to trouble them.

Beyond these were the allies abroad, actual and potential, and in the first place the International Miners' Federation. Frank Hodges, installed as Miners' International Secretary, was expected as coming from Britain and from South Wales in particular, to take an attitude at any rate in consonance with the bodies who had been responsible for his election. The contrary however proved to be the case when Hodges had given evidence before the Samuel Commission. Furthermore, he had indicated that the miners of Britain should be prepared to work longer hours, a standpoint considered very reprehensible by many South Wales Miners. At a SWMF Special Conference in the Co-operative Hall in Cardiff record tells:

"Strong resentment against the attitude of Mr. Frank Hodges, the Secretary of the Miners' International, was expressed by some of the delegates; and a resolution was moved calling for his resignation. But on the suggestion of the President it was agreed to defer consideration of this question until a later conference after the crisis was over, when an opportunity would be given for dealing with the matter" (15 iv 1926).

Thus the trust which they had been led to repose in the Miners' International, after the 27th International Congress held in Prague in summer 1924, was weakened by the fact that the man they had installed as its secretary was publicly operating against the British miners' policy.

There remained other international connections. They were linked, somewhat tenuously through the TUC, with the International Federation of Trade Unions: and more directly in the TUC's Anglo-Russian Committee, appointed a year earlier, on which the miners were represented. On the friendship and loyalty to international causes of the Russian workers they were to learn to place great reliance. But at moment most of this was in the future.

There were, however, others whose aid they were ready and willing to accept. Not only the Miners' Minority Movement, carrying forward the principles of the Unofficial Reform Committee Movement, but the Minority Movement as a whole (in which the Miners' Movement were now one section), were ready to give their aid. Since it owed its origin partly to the initiative of the Communist Party leaders Willie Gallacher and Harry Pollitt: and since its Chairman was the veteran Tom Mann who had given them signal help at Tonypandy in 1910, the miners in South Wales felt they could look to it also for support.

In this connection they voiced their disapproval of the vendetta carried on against the Communists by Ramsay MacDonald, Philip Snowdon and Frank Hodges. They felt that the Liverpool Conference of October, 1925, excluding Communists had been a great mistake. This critical standpoint was regularly uttered in their monthly organ right into 1926 by the treasurer, Oliver Harris, who was regarded in many of the lodges as very far from being a revolutionary:

"The decision of the South Wales District of the Independent Labour Party to support the acceptance of the Communists into the Labour Party is an indication that the view is growing that the decision of the Liverpool Labour Party Conference was a serious blunder, which should be rectified as soon as possible. A large number of local Labour Parties, Trades Councils, etc., have refused to carry out that decision, and have declined to ban members of the Communist Party, who usually are among the most active supporters of the cause of Labour. This is quite consistent with the policy of the South Wales Miners' Federation, which has in past Conferences emphatically declared in favour of active co-operation with our Communist comrades.

"The Labour Party should be broad enough to accept all schools of thought that support the policy of emancipating the workers from the grip of Capitalism. It is already tolerant enough to accept many politicians of reactionary tendencies, whose adherence to the Labour cause is merely one of expediency. If we can accept men of that type we should have no difficulty in also accepting men like Tom Mann, Pollitt, Page Arnot and others, who have rendered yeoman service for many years to the cause of the workers (February, 1926)."

The South Wales Miners' Federation had not been a member of the Labour Party until well on in the 20th century, while the valley unions had been also electoral organisations with local and county councillors and M.P.s in the House of Commons for over a quarter of a century. With this past history and with the way in which the colliers looked to the South Wales Miners' Federation to do everything for them that a political party could possibly do, there was not the same submissiveness to the Labour Party Committee in Westminster as happened with some of the newer constituents of the Labour Party.

But Vernon Hartshorn[1], the former SWMF president who had been favoured with a seat in the 1925 Cabinet by Ramsay MacDonald, strenuously sought in his own part of South Wales to break the miners' consistent opposition to the policy of expulsion.

It was not by any means easy as is told by the former compensation officer of the SWMF in Cardiff, Mel Thomas (then of the ILP), who writes:

"There was an incident at Bridgend when Vernon Hartshorn called for the police to evict Communist members from the Annual General Meeting of the Ogmore Divisional Labour Party, which would have meant throwing out the majority of delegates."

[1]Vernon Hartshorn, like John Evans, M.P., and two or three others were exceptions to the rule that miners' leaders in the South Wales coalfield had been local preachers in their youth or otherwise prominent in non-conformist churches and chapels.

CHAPTER TEN

SEVEN MONTHS' LOCKOUT

1 CRISIS LOOMS NEARER

In the valleys of South Wales the first five months of 1926 rolled on amid hopes and fears. Their hopes were based on the achievements of their Union in the twelve months up to 31st July, 1925 (Red Friday), and on the trust reposed in their National Secretary and their representatives on the MFGB Executive Committee. Their fears and anxieties arose from the developments of the autumn and winter of 1925, culminating half way through the nine months' subsidy period in the truculent speech of the Chancellor of the Exchequer, Winston Churchill, on 10th December, 1925.

In mid-April at an SWMF Special Conference in the Co-operative Hall, Cardiff, 243 delegates (representing 150,921 members) unanimously accepted the recommendations of the miners' national conference.[1] It was after the reports given by Enoch Morrell and S. O. Davies and after some discussion that Councillor W. Hammond, Rhymney Valley, had moved and Councillor Aneurin Bevan, Tredegar, had seconded the acceptance. In a very sober mood it was then resolved to urge the MFGB Executive Committee to make a direct appeal to the Prime Minister on behalf of their captives:

[1]"That this Conference, having considered the Report of the Royal Commission and the proposals of the colliery owners thereon, recommends the districts as follows: (a) That no assent be given for any proposal for increasing the length of the working day. (b) That the principles of a National Wage Agreement with a National Minimum Percentage be firmly adhered to. (c) That inasmuch as wages are already too low we cannot assent to any proposals for reducing wages. These recommendations to be remitted to the districts for their immediate consideration and decision, after which a further Conference be called as speedily as possible for the purpose of arriving at a final decision" (9 iv 1926).

Ten days earlier a Conference of Minority Movement Groups from the various coalfields met and passed the following resolution:

"This Conference of militant miners from every coalfield in Britain, resolves to work vigorously and perseveringly for the full and complete rejection of the Royal Coal Commission Report. We recognise the Report to be a subtle manoeuvre on the part of the British Capitalism to be relieved of the subsidy to the mining industry, through the lowering of wages and working conditions of the miners, which it hopes to achieve in consequence of the pseudo-socialistic bait embodied in the Report which is intended to divide the miners into factions for and against the Report. We, therefore, call upon the miners to concentrate upon securing 100 per cent organisation and to prepare to fight for the guaranteed Weekly Minimum Wage, commensurate with the increased cost of living, whilst recognising that the necessary re-organisation, so far as to permit this, is only possible by the nationalisation of the mining industry without compensation, and with workers' control" (28 iii 1926).

"To exercise his good office and authority to obtain the immediate release from prison of the four workmen in Swansea Gaol, the Conference believing that in the interest of peace and goodwill during the serious crisis now prevailing in the coal industry such an act of clemency would very materially assist to create the desired effect upon the workers in the Anthracite area in particular and the miners of the country in general" (15 iv 1926).

The Executive Council, recently reinforced by three new members (A. L. Horner from Rhondda No. 1, James Griffiths from the Anthracite, Bryn Roberts from Rhymney Valley), had been dealing so far largely with local matters and awaiting the results of national negotiations.

On 16th March, an invitation to the Miners' Minority Movement National Conference[1] of 21st March was refused.

That Spring the District Meetings discussing the future felt they could only await events. In one case, however, there was a difference, as minutes show:

"The Ordinary Monthly Meeting of the Rhondda No. 1 District was held at the Miners' Offices, Porth, on Monday, 29th March, 1926. Guardian W. J. Parry, J.P., presided supported by Mr. James J. Lewis, Vice-Chairman; Mr. W. H. Mainwaring, Agent; Alderman David Lewis, J.P., Secretary; Mr. Arthur L. Horner, E.C. Member; Messrs. Watts Morgan and Will John, Members of Parliament, were also present.

"The coming Crisis was further considered in relation to proposed closer relations between the Trade Unions and the Co-operative Movements. For some time the question has been under discussion, and the possibilities of some working agreement being arrived at. The difficulties surrounding the question became immediately apparent since the situation had not been provided for in any way. It is useless expecting any body coming to our assistance without definite safeguards, and it is the provision of adequate guarantees that form the main difficulty. The Delegates felt, whatever may be done for the immediate Crisis, it is highly necessary that some provision be made for the future. A settled plan on some agreed lines should be forthcoming. To this

[1]The *Colliery Workers' Magazine* of May 1925 (vol. III No. 5), stated:

"With the second pamphlet there will not be the same general agreement. To most of us it would appear that the work which the Minority Movement has set out to accomplish, could very well be done from within the Trades Unions themselves. The British Trades Unions are the most democratic in the world, and there is nothing to prevent any member from pressing his views on his organisation and securing their adoption if and when he can convert his fellow-members to his point of view. A sectional organisation has dangers which are hardly worth incurring for the sake of the problematical advantages of such a policy."

Actually, the National Minority Movement held a "Conference of Action" at Latchmere Baths in Battersea under the chairmanship of Tom Mann with 883 delegates attending from 547 organisations including 52 trades councils (among them Manchester, Sheffield, Leeds and Coventry) 61 Minority groups and shop stewards' committees and 33 organisations of the unemployed. After Tom Mann's keynote speech, a resolution on the capitalist offensive was moved by Arthur Horner—seconded by Peter Kerrigan (National Minority Movement) and a call for the development of all-embracing Councils of Action for the struggles ahead.

end it was decided to forward the following suggestions for discussion in South Wales, thence to the MFGB and the Trades Union Congress:

(a) That the provision of the minimum needs of the Workers in respect of food would be of immense assistance during industrial conflicts, and that it is necessary to make some preparation to ensure such for the future.

(b) That a proportion of Trade Union Contributions should be laid aside for this special purpose.

(c) A closer relation between Trade Unions and Co-operative Movements. The Co-operative Movement to function as Purchasers and Distributors of Supplies.

(d) Mutual arrangements between Trade Unions for assistance by way of direct money assistance and credits.

The course of events after the MFGB mid-April Conference with the huddled sequence of nearly continuous or overlapping conferences was, as before April, relayed to the miners by regular representatives' reports to the Executive Council (and thence to valleys and lodges) to the District Meetings, to the Coalfield Conferences with up to 200 delegates reporting back to lodges. It was an exercise, regularly carried out, in democratic representation and reporting to the people.

To the MFGB Special Conference of 197 delegates, with 784,786 in unions, in Kingsway Hall, London, on Wednesday, 28th April, 1926, 52 delegates came from South Wales (with 129,150 in unions). The mounting tension was shown on the four successive days of the Conference, partly by its very short and broken sessions. On the second day (Thursday, 29th April) they met again and adjourned until 12.30 p.m., when after a statement read by Cook they adjourned till six o'clock and then to the following morning. On Friday, 30th April, Herbert Smith, in the Chair, told how "we got to the Prime Minister at twelve o'clock midnight and were with him until one o'clock, and had to go back to the Committee, and finished about twenty minutes past one." After this it was agreed to adjourn till half-past twelve and to reassemble at three o'clock. Then the delegates were told (after some account of what had happened in the meantime) to adjourn again until five o'clock. The Conference reassembled at eight but did not commence proceedings until 11.30 p.m. when Cook came to suggest adjournment until nine o'clock in the morning. He said: "The TUC has been backward and forward almost too many times to remember. We have been with them on some of the occasions."

Next morning, Saturday 1st May, Cook read out the proposals of the TUC General Council "for co-ordinated action of trade unions", and the miners' delegates adjourned till two o'clock.

2 BEHIND THE SCENES

Meantime, in the last week of April 1926, there had been meetings of many parties, meetings of all kinds day after day—some publicly reported and some behind the scenes.

On Thursday, 22nd April, negotiations between owners and men having broken down on the question of District and National wages, the owners finally raised with the men the question of hours. Later that same day, the Prime Minister, seen by the Industrial Committee of the Trades Union Congress General Council and by them urged to invite parties to accept his mediation, issued invitations accordingly for the following day.

On Friday, 23rd April, at 11 a.m. a joint meeting of owners and miners was chaired by Baldwin, who then listened for twenty-five minutes to the owners' chairman, Evan Williams, and for twenty minutes to Herbert Smith, neither of them making any change in previous standpoints. At the end Baldwin suggested three from each side meet with him in the afternoon, the miners at 3 p.m. to 4.30, the owners an hour later. Thomas Jones, acting secretary to the Cabinet and confidential henchman of Baldwin, was present at many if not most of these April meetings, often enough with senior civil servants and also two or three Cabinet members, especially Steel-Maitland, Minister of Labour. In his private diary of that Friday, 23rd April, Thomas Jones, after recording that at 5.45 the owners' small committee arrived, made the following comment:

"It is impossible not to feel the contrast between the reception which Ministers give to a body of owners and a body of miners. Ministers are at ease at once with the former, they are friends jointly exploring a situation. There was hardly any indication of opposition or censure. It was rather a joint discussion of whether it were better to precipitate a strike or the unemployment which would result from continuing the present terms. The majority clearly wanted a strike."[1]

After the meeting Tom Jones, taking a hint, walked in the park with the perplexed Prime Minister, to whom he gave his sapient comments and advice. They walked together towards Pall Mall where, in Steel-Maitland's club (the Travellers) Baldwin was to have a quiet dinner with Evan Williams while Tom Jones went off to dine with Sir Alfred Cope (Chairman of Amalgamated Anthracite Colliery Ltd.), the henchman of Mond and his multi-millioned ICI, to learn what had happened at the Savoy Hotel where some monopoly capitalists disagreed with the spokesmen of the Mining Association of Great Britain. On this a memorandum was to be sent by Sir Alfred Mond to Baldwin.

Next morning the Prime Minister, the Minister of Labour and Sir Horace Wilson, its Permanent Secretary, the Permanent Under-Secretary for Mines and the Principal Assistant Secretary at the Mines Department

[1] *Thomas Jones, Whitehall Diary*, edited by Keith Middlemass, Oxford University Press, 1969.

gathered at Downing Street. The PM, wrote Jones in his diary, "took me aside to ask would I mind spending the week-end alone with him at Chequers." So that Saturday evening in Chequers the two of them were discussing "coal". Baldwin, whose ideas "were slowly clarifying", proceeded, so Jones guessed, to reflect ideas "which had circulated round the table at the Travellers' Club last night when he dined with Evan Williams, Lord Weir and Steel-Maitland". He was all for trying to get "the power of the MFGB Executive broken without resorting to a strike".

On Sunday, 25th April, the Prime Minister and his Fabian henchman set out for a walk through the woods of the Chiltern Hills, where Baldwin turned over "various combinations" of possible solutions until Tom Jones, whose hint at "bringing Tawney down today, or even Cook" had been negatived, suggested asking Arthur Pugh, President of the TUC and Chairman of its Negotiating Committee. "We walked on and on with remarks about the weather, the beeches and the bluebells, and after five or ten minutes he agreed that I should summon Pugh but should keep the visit secret."

Before lunch Jones telephoned Sir Horace Wilson who arrived with Pugh at 4.30. They stayed for two hours. The PM showed them over the house and gave them tea in what he called "the finest room in England". They were shown Queen Elizabeth's ring and the letter Nelson wrote about the frigates after the battle of the Nile. Jones got Pugh talking of the days he worked at Cwmavon for Wright and Butler a firm well-known to S.B., and this set them at their ease. At 5 p.m. they got down to business, the PM starting off with "What did Mr. Pugh think should be done ?"

Jones's Diary goes on:

"When the talk had been going for an hour, the PM rang for some whisky and soda and I beguiled Wilson to the lounge, leaving the PM alone with Pugh. After they had gone, the PM said the talk had been invaluable to him and he joined Mrs. Baldwin in her room while I drafted the outlines of two speeches, one to the TUC, and one to the Owners for tomorrow's meetings" (25 v 1926).

On Monday, 26th, the Prime Minister, back in Downing Street, continued his separate meetings with the leaders of all parties. The same process was repeated day after day up to 30th April, with Baldwin on Tuesday, 27th, taking the chair at 7 p.m. at a Conference of Owners and Miners, while the Cabinet and other "interested parties" were also busily conferring.

On Friday, 30th April, at long last the coal masters tabled their revised terms. These Baldwin passed on to the men. The miners rejected them. The TUC General Council intervened and urged that notices be postponed. A Royal Proclamation proclaimed a State of Emergency and the special machinery prepared in advance was set in motion. "Hostilities" had begun, several hours before the first ultimatum.

That last day of April in the Memorial Hall in Farringdon Street, off Ludgate Circus, a Special Conference of Executive Committees of Affiliated Unions began its second session at 11 a.m., adjourned till 11.45; adjourned again till 3 p.m.; then till 5 p.m.; again till 6.15 p.m.; then till 7.15 ; again till 9 p.m.; then till 11 p.m. and again till 11.25 p.m. During most of these times this Sanhedrim of over seven hundred representatives were kept waiting. They were told periodically by Mr. A. A. Purcell that "the position is exceedingly grave" (11.45 a.m.); secondly, that the Industrial Committee are "still in negotiation with the Prime Minister" and "are still continuing their efforts" (3 p.m.); thirdly, that the whole of the Special Negotiating Committee "are still in with the Prime Minister", and that they should stay in their seats in the hall : the situation was "severely grave" (5 p.m.); fourthly, that the miners had been called in to stand by, and conversations with the Prime Minister "have been resumed" : he had told the Special Negotiating Committee that "you were singing (they sang *Lead Kindly Light*); and there was no sign of downheartedness" (6.15 p.m.); fifthly, that the Conference between the Negotiating Committee, the Prime Minister, Lord Birkenhead and Sir Austin Chamberlain, "has now been resumed with the Miners' representatives" : that the position has not improved and is not "in what we would regard as a satisfactory state" (7.15 p.m.); sixthly, that "our representatives were about to leave but they have now been called in to see the Government" (9 p.m.); seventhly, that "the Special Industrial Committee is still with the Government" : but that "we have sent a message" to see if it be possible to spare two representatives "to come down to the meeting here at once" (11 p.m.).

Finally, shortly after 11.25 p.m., Arthur Pugh (accompanied by the members of the General Council and representatives of the Parliamentary Labour Party) took the chair and reported on the discussions they had had with the Prime Minister and others throughout that Friday : the negotiations had broken down completely.

The Press were invited to enter at this stage. They heard a full statement from the Rt. Hon. J. H. Thomas, MP, who may be said to have summed it all up when he told how the full Cabinet had been summoned to give their final decision. "Their final decision", said J. H. Thomas, "was a refusal to accede to your request. Please observe, not to effect a settlement, but a refusal to accede to your request for a suspension of the notices so that the negotiations could continue."

There were already scores of thousands of miners locked-out by the owners as this final report was being made.

3 THE NINE DAY STRIKE

"Tuesday, 4th May, started with the workers answering the call. What a wonderful response ! What loyalty ! ! What solidarity ! ! ! From John o'Groats to Land's End the workers answered the call to arms to defend us, to defend the brave miner in his fight for a living wage.

"Hurriedly the General Council formed their Committees, made preparations to face this colossal task—the first in the history of this country. No one could over-estimate the greatness of the task that faced the General Council, and to the credit of many of the members—especially Ernest Bevin—they made every effort possible to bring into being machinery to cope with the requirements.

"The difficulties of transport, of communication, of giving information, were enormous; but the foresight and energy of the officials in the country and of the rank and file rose to the occasion. Links were formed, bulletins were issued; officials, staff and voluntary workers of the TUC and the Labour Party worked night and day to create the machinery necessary to link up the whole movement—machinery that would have been prepared by common-sense leadership months and months before.

"It was a wonderful achievement, a wonderful accomplishment that proved conclusively that the Labour Movement has the men and women that are capable in an emergency of providing the means of carrying on the country. Who can forget the effect of the motor conveyances with posters saying: 'By permission of the TUC'? The Government with its OMS were absolutely demoralised. Confidence, calm, and order prevailed everywhere, despite the irritation caused by the volunteers, blacklegs, and special constables. The workers acted as one. Splendid discipline! Splendid loyalty!" (From *The Nine Days*, by A. J. Cook).

A. J. Cook's enthusiastic description, there seems no doubt, applied broadly to the whole of the country. Apart from a few exceptions, such as in the university towns and cathedral cities of the south of England, the response to the strike call was beyond expectation and well-nigh complete. All the detailed preparations over nine months failed entirely in their purpose to break the strike. The rally of the upper and middle classes "for King and Country" against the working class withholding their labour not only failed to break the strike but indeed served mainly, as by successive flashes of lightning, to have lit up the whole social landscape so as to display not the familiar England, Scotland and Wales as represented in Press and Parliament, implanted at school, inculcated in colleges, hymned and limned in church and studio, but a Britain riven by a class struggle.

"Never before in the history of the world has there been such a display of industrial solidarity by the rank and file"—so ran the opening editorial note in June of *The Colliery Workers' Magazine*, which then went on in a special article to survey the developments "since 1st May and the events that led to the miners alone being left to fight", as follows:

"On Monday night and Tuesday morning, 4th May, the strike order came into operation and the response was simply marvellous. Never before in the history of the world has there been such a manifestation of working class solidarity. Everywhere there was a solid enthusiasm. Men with responsible posts and big salaries had come out as solidly as any. Thousands of men who had never been on strike before responded as readily as any. In remote villages, equally with the industrial 'storm' centres, the men and women came out with a determination that the miners were not to be let down this time. What criticism there was came from the men who were still at work. Why were they not called out? They, too, wanted to strike a blow in this great adventure on behalf of the miners.

"It immediately became evident that the wireless, BBC, would be used by the Government as a means of propaganda against the strike. Definitely false news, coloured news, and news with a decided twist were sent out in a continuous stream. One day it was reported that work was proceeding normally at the Cardiff docks, when in fact they were at a complete standstill, except for two small boats that were being dealt with by a few scabs."

The Colliery Workers' Magazine of June runs as follows:

"On Wednesday morning 5th May, the Government brought out their own newspaper, the *British Gazette*, printed on the machines of the *Morning Post* by blackleg labour. With all the resources of the Government at its disposal, this paper was distributed all over the country, large numbers of them being given away. It was a purely anti-strike newsheet on a par with the news broadcasted by the BBC.

"The object of course was to create a defeatist mentality among the mass of the workers by suggesting that the strike was breaking down in various parts of the country. It recalled the early days of the war, when the British public were roused to the necessary war-like pitch by carefully concocted stories of 'Hun' atrocities. It is useless to blame the Government for adopting these tactics: they realised that they were engaged in a war with the most important section of the community—the workers—and as they had been placed in the most favourable position to fight, having all the organised resources of the State at their disposal, they cannot be blamed for using those resources for their own ends—the defeat of the workers and depriving the miners of some of their already inadequate wages. It is to be hoped that Labour leaders have learned a lesson by this experience, and that the next Labour Government will be equally ruthless in securing to the workers an adequate reward for their labour.

"It is not often that the Churches are found on the side of the workers, but the unreasonable and tyrannical attitude of the Government was too much even for the high dignitaries of the Church. The Archbishop of Canterbury, the Bishop of Oxford, and representatives of the Nonconformist Churches, met and issued an appeal[1] on Friday, 6th

[1]The appeal was as follows:

"After full conference with leaders of the Christian Churches in this country, the Archbishop of Canterbury desires to make public the following expression of considered opinion:

'Representatives of the Christian Churches in England are convinced that a real settlement will only be achieved in a spirit of fellowship and co-operation for the common good, and not as a result of war. Realising that the longer the present struggle persists the greater will be the suffering and loss, they earnestly request that all the parties concerned in this dispute will agree to resume negotiations undeterred by obstacles which have been created by the events of the last few days. If it should seem to be incumbent on us to suggest a definite line of approach, we would submit, as the basis of a possible Concordat, a return to the status quo of Friday last. We cannot but believe in the possibility of a successful

May, but the Government refused to publish that appeal in *The British Gazette* and prohibited the BBC from broadcasting it.[1]"

In *The Colliery Workers' Magazine*, Vol. IV, No. 6 June, 1926, Oliver Harris made the following comments :

"Not the least result of the strike was the final death-blow it gave to the Liberal Party. The clear and unequivocal declarations of Lord Oxford, Earl Grey, Sir John Simon, and others, in Parliament that they were supporting the Tory Government against the workers revealed in a glaring fashion that there is now no difference between the Tories and Liberals in their attitude towards the just claims of the workers. Some of us have been conscious of this for a long time, but there were considerable numbers of workmen still under the glamour of the traditional Liberal Party and its achievements in past generations. The strike brought the parties face to face with a tremendous economic issue—whether the welfare of the workers, the people upon whom the whole fabric and the very existence of the community depends, was to be the first consideration. The Tory Government said, 'No, the wages of the miners must come down; the workers must be sacrificed,' and the official leaders of the Liberal Party supported them in this policy. Fundamentally, that was the issue involved in the General Strike, and the inevitable doom of the Liberal Party was hastened by their decision."

Harris's narrative of events continued :

"Before the end of the first week the *British Worker* appeared as a counterblast to the Government paper. The first number was seized by 'Jix' and his minions for 'inspection', but after some delay the paper was allowed to come out. Incidentally, we may say that many thousands of copies of the *British Worker* were printed by the Cymric Federation Press, Cardiff, the SWMF having placed the plant at the services of the movement.

"The end of the first week of the General Strike found the workers standing solid, and hopes ran high. Mass meetings were held all over the country, attended by tens of thousands of men and women, at which resolutions were unanimously passed to stand firm until justice had been secured for the colliery workers. The appeal of the Churches was having effect, and the large, more or less neutral, section of the community were being swung definitely against the Government and in support of the policy outlined in the appeal.

"But it now appears that the General Council were already beginning to have cold feet. Rumours had reached Eccleston Square, it is said, that the Government intended to arrest the General Council and local Strike Committees; that the Army Reserves were to be called up, and

issue. Our proposal should be interpreted as involving simultaneously and concurrently (1) The cancellation on the part of the TUC of the General Strike; (2) Renewal by the Government of its offer of assistance to the Coal Industry for a short definite period; (3) The withdrawal on the part of mine-owners of the new wages scales recently issued'."

[1]Actually the BBC was not prohibited from doing anything. Nor was it taken under control as Churchill demanded. An interview between Baldwin and John Reith was enough. Thereafter the BBC exhibited a servile alacrity to serve the purposes or the whims of the Government.

that Bills were to be rushed through the present packed House of Commons to curtail the powers of Trade Unions and to seize Trade Union funds. We are not sure whether these statements are correct, and it is only fair to the General Council that we should suspend final judgment on their subsequent actions until they have had an opportunity of telling us the whole story and the reasons why they took the action which was ultimately taken.

"On Monday, 10th May, Sir Herbert Samuel appeared on the scene, and there can be no doubt that privately he had some consultations with the Prime Minister. Meetings took place between the General Council and Sir Herbert, and on Tuesday, the 11th, the stage was set for the great surrender. Without consulting the officials of the Miners' Federation, the General Council and Sir Herbert Samuel agreed upon a series of propositions as a basis for negotiations."

These, especially the correspondence, are of historical interest.[1]

4 THE MINUTES OF A COUNCIL OF ACTION

The experience of the South Wales Miners and of the men and women called out on strike in their aid was very much the same as in the other nine districts. In South Wales no other than the Earl of Clarendon, a Junior Minister but one high in the counsels of the Court at Buckingham Palace, was in charge, together with an admiral and a general, as well as having at his disposal all the armed forces of the Crown, police forces, special constabulary, local government offices, as set forth in the Government Circular so instructing them of 24th November, 1925. What was done on the workers' side in South Wales as in every other part of the country was largely a matter of improvisation. The absence of preparedness, coming up against the highly-

[1]The following letters were exchanged between Sir Herbert Samuel and the General Council of the Trades Union Congress. "Dear Mr. Pugh, As the outcome of the conversations which I have had with your Committee, I attach a memorandum embodying the conclusions that have been reached.

"I have made it clear to your Committee from the outset that I have been acting entirely on my own initiative, have received no authority from the Government, and can give no assurances on their behalf.

"I am of opinion that the proposals embodied in the Memorandum are suitable for adoption, and are likely to promote a settlement of the differences in the Coal Industry.

"I shall strongly recommend their acceptance by the Government when the negotiations are renewed. Yours sincerely, (signed) Herbert Samuel.

"Sir Herbert Samuel, London.

"Dear Sir, The General Council, having carefully considered your letter of today, and the memorandum attached to it, concurred in your opinion that it offers a basis on which the negotiations upon the conditions in the Coal Industry can be renewed.

"They are taking the necessary measures to terminate the General Strike, relying upon the public assurances of the Prime Minister as to the steps that would follow. They assume that during the resumed negotiations the subsidy will be renewed, and that the lock-out notices to the miners will be immediately withdrawn.—Yours faithfully, (signed) Arthur Pugh, Chairman, Walter M. Citrine, Acting Secretary" (12 v 1926).

prepared provocative plans and actions of the Government, was eked out by the voluntary and spontaneous efforts of the trade unionists and their friends. In this situation there was little possibility of co-ordinated action directed from Cardiff or within each valley of the six designated counties. But here and there effective joint working between the miners locked out and the strikers was carried through.

The Executive Council of the SWMF met three times in May, once before and twice after the *Nine Days*. No coalfield conference was held; nor could there be, due to the cessation of locomotive engines on trains or other means of transport. The printed minutes of the Rhondda No. 1 District ceased after mid-April, not to be resumed for another nine months. Nor has there been found record of any other District meetings in the first half of May 1926.

Thus, in the main, whatever happened was like the conflict at Inkerman in the Crimean War, essentially "a soldier's battle". It was the rank and file on their own responsibility who had to carry through whatever was necessary to be done. Fortunately there exists a day to day record of one portion of one district, where careful and complete minutes were kept of a new organisation improvised to meet the unprecedented situation. The locality was Bedlinog in the north-east of Glamorgan, some five miles south of Dowlais. Bedlinog is a ward of Gelligaer Urban District and Parish, on the eastern border of Glamorgan, some fourteen miles north of Cardiff. Gelligaer had a population of just over 40,000 a quarter of a century later.

Dowlais itself, with a railway station at an altitude of 1,000 feet, lying high up in the parish of Merthyr Tydfil, and possessing large iron works and collieries, lay five miles to the north of Bedlinog. The Dowlais district of the South Wales Miners' Federation was one of the smallest. At one time the Dowlais district had had a record of non-unionism; its struggle against that non-unionism and its final extirpation in 1923 by measures devised by its agent, S. O. Davies, have been briefly recounted in an earlier chapter of this book.

Through the valley from Gelligaer north-eastwards there ran the railway line through Bedlinog and on to Merthyr Tydfil. To the east there was a parallel railway line running up to the next valley. Between them lay a Roman road running almost due northward. This, then, was the locality in which the locked-out miners and the strikers improvised a joint organisation to meet the emergency. There was no detailed plans to be put into operation at an hour's notice as in the case of their opponents.

Dowlais, though a small district, had been one of those most committed during the previous five years to support of the Red International of Labour Unions and subsequently had been very favourable to the aims of the National Minority Movement (and the Miners' Minority Movement) headed by Tom Mann. These proclaimed the need, in case of an emergency, to form Councils of Action. On Tuesday, 4th May, 1926, there was called into being a Council of Action in

Bedlinog. Its minutes furnish us with a vivid picture of what it meant to be in the strike.

The Minutes of the Bedlinog Council (given throughout this section as footnotes) begin with the first day.[1]

Tuesday, 4th May : First Day of General Strike.

The stoppage was complete and, indeed, began several hours before Monday midnight. As the day shifts ended, the night shifts in transport, printing and other nocturnal trades did not begin. In every trade called out, the organised workers responded : for the most part the unorganised responded also : the unemployed stood fast. A few unions lagged behind. The TUC General Council announced response beyond expectation and reported difficulty in keeping other workers in. The BBC issued three-hourly bulletins, announcing "Everything quiet," etc. Arrest of Shapurji Saklatvala, Communist MP for speech on first of May.

Wednesday, 5th May : Second day of General Strike.

House of Commons debates the Regulations under the Emergency Powers Act as tabled on Monday, 3rd May, and now moved by the Home Secretary, Sir W. Joynson-Hicks. Government takes over *Morning Post* equipment and under super-editorship of Mr. Churchill, and with blackleg labour, issues official *British Gazette*. In evening, TUC General Council takes over *Daily Herald* equipment and produces *The British Worker* issued after preliminary confiscation by Home Secretary, Joynson-Hicks, had been cancelled by Government. The first number of *British Gazette* calls it a "conflict between the Trade Union leaders and Parliament." In the first number of the *British Worker* the General Council emphasises that the strike is an industrial dispute, and calls for peaceful behaviour. At Liverpool warships land supplies. A destroyer and submarine are berthed in the Tyne. Sir Kingsley Wood, Commissioner in Newcastle (where OMS had broken down completely), together with General Kerr Montgomery, go to Miners' headquarters to negotiate with the Joint Strike Committee. In the *British Worker* there was printed a manifesto of the Miners' Federation of Great Britain as follows :

[1]**Council of Action, Bedlinog, Tuesday, 4th May, 1926.**

Appointment of Officers. Chairman: Morgan William Thomas; Secretary: Hy Morgan; Treasurer: George Roberts. Delegates present: Lewis Williams, Edgar Evans, Edi Ingram, George Roberts, W. R. Davies.

The following resolutions were passed: 1. That we write to the Secretary of the Dowlais Co-op Management Committee asking them to appoint delegates from the Committee and Employees of the Co-op, to the Bedlinog Council of Action. 2. That we write to the Secretaries of the NUR and NUT asking for representatives. 3. That we call a public meeting of the women of Bedlinog to discuss the question of feeding the children during the crisis. 4. Method of calling meeting: (a) that we ask for volunteers from the various religious bodies to attend a meeting on Monday next, 10th May, 1926, at 4.30 p.m.; (b) that we make an application for Gosen Hall to hold the meeting. 5. That the TUC be notified that a Council of Action has been formed at Bedlinog and that any instructions to be issued to the localities should be issued to this body in so far as Bedlinog is concerned.

Comrades, the struggle has begun. Menaced with an onslaught on their standard of life by the mineowners and the Government, the Miners' Federation of Great Britain submitted their case to the judgment of their fellow trade unionists. The General Council and Conference of Trade Union Executives considered it with a full sense of their grave responsibility and pronounced it just beyond all possibility of question. Today the whole body of British workers stands united as one man in their unconquerable determination to resist demands which were a calculated and deliberate attack, not only upon the miners, but on every worker in the country and upon the very existence of the Trade Union Movement itself.

On behalf of the Miners' Federation we express our heartfelt thanks for the magnificent loyalty with which you, our fellow-workers, have responded to our appeal for aid. We have laboured for a peaceful settlement, but the Government, not only by its words, but by its actions, has shown only too plainly that peace is not what it desires. In insisting that the miners should pledge themselves to accept a reduction in wages before even entering negotiations, advanced an unheard of demand which no body of Trade Unionists could accept.

In suddenly breaking off negotiations with the General Council and the Miners' Federation on Sunday night, it revealed its determination to force upon the Trade Union Movement a struggle for which the Government had long prepared. It is on the Government, and the Government alone, that the responsibility for the present situation rests. There is no need for us to call for your assistance, for you have already given it. With you we shall stand firm to the end in defending the rights of the organised workers. With you, we know that justice is on our side. With you, we are confident that the resolute action of a united movement will bring victory to the cause of the workers.

Thursday, 6th May: Third Day of General Strike.

The TUC General Council established five sub-committees for the guidance of the strike on transport and communications; information; food supply; control and instructions; finances; and published a list of 82 unions who were on strike. The Government in an official report announced that in several parts of the country the Fleet had been called in to assist the civil power. It made a further promise assuring all blacklegs that it would take measures to protect them. Shapurji Saklatvala, MP, is sentenced to two months imprisonment.[1] In Glasgow

[1] Bow Street Police Court, 6th May, 1926.

Sir—Adverting to my letter of the 4th instant, I have the honour to inform you that I have this day committed Mr. Shapurji Saklatvala, Member of Parliament, to His Majesty's Prison at Wormwood Scrubs for making default in obeying an Order to enter into a recognisance in the sum of £500, with two sureties each in the sum of £250, to keep the peace and be of good behaviour towards His Majesty and all his liege people for the term of twelve months. The Order was made upon the proceedings instituted by the Director of Public Prosecutions, in respect of which Mr. Saklatvala was arrested as reported in my previous letter. Upon his making default in complying with the Order, I committed Mr. Saklatvala to the said Prison, in the Second Division, for the space of two months, unless he should sooner comply with the Order.

I have the honour to be, Sir, Your obedient servant, C. Biron, Chief Magistrate
To the Rt. Honourable The Speaker of the House of Commons.

18 CO-OPERATIVE MINING IN 1926 AT GLYN-NEATH SOVIET LEVEL

19 SOUTH WALES MINERS SINGING FOR THE CAUSE IN LEICESTER SQUARE, 1926

66 arrests were made and in the clashes between police and strikers there were several injured.

Mr. M. Connolly, MP for Newcastle East, states in the House of Commons:

The position in Newcastle is that the OMS has entirely broken down, that the authorities have approached the trade unions, and asked them to take over the vital services, and that the trade unions have consented to do so on condition that all extra police, all troops, and all OMS services shall be withdrawn. That has been done, and the city is going on all right.

Friday, 7th May: Fourth Day of General Strike.

Government announces on wireless an indemnity to troops for any actions necessary to maintain order. War Office states: "The spirit of the troops is excellent." Archbishop of Canterbury's proposals for settlement printed in *British Worker* but *British Gazette* refuses to print, and BBC refuses to broadcast. Collisions with police in many towns. In London 36 arrests. Home Secretary broadcasts an appeal:

I want 50,000 Special Constables by Monday morning. It may be that men have a right to withhold their labour, but it is absolutely certain that in a free counry men have a right to work if they wish to do so. I do not wish to be an alarmist, but naturally all the attacks on omnibuses, lorries, vans, and so forth are reported to me. In the aggregate, the number is small, but the law of England provides that no single man should be molested in the performance of his duties.[1]

Saturday, 8th May: Fifth Day of General Strike.

[1]Meeting (of Bedlinog Council of Action) held on Friday, 7th May, 1926.

Chairman: Morgan William Thomas; Members present: W. J. Phillips, J. Powell, Edi Ingram, George Roberts, D. Ph. Davies, Dd. Gittens, W. R. Davies, Ior Evans, H. Bolwell, Allen Hughes.

Business. Report given by Dd. Gittens re Workmen of Taff Merthyr. The following resolutions were passed: 1. That we stop all men, apart from those engaged in making the Underground Lodge Room, which they consider as safety men, until the Agent, Mr. S. O. Davies, can discuss the question with the Council of Action on Sunday; 2. Re Screenmen at Taff Merthyr: Comrade Gittens to inform the Screenmen that the Council of Action will allow them to carry on with their work on the understanding that they join their respective Unions or the Miners' Federation. Their case to be further considered on Sunday next; 3. That Edi Ingram accompanies Dd. Gittens to Taff Merthyr to give report; 4. Re Nantwen Lodge and Non-Unionists: That we appoint a deputation to interview Lewis Rees Davies asking him to join the Union or he would be replaced by Union man. Deputation appointed: Hector Bolwell and George Roberts; 5 Re Mynyddislwyn Colliery: that we appoint a deputation to interview Mr. Samuel Williams, the Owner, asking him to stop working. Deputation appointed: Morgan William Thomas, W. R. Davies, and W. J. Phillips. Same condition to be applied to Safety men re Union; 6. Re bus running between Trelewis and Bedlinog: that we appoint a deputation to interview the drivers stating that if they do not stop running the bus a demonstration would be organised to stop them. Deputation appointed: Lewis Williams, D. Ph. Davies, Allen Hughes; 7. Owing to the fact that no letters have been received to our letters to the TUC, that we send a letter by dispatch through Merthyr.—W. M. Thomas."

Friday, 7th May meeting. The meeting decided to appoint pickets for Taff Merthyr. Pickets appointed: Morgan William Thomas, Lewis Williams, Dd. Ph. Davies, W. R. Davies, J. Bolton Thomas, Ior Evans and Sec.

The Government forms a new body, the "Civil Constabulary Reserve", to be composed entirely of ex-soldiers as special auxiliary constables, and to be equipped with steel helmets and truncheons, and to be paid considerably more than the workers in the mines. It is reported that 15 Councils of Action are functioning in London. Collision between police and strikers in various parts of the country, but no incidents reported in South Wales. Prime Minister Baldwin ends a Saturday evening broadcast with the words :

I am a man of peace. I am longing and working and praying for peace, but I will not surrender the safety and the security of the British Constitution. You placed me in power 18 months ago by the largest majority accorded to any Party for many years. Have I done anything to forfeit that confidence ? Cannot you trust me to ensure a square deal, to secure even justice between man and man ?[1]

Sunday, 9th May : Sixth Day of General Strike.

The *British Worker* issues a reply of the General Council to the speech broadcast by Baldwin. It says that the General Council is ready to renew negotiations at the point at which they were broken off. The General Council denies that it in any way is threatening the food supply of the population or that it has in any respect broken the constitution.

Mr. J. H. Thomas, speaking at Hammersmith, said : "I have never disguised that I did not favour the principle of a General Strike."

Purcell (Strike Organisation Committee) declares at meeting that Government has issued warrants for arrest of himself and of Ernest Bevin. (Three weeks later in *Lansbury's Labour Weekly* of 22nd May it is stated that the Government decided to arrest the members of the General Council and of local strike committees, to call up the army reserves, and to repeal the Trades Disputes Act). International Transport and Mining Federations at Ostend resolve to stop export of coal to Britain or bunkering of ships. On this day, while Baldwin visited the Zoo, Cardinal Bourne, at High Mass, made a declaration that the

[1] Meeting of Bedlinog Council of Action held Saturday morning, 8th May.

Chairman, Morgan William Thomas. Members present: W. J. Phillips, Dd. Ph. Davies, Ior Evans, Hector Bolwell, Allen Hughes, Edi Ingram, J. B. Thomas, Lewis Williams, B. Phillips.

Minutes read and confirmed. Business, Reports: 1. Re Taff Merthyr, given by Edi Ingram; and accepted. 2. Re bus, given by Lewis Williams; and accepted. 3. Report given by Morgan Wm. Thomas; and accepted. 4. Re Lewis Rees Davies, given by Hector Bolwell; and accepted. 5. Re Taff Merthyr Washeries: that we allow them to work until S. O. Davies visits us on Sunday to discuss the case, with the understanding that they join the Union. 6. That we send a dispatch rider to Treharris for news from the TUC. 7. Re the Mynyddislwyn Colliery: that we send a dispatch rider to Deri to get their view of the above colliery, also their activities re the Crisis.

Meeting held Saturday afternoon.

1. Re Mynyddislwyn Colliery: that the Colliery be picketed on Monday morning. 2. That we ask for volunteers at the mass meeting to be addressed by S. O. Davies.

General Strike was a sin against God.[1]

Monday, 10th May: Seventh Day of General Strike.

On a question being raised in the House of Commons by Sir Nicholas Grattan Doyle, about the statement made on 6th May by the Member for Newcastle East, one of the most junior members of the Government, Sir H. Barnston (Controller of His Majesty's Household), was put up to carry the can, by uttering a denial in a case where the truth would have seriously impaired the morale of the Government side, saying: "There is no foundation for any of these statements. The organisation in Newcastle has worked quite satisfactorily. It was working well on the day referred to, and is working still better today." And being from his military experience an intrepid liar, this most junior of all members of the Government went on: "I am informed that all those statements are absolutely untrue, and I am a little bit surprised that the Hon. Member is not ashamed to repeat them."

Sir Herbert Samuel approaches the General Council. Negotiations proceeding between the General Council and the Co-operative Wholesale Society for credits to the Trade Union Movement. BBC announces arrests and imprisonments of up to six months. *The British Worker* reports 374 arrests in the previous few days. Arrest of Noah Ablett, member of the Executive Committee of the Miners' Federation of Great Britain. All India Trade Union Congress cables further £300. Five per cent levy on all trade unionists not called on to strike required by

[1]Meeting of Bedlinog Council of Action held Sunday afternoon, 9th May.

Chairman: Morgan William Thomas. Members present: Lewis Williams, Edi Ingram, George Roberts, Dd. Ph. Davies, Joe Powell, Alf Lewis, W. R. Davies, Ior Evans, D. Gittens, Benji Phillips.

Minutes read and confirmed. The following resolutions were passed: 1. That we try to get in touch with Miners' Office, Dowlais, by phone or dispatch to enquire for S.O.D. 2. Re Mynyddislwyn Colliery: that we call a public meeting tonight on the Co-op field, at 8 o'clock, whether S.O. comes or not, to appoint pickets to picket Mynyddislwyn Colliery. Other matters to be dealt with at meeting: that Bedlinog Council of Action be enlarged by appointing additional representatives from the various organisations. Also to appoint pickets for Taff Merthyr Colliery. Number of pickets for Mynyddislwyn 12. For Taff Merthyr 4. 3. That the meeting be called by sending announcements to the various religious organisations. 4. Re washery men at Taff Merthyr: that we make enquiries at Dowlais re their position.

Meeting Sunday night. —

Chairman: Morgan William Thomas. Members present: J. B. Thomas, H. Bolwell, A. Hughes, W. J. Phillips, George Roberts, Lewis Williams, Edi Ingram, Dd. Ph. Davies, Ior Evans. S. O. Davies present. The following resolutions were passed:

1. Re Mynyddislwyn Colliery: that a deputation meet the men as they come from the pit on Monday afternoon to try and persuade them to finish working. Deputation appointed Lewis Williams, Hector Bolwell and Dd. Ph. Davies. 2. Re Taff Merthyr Colliery: (a) that we appoint four pickets to picket the Colliery on Monday: pickets appointed Lewis Williams, J. B. Thomas, Hector Bolwell, A. Hughes, Ior Evans; (b) that a deputation be appointed to interview the Manager of Taff Merthyr asking him to comply with the request of stopping all but safety men: failing his complying with our request that the safety men would be withdrawn. 3. That those employed at the Washery at Taff Merthyr be called out. A letter was read by the Secretary from the Secretary of Gosen Hall stating that we could have the use of the Hall as from tomorrow, Monday.

General Council. General Council issues message at opening of second week: "Stand firm, be loyal to instructions and trust your leaders."[1]

Tuesday, 11th May: Eighth day of General Strike.

General Council issues strike order calling out from midnight all engineering and shipbuilding workers not yet affected by the strike. Persons arrested in Glasgow tried before three Special Tribunals and 100 of them sentenced to three months imprisonment. In Hull 25 persons sentenced to between three months and nine months imprisonment. Reported that in London 40,000 police volunteers registered and in provinces 200,000; Noah Ablett in London bound over; Cook declares, after all day session of Miners' EC, all districts are against any compromise on hours and wages.

Two days earlier Cook had said: "A drunken man, a rowdy man, is your enemy and mine. If I had my way I would shut every pub down. We need clear heads in this struggle."

[1]Meeting of Bedlinog Council of Action held Monday, 10th May, 1926.
First Session 10 a.m.

Chairman: Hector Bolwell. Members present: Elias Jones, J. B. Thomas, Thomas Williams, John T. Jones, Owen Jones, W. J. Phillips, A. Hughes, Edi Ingram, John Ingram, George Roberts.

1. Minutes of yesterday read and confirmed. Report of Pickets of Taff Merthyr given by Hector Bolwell and accepted. Result two platelayers and one striker returned home. 2. Moved that the Deputation to interview the Manager of Taff Merthyr should be: Owen Jones, John Ingram, J. T. Jones and Secretary. 3. Re Feeding the Children: that a deputation be appointed to interview the various heads and the School Managers seeking information as to what has been done by the Education Committee. Deputation appointed: Hector Bolwell and Elias Jones. 4. That a Committee of Women be appointed from tonight's meeting to meet the Council of Action to discuss the food question, children and adult.

Second Session 2 p.m.

Chairman: Morgan William Thomas. Members present: W. J. Phillips, Edi Ingram, Allen Hughes, George Roberts, Elias Jones, J. T. Jones, Owen Jones, Thomas Williams, J. B. Thomas, John Ingram, Alf Lewis, John Thomas.

Report received from the various deputations. Deputation from Taff Merthyr reported through the Secretary to the effect that Dd. Hughes, the manager, refused to stop the men but gave an undertaking that the Foreman would send for any man. Report was accepted.

On this report the Council decided to communicate with Treharris Council of Action asking them to take responsibility for picketing the Trelewis end and that Bedlinog would be responsible for this end. The Secretary reported transaction between the deputation and the Foreman of the Construction Gang on the Washery to the effect that a letter had been received by the Secretary of Taff Merthyr Lodge asking him to forward a written statement of the decisions of the Council of Action re the Washery men. The deputation decided that, being that the Secretary of the Council of Action was on the Deputation, he hand to the Foreman a written statement of the decision arrived at. The Council endorsed the action of the Secretary.

Report of Deputation to Mynyddislwyn Colliery given by Edi Ingram (and accepted) to the effect that the workmen there would join the strikers. On this report it was passed that the boy who worked the pump would be allowed to work on the understanding that he join the Miners' Federation at Nantwern Lodge. The owner, Mr. Samuel Williams, to be notified of this by letter.

Comrade Lewis Williams raised a question and asked the Council to decide if he should allow his name to go forward for the post of Assistant Relieving

Memorandum by Sir Herbert Samuel handed to General Council which unanimously decides to accept it and call off General Strike. They then hand it to Miners' Executive, who reject it, regret that they have not been consulted and point out that the memorandum means reduction in wages which was what the General Strike was declared against. Notice from Gosling and Ernest Bevin of Transport and General Workers' Union published today in *British Worker*: "We shall continue steadfast in our stand for justice and right. Hold fast. (Signed) H. Gosling. We must see the miners through (Signed) Ernest Bevin."

At Cardiff a woman got one month for breaking a tram window: and a girl was fined 20 shillings for obscene language to a tram-driver. At Newport a man was fined £5 for pulling down Government notices as to the protection of men returning to work.

Officer. The Council decided that his name be allowed to go forward. The Council decided to call on those men who volunteered as pickets, at the public meeting held Sunday night, to attend a meeting of the Council on Monday night, 6 p.m.

A public meeting of the women was held at 4.30 to discuss the food question. This meeting decided to form a committee to work in conjunction with the Council of Action. Secretary appointed: Mrs. Morgans, 35 Oakland. They appointed two delegates to accompany the delegates of the Council of Action to interview the various heads of the schools and the School Managers at 11.30 a.m., Tuesday.

Third Session.

Chairman: Morgan W. Thomas. Members present: Hector Bolwell, J. T. Jones, Owen Jones, Joe Powell, Llewellyn Jones, Wm. Arthur, Edi Ingram, John Ingram, Thomas Williams, D. Jones, J. B. Thomas, George Roberts, Dd. Ph. Davies, Alf Lewis, Dd. Gittens, W. R. Davies, Rees Davies, Edgar Evans, Elias Jones.

The following resolutions were passed: 1. Report of Women's meeting given by Secretary and accepted. 2. Appointment of Pickets for Taff Merthyr. Pickets appointed: Thos. Williams, D. Jones, J. B. Thomas, Tom Stephen Rees, Alf Lewis, Wm. Arthur. 3. Appointment of pickets for Mynyddislwyn Colliery: that we call five out of the volunteers who volunteered at Sunday night's meeting: Emlyn Thomas, Evan Watkins, Arthur Telwood, Hector Bolwell, J. Williams. 4. Re application of Taff Merthyr Manager for inclusion of Blacksmith's striker in list of safety men: that the striker be allowed to work providing he joins the union. 5. Re Non-Unionists at Taff Merthyr: that we appoint Dd. Ph. Davies and W. R. Davies to accompany D. Gittens to interview them. 6. The Chairman, Morgan William Thomas, tendered his resignation from the chairmanship of the Council owing to deafness. The Council accepted the resignation with regret and appointed Hector Bolwell to the Chair. 7. Re Washery men at Taff Merthyr: that we promise the men from England, working on the Washery, that this Council would communicate with the Council of Action operating in that district asking them to look after the families of the men owing to the position in which they find themselves. 8. That we ask one of the riders to take W. R. Davies over to Mardy to enquire into the scheme they have in operation there for feeding the children and adults. 9. The question of finding oil and petrol for our dispatch rider was raised: (a) Passed that the Secretary of the Council of Action supply the rider with a note to take to the garage for supply of oil and petrol; the Council to be responsible for same; (b) that a sub-committee be appointed to deal with the question of the insurance of the bicycle and rider. 10. That we appoint two delegates to attend the Treharris Strike Committee, at 12 noon on Tuesday, to give report of Taff Merthyr. Delegates appointed: Owen Jones and J. T. Jones.

Arthur Cook issues statement on standpoint of the Miners' Federation Executive Committee.[1]

Wednesday, 12th May: Ninth day of General Strike.

BBC 10 a.m. bulletin states "the position as a whole is still one of deadlock." New decree published under Emergency Powers Act empowering Government to confiscate money sent from abroad for the strike. General Council issues denial that it had called out engineers and shipbuilders. Eighty miners arrested in the Doncaster region as a result of a collision with the police; but still in South Wales no report of any incidents or of any arrests.

At mid-day official Government wireless message declares "General Strike ceases today." TUC General Council arrives at 10 Downing Street and informs the Prime Minister, with most of the Cabinet present, that "We are here today, Sir, to say that this General Strike is to be terminated forthwith." Baldwin made brief reply. The news was broadcast at one p.m. The King, George V, issues a statement urging co-operation and amity.

[1] Meeting of Bedlinog Council of Action held Tuesday, 11th May, 1926.

Morning Session. Chairman: Hector Bolwell. Members Present: W. J. Phillips, Edi Ingram, J. B. Thomas, Thomas Williams, Llew. Jones, Allen Hughes, Arthur Selwood, Evan Watkins, George Roberts, J. T. Jones, Tom Thomas, Mrs. Morgan and Mrs. Rowe present from Women's Section.

Business transacted: welcome of Tom Thomas as delegate from Taff Co-op. 1. Report of pickets of Taff Merthyr given by Llew Jones, and accepted. Out of Report the Council decided to appoint a deputation to interview Dan Roberts of Bedu Road, Bedlinog, to ask him for the name of the Lodge Sec. (Brick Layers Union) Deputation appointed: Arthur Selwood and Llew Jones. It was also passed that we appoint a deputation to interview Jack Bennet. Deputation appointed: Hector Bolwell and Allen Hughes. 2. Report of Mynyddislwyn Colliery pickets given by Arthur Selwood and accepted. Reported all out at this colliery. 3. Re Screen men at Taff Merthyr: pass that the Screen men be withdrawn, the foreman be notified. That Treharris deputation hand in letter on the way. That the Sec. have power to co-opt a delegate from the Washery men (union man) from England on to the Council of Action.

Afternoon Session.

Chairman: Hector Bolwell. Members present: George Roberts, D. Jones, Thos. Williams, A. Hughes, J. Ingram, Tom Thomas, Alf Lewis, Llew Jones, Wm. Arthur, Elias Jones, Morgan Wm. Thomas, Owen Jones, J. B. Thomas, J. T. Jones, Lewis Williams, W. R. Davies.

1. Report of deputation to Treharris by Owen Jones: called at Taff Merthyr but failed to deliver letter instructing foreman of Screens of decision of Council. Reported that Treharris Council of Action would appoint 12 pickets to picket the Taff Merthyr Colliery on Wednesday morning and that they would require a list of Safety men. Report accepted. (a) Passed that we appoint pickets to picket Taff Merthyr, Bedlinog end, Wednesday morning. (b) That list of Safety men be sent to Treharris Strike Committee. Pickets appointed: Lewis Williams, Llew Jones, Wm. Arthur, Emlyn Jones, Thos. Williams, John Ingram.

2. Report of Deputation to interview the various heads of the schools and the school managers given by Mrs. Morgan. The Women's Committee having been called in on this report, it was moved that the Sec. write to F. F. James, 134 High Street, Merthyr; Dr. James, Chief Education Officer, Cardiff; Councillor Hopkins, Bargoed, asking for information. Amendment: that a sub-committee be formed to deal thoroughly with the matter. The amendment was carried. It was decided to appoint a committee of six, three males and three females.

At 7 p.m. stenographic report of termination of General Strike broadcasted, followed by broadcast of a message from the King; followed by a message from the Prime Minister at 9.30 p.m.; followed by a valedictory from the British Broadcasting Company, as follows:

Our first feelings on hearing of the termination of the General Strike must be of profound thankfulness to almighty God who has led us through this supreme test with national health unimpaired. You have heard the message from the King and the Prime Minister. It remains only to add the conviction that the nation's happy escape has been in a large measure due to the personal trust in the Prime Minister not misplaced. As for the BBC we hope your confidence in, and goodwill to us, have not suffered.

"Jerusalem," by William Blake, was then recited or, at any rate, four verses of it.

The Miners' Federation Committee met at 10 a.m. to review the whole situation. The Strike Committee of the Council was sent up by the General Council to interview them, and to appeal to them to concur in the action of the Council for the sake of the wider movement.

Members appointed on Committee: Mrs. Morgan, Mrs. Rowe, Mrs. Evans, Tom Thomas, Lewis Williams, W. R. Davies. Elias Jones was appointed to act as deputy for Tom Thomas in the event of his being called away. 3. Re Recreation and Social Entertainments: that a Committee of six be appointed to deal with the question: Emlyn Jones, J. T. Jones, Owen Jones, Llew Jones, Mrs. Thomas, Mrs. Thomas.

Evening Session.

Chairman: Hector Bolwell. Members present: Allen Hughes, Edi Ingram, Dd. Ph. Davies, Alf Lewis, John Ingram, D. Gittens, Llew Jones, George Roberts, Owen Jones, J. Powell, J. B. Thomas, W. J. Phillips, Thos. Williams, D. T. Jones, Tom Thomas, W. R. Davies, Lewis Williams.

1. Report given by Llew Jones re deputation to interview Dan Roberts. Report accepted. Out of report it was decided to send a Rider to the Sec. of Nelson Strike Committee asking them to see the Sec. of the Bricklayers Union to enquire if he was a member of that Union and, if so, to instruct him to finish working. 2. Report of interview with Jack Bennet given by Hector Bolwell. The Council decided that he be allowed to work on condition that he does his own work and joins the Union. 3. Report given by D. Gittens of the Deputation to see the non-Unionists at Taff Merthyr: that a deputation be appointed to interview these non-Unionists. Dep. appointed : Lewis Williams, W. R. Davies. 4. Re increasing the numbers of the Council of Action: that the officials of various organisations appoint additional members from their lodge on to the Council. 5. Re Blackleg Press: passed that the local newsagent be interviewed. Deputation appointed: Tom Thomas, W. J. Phillips. 6. Report of Food Committee given by W. R. Davies. (a) That we call on the women to attend a meeting of the Council on Wednesday at 6 p.m. (b) That the Board of Guardians would be approached re feeding the adults. Report adopted. (c) That we recommend the delegates on this Council have the Taff Merthyr Lodge Treharris to ask them to pay the money due to the Bedlinog Paying Station from the Treharris Lodge Fund to a body organised in this place to feed the children and adults. 7. Re picking coal on the tip: that a notice be placed in the window asking people not to sell coal picked on the tip. 8. Report received from Nelson, re Dan Roberts: that he be approached on the Road on Wednesday morning by the pickets. 9. Communication from East Glamorgan Federation of Trades Councils to the effect that a Conference would be held at County Hall, Pontypridd, on Wednesday, 12th May, at 6 p.m. Lewis Williams appointed to attend the Conference.

The Committee were then informed by Mr. Bevin that the General Council had now definitely decided to call the strike off at noon that day, and that an interview with the Prime Minister had already been arranged to inform him of this decision. The Strike Committee was sent to make a last appeal to the Executive Committee to fall into line with this decision, and to accept the draft proposals as a justification for the cancellation of the General Strike on the strength of the recommendation by Sir H. Samuel. Messrs. Bevin, Purcell and Ben Turner all made appeals. The burden of all their appeals was that the General Strike could not be maintained, as it had reached a point when any further continuation was a menace to the whole movement, and when in view of the financial and other difficulties of the unions it was essential to terminate it in order to prevent the movement being disrupted, and the whole thing degenerating into a rout. After the Strike Committee had retired, the Federation Committee again considered the matter and passed:

That having heard the report of the representatives of the TUC we reaffirm our resolutions of 11th May, and express our profound admiration of the wonderful demonstration of loyalty as displayed by all workers who promptly withdrew their labour in support of the miners' standards, and undertake to report fully to a conference to be convened as early as possible.[1]

Thursday, 13th May:

General Strike, called off in the afternoon by the General Council, continues unofficially on Thursday. British Broadcasting Bulletin

[1] Meeting of Bedlinog Council of Action held at Gosen Hall, Wednesday, 12th May, 1926.

Afternoon Session. Chairman: Hector Bolwell.

Members present: Wm. J. Phillips, George Roberts, A. Hughes, Arthur Selwood, W. R. Davies, J. E. Jones, Lewis Williams, Owen J. Owens, Llew Jones, Wm. Arthur, Emlyn Jones, H. O. Jones, Hector Bolwell, Edi Ingram, J. B. Thomas, Dd. Ph. Davies, Thos. Williams, J. Thomas, Alf Lewis, Hy. Moyan, Ior Evans, J. Powell, Tom Thomas, Thos. J. Hughes, D. Jones.

That Evan Davies be co-opted on to the Council. 1. Minutes of yesterday read and confirmed. 2. Report of Taff Merthyr pickets given by Emlyn Jones. Dan Roberts passed without stopping and J. Bennett promised to join the Union as soon as possible. They also reported that the Screen foreman wished to see the Sec. of the Council. On this report the Council decided to call upon the Screen foreman to attend a meeting of the Council. 3. Report of non-Unionists at Taff Merthyr given by W. R. Davies: that we await report from Treharris before we discuss the report further. If no report is received, that the question be further discussed by this Council. 4. Re Blackleg Press: that we accept report given by Tom Thomas and that we boycott the papers as much as possible by agitation. 5. Passed that we accept all reports. 6. A letter addressed to Dan Roberts was brought by dispatch rider to the Council to be delivered. Also a letter re the above from the Bricklayers' Union was read to the Council. The Council decided that the letters be delivered and the position explained by a deputation. Deputation appointed: Hector Bolwell and Wm. Arthur. Passed that J. Thomas be co-opted on to the Recreation Committee. 7. Report of Insurance Committee given by George Roberts. That the question be left till tomorrow morning pending the report from Tom Thomas.

Evening Session 6 p.m. Chairman: Hector Bolwell.

throughout the day displays surprise that work has not been resumed. It became known that the settlement did not involve the withdrawal of the lockout notices to the miners, and that the MFGB had refused to agree to the settlement. The employers in various industries demanded impossible conditions of reinstatement, and the strike continued without any sign of weakening. The *Times* opens National Police Fund.

The industrial outlook in the Swansea district is not very reassuring, as the dock workers, millers and railway men are still idle and are awaiting assurances from the employers.

Parliamentary Labour Party issues protest against "unfounded" inaccurate and provocative statements that the General Council had unconditionally surrendered." Ninety-five persons sentenced to various terms in different parts, including twelve Communists. In the evening there had been no return to work. Baldwin has interview with Miners' Executive Committee. The Communist Party issues appeal to all beginning :

The General Council's decision to call off the General Strike is the greatest crime that has ever been permitted, not only against the miners, but against the working class of Great Britain and the whole world. The British workers had aroused the astonishment and admiration of the world by the enthusiasm with which they had entered upon the fight for the miners standard of living. But, instead of responding to this magnificent lead by a call to every section of organised labour to join the fight against the capitalists, the General Council have miserably thrown itself and the miners on the tender mercies of the workers' worst enemies—The Tory Government.

Women's Committee present to discuss the feeding of the children. 1. Report of Interview with Guardian Bolwell given by Lewis Williams and accepted : (a) that the parents send their children to school on Friday morning without breakfast and the children if asked by the teacher or schoolmaster, to say so; (b) that the whole of the question of feeding the children and adults be left in the hands of the Sub-Committee appointed to deal with same. 2. Report of Deputation interviewing Dan Roberts given by William Arthur and accepted. It was reported that he definitely refused to stop working. Passed that owing to the reports received re development of Strike that the matter be left in abeyance. 3. Discussion risen on the notice to be issued by the local Secretary of MFGB. Decided that it be worded as follows : "That no miner should resume work before the National Conference to be held on Friday next."

4. A discussion was raised as to whether the Council of Action should dissolve. It was decided that the Council of Action should continue to function and it be placed on the agenda for the next meeting : "The question of appointing a Sub-Committee to draft Standing Orders for this Council." Report of Food Committee given by W. R. Davies. He submitted three resolutions passed by the Committee to be endorsed by the Council : (a) that all persons receiving food notes from the Guardians should throw them into a common pool; that the purchase of food be made in bulk; and that all strikers and their wives be fed from a communal kitchen; (b) that a mass meeting be called on Monday next 17th May, at 11 a.m., this matter to be placed on the agenda; (c) that the Secretary of the Food Sub-Committee work out a plan to this effect down to the last detail by Monday. Passed that the resolutions be endorsed by this Committee. 5. Report of Recreation and Social Committee given by Emlyn Jones. Reported that Lewis Williams be authorised to interview the Treharris Band asking them to give a concert at Bedlinog. Report accepted.

Message from TUC General Council:

Fellow Trade Unionists the General Strike is ended. It has not failed. It has made possible the resumption of negotiations in the coal industry and the continuance during the negotiations of the financial assistance given by the Government.[1]

A second Message from the TUC General Council:

Let there be no mistake. The Trade Union movement is not suing for mercy. It is prepared to help the peace as man to man. It is not beaten, and it is not broken. Its strength is unimpaired, and reinforced by the solidarity which the response to the General Strike revealed. If one class of employers, misrepresenting the calling off of the strike, thinks it can seize the opportunity to disrupt and degrade the Trade Union movement, the situation is grave indeed, for to that the movement cannot and will not submit.

Friday, 14th May:

BBC begins, "There is as yet no general resumption of work." Delegate Conference of Miners' Federation of Great Britain, meeting in London, received reports and adjourned till Thursday, 20th May. *The Western Mail* (owned by Berry Coal Combine) calls for dissolution of Communist Party and Minority Movement as illegal organisations.

That night, the Prime Minister submitted a series of nine proposals for settlement of mining dispute on lines of Royal Commission's Report to the Conference which decided to adjourn for six days in order that

[1]Meeting of Bedlinog Council of Action held Thursday, 13th May, 1926. Morning Session 10 a.m.

Chairman Hector Bolwell.

Owing to developments it was decided to stand adjourned till 2 p.m. waiting news.

Afternoon Session 2 p.m.

Chairman: Hector Bolwell.

1. Minutes of yesterday's meeting read and confirmed. 2. Re appointment of Sub-Committee to draft Standing Orders for the Council; that question be deferred till Morgan William Thomas, the mover of the notice of motion, be present. 3. Correspondence re position of Railwaymen read to Council: that the news contained and the terms offered to railwaymen be posted up in the usual place. 4. Passed that the next meeting be held at 2 p.m., Friday. Secretary received communication from Treharris which necessitated the calling of a meeting of the Council. In answering the letter the Secretary stated that Bedlinog Council of Action would undoubtedly help Treharris in picketing the stations. The action of the Secretary was endorsed by the Council and it was passed that pickets be appointed. Pickets: John Thomas and J. B. Thomas. It was passed that Taff Merthyr be picketed tomorrow morning (Friday). Pickets: J. T. Jones, Alf Lewis, Hector Bolwell, Hy. Owen Jones, Llew Jones, Wm. Arthur, Harry Howells. 3. It was passed that Harry Howells of Taff Merthyr Colliery be co-opted on to the Council. 4. The notice of motion put forward by Morgan Wm. Thomas: "That we appoint a Sub-Committee to draft Standing Orders for this Council," was passed. Four members with the chairman and secretary were appointed: Morgan Thomas, Tom Thomas, Lewis Williams, John Thomas. 5. Passed that a deputation interview Jack Bennet re paying the Union. Deputation appointed: D. Gittens, Hy. O. Jones. Passed that Resolution 4 of the afternoon session be rescinded and that we meet at 10 a.m. Friday.

the districts might have an opportunity of considering them.[1]

Saturday, 15th May.

Adjourned Delegate Conference of MFGB meets, discusses position taken by EC and refers Baldwin plan to Districts to receive replies on Thursday, 20th May.

The Conference, reassembling on Thursday, 20th May, rejected Baldwin's proposals, as did the coalowners. On the next day, the Treasurer, W. P. Richardson, told of a telegram received from the President of the Russian Miners' Union, who were sending £260,000 for the support of the British miners and their families. From other sources there were altogether £3,000. Richardson said:

We have received subscriptions from 1/- to £500, in round figures something like £3,000. They represent 750 donations, which you see is round about an average of £5. As I have said we have received shillings, which in probability represent to those people just as much

[1] Meeting of Bedlinog Council of Action held Friday, 14th May, 1926. Morning Session.

Chairman: Hector Bolwell. Members present: Wm. J. Phillips, Allen Hughes, Dd. Thomas, Evan Davies, Hy. Howells, John Ingram, Llew Jones, Hector Bolwell, J. B. Thomas, Thos. Williams, Hy. Morgan, Tom Thomas.

Minutes of yesterday's meeting read and confirmed. 1. Report of pickets appointed to picket Bedlinog Station given by J. B. Thomas. Report adopted. Report satisfactory. 2. Report of Taff Merthyr pickets given by Llew Jones. Report very unsatisfactory. Passed that we report to Treharris Council of Action asking them what action can be taken to deal with these men. 3. It was reported to the Council that a Colliery, known as the "House Coal Colliery," was working at Nelson and that the Nelson Strike Committee had decided to allow this Colliery to work. This Council decided that a protest be sent from this Council to the Nelson Strike Committee protesting against their action. 4. Report of Sub-Committee appointed to draft Standing Orders given by Secretary. Passed that Standing Orders drawn out by the Committee be adopted.

Friday, 14th May, 1926. Evening Session.

Chairman: Hector Bolwell.

1. A resolution was passed that a resolution of protest be sent to the TUC expressing our disgust at the way in which the settlement was made and the strike called off. 2. A correspondence from Treharris in answer to our letter re picketing Taff Merthyr Colliery. Passed that the suggestion of Treharris Council of Action be adopted by this Council: (a) "That we leave the matter in abeyance for a day or two pending developments"; (b) "that the names of persons who made certain statements re the House Coal Colliery, Nelson, be sent to Nelson Strike Committee for investigation." 3. Report of Food Committee given by W. R. Davies. Two schemes of feeding were submitted to the Council: (a) Direct feeding by the Education Committee; (b) Canteen feeding. Passed: that the Council of Action recommend to the Head Teacher to institute the Canteen method of Feeding the Children. 4. Passed: that the deputation be appointed to interview Head Teacher. Deputation appointed: W. J. Phillips and Hector Bolwell. 5. Passed: the offer of Tom Thomas to interview Councillor Hopkins, Bargoed, re his statement of the plan of the County Council of instituting a penny rate to meet the expenses of Feeding Children. 6. Passed: that a small committee be appointed to meet at Secretary's house on Saturday afternoon as the room at Gosen Hall was not available. Committee appointed: W. J. Phillips, Nantwen; W. R. Davies, Taff Merthyr; J. Jones, Treharris; Edi Ingram, Labour Party; E. Jones, Unemployed; T. J. Hughes, Co-op.; Joe Powell, Post Office; Ior Evans, Communist Party; Edgar Evans, Chamber of Trade; D. Jones; Griff Jones, Woodworkers.

in their view as those sending £5. We have had £50. We have had £500 sent to us from Mr. Oswald Moseley.

I am going to give you one or two donations which have come to us. We have received from the Austrian miners £145. I may tell you that is a very big sacrifice for them. The Leicester Hosiery people have sent us a cheque for £250. There are two or three £50, and the total amount—calculating the Russian money—the figure is £263,000 and that is the figure we are working on for the purpose of disbursement.

Thereupon the Conference placed on record "its appreciation of the splendid sum received from the Russian mineworkers, and also all the subscribers to the Fund."[1]

5 THE VENGEANCE OF THE AUTHORITIES

In South Wales, unlike the rest of Britain, there were no reports of arrests or imprisonments in the first fortnight of May. The extended machinery for maintaining law and order, as well as for strike-breaking, set up in every county of South Wales under Lord Clarendon (Commissioner to enforce the Regulations made under the Emergency Powers Act) was not brought spectacularly into play. As far as public reports

[1]Meeting of Bedlinog Council of Action held Monday, 17th May, 1926. Morning Session.

Chairman: Hector Bolwell. Members present: W. R. Davies, J. T. Jones, Emlyn Jones, Thomas Williams, Elias Jones, Harry Jones, W. J. Phillips, Dd. Ph. Davies, Llew Jones, J. B. Thomas, J. E. Jones, Dd. Thomas.

Business. 1. Report of Interview with Mr. Daniels given by Hector Bolwell and accepted. 2. Correspondence from Bargoed Joint Trades Council of Action re separate meat tickets. Passed that a resolution to the same effect be sent by this Council to the Merthyr Board of Guardians. 3. That we send a resolution to the Miners' EC calling upon them to stand firm for the three points put forward, viz:—No district agreements; No reduction in wages; and no lengthening of hours. 4. That the Secretary of Nantwen Lodge phone to the Dowlais District headquarters to see if S. O. Davies or Chairman of the District could come to Bedlinog to explain the position.

Meeting of the Council of Action held at Gosen Hall on Wednesday, 9th June, 1926.

Chairman: Morgan W. Thomas. Members present: Llew Jones, Thos. Williams, J. B. Thomas, Emlyn Jones, Alf Lewis, Wm. Arthur, John Ingram, John Thomas, W. R. Davies, Ior Evans, Edi Ingram, Edgar Evans, Hector Bolwell, Alun Hughes.

The following resolutions were passed: 1. Reorganising of the Washery men at Taff Merthyr. That the correspondence from Mr. J. Twomey of Swansea, Organiser of the Transport and General Workers' Union, be handed over to the Lodge officials at the Taff Merthyr for their consideration and that the organiser be notified of this step. 2. Reports of Sports Committee given by Comrade J. Thomas and accepted. 3. Re Victimisation of members who have taken active part on Council of Action during strike: case of W. R. Davies reported to Council, on this case it was reported that the case was in the hands of S. O. Davies, Miners' Agent. It was decided that W. R. Davies interview S. O. Davies to see if anything was being done and that the question be left in abeyance till we receive a report. 4. Sammy's Pit: that a mass meeting be called as early as possible and that we invite S. O. Davies to

were concerned, it was all quiet on the South Wales Front. But once the strike was called off the wheels were set in motion. News of arrests, trials and sentences by magistrates, too numerous to appear in the national dailies, filled columns in the local newspapers. As the repression became more intensive throughout the coalfield in the summer and autumn, and as more and more women were brought up for trial the situation in each valley took on the aspect of persecution and of vengeance. In the West of the coalfield where Welsh was more widely spoken and where, especially in the chapels, there was frequent resort to scriptural analogies, it seemed as though the Chief Constable of the County had taken as his motto Deuteronomy Ch. 32, Verse 42: "I will render vengeance to mine enemies."[1]

A selection of incidents, chosen at random from a perusal of the *South Wales News and Western Mail*, indicates the content of many columns month by month of the local Press in the partlv summarised excerpts that follow, and gives a vivid picture of the first five weeks of repression after the General Strike ended.[2]

May 14th: Communist sent to Gaol. At Bridgend yesterday Bertram Slack (23), Secretary of the Aberavon Communist Party and residing at Thornborough, New Road, Porthcawl, was sentenced to two months with hard labour for being in possession of documents,

address the meeting. 5. Re transforming the Council of Action into a Trades and Labour Council. That the Secretary of the Council of Action circularise the various Labour organisations asking them to appoint representatives to attend an informal meeting to discuss the advisability of converting the Council of Action into a Trades and Labour Council.

6. Re scheme to assist mothers: that a deputation be appointed to interview the various midwives for information as to the number of cases at Bedlinog so that we can report same to the "Women's Committee for the relief of miners' wives and children." (Secretary of Committee) Central Area, D. H. Daines, 12 Tavistock Place, W.C.1.

7. Circularised the following Lodges re transfer from Council of Action to Trades Council:

1. Taff Merthyr, D. Gittings, Miners.
2. Nantwen, W. J. Phillips, Miners.
3. Treharris, Lewis Williams, Miners.
4. Unemployed, J. B. Thomas, Miners.
5. NUR. F. W. Berry Nelson, Railwaymen.
6. Shop Assistants, W. Sheen, Dowlais.
7. Co-op Committee, The Secretary, Co-op Dowlais.

[1]The antagonism between capital and labour was carried sometimes into the religious bodies as, for example, the arrival of a new manager in the Anthracite. When he attended chapel several of the flock would leave to attend another chapel of the same denomination! Or, again, when for the years after the lockout, the game of rugby football would be so arranged in each village that the teams would tend to represent on the one hand the management or upper or lower officials, and on the other hand the face workers and the men on the surface. A consciousness of class infused both the religion and the sport that were cherished in the western valleys.

[2]These excerpts are given, by the kindness of Mr. Hywel Francis, from a more extensive record of disturbances and prosecutions he compiled when engaged in the preparation of his paper in the May number of *Llafur* 1973.

the publication of which was likely to cause disaffection among the civilian population. Harry Lewis, on instruction from Chief Constable of Glamorgan, prosecuted under Section 21 of the Emergency Regulations; "His conduct had caused great anxiety in policing the area." *(S.W. News).* Defendant, after affirmation, said that for 18 months he worked at Port Talbot as a wagon repairer and previously at Cardiff and Gloucester. Member of Communist Party since July 1924. Pleaded Guilty.

May 15th : Pontypool Demonstration. 8,000 took part headed by bands : contingents from Blaenavon, Abersychan, Cwmbran, and Griffithstown. Blaenavon contingent had banners "Workers of the World Unite." Cwmbran banner "Give Us Our Daily Bread."

May 18th : (1) Rhondda men before the magistrates at Pontypridd. Frank Bright (35), colliery repairer, Ynyshir, a householder (had four children of school age, wife in hospital); Emrys G. Llewellyn (24), labourer; Bd. James Lewis (22); Isaac Lewis (17), colliers of Porth. Charges of being in possession of seditious literature likely to cause disaffection amongst people (police, fire brigade or civilian population). The two brothers resided with their mother at Gethin Terrace. Her husband killed underground four years ago. In last nine years Mrs. Lewis had lost four children. She was very upset at two sons being arrested. Bail refused—although all wanted it.

(2) Aberaman Arrests : Question of Bail at Aberdare. Robert Owen (30), a miner, residing with his parents at Margaret Street, Aberaman. Max Goldbert (27), railway worker, lodging at Lewis Street. K. Wilde, collier (23), residing at Hill Street, Aberaman. Had been in area for two years—done no work except acting secretary of unemployed. All charged with being in possession of certain documents, reports and statements, the publication and circulation of which among other persons would be a contravention of the Emergency Regulations. Admitted to bail in the sum of £100 each and sureties of £200 each. One had duplicating machine evidently used to disseminate literature of this kind.

(3) Maesteg and Pontycymmer Men Charges : Three alleged Communists, Aneurin Jones, Greenfield, Maesteg; Wm. Mullins, Maiden Street, Garth; Illtyd Beere, Alexandre Road, Pontycymmer, remanded until Thursday at Bridgend Court on charges of having in their possession certain documents, the publication of which was likely to cause disaffection among the civilian population and to impede transit. Houses of each were raided. Bail granted in the sum of £100 in respect of each of the defendants plus two sureties of a similar amount. Gave undertaking not to carry out any propaganda in the meanwhile.

20th May : "Under the Emergency Powers," (1) Thomas Davies, a labourer, Secretary of the Neath District CP, two months hard labour for being in possession of documents likely to cause disaffection. Accused said he had only been able to work for seventeen weeks in the last three years. Before that he had been employed at the oil works. Formerly in ILP and afterwards Secretary of Local Unemployed Workers' Union but gave that up, he thought they were too slow in moving. Then joined CP February 1926 and two months ago appointed as Secretary. About seventeen members in branch. Not paid. Left ILP—he thought they had failed in their purpose.

(2) Pontypridd Cases: A formal notice of appeal. Mr. Hammond defended on the instruction of the CP. Addressing the two Lewises and Llewellyn, the Stipendiary said that he was prepared to take a certain course in their cases if they would now give an undertaking to abstain from taking part in the propaganda work or circulate or distribute literature of the type which they had before them that day for the next 12 months. Each of the three defendants declined to give three guineas costs. Llewellyn: fined £8 plus two guineas costs or one month in the 2nd division. Daniel James Lewis: fined £8 plus the pledge. Bright: two months in 2nd division and asked to pay two guineas costs or three weeks in the 2nd division. Isaac Lewis: bound over in the sum of £10 to be of good behaviour for six months plus one guinea costs. Formal appeal—granted.

22nd May: Frank Joseph Ceriez (26), a labourer, charged with being found in an enclosed area at the Penylan Bowling and Lawn Tennis Club, Marlborough Road, for an "unlawful purpose" and he was further charged with assaulting Special Constable Harry Terence Hayes, an accountant residing at Marlborough Road. First charge dismissed. Magistrate fined prisoner £5, or one month, for the assault.

22nd May: Thousands of demonstrators from Risca, Abercarn, Cross Keys, Nine Mile Point, Pontymister, Bedwas and Machen—all under jurisdiction of Board of Guardians. Stopped at Bassaleg by police—order read to them by police and Chief Constable of Newport prohibiting, under Emergency Regulations, a procession through the town. Leaders were: Communist, Eddie Morton, Risca; Messrs. Will Lewis, Rd. Clarke, John Jones, Nine Mile Point; Ted James, Machen. decided to send a deputation. Communist, Casey, Newport on deputation—represented Newport Labour Party. Communist Ted James said not much done on Board of Guardians only 21 out of 80 Labour at it. Later Newport Labour Party sent out to Bassaleg for the demonstrators. 200 loaves, 200 lbs. of cheese and 200 gallons of mineral water.

24th May: Two cases of offences calculated to cause sedition and disaffection among the civilian population were dealt with by the Pontypridd magistrate, on Saturday, 22nd, when Anten O' Pulsky (32), a Russian living at Abercarn was sentenced to three months imprisonment and recommended for deportation. Frederick Chapman, a well-known newsagent, of Pontypool and Abersychan, was sentenced to one month's hard labour. Both pleaded not guilty. Chapman was a manager of the firm of "Chapman & Wills" small newspaper vendors and, among other things, had a shop at Abersychan. On 12th May, poster in shop containing short catechism between father and son on the definition of blackleg.

The child, added Mr. Lyne, was supposed to be asking his father "What is a blackleg, daddy?" And his father replied, "A blackleg is a traitor, my boy, who knows not honour or shame." Then the child asked, "Are there any in the Eastern valley, dad?" Father: "No my boy, only the station manager at Abersychan, and two clerks at Crane Street Station." Child: "I am glad your not a blackleg, daddy."

Lyne said: Likely to cause trouble. Poster had been headed "Eastern Valley Joint Industrial Council." Hammond disclaimed all responsibility. Space in window let to "EVJIC." O'Pulsky was a Russian and a Communist and believed to be either local secretary or some other official of the Communist organisation. Came to England in 1913 and, in 1918, being of military age he entered the Army, serving in a Labour Corps. After the war, in army of occupation in Germany. There he met with an accident in respect of which he received a full pension of £2. "His way of showing gratitude to this country was by taking up Communistic work." Also obtained a pedlar's certificate and coupled with peddling the distribution of pamphlets. He distributed leaflets when a notorious Communist named Cant addressed a meeting at Abercarn. O'Pulsky had refused legal advice.

31st May: Pencoed Miners' Leader: Stopped Buses running. Considerable interest was taken in the case at Bridgend on Saturday in which Mervyn Payne, a well known Pencoed miners' leader, who formerly sat on the Glamorgan CC, was charged under the Emergency Regulations with doing an act calculated to impede means of locomotion. Mr. W. M. Thomas defended. Mr. Harry Lewis appeared to prosecute on instructions from the Chief Constable of Glamorgan. Tried to stop buses with blacklegs. Fined £50 or two month's imprisonment. Rd. Griffiths (bus proprietor) of Pontycymer fined £20 or one month and Idrislwyn David (a bus conductor) Pontygog, Pontycymmer, fined £10 for doing an act calculated to restrict locomotion by calling upon Joseph Henry Perkins, a driver in the employ of the S. Wales Commercial Motors Ltd., to drop his bus at Bryncethin on the 6th May.

5th June: Minister fined: Neath court story; sequel to Strike Incidents.

The Rev. Edward Teilo Owen, minister of the Siloh Congregational Chapel, Cwmgwrach, was at Neath yesterday fined £20 or two months on one charge, bound over on another charge arising out of incidents during the General Strike. A third charge not proceeded with. Accused, according to police witnesses, was alleged to have said in Welsh: "We have been squeezed. It is now time to rebel I have turned rebel." Prosecution said: "Likely to cause dissaffection among civilian population during the strike."

To the comrade Thomas Bell
(Lux 154)

Dear comrade,
I thank you very much for your letter, d. 7/8. I have read nothing concerning the english movement last months because of my illness & overwork.

It is extremely interesting what you communicate. Perhaps it is the beginning of the real proletarian mass movement in Great Britain in the communist sense. I am afraid we have till now in England few very feeble propagandist societies for communism (inclusive the British Communist Party) but no really mass communist movement.

If the South Wales Miners Federation has decided on 24/VII to affiliate to the III Int. by a majority of 120 to 63, — perhaps it is the beginning of new era (How much miners there are in England? more than 500 000? How much in South Wales? 25000? How much miners were really represented in Cardiff 24/VII 1921?)

If these miners are not too small minority, if they fraternise with soldiers & begin a real "class war", — we must do all our possible to develop this movement & strengthen it.

Economic measures (like communal kitchens) are good but they are not much important now, before the victory of the proletarian revolution in England. Now the political struggle is the most important.

English capitalists are shrewd, clever, astute. They will support (directly or indirectly) communal kitchens in order to divert the attention from political aims.

What is important, is (if I am not mistaken) 1) to create a very good, really proletarian, really mass communist party in this part of England, — that is such

20 PHOTOGRAPH OF LENIN'S LETTER ON THE SOUTH WALES MINERS (continued overleaf)

party which will really be the leading force in all labour movement in this part of the country. (Apply the resolution on organisation & work of the party adopted by the 3 congress to this part of your country)

2) To start a daily paper of the working class, for the working class in this part of the country.

To start it not as a business (as usually newspapers are started in capitalist countries), not with big sum of money, not in ordinary & usual manner, — but as an economic & political tool of the masses in their struggle.

Either the miners of this district are capable to pay halfpenny daily (for the beginning weekly, if you like) for their own daily (or weekly) newspaper (be it very small, it is not important) — or there is no beginning of the really communist mass movement in this part of your country.

If the communist party of this district cannot collect few £ in order to publish small leaflets daily as a beginning of the really proletarian communist newspaper, — if it so, if every miner will not pay a penny for it, then there is not serious, not genuine affiliation to the III Int.

English government will apply the shrewdest mean in order to suppress every beginning of this kind. Therefore we must be (in the beginning) very prudent. The paper must be not too revolutionary in the beginning. If you will have three editors, at least one must be non communist.[?] (at least two genuine workers) If 9/10 of the workers do not buy this paper, if 2/3 workers $\left(\frac{120}{120+53}\right)$ do not pay special contributions (f.i. 1 penny weekly) for their paper, — it will be no workers' newspaper.

I should be very glad to have few lines from you concerning this theme & I beg to apologise for my bad English.

With communist greetings Lenin.

Defence said wrong interpretation on the words.

Was last candidate (unsuccessful) at Carmarthen against Sir Alfred Mond in last election. Spoke at May Day meeting in Neath district. Moved from Llangeler, Carms. to Cwmgwrach November, 1925.

The three summonses were on the grounds that on 6th May he made a speech likely to cause disaffection amongst the civilian population: that on 12th May he said to Miss Anne E. J. Morgan, an assistant teacher at the Cwmgwrach schools (at Glynneath Station): "Don't come up by this train and support the blacklegs or your services will not be required here." That he made a statement to PC Dd Evans (Cwmgwrach): "I am surprised at you sending your child to a school by a train driven by blacklegs. I will have something to say about that Inspector of yours later. Fancy him shepherding a gang of children from Glynneath to go by train worked by blacklegs and refusing to allow the pickets to speak to them." Mr. Daniel Hopkin, prospective Labour candidate for Carmarthen, defended.

8th June: Pencoed Stir: Werntarw Lodge convened a meeting to discuss non-support given to Mervyn Payne in recent conviction. Two miners' agents, Evan Williams (Maesteg) and Ted Williams (Garw), blamed at a public meeting of trade unionists at the public hall, Pencoed, yesterday for not standing by Mr. Payne, as both agents were members of the Industrial Council which, it was alleged, had issued instructions regarding "bus traffic during the strike." Payne reckoned case would not have succeeded to the extent it did but for the fact that "Mr. Ted Williams had informed the superintendent of police that he (Mr. Payne) was acting without authority in stopping the buses."

21st June: Monmouthshire police Chief asked to resign. By eight votes to seven the Monmouthshire Standing Joint Committee, at Newport on Wednesday, decided to ask the Chief Constable (Mr. Victor Bosanquet) to resign "inasmuch as his actions during emergencies were calculated to disturb the peace of the country." Pointing his finger at the Chief Constable, Mr. Vaughan added with some emphasis:

> They say you are deliberately trying to break the peace. I don't think so, I think it is sheer stupidity, a failure to understand the psychology of our people. When the restraint of the people was wonderful you were irritating them with these prosecutions. It is not Lewis and Gilchrist (two leaders of march to Newport who had been prosecuted) who ought to be prosecuted. The man who ought to be prosecuted as a disturber of the peace is there (pointing to the Chief Constable). The man who ought to be in the dock is there, and his name is Victor Bosanquet."

Sir H. Mather Jackson said that no action could be taken without the leave of the Home Office. It was decided "to confirm the resolution and that the Home Office be so informed." The Standing Joint Committee numbers 26 members, 13 representing the Court of Quarter Sessions and 13 the County Council—all Labour. The Chief Constable was appointed on 1st January, 1894.

6 THE MINERS FIGHT ON

With the double rejection of the Government's mediation proposals of 14th May (by miners and coalowners on 20th May and 21st May respectively) it seemed as though all had gone back to square one of the lockout, and that the two sides were once more in full confrontation. On the miners' side, however, the reckoning had to be not only with the coalowners but with the increasingly hostile attitude of the Government. The Baldwin-Churchill Cabinet at the time of their ignominious retreat[1] on Red Friday, before the TUC threat of industrial action, had given its backing to the mineowners. Then in conceding the owner's full claim (for this is what the subsidy implicitly did) Baldwin completely ignored the critical recommendations of the McMillan Court of Enquiry, including the highly-skilled advice of Sir Josiah Stamp, leading economist and, as Chairman of the Midland Railway, leading capitalist of Britain.

The same Government, which over seven months later had been compelled against its own preconceptions to accept on the 24th March the report of the (Samuel) Royal Commission on the Coal Industry, now took the first opportunity of withdrawing from its conditional acceptance. From their point of view the Samuel Commission had served its purpose: and, with the General Strike ended in a surrender to the Cabinet on the 12th May, their arguments against subscribing to the Samuel Commission resumed their full force. But this did not mean that the Government "resumed a position of neutrality": on the contrary, even while nominally subscribing to the Samuel Commission Report, they had in the last days of April been sending out "guidance" recommendations to the newspapers to bring up and stress the question of longer hours against which the Samuel Commission had given its report.

A month later, having withdrawn its propositions of 14th May, put forward (as it appeared to many at the time) in Baldwin's hours of sudden panic that the arranged surrender might not be effective (as shown in the speech broadcast on the night of Thursday, 13th May) and that the workers would not obey their leaders' call to return to work, but would continue the General Strike,[2] the Government now,

[1]*Commons Hansard* 6 viii 1925.

[2]**Baldwin on Thursday evening** *(Hansard)*: "The supreme interest of this country today requires that the largest body of men possible should be brought back to work at the earliest possible moment.

"I will not countenance any attack on the part of any employers to use this present occasion for trying in any way to get reductions in wages below those in force before the strike or any increase of hours.

"At a time like this there are some who like fishing in troubled waters. **Let us get the workers calm as soon as we can, lest their work spoils the work of half a century."**

Extracts from *The General Strike, May 1926*: *Its Origin and History* by R. Page Arnot for the Labour Research Department.

step by step, yielded to the successive standpoints put forward by the Mining Association of Great Britain.

The miners, therefore, during the rest of the summer and autumn had to reckon with the Government seemingly carrying out the function of an "impartial government," but actually, both legislatively and otherwise, giving its full support to the coalowners. It was an unequal struggle.

To many, after the lapse of half a century, it may seem inconceivable that a Government equipped with all the necessary economic and statistical information should have swallowed the propaganda of an interested party, should apparently have believed that once the men underground were working longer hours and with lower wages, then prosperity would return to the coal industry, unemployment would vanish and the whole of British economy would get back on a sound basis. Today, of course, it is clear that the unorganised industry stubbornly sticking to the competitive system of the early 19th century, had been a chief obstacle to the reconstruction of British economy after the war of 1914/1918.

But the Government blindly trusted to the prescience of the coalowners who, with no obligations except to their shareholders, continued all their previous practices with complete unconsciousness of sin. Except as citizens they had no responsibility for British economy as a whole. Their standpoint that their favoured mid-19th century position in the markets of the world could be sustained mainly by long hours and low wages was derived from their continuance with a capital structure that was already obsolescent in the eighties and early nineties when their rivals in Germany and the United States were already making market conditions difficult. These two rivals reorganised, or rather organised, the coal industry both in the gigantic Pennsylvania coalfields, and in the German Ruhr with the Westphalia Coal Syndicate. In spite of the warnings by the ablest for this period of British capitalist coalowners, Sir George Elliot, who proposed a National Trust with a board of nine men in 1893, the industry continued as though there had been no change since half a century earlier in national and world conditions. The British owners in their several thousand pits had chosen more and more immediate profits rather than undertake the task of re-equipping their industry to cope with their emergent rivals, and the ever-changing market conditions.

Whatever may appear now to have been the historic short-sightedness of the Government in embracing an industry whose obsolescence, signalled by successive Royal Commissions, had been demonstrated by its history in the 20th century as a menace to the continued prosperity of the economy as a whole, there can be no doubt that at the time the yielding of the Baldwin/Churchill Cabinet to the most extreme demands of the coalowners was immediately detrimental. It was a self-inflicted blow, marking a stage in decadence and in the decline of the British Empire.

The effect of the Government's action was immediately to be seen both at home and abroad, alike in Europe and the Far East, where the miners' seventh-months lock-out was a shield to the Chinese Revolution.

Finances, already on a narrow edge by the Churchill return to Gold Standard of Spring 1925, were rocked in their prospects. The balance of payments went by the board. On the 20th May, Churchill, as Chancellor of the Exchequer, in the House of Commons, put direct expenditure by the Government as well-nigh a million pounds. As to other costs of the strike or lock-out, he considered that up to three weeks would not make much difference as it could be repaired within a year; but that, if these conditions (that is, the lock-out) were to continue for another thirteen weeks, the damage to British economy would be such as to set them back for many years. In the event, it was to last over twice as long and the damage was not twice as great, but as he himself indicated, immeasurably greater.

At the end of the unequal struggle between miners on the one hand and mineowners plus Government on the other, the miners were defeated; but the others were not victorious. All three were plunged into ruin. Not greed on the part of the embattled coalowners was primarily responsible; but rather the Government's insensate commitment to backing an example of "private enterprise" (forsaking the ordinary dictates of statesmanship and political prudence) that was economically, industrially and technologically obsolescent.

In the annals, tales and legends of antiquity from which so much of "Western" civilisation is derived, one of the practices least acceptable to modern opinion, whether capitalist or socialist, was that found amongst militaristic Lacedoemonians whereby each year, ritually, the Spartan ephors declared civil war upon their helots, outlawed them, put them beyond the pale, subjected them to special penalties and indignities. A society wherein lip-service had come to be given to democracy and liberty and equality before the law had reached a stage, at the end of the War of Empires (1914/1918), where the methods to maintain the effective and unquestioned dominance of the ruling class became subject to great stress periodically. Thereupon the Emergency Powers Act of November 1920 converted Britain to what Churchill himself called a "Police State." The Royal Proclamation was signed on 30th April, 1926. For the better prevention of clandestine outlawries, there was provision that Regulations be debated. They went through the House of Commons on 3rd May.

By mid-May it was obvious that the danger proclaimed (but hardly anticipated) had vanished. Nevertheless, the Proclamation was renewed in June. This ritual declaration of civil war upon the miners and their families, uttered each month and each month debated in Parliament, was to continue until the rulers were satisfied that the miners had been utterly and completely defeated.

The apparatus of these hostilities was sufficiently massive. In the speeches of Joynson-Hicks, the Home Secretary, it was revealed in the first week of May that not only had the country been partitioned into ten districts, in each of which a Civil Commissioner excercised dictatorial powers, subordinating to himself all the powers for enforcement of law and order of all local authorities (and in particular all the police and all the armed forces of the Crown, naval and military), but that no less than 250,000 Special Constables, drawn from the middle-classes, were enrolled to cope with the widespread strike situation, and that they were armed in certain areas with what Joynson-Hicks estimated at 47,000 truncheons. But these somewhat inordinate preparations were not considered necessary to anything like the same degree for each monthly period.

In the longer period of nearly seven months, from mid-May onwards, the miners and those workers who sympathised with them had therefore each month to reckon with the regular forces at the disposal of the Government, plus a varying amount of middle-class opponents aroused into hostility by the Home Secretary and his policy of setting "class against class."

Against this the miners could reckon on working class sympathy and help. While abroad they could find in every country, however remotely, a measure of support expressed in messages and in money, from small amounts to the gigantic contribution of the trade unionists within the USSR totalling over £1,200,000.

Within Britain the Tory Cabinet did not have the entire support of the other parties or interests. Although the majority of the Liberal Party had gone over "lock, stock and barrel" to solidarity with the Tories, acute criticism was delivered by Lloyd George: nor did the Archbishop of Canterbury or the leaders of the Free Churches give support to mineowners and Government—points of view that found occasional expression.

But for the most part the owners and their Cabinet had the full backing of the main capitalist Press with combined circulation approaching twenty millions, together with all the popular and the learned periodicals.

In stark contrast the miners' supporters in the Press were a feeble band and few. The *Daily Herald*, being mainly controlled by Labour leaders and members of the General Council, could not give that support with the same degree of whole-heartedness as most of its readers and trade unionist employees would have wished.[1]

[1]A miner who sat on the Executive Committee of the national Labour Party wrote in mid-July:

"After eleven weeks of the most bitter struggle that has ever been waged, when all the forces of the most merciless ruling class the world has ever seen have been brought to bear on the miners, when imprisonment has been the lot of hundreds of their fellows, we read an advertisement in Labour's only daily that the mines can only pay if we submit."

There was support of the various party organs such as the *New Leader* for the ILP and the *Workers' Weekly* for the Communist Party, while amongst the independent weeklies *Lansbury's Labour Weekly* played a very big part, having as its regular writers many who were devoting their energies to the miners' cause, such as Ellen Wilkinson, MP.

Then there was the *Sunday Worker* which, as we have seen, was to some extent an organ of A. J. Cook, as well as of the Left Wing trade unionists in alliance with the Communist Party.

Amongst the monthlies, *Trade Union Unity*, the organ of the Anglo-Soviet trade union alliance to bring about an international merger, edited by the Chairman of the International Federation of Trade Unions, Alfred A. Purcell, had, from its beginning in April, 1925, supported the miners' cause.

The organ of the National Council of Labour Colleges, the *Plebs*, born in 1909 from amongst the students of the South Wales Miners' Federation, and having as its presiding spirit Noah Ablett, gave as always its support to the miners' cause.

The *Labour Monthly*, from which in the early months of 1924 had come the first impetus to the formation of a Left Wing in the General Council and amongst leading trade unionists, had from summer 1924 onwards so conducted the ideological struggle that in some quarters it came to be regarded almost as though it were an external organ of the Miners' Federation of Great Britain, with regular articles in it by Herbert Smith and A. J. Cook, and by A. A. Purcell and others.

The Miners' Federation was able to take advantage of these periodicals, all putting forth considerable encouragement. For day to day purposes, however, the Executive Committee of the Miners' Federation relied on the connection built up with the Labour Research Department, which had provided all the statistical and other material both for the Buckmaster Court of Inquiry in the spring of 1924, and for the joint enquiry asked for by the owners in the autumn of 1924, in which its staff had been accustomed to work with the Miners' Executive at their head office in 55 Russell Square. In the preparation for the Royal Commission on the Coal Industry, the Labour Research Department had again been called in to aid : and on 15th February, 1926, added to its mining publications *The Coal Crisis* : *facts from the Samuel Coal*

Dealing with the argument "that to refuse such an advertisement would be interfering with the liberty of the Press," he answered :

"That was not said when the advertisement of the Minority Movement was refused. Liberty of the Press when we are fighting for the liberty to exist. O, Liberty, what crimes are still committed in thy name. Freedom of the Press, and a Labour Press, to which the miners have given their all, when we are fighting in the North to retain the shorter working-day that was won for this generation half a century ago."

(*The Miners' Struggle in the North* by Will Lawther, *Labour Monthly*, August 1926 (page 473)).

Commission, of which 2,500 copies were sold in the first week. The price was one shilling and within a month a cheap edition was being sold to affiliated societies at five shillings a dozen.

After 12th May, the day of the TUC General Council's surrender, with little help to come from the headquarters of either TUC or Labour Party—or their entourage—the Labour Research Department was called upon more than ever to help to meet new problems that successively emerged in the two hundred days that followed.

From the end of May, throughout the greater part of the lock-out, the LRD staff (including Emile Burns, Dame Margaret Cole, Eva Reckitt and D. J. Parsons) from their office beside Eccleston Square (then jointly occupied by the TUC and Labour Party) was in daily contact with the MFGB offices in Russell Square where, latterly, a room was occupied by the Secretary of the LRD who also, on occasion, accompanied the national officials to Paris and elsewhere in the endeavour to maintain a flow of assistance as a token of international working class solidarity. Thus, it was possible to help at speed with the issue of statements or other weapons in the armoury of the ideological warfare and propaganda: and by 1st June this was regularised when R. Page Arnot was appointed chief strike propagandist by the MFGB.[1]

At a later stage, when after eleven weeks of lock-out in certain areas pits were opening up, the leak in the dyke was plugged up by a renewal and intensification of propaganda, both written and spoken, especially by meetings at or near the collieries affected. The malign hopes of further weakening, expressed by the employers and in the newspapers, were dashed to the ground by the effectiveness of the propaganda. The written propaganda included six new leaflets for distribution at meetings "prepared in conjunction with the Secretary of the Miners' Federation of Great Britain by the Labour Research Department, 162 Buckingham Palace Road, SW1, and printed by the Co-operative Printing Society, Tudor Street, London EC4," namely No. 1, Bad Organisation: 2, The Drain of Royalties; 3, The Drain of the Middleman: 4, Miners' Wages: 5, Mussolinis and Hours; 6, Coal Boss Baldwin. Later there followed "Miners' Leaflets" Nos. 7 to 25.

At the end of the third week of July, it was recorded that there "was a great decrease in the number of miners working in Warwickshire

[1]The *Morning Post* of Friday, 18th June, 1926, (on the anniversary of the Battle of Waterloo) in an angry editorial seeking to prove that the "industrial dispute" was not very different from a "revolutionary conspiracy" fomented by communists, wrote:

"Again, the man who has been appointed by the Miners' Executive to assist Mr. Cook in propaganda is that notorious Communist and Revolutionary, Mr. R. Page Arnot. If any miner has any lingering doubts as to the opinions of the man who has been appointed to present the miners' point of view to the public, let him read the extracts from an article by Mr. Arnot which appears in the *Labour Monthly*. His is evidently one of those ensanguined minds which busy themselves continually in a horrible nightmare of class war. He lives but to use the working class as an instrument of his violent designs."

as a result of Mr. A. J. Cook's weekend campaign". These weekend campaigns, which had begun earlier, now became an outstanding feature of the struggle of a kind that could hardly ever have occurred on the same scale before in the history of trade unionism. Each weekend, in one coalfield or another A. J. Cook addressed meetings that summer and autumn in the open air—meetings of miners only, coming by omnibus or other vehicle from every part of their county to get inspiration and encouragement from the burning eloquence of A. J. Cook. Other miners' leaders seconded him, together with, as a matter of course, all the 42 miners' Members of Parliament.[1]

7 A RIFT IN THE LUTE

For the first eight weeks of the lockout the South Wales' Miners Federation were in full accord with the MFGB Executive Committee and the National Officers. But then came a rift in the lute. In Cardiff the Executive Council discussed the national situation and decided that Smith and Cook be told of the "disapproval of this Council of statements made in public contrary to the National Conference proceedings" (26 vi 1926). To this same Executive Council meeting Aneurin Bevan came on deputation to complain "that while the working levels and sale of coal was stopped in the Tredegar District, it had not been stopped in Ebbw Vale and this was resented."

Three weeks later, to the full Executive Council with 37 present, Vice-President S. O. Davies disclosed proposals (which were "not to be divulged" by members of the MFGB Executive Committee) whereupon it was resolved:

[1]The author was present along with Cook at a meeting in summer 1926 at Haydock, near St. Helens, in the Lancashire coalfield where Joe Tinker (1875-1957), the local MP, was the other chief speaker. The scene was impressive to a degree. In a field which sloped slightly upwards, almost with the effect of an amphitheatre, to the high wall at the back of a gas works there were seated on the ground, in row after row, tens of thousands of miners. A platform had been erected and on this Cook moved about a little, speaking to one quarter of the field after another. As he spoke he kept repeating himself three to four times and as the points he made went home the applause beginning in one segment of the field would spread to another, and then to another. If there were biting jests uttered or simple jokes that went home to the hearts of the colliers the ripple of laughter could be seen spreading from those seated in the front right up through all the innumerable rows to the furthest back segment. Some of the London Press overstated the attendance as beyond 80,000 on the ground. The "quality Press" or some of them, put it at 50,000; while the *Manchester Guardian*, ever cautious and designedly prone to understatement, estimated 35,000 present: a solitary guess amongst the skilled estimators of Fleet Street and the provincial Press. It may be there are police estimates but it is very doubtful as the police kept strictly away from these gatherings. There was not yet the use of amplifiers, there were no mikes, no loudspeakers, nothing but the human voice rivalling in its sonority and its resonance the legendary speaking powers of the missionary St. Columba (whose voice we are told reached for over a mile in the West of Scotland) or of that orator who could move the very stones to rise in mutiny.

There was indeed something legendary about Arthur Cook.

That having before us the intimation that the National Executive has empowered a deputation of Church leaders to approach the Government in order to put before it terms which are in opposition to Conference decisions, this Council instructs the Secretary to communicate with the MFGB Committee urging that the authority to present these proposed terms of settlement be withdrawn pending the calling of a National Conference to discuss the matter (17 vii 1926).

At the same time the Secretary of the Durham Miners' Association had been similarly instructed:

Dear Mr. Cook—At a meeting of our Executive Committee yesterday the enclosed resolution was passed, and I was instructed to forward same on to the Miners' Federation Executive Committee. I shall be glad, therefore, if you will submit same to the next meeting of the Executive Committee. Yours faithfully, W. P. Richardson.

Durham Miners' Association, Red Hill, Durham.

Resolution.

As an Executive Committee we protest against the action of the National Executive in empowering the members of the Christian Fellowship Society to meet the Prime Minister on behalf of the miners on definitely arranged terms, which suggest that a subsidy should be continued for a short period and re-organisation work to be thoroughly gone into, at the end of which short period if no settlement is arrived at on the matters in dispute an independent chairman must be appointed to decide between the two parties, which is accepting the principle of compulsory arbitration which the miners have already refused. The procedure, in an important step like this, ought to have been that the districts should at first have considered and decided upon such a step and then been confirmed, or otherwise, by a national conference. This, in our opinion, is subversive to the policy of the Federation.

At the MFGB Special Conference a fortnight later, on Friday, 30th July, South Wales delegates turned up in strength, mustering 58 out of 169 delegates present. Enoch Morrell, JP, president, was able to report that "our men are solid with the exception of about 100. There is one little colliery in Little England, where there are 20 men employed. Another colliery is being developed, a new colliery, where I understand about 50 men are employed."

After Cook had reported upon "proposals agreed with representatives of the Christian Churches," Morrell put forward the South Wales criticism and was followed immediately by James Robson of Durham who said:

We protest against the action of the Executive Committee in connection with this document, because we hold it embodies a serious departure from the policy of the Federation. We realise the position of the officials, but the thing is that it is a clear departure from the fixed, decided and determined policy of this Federation. At the very last Conference we had you submit a resolution yourself in which you protested against a clause in the Government's proposals which made provision for an independent chairman to determine whether agreements that maybe come to had to be national or district. There might be some little difference in the circumstances surrounding the two documents but the principle is the same.[1]

There was then a sharp exchange in debate, personalities were exchanged between Herbert Smith and Arthur Horner and on the other hand between Cook and George Spencer, MP. Horner said, "that he regretted the personal attack that was made based on what was contained in his article written to *The Sunday Worker* on the Bishops' proposals", wherein the only reference to the officials had been : "Cook and Smith and the rest of the Executive must be told that we refuse to follow them because of their policy and not because of themselves." Then Jack Williams, formerly of the Garw Valley and now Secretary of the Forest of Dean Miners' Association, rose to contravene what Cook had said, as follows :

It has been Mr. Cook's slogan 'Not a minute on a day, not a penny off the pay'— and even up to a few days ago he declared that we must stand loyally by the position that we have taken up hitherto . . . I wish to say that with regard to Mr. Cook's reference to the Forest of Dean I am going to challenge him to come to the Forest of Dean to a mass meeting on Sunday and repeat his statement there, making an attack on the Forest of Dean (30 vii 1926).

Cook interjected, "Keep to the facts if you can," the chairman intervened, "Let's have order." Aneurin Bevan, from South Wales, then said :

I did not intend, like quite a number of my colleagues, to say anything at all until we had the extraordinary speech of Mr. Cook and Mr. Spencer. I don't know what has come over the psychology of the Conference. I say this that many of us remember 1921. Some of the younger men remember even more than the older men. I am speaking for my colleagues in South Wales, and say that if we go back home from

[1]**Proposals agreed upon with representatives of the Christian Churches.**

1. Immediate resumption of work on conditions obtaining on 30th April, 1926, including hours and wages. The settlement, when arrived at, shall be on the basis of a national agreement.

2. A national settlement to be reached within a short defined period, not exceeding four months. In order to carry through Clause 1 financial assistance be granted by the Government during the defined period, under a scheme to be drawn up by the Commissioners who prepared the Report. The Commissioners shall be reappointed for this and for the other purposes mentioned in the following clauses.

3. The terms of the reorganisation scheme and the reference to wages in the Report to be worked out in detail by the Commissioners, and the results to be incorporated by them, as far as may be necessary, in a Parliamentary Bill or Bills.

4. Those parts of the reorganisation scheme capable of early application to be put into operation at the earliest moment practicable.

5. The Government to give assurance that those parts of the Report which require legislative sanction shall be placed on the Statute Book at the earliest possible moment.

6. At the end of the defined period, if disagreements should still exist, a Joint Board, consisting of representatives of both parties, shall appoint an independent chairman, whose award in settlement of these disagreements shall be accepted by both parties.

this Conference giving an account of the defeatist speeches we have listened to this morning we shall be in practically an impossible position to rebuild the South Wales Miners' Federation for a number of years. It would be better for our men to be defeated as a consequence of their own physical exhaustion than it would be to be defeated as a consequence of any moves we are taking. We know what has taken place since 1921, and I am saying this with perfect sincerity.

Mr. Pearson of Durham said :

It has been a revelation to me. This is my first appearance at a National Conference as a delegate from a district, and if any one would have told me I should have heard such utterances from our leaders I would not have believed them, not even if they were the Archangel. What about the rank and file; is there not their morale ? (30 vii 1926).

Gill, of Bristol, counter-attacked Aneurin Bevan while Fred Swift, of Somerset, was in agreement with George Spencer. When it came to be moved : "That the proposals be sent back to districts with a recommendation for their acceptance and that a Conference be called if necessary" (30 vii 1926). Voting was 451 for and 339 against. The minority was made up of 130 from South Wales, 120 from Durham, 75 from Lancashire, 5 from Forest of Dean, and 9 from Cumberland. A sharp division of opinion was clear.

By 10th August, 1926, the result of the District voting on the proposals agreed upon with the representatives of the Christian churches was known.[1]

A Special Conference of the South Wales Miners' Federation was held at the Cory Hall, Cardiff, on 7th August, 1926. Mr. Enoch Morrell,

[1] **Result of District vote on the proposals of representatives of the Christian Churches.**

District	No.	In favour of proposals	Against proposals
Bristol	1,900	1,900	—
*Cleveland	5,000	—	—
Cokemen	4,200	4,200	—
Cumberland	8,500	—	8.500
Derbyshire	35,000	35,000	—
Durham	120,000	120,000	—
Group No. 1	19,600	19.600	—
Forest of Dean	5.000	—	5,000
Kent	2,000	2,000	—
Lancashire	75,000	—	75.000
Leicester	7,000	7,000	—
Midlands	60,000	60,000	—
Northumberland	37,836	37,836	—
North Wales	10,000	10,000	—
Nottingham	25,000	25.000	—
*Scotland	80,000	—	—
Somerset	4,500	4,500	—
South Derby	6,000	6.000	—
South Wales	129,150	—	129,150
Yorkshire	150.000	—	150,000
Totals	785.686	333.036	367.650

* No vote taken.

JP, President, (in the Chair) gave a report of the progress of the dispute since the last Conference, and explained how the proposals for a settlement known as the "Churches' Formula", came before Conference. He also dealt with the Eight Hours Act passed by Parliament, intimating that there must be a continuous fight until this Act will be repealed: this action of the Government was an indication that they had combined with the coalowners to crush the miners. He emphatically stated that the miners of Britain cannot be crushed, and will not rest content until justice and fair play are meted out to them.

After some discussion by the Conference the suggested terms of settlement were rejected by 165 votes to 78.

Baldwin and his "American cable" brought a resolution:

This Conference expresses its strongest possible protest and indignation with the action of the Prime Minister in his further attempt to support the coalowners in their fight to starve the miners and their families into submission. We consider his American communication as despicably mean and untrue, as well as a dishonourable degradation of the office of Prime Minister of this country. It is also a complete disclosure of his hypocritical protestations that during the whole of the proceedings in connection with this struggle he has not supported the coalowners (7 viii 1926).

The comment in the September issue of the *Colliery Workers' Magazine* ran as follows:

It is difficult to imagine anything more mean, contemptible and misleading than the cable which Mr. Baldwin sent to the American Press to prejudice the efforts of the representatives of the Trade Union Movement in their appeal for funds on behalf of the miners and their dependants. He must know that his allegation that there is no distress in the coalfields is untrue, for this has been clearly revealed by Mr. Chamberlain, the Minister of Health, in dealing with the estimates and the administration through the Boards of Guardians for Poor Law Relief.

At the MFGB Special Conference in the Kingsway Hall, London, on Monday, 16th August, at 2 p.m., there was a resumption of the debate and a motion was made by George Spencer to open up negotiations. The number at work was given and after two days of rather sharp discussion, with Ebby Edwards now entering the fray, there was a decision on two matters. The first was Baldwin's message to America; in similar terms to the South Wales decision already quoted, it voiced their protest[1] and drew conclusions.

[1]That this Conference emphatically protests against the action of the Prime Minister in sending an untrue communication to the American Press timed to reach America when the Miners' Federation delegation landed in that country. This was done obviously with the object of preventing, so far as he possibly could, the American Trade Unionists and general public from subscribing to the fund for the relief of the wives and children of the British miners who are the principal sufferers through the lock-out of the miners by the mineowners. This affords further evidence that the Government has definitely decided to assist the mineowners to defeat the miners by starvation (16 viii 1926).

The second decision was that "the principle of opening up negotiations be accepted". This was carried by 428 votes against 360, the minority being made up of South Wales, Lancashire, Forest of Dean and Yorkshire, who were no longer backing Herbert Smith.

The view of the South Wales delegation upon the whole matter had been largely determined by the vote of the South Wales Conference, when a majority decided to turn down the Churches' proposals so that the spokesman for South Wales and the South Wales vote favoured the position of no compromise.

In the light of the subsequent meeting held on the 19th August, of the coalowners and our National Executive members, I have no hesitation in saying that had the Conference anticipated the reception we received, the decision would have been different. It is very difficult to conceive of anything more callous than the treatment meted out to our representatives by Mr. Evan Williams, the coalowners' chairman. His opening remarks were:

'I do not know whether with your recent ecclesiastical associations you have developed the habit of starting the proceedings with prayer and a hymn, and I hope you will not find it strange if we do away with that this afternoon, and get straight on to business.'

Needless to say the meeting was abortive, and that the coalowners' position is that there is to be an increase in the working day. There is to be no National Agreement with a National minimum, but that wages must be determined by the capacity of each District to pay. We are therefore faced with a new issue which overwhelms all others, and that is, that the coalowners are determined to smash the Miners' Federation. Upon this there can be but one voice, viz, a fight to a finish.

8 THE WAR OF ATTRITION (JULY TO DECEMBER)

By the beginning of July 1926 the miners' struggle had already lasted over nine weeks and, just by this, had shattered the Government's hopes (the nine-day General Strike past) of a speedy ending to it all. Thereafter came a war of attrition, with the Cabinet seeking to wear down the resistance of a community of nearly five million men, women and children whose main resource was help from other trade unionists at home and abroad, above all from those in the USSR. It was a stretch of civil strife, whence came, in the end, defeat upon the mining community but no victory to the Government, sitting in Whitehall amid the ruins of its economy, vainly seeking comfort in the assurances of what would come in the promised land of lower wages and longer hours.

In a contemporary magazine it was written of the miners' struggle at midsummer:

"What of the miners themselves? Of them it is as it was in the *Song of the Fight at Maldon* well-nigh a thousand years ago:

Mind shall be harder,
Heart the keener,
Mood shall be greater
As our might lessens."

From South Wales this greater mood spreading throughout the coalfields brought a stiffening of resolve and a strengthening of the strategy. The "seven-month lockout" lasted for over thirty weeks until the last day of November. Then, and then only, the Executive Council of the South Wales Miners' Federation met the Monmouthshire and South Wales Coal Owners' Association to accept their terms. Two features of this epic, with all its episodes over 200 days in 20 valleys may briefly be recalled. The first being the behaviour of the authorities and, second, the democratic policy of the SWMF Executive Council, as laid down by successive delegate conferences and as ratified, or otherwise, by ballot vote of the members themselves.

From the Royal Proclamation on 30th April the Emergency Powers' Act was enforced. Month after month the Emergency Regulations were debated in Parliament. In practice the duty of repression fell largely upon the Chief Constable of each county with the consequence of his behaviour coming under public scrutiny. Victor Bosanquet, Chief Constable of Monmouthshire, was asked to resign by the Standing Joint Committee. Next month the matter came up of the Carmarthenshire Chief Constable. What the behaviour of Chief Constables or of their subordinate officials was and how it was received, can be judged by excerpts (given below from the *South Wales News* and *Western Mail)* from mid-summer to the end of 1926.

13th July: In his quarterly report to the Standing Joint Committee (Col. F. D. W. Drummond, CBE, presiding) the Chief Constable, Mr. W. Phillips, stated that miners' conduct had been exemplary; that police were using motor cycles to advantage but that such vehicles were also used by "Communist despatch riders." Of the Council of Action at Llanelly, he said "its bark was worse than its bite." A fortnight later an Ammanford public meeting called for the resignation of Chief Constable and a resolution to this effect[1] submitted by Edgar Bassett

[1]"That this public meeting of the citizens of Ammanford and district enters its protest against the action of the Chief Constable and the Standing Joint Committee in sending extra police into the town and neighbourhood. It expresses its indignation of this insult to the community that has for 12 weeks been engaged in a struggle for the right to a decent existence without causing the slightest disturbance of the peace. It also protests against the shameful squandering of the peoples' money on parasitic police when relief to the miners' wives and children is being shamefully cut down all over the country. It protests against the Chief Constable's interference in the merits or demerits of the dispute in the mining industry, an industry of whose economics the Chief Constable displays such a profound ignorance.

"It calls upon the Labour representatives on the County Council to take steps to prevent the Chief Constable of Carmarthenshire menacing the peace of the county by tabling a resolution demanding his resignation, on the grounds that he is not a fit and proper person to be in charge of the maintenance of the peace in the Carmarthen district."

and seconded by D. Price of Tycross, was carried unanimously.

How much the police took account of complaints from elected representatives was shown at the end of August in Monmouthshire:

31st August: Under the heading, "Baton Charge at Pontypool," the newspaper reports a demonstration against men working at the Quarry Lane, Pontypool. A squad of police under Superintendent Spendlove drew their truncheons and charged 900 to 1,000 miners, several of whom were injured. A deputation of Jenkins, Coldrick, Edwards and others, appointed at an earlier meeting to interview the 39 workmen who have returned to their employment on pre-stoppage terms and cards reported. The crowd of 200 booed when told by deputation that men refused to stop work. Stones were thrown; police already there; police attacked demonstrators with their batons. A crowd of women shouted at the police, "You dirty swine," "You miserable cowards," etc.

Mr. Arthur Jenkins, the Miners' Agent, mounted a coal truck and shouted that the police had acted with terrible ferocity. He had seen an old man, who was sitting down peaceably, struck by a truncheon in a most wanton manner. Police reinforcements were rushed up from all parts of the country in motor cars, and eventually the crowd dispersed."

★ ★ ★

14th September: "A Police Ban on Miners' March". The march from Rhondda Valley to protest against Pontypridd's Board of Guardians' cuts in relief scales was vindicated by the Standing Joint Committee at its quarterly meeting in Cardiff on 13th September. G. Dolling (Ynyshir) proposed resolution against Lindsay's action. Sir Rhys Williams, Bart., DSO, KC, defended Lindsay but was defeated by a large majority.

In other discussion warm tributes were paid to the general conduct of the people of the County during a most trying period. It was mentioned that an area near Pencoed was "ringed off" to forbid meetings owing to "influences at work from London." The ban is now removed. This too was included in Chief Constable's report. Resolutions were received from SWMF lodges and other bodies protesting against Lindsay's action. Lindsay said that he had no instances of the police interfering with peaceful picketing.

★ ★ ★

25th September: Ogmore Vale miners and women sent for trial (further charges of intimidation and unlawful assembly brought against some of them). Committed to the Assizes.

28th September: Ton Pentre August Scenes. Unlawful assembly and intimidation on 23rd August against:

Charles Clarke
Walter J. Hunt
William Eynon
John D. Phillips

Unlawful Assembly against:

Wm. J. Mears
J. Orledge
John Howard
John Regent
Edgar Lewis
Alf Harris
Alf Bridgeman
Rose Keast
Agnes Lowe
Cissie Jones
Martha Clemens
May Clemens
Annie Howells
Thos. Davies
Alf C. Clarke
Wm. G. Hunt
Catherine Williams

Assault on Arnold Barnes:

Rose Keast
Agnes Lowe
Cissie Jones
Kate Jones
May Clemens

★ ★ ★

14th October: Rhondda Urban District Council passed resolution protesting against the introduction of police into the Treorchy and Cwmparc districts, calling for an investigation as to how and why they were introduced and whom was to bear the cost of their introduction.

★ ★ ★

Headlines of 15th October: Lorry Set on Fire; More Ugly Scenes at Cymmer; Police Charge Crowd after Stone Fusillade; Officer Hauled off Motor Cycle by Boulder; Driver Pulled off Motor Lorry; Police Charabanc Arrives; Police Charge Crowd.

★ ★ ★

Headlines of 16th October: Twelve Police Injured; More Rioting at Cymmer; Sanguinary Encounters; Women Hurt in Police Charge; 47 Miners Injured (including three women); The Village is stated to be in a terrified state; Fetch Them Out.

Mrs. Elvira Bailey, an elderly woman, of High Street, Treorchy, was given two months for throwing a stone at P.C. Thos. McCullough. Rhondda Stipendiary (D. Lleufer Thomas): "You threw the first stone at the P.C. and you set a very bad example to the women of the district. I find that the women have been taking too prominent a part in these disturbances, and I must impose a penalty that will be a deterrent to others" (3 xi 1926).

8th November: Communist Meetings banned by Police. Aberdare Communist Party meeting (speaker Joseph Vaughan, ex-mayor of Bethnal Green) banned by Home Office—first in Aberdare Valley under Emergency Power Regulations.

★ ★ ★

19th November: Glamorgan Assizes: Record Crime Calendar. 395 intimidation charges. Heaviest on record for Swansea. Of 395 persons named, 344 were charged with riot, intimidation, unlawful assembly, or other kindred offences arising out of the circumstances connected with the coal dispute in groups of from 2 to 45 (latter Pontypridd area). All these cases would be taken after 29th November.

★ ★ ★

23rd November: Ammanford Communist Fined. Lauchlan M. Stewart summoned on two counts under Emergency Powers Regulations. (1) Having done a certain act calculated to prevent proper working of Emlyn Colliery, Penygroes, by publishing document inciting workmen to cease work on 27th October; (2) For distributing a document containing statement the publication of which was likely to cause disaffection amongst the civil population. Fined £20 or two months. Paid by a person in court.[1]

★ ★ ★

24th November: Panteg, Pontypool disturbance of 30th October. Arthur Jenkins, agent, 42 (County Councillor) also charged with inciting his co-defendants to riot. All charged with riotous assembly. Riot took place at Quarry Level Colliery. Case adjourned until today.

★ ★ ★

25th November: Tylorstown Cases. Dock in the Criminal Court at Swansea too small. 47 of 48 accused accommodated in the public gallery of the court which had been cleared for the occasion. Thomas Evans (a prisoner) failed to surrender to his bail.

Prisoners were:

Wm. Parfitt (31), checkweigher
Rd. Williams (27), labourer
Geo. Maslin (34), stoker
Stephen Davies (39), labourer
Emlyn Davies (30), collier
Thos. Thomas (30), collier
John E. Jones (26), engine driver

[1]These "documents" were sometimes single sheets of paper comparable to the leaflets with which local shopkeepers promote their wares—or, in some cases, a typewritten or stencilled sheet of the kind normally and frequently issued by churches and voluntary organisations.

Joseph Harrison (29), haulier
Henry Collingbourne (39), labourer
George Jones (28), labourer
Benj. Lewis (30), labourer
John Hughes (35), collier
Edward Davies (50), collier
Wm. Coombes (43), collier
Ward Davies (38), labourer
James Cooksly (38) haulier
Edward Ballings (26), collier
Wm. John Davies (28), labourer
Edgar Jacob (28), collier
Thos. Morgan (52), collier
James Mathews (37)
John Lewis Richards (30), labourer
Wm. Davies, collier
Geo. Stiff (42), labourer
John Davies (51), collier
Thos. Maslin (30), repairer
Wm. Goodwin (44), labourer
Ed. Goodwin (23), labourer
Alf Brushfield (32), labourer
Ben Davies (25), collier
Thos J. Morgan (51), collier
Jas. Hopkins (42), collier
Josiah Bowen (28), stoker
Alf Lewis (45), hitcher
Peter Hughes (20), labourer
Thos. Evans (45), labourer
John Leo (30), labourer
Dd. R. Lewis (22), collier
Fitzroy Lydead (44), collier

★ ★ ★

16th December: Pentre Riot cases at Swansea

Wm. John Mears, colliery labourer
Joseph Orledge, engine cleaner
John Howard, collier
Rose Keast
Agnes Lowe
May Clemens
Cissy Jones
Annie Howell
Eliz. Jane Hary
John Regan, collier
Edgar Lewis, collier
Alf Harding, collier
Alf. Edw. Bridgeman, collier
Tom Davies, collier
Alf Davies, collier
Alf. Charles Clarke, labourer
John Hunt
Wm. John Eynon, collier
Cath Williams

All charged with riotous assembly and intimidation.

★ ★ ★

17th December: (1) Cymmer rioters—second batch. Dd. John Jones admitted he was secretary of International Class War Prisoners' Aid. (2) Pentre. When 14 found guilty, three women fainted in dock (four not guilty—Davies, Clarke, Hunt and Eynon).

Already, seven weeks before the end of their agony, in studiously moderate phrases Oliver Harris wrote in *The Colliery Workers' Magazine*:

The way in which the workers have been persecuted under EPA and under common law, since the General Strike, has driven home to the mind of the public how completely is the administration of "justice" in the hands of the enemies of the working classes. Trivial offences of a technical character are magnified into serious crimes, and the most vicious sentences are imposed if the person charged is a working man, and especially if he is an active trade unionist. The evidence is often of the flimsiest character; words are twisted and turned to suit the purpose of the persecutors, and the whole procedure is generally a mere travesty of justice.

The Courts, from the lowest to the highest, are administered by men whose whole training and upbringing has created within them an attitude of mind prejudicial to the workers, and when a member of the working class is brought before them he is already condemned, unless he can bring overwhelming evidence to rebut the charges brought against him. The Police Courts and Quarter Sessions are packed with men whose sole conception of the workers is that they are creatures who were created to work upon any terms the "masters" chose to give, and if they refuse to work on these terms, they are regarded more or less as criminals, who should be put down at any and every opportunity.

Far otherwise, of course, is the attitude of these courts towards any individuals who are regarded as being above the workers. In their cases every effort is made in the other direction, and the utmost leniency is shown. A Carson, a Jix, or a Churchill can organise rebellion in Ulster with impunity, and given the highest offices in the State thereafter, but if a worker whispers that the workers should arm to dethrone their oppressors, he is at once hawked before the courts and savagely sentenced.

Every care is taken that the vast majority of the magistrates belong to the other class. Members of the House of Lords can claim to be tried by their Peers; that is, by members of their own class, and it is full time that the workers should put forward a similar claim, and insist that they also shall be tried by members of their own class and not by their enemies. It is one of the problems that a real Labour Government should tackle at the earliest opportunity.

9 STAUNCH TO THE END

At the SWMF Special Conference on Tuesday, 5th October, the following motion was moved and seconded and carried almost unanimously :

That the Welsh Representatives to the National Conference to be held on Thursday next, October 7th, be instructed to demand the *status quo* conditions. In order to obtain this, the policy of the MFGB on the following items to be as follows :

Safety Men.—All such to be withdrawn from every Colliery.

Embargo.—That we urge this on all foreign produced coal.

Outcrop Coal.—That the MFGB immediately orders the cessation of this practice.

Levy.—That a special congress of the Trades Unions be called specifically to deal with this matter.

Propaganda.—(a) That we send speakers to all "black" areas; (b) That Labour MPs be marshalled for a nationwide campaign.

At the Kingsway Hall, London, on Thursday, 7th October, the President, Herbert Smith, characterised the South Wales proposition as closing the door for future negotiations, and expressed the hope that the Conference would not adopt it.

When the South Wales proposal was put to the vote, it was carried by a large majority. The figures were:

For	589,000
Against	199,000

The SWMF Special Conference which was held on Wednesday, 17th November, met for the purpose of deciding whether to accept or reject the terms of settlement as recommended by the General Conference of the MFGB. The President stated that the lodges had given the delegates their instructions in reference to the matter.

The result was:

For	823
Against	2,403

Each vote represents 50 members.

November 23rd and 24th.—South Wales Miners' Executive meet South Wales Coalowners: and fail to agree.

November 25th—A Special Conference decided to ballot men on the question of authorising the E.C. to settle.

November 29th—South Wales Miners' ballot decide in favour of authorising a settlement.

November 30th—South Wales E.C. and South Wales Coalowners again meet. Terms accepted.

December 1st—General resumption of work in the South Wales Coalfield.

In *The Colliery Workers' Magazine*, in his "Notes and Comments" on the "End of the Great Lockout," the Editor wrote:

The great struggle that has been raging in the British Coal Industry from 1st May to 1st December has ended with the defeat—the utter and complete defeat—of the workmen. It has been the greatest contest in industrial history—great not only in the heroism displayed by the men and women in the mining areas in defence of their meagre standard of life, but also because of the tremendously callous and brutal forces that were brought against them. The community as a whole has had to pay dearly for the stupidity of the electors in 1924 in electing to power a gang of men who have so ruthlessly exercised their authority against the workers; but it is the miners in particular who have had to bear the brunt of the stupid mistake.

We have had bad and incompetent Governments before, but it is doubtful whether there has ever been a Government so completely a tool of the Capitalist Class as this Tory Government has proved itself to be. We have a Colliery Shareholder at the head of it in the person of Mr. Stanley Baldwin—the arch-hypocrite, who could blasphemously cry, "Give us peace in our time, O Lord," while at the same time he was using all the authority of the State to secure further degradation of the standard of life in the mining areas.

Every department of the State has been utilised to secure our defeat. The Home Office, under the direction of "Jix," who, being a devout Churchman, is probably a bigger hypocrite than Baldwin, has exercised the powers given it by this Tory Parliament, under EPA, to intimidate the workmen by means of police, baton charges and prosecutions. The Judiciary, from the highest Court to the lowest, was already packed with men who were entirely out of sympathy with the aspirations of the workers, and who were ready tools in the hands of our enemies, for carrying out a policy of repression.

Hundreds of our men have been sent to prison or fined on the flimsiest evidence uncorroborated by anyone outside the police themselves, and the most vicious sentences have been passed revealing quite clearly the class bias of those in charge of the administration of the law.

Often, as in the recent cases from the Eastern Valleys of Monmouthshire, the Judge adds insult to injury by lecturing the men who are infinitely better than himself, while at the same time he passes unjust sentences upon them. The Ministry of Health, under the guidance of that superior person, Neville Chamberlain, has been notoriously active in bringing pressure to bear upon Boards of Guardians to reduce relief to starvation point—all for the purpose of destroying the morale of the workmen and bringing about their defeat.

The Press, of course, have done their worst; the newspapers have, indeed, been the most useful instruments in the hands of the Coalowners.

* * *

The stoical but sombre tone of the above editorial by Oliver Harris in the union's magazine may be taken as representing the general outlook of Executive Councilmen as well as the lodge officials and conference delegates. The bitter resentment against the whole oppressive apparatus of Government—executive, legislative and judicial, against the three estates of the realm—King Lords and Commons (and also against the venal "Fourth Estate", the Press) smouldered on in the valleys for year after year.

But there were some who saw a deeper meaning in the struggle: and who sought not only to probe, however critically, into the causes but to snatch from the jaws of this "utter and complete defeat" plans for a new strategy and for new forms of organisation that in the inevitable future conflicts would yield good hope for success.

One such was the checkweigher of Mardy in the Rhondda, Arthur Horner, who on Saturday, 4th December, 1926, gave an interview to the representative of the *Sunday Worker*, which for twenty months had voiced the outlook of A. J. Cook and his supporters.

"NATIONAL UNION

Miners' Minority Movement Opens Campaign

(From our Own Correspondent)

Porth, Saturday.

"After attending the mass trial of South Wales miners at Swansea, I saw Arthur Horner, the young leader, whose plan for strengthening the miners' organisation has created much interest in the British coalfields.

Horner is very emphatic regarding the weakness of the Miners' Federation as a fighting weapon against the united forces of the employers.

In reply to my request for a brief explanation of his position, Horner said : 'The struggle has revealed that the Miners' Federation is only a loose combination of district organisations. At every moment of the crisis, during the lockout, there was a tendency for the weaker districts to fall out of the struggle.

'This explains why renegades like Spencer were able to weaken and ultimately to betray their district.

'My plan,' said Horner, 'is to make the Federation into a National Industrial Union of Mineworkers. The campaign to realise this has already been taken up by the Minority Movement.

'Side by side with the change in structure there must take place a change in leadership. Among the miners' leaders are many who are both honest and courageous, but they are unable to adapt themselves to the new methods of industrial struggle where the employers fight with the whole organised force of the government, and even of Labour leaders, behind them.

'It is necessary,' urged Horner, 'for the miners to transform and strengthen their organisation, because big struggles are facing us in the coalfields. The steady decline in British industry will drive on the employers to attack us, again and again, and we must improve our fighting machine.

'It is easy for Labour privy councillors who receive high salaries, and who earn fabulous sums by writing in the capitalist Press, to preach industrial peace. They have climbed on the back of the workers and have lifted themselves out of the industrial struggle. We who are working in the coalfields, and who know what the conditions are, say very definitely that there can be no peace in the coal mining industry.

'The struggle must go on,' concluded Horner, 'and I urge my comrades to build up a National Union for Mine Workers, so that we can defend ourselves and attack our enemies.' "

It was to be many years ahead, years of unmerited suffering and of many tribulations, before the plan so boldly advanced by Arthur Horner at the very nadir of their fortunes was to reach its triumphant fulfilment.

APPENDIX I

RUSSIAN CONTRIBUTIONS TO THE BRITISH MINERS' RELIEF FUND.

(from *The Colliery Workers' Magazine*, Vol. IV, October, 1926).

The Trade Union Bulletin of the Russian Central Council of Trade Unions gives details of the contributions of the Russian workers to the British miners, and very effectively gives the lie to the statements of the British capitalist Press that the money is given by the Soviet Government.

Table 1 gives the names of 61 centres, and the amount contributed by each during the months of May and June, making a total of 2,156,602 roubles. Table 2 gives the contributions of various classes of workers (railwaymen, metal workers, printers, etc., etc.) Table 3 gives contributions from newspaper offices, individuals and various institutions.

Summary of Receipts.

	Roubles.
Table No. 1	2,156,602.30
Table No. 2	645,764.93
Table No. 3	245,408.93
Advanced by C.C.T.U. against future receipts ...	673,000.00
Grand Total ...	3,720,776.16

APPENDIX II

Accountant's Report to South Wales Miners' Federation re Cymric Federation Press.

The following Statement of Account covers the first trading period of the Printing Works, which is a branch or Department of the South Wales Miners' Federation.

The only Working Capital provided by the Federation was £200, of which £126 17s. 10d. remained at the Bank at 31st October, 1921.

The gross profit of £452 14s. 11d. is accurately arrived at after fully allowing for the proper charges against income, excepting that no debit is made in respect of the capital outlay upon premises, plant or working capital.

A few improvements have been effected during the year upon plant and equipment, and these have been dealt with in the Trading Account.

As to the Statement of Accounts, the amount outstanding is £505 8s. 4d. Of this, £156 9s. 11d. has already been collected since the accounts were closed at the end of October, and all are considered good debts with the exception of about £20, in respect of which no provision is made by allocation to a reserve.

As to the disposal of the gross profit, I suggest that, subject to payment of a bonus to the Managers as agreed, the balance should be carried forward as working capital.

6 Cathedral Road, Cardiff, WILLIAM ROBERTS
December, 1921. Accountant.

APPENDIX II (continued)

CYMRIC FEDERATION PRESS

TRADING ACCOUNT FOR YEAR ENDED 31st OCTOBER, 1921.

	£ s. d.	£ s. d.		£ s. d
Paper and Materials ...	1029 15 1		Sales	2811 15 11
Wages	1129 13 8		Discounts	7 6 5
Fuel, Light and Power ...	52 10 0		Bank Interest	3 17 7
Rates, Taxes & Insurance	72 7 5		Stock & Work in Progress	99 3 6
Repairs & Renewals ...	133 10 0			
Expenses (Printing Office)	51 12 4			
		2469 8 6		
Profit (Gross) ...		452 14 11		
		£2922 3 5		£2922 3 5

STATEMENT OF ACCOUNTS AS AT 31st OCTOBER, 1921.

LIABILITIES	£ s. d.	ASSETS		£ s. d.
Advances from SWMF	200 0 0	Stock & Work in Progress		99 3 6
Sundry Trading Creditors	79 18 1	Sundry Debtors		505 8 4
Gross Profit as per Trading Account ...	452 14 11	Cash in Hand	1 3 4	
		Cash at Bank	126 17 10	
				128 1 2
	£732 13 0			£732 13 0

APPENDIX III

LENIN'S LETTER TO TOM BELL.

Tom Bell (1882-1944), an early associate of James Connolly in the Socialist Labour Party, set up in Scotland in 1903, and for several years President of the Executive Council of the Ironmoulders' Union, played a leading part in the formation in 1920 of the Communist Party of Great Britain.

After the Unity Conference of the Communist Party of Great Britain in January, 1921, Bell went to Moscow in the early spring to sit as the first representative of the unified party on the Executive Committee of the Communist International. In the summer of 1921 the mining lockout came to an end and several colliers attended the first congress of the Red International of Labour Unions as delegates, notably Hewlett of Abertillery (killed, together with Sergeiyev Artyom, the leader of the Russian miners, in an accident), Proudfoot of East Fife and Stewart of West Fife. They had given Tom Bell details of the kind of struggle that had gone on in the thirteen-week lockout from 31st March to the beginning of July, 1921. These particulars together with the news that the South Wales Miners' Federation, at its Annual Conference in Cardiff, had passed by 120 votes to 63: "That the Miners' Federation of Great Britain, at the Annual Conference of that body, be urged to affiliate and actively identify itself with the Third International" (23 vii 1921), caused Tom Bell to write an informative letter to Lenin, one of his five Soviet Russian colleagues on the Executive Committee of the Communist International.

A few days later Bell, then in Room 154 of the Lux Hotel, received a reply[1] from Lenin which is illustrated earlier in this volume and reproduced below exactly as the original.

[1]To the comrade Thomas Bell (Lux 154).

Dear Comrade,

I thank you very much for your letter, d.7/8. I have read nothing concerning the English movement last months because of my illness and overwork.

It is extremely interesting what you communicate. Perhaps it is *the beginning* of the real proletarian mass movement in Great Britain *in the communist sense.* I am afraid we have till now in England few very feeble propagandist societies for communism (inclusive the British Communist Party) but no really *mass* communist movement.

If the South Wales Miners' Federation has decided on 24/VII to affiliate to the III Int. by a majority of 120 to 63—perhaps it is the beginning of new era (how much miners there are in England? more than 500,000? How much in South Wales? 25,000? How much miners were *really* represented in Cardiff 24/VII/1921?)

If these miners are not too small minority, if they fraternise with soldiers and begin *a real* "class war"—we must do all our possible to *develop* this movement and strengthen it.

Economic measures (like communal kitchens) are good but they are not much important *now*, *before* the victory of the proletarian revolution in England. *Now* the *political* struggle is the most important.

English capitalists are shrewd, clever, astute. They *will* support (directly or indirectly) communal kitchens *in order* to divert the attention *from political aims.*

What is important, is (if I am not mistaken) (1) to create a very good, really proletarian, really mass *communist party* in this part of England—that is such party which will *really* be the LEADING force in *all* labour movement in this part of the country. (Apply the resolution on organisation and work of the party adopted by the three congress to this part of Your country).

(2) To start a daily paper of the working class, for the working class in this part of the country.

To start it not as a business (as usually newspapers are started in capitalist countries), not with a big sum of money, not in an ordinary and usual manner—but as an *economic and political* tool of the MASSES in their struggle.

Either the miners of this district are capable to pay *halfpenny* daily (for the beginning *weekly*, if you like) for their OWN daily (or weekly) newspaper (be it very very small, it is not important)—or THERE IS NO BEGINNING *of the really communist mass "movement in this part" of Your country.*

If the communist party of this District cannot collect a few pounds in order to publish *small leaflets* DAILY as a beginning of the really *proletarian* communist newspaper—if it so, if *every* miner will not pay a penny for it, then there is *not serious*, not genuine affiliation to the III Int.

English government will apply the shrewdest means in order to suppress every beginning of this kind. Therefore we must be (in the beginning) very prudent. The paper must be *not too revolutionary* in the beginning. If YOU will have three editors, at least one must be *non communist* (at least two genuine workers). If 9/10 of the workers do not buy this paper, if 2/3 workers (120/120+63) do not pay special contributions (f.i. 1 penny *weekly*) for their paper—it will be no workers' newspaper.

I should be very glad to have few lines from You concerning this theme and I beg to apologise for my bad English.

With communist greetings, Lenin.

INDEX OF SUBJECTS

INDEX OF NAMES

DETAILS OF ILLUSTRATIONS

8 CWMLLYNFELL MINERS' GLEE PARTY, 1923

Back Row: Daniel Owen Jones (Dan Brickman); David William Morgan (Dai Wat Ben); William Kendrick (Wil y Sincwr); Emlyn Jones (Emlyn Gwilym Wyn); David Jones (Dai Wil Dick); David Lewis Edwards (Dai Lewis).

Middle Row: David Rowlands (Dai Aberafon); Mr. G. Gardner (owner); David Williams (Dai Lady); John Penry Davies (John Penry Aberdâr); John Walter Williams (Wat Bach); William Gwilym (not a miner, schoolmaster at Rhiwfawr).

Front Row: Jim Davies; Griffith William George (Gute George); Arthur Thomas (Arthur y Boblen); Will Thomas (Wil y Boblen).

10 RELEASE OF ANTHRACITE STRIKERS, 1925

Stanley Evans, first of the 59 imprisoned miners to be released, is welcomed by family and friends who pose with their hero at a photographer's studio.

Back Row: Dai Ladd Davies; Jack Parry; Rhys Thomas; Jim Jenkins; Twm Thomas; Johnnie Vaughan; Coun. Dai Price; Coun. Tom Haines

Second Row: Will Thomas; Elfet Thomas; Jack Davies; Dai Harris; Mrs. Dollie Bassett; Edgar Bassett, General Manager, Ammanford Co-operative Society; Jim Phillips; County Councillor Gwilym Thomas; Rhys Griffiths; Bryn Thomas; Eddie Bowen; Will 'Aberdâr' Williams; Will Allen.

Third Row: Dai Lloyd Davies, International Class War Prisoners' Aid representative; Evan (Ianto) Evans (brother); Mrs. Evans (sister-in-law); Mr. Evans (father); Stanley Evans; Mrs. Evans (mother); George Thomas; Lauchlan Stewart, Glasgow University lecturer.

Front Row: Myrddin Morgans; Will Thomas; Aneurin Williams; Ieuan Evans (nephew); Garfield Williams; Dai William Lewis; Sid Lloyd

ERRATA

Page 16	Delete 5th line from the bottom and substitute: 'Fabian socialist dissenters, had from the spring of 1912 intensified a'
Page 28	12th line, '9th' should read '11th'
Page 103	Second to last line of footnote "Nr." Openshaw should read "Hr." Openshaw.
Page 106	Line 27 "Enoch Morrel" should be "Enoch Morrell".
Page 124	14th line from bottom of page "contractural" should read "contractual".
Page 133	9th line from top, '1971' should read '1917'
Page 135	19th line from top of page "Davenport" should read "Devonport".
Page 137	On 2nd line of the 3rd paragraph, 'Railways' should be 'Railway'
Page 150	1st footnote, 5th line from the end of that footnote delete the word "ran" (9th word in sentence).
Page 167	13th line from top, second word should be 'gentleman' not 'gentlemen'
Page 183	14th line from bottom "Non-conformity" should read "Nonconformity".
Page 193	17th line from top of page "battening" should read "batoning".
Page 203	13th line from top of page 4th word from end of line "sytem" should read "system".
Page 214	6th line from top, sixth word should be 'thirty' not 'thitry'
Page 225	8th line down from top "Internationale" should read "International".
Page 233	9th line from bottom of page first word "Emmanuel" should read "Emanuel".
Page 286	25th line down from top "Engel's" should read "Engels' ".
Page 290	8th line from bottom "Snowdon" should read "Snowden".
Page 295	In footnote, "Middlemass" should read "Middlemas".
Page 297	Line 18, "Sir Austin" should read "Sir Austen".
Page 305	20th line from top of page "counry" should read "country".
Page 305	Line 2 of footnote "Dd Gittens" should be "Dd Gittings".
Page 318	Line 16 "Bd James Lewis" should read "Dan James Lewis".
Page 320	9th line down from top, "your" should read "you're".
Page 320	Line 3 from foot of page, a colon should be inserted after "It is now time to rebel:" before "I have turned rebel".
Page 326	4th line down of footnote "O," should be "Oh".
Page 336	Lines 26 and 27 in the second list of names "Cissy Jones" should be "Cissie Jones" and "Annie Howell" should read "Annie Howells".

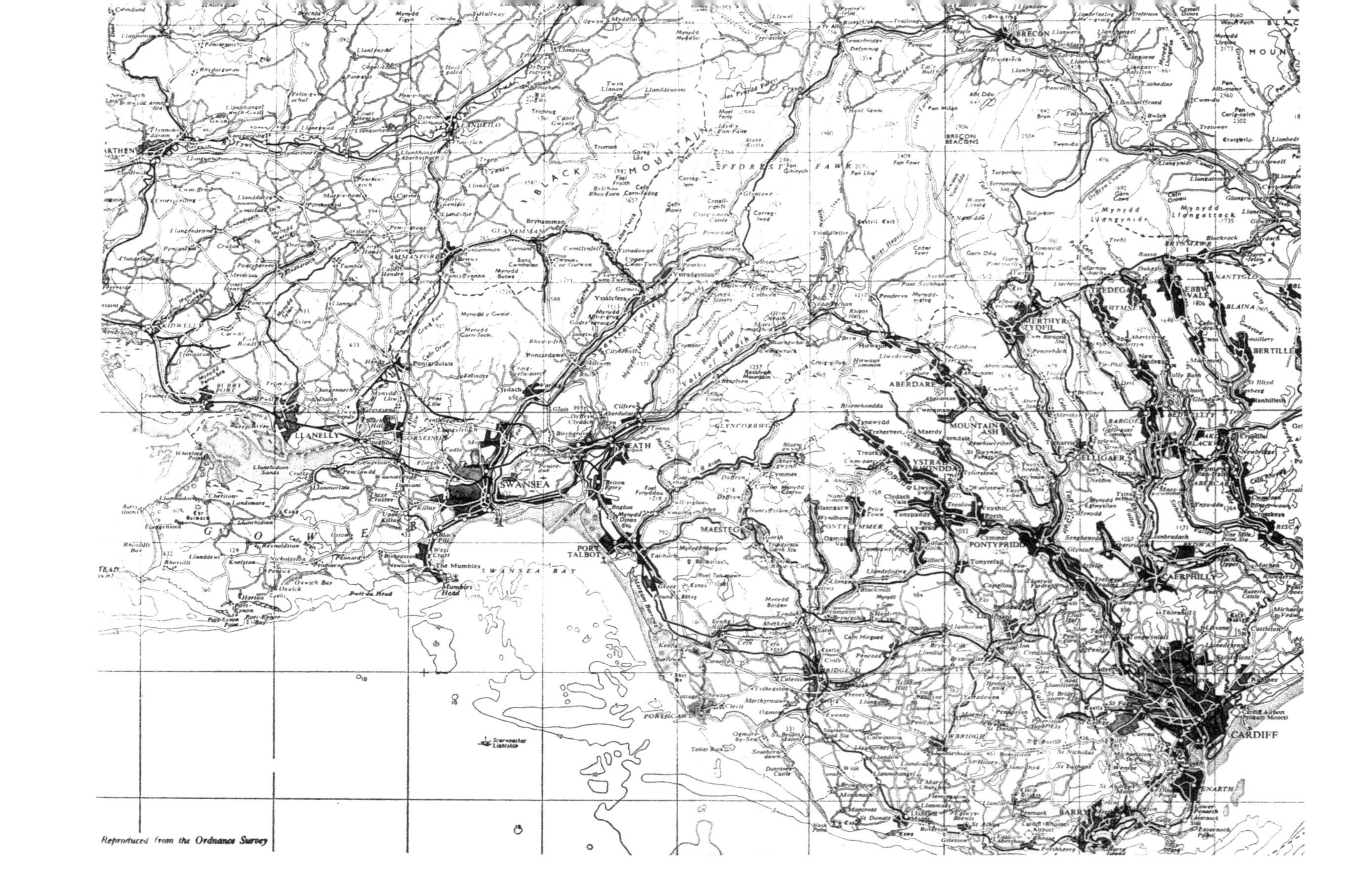

BRECON
BRECON BEACONS
LLANDEILO
AMMANFORD
GLANAMMAN
BLACK MOUNTAIN
FFOREST FAWR
KIDWELLY
LLANELLY
GORSEINON
SWANSEA
SWANSEA BAY
The Mumbles
Mumbles Head
NEATH
PORT TALBOT
Margam Burrows
MAESTEG
ABERDARE
MOUNTAIN ASH
MERTHYR TYDFIL
TREDEGAR
EBBW VALE
BLAINA
ABERTILLERY
NANTYGLO
BRYNMAWR
GELLIGAER
PONTYPRIDD
CAERPHILLY
CARDIFF
PENARTH
BARRY
BRIDGEND
COWBRIDGE
PORTHCAWL
GOWER
Mynydd Llangynidr
Mynydd Llangattock
Vale of Neath
Swansea Valley
Scarweather Lightship

For Product Safety Concerns and Information please contact our EU
representative GPSR@taylorandfrancis.com
Taylor & Francis Verlag GmbH, Kaufingerstraße 24, 80331 München, Germany

www.ingramcontent.com/pod-product-compliance
Ingram Content Group UK Ltd.
Pitfield, Milton Keynes, MK11 3LW, UK
UKHW011451240425
457818UK00008B/283

* 9 7 8 1 0 3 2 5 3 9 1 7 1 *